An Introduction to Structured Programming
Using PL/I and SP/k

INTRODUCTION TO STRUCTURED PROGRAMMING
Using PL/I and SP/k

Richard Conway
David Gries
Cornell University

David B. Wortman
University of Toronto

contributions by
John E. Dennis, Jr. and Jorge Moré

Winthrop Publishers, Inc.
Cambridge, Massachusetts

Library of Congress Cataloging in Publication Data

Conway, Richard Walter
   Introduction to structured programming, using PL/I
and SP/k.

  (Winthrop computer systems series)
  Includes bibliographies and index.

  1. PL/I (Computer program language) 2. SP/k
(Computer program language) 3. Structured programming.
I. Gries, David, joint author. II. Wortman,
David B., joint author. III. Title.

QA76.73.P25C653   001.6'424   77-7973
ISBN 0-87626-412-7

Cover graphic by Roger Vilder
from the series *Cyclic Progressions* (1976).
Courtesy of Galerie Gilles Gheerbrant, Montreal

Cover design by Harold Pattek

© 1977 by Winthrop Publishers, Inc.

17 Dunster Street, Cambridge, Massachusetts 02138

CONTENTS

Appendices

Preface

If someone approaching programming for the first time already
has a systematic, well-disciplined approach to problem analysis
in general, then learning to program a computer just means
learning the nature and syntax of a programming language. In
this case a book that concentrates upon the syntactic details of
a programming language is probably adequate. However, few
students have this prerequisite training in problem solving.
For them a course in programming is a unique opportunity to
develop this skill in a particularly useful and interesting
context. The approach and method of analysis are then more
significant than the details of the programming language. This
book is our attempt to provide a text that will help an
instructor who takes this view of his task.

Nothing in our approach is really new. We are simply trying
to apply the classical "scientific method" to the production of
computer programs. We have been surprised how directly the
recommendations of the scientific philosophers -- Descartes,
Mill, Polya -- can be applied to this new field, and we have
drawn heavily upon their views and procedures. Edsger Dijkstra
has pioneered the application of these ideas to programming and
we have benefited tremendously from his work.

This approach to programming leads to a strong concern with
the organization of programs. The structure of a program should
clearly reflect the structure of the problem that it represents,
and the pattern of analysis that the programmer has followed.
For non-trivial problems this approach offers the only hope of
being able to adequately demonstrate the correctness of a
program. If necessary, we are willing to accept slower programs
to achieve clarity of structure and reliability. It makes no
sense to use an unclear program of uncertain correctness no
matter how efficient it might be. Actually, the major source of
program efficiency lies not in clever tricks but in a clean and
logical approach to the problem. Clarity and good programming
style often lead to more efficient algorithms.

We enthusiastically embrace the philosophy of "structured
programming", because it lends so much insight into what the
best programmers have been doing all along, and gives us
concepts that can be taught to new programmers. Emphasis on
structure, on the use of program elements that most clearly
reflect that structure, and on program correctness, results in
superior programs and more capable programmers.

Programming has too long been regarded as a highly individual art. Very little attention is given to encouraging consistent form, style and conventions in programming, and in fact highly individual and even peculiar styles are tolerated. However, the practice of programming has long since passed the point where it is entirely a private activity. To be sure, many engineers and scientists still write their own programs, use them once, and then throw them away. But the real difficulties in programming arise in larger problems, where the programmer is not working on "his own". He is given an assignment that represents only one aspect of the complete problem; he must produce a section of program that will work properly with other sections he has never seen; and the entire program must be usable by people who know little or nothing about how it is constructed. Often such programs have a relatively long lifetime -- measured in months or years rather than hours or days -- and will be subject to significant modification during this time. In this context programming is not an art form; it is a technical communication process. It is crucial that programs be cleanly divided into functional modules and that the interfaces between these modules be specified in explicit detail in program documentation. We try to illustrate and encourage this practice by employing it even for simple introductory examples, where it is obviously not really necessary and where it may require writing extra statements. The fraction of lines devoted to control structures and comments is oppressively large in some of our short examples, but of course, this proportion diminishes as the same style is applied to problems of more substance. Programming practices needed for large problems can be used for small problems, but not conversely. Although most students will regard programming only as one of many tools, and use it only occasionally, we see no disadvantage in introducing them to programming as if they were going to be serious about it.

Most writers of programming texts and teachers of programming courses are themselves more or less serious programmers, understand and believe in the virtues of such things as highly modular, adequately documented programs. They appreciate the substantial fraction of total programming time and effort that goes into testing. Yet the usual text or course does little to convey this concern. Compare the number of pages in a typical text devoted to syntactic details to the number devoted to discussion of strategy and style, to the process of constructing programs, and to how programs should be designed for systematic and exhaustive testing. Even worse, whatever material is included on strategy, structure and testing is usually relegated to the final chapters and lectures. In that position it is often omitted when things get behind schedule. It also means that throughout his initial exposure and experience the student is unguided on these important matters, and even encouraged into some very bad habits which a few parting admonitions cannot overcome. We have tried to emphasize these issues from the very beginning. Something must yield, of course, to allow the time and pages for this emphasis and we sacrifice breadth of coverage and syntactic detail. Our reader and student may know less of PL/I than if he had followed a more conventional text, but he will better understand what he is doing and can perhaps use what he knows more effectively. We would like to give him a clear understanding of the fundamental concepts of computing so that he can later, on his own, expand his knowledge of this or any programming language.

Some comment on our choice of programming language is in order. This approach to programming could certainly be used with FORTRAN, COBOL, or even assembly language, and should result in better programs in any language. However, it is easier to teach this approach using a language whose control structures encourage a natural "top-down" description of a program. In terms of this approach PL/I, PASCAL and ALGOL are higher-level languages than FORTRAN. That is, in the level-by-level reduction from problem statement to program, one would require an extra level if the target language were FORTRAN rather than PL/I. Stated in another way, given a description in a PL/I-like language as the next-to-last level one could proceed from there to write a FORTRAN program.

PL/I is, in most respects, less attractive than PASCAL or ALGOL, both for programming and as a vehicle for teaching programming. But it is also more widely used. In many places this makes it the only alternative to FORTRAN or COBOL that is politically acceptable for an introductory course. PL/I is not easy to love, but if FORTRAN or COBOL are the only alternatives one can learn to live with PL/I.

PL/I has some unfortunate characteristics. In spite of claims to the contrary it is not adequately modular; too much must be known before one really understands certain constructions. Many common student "errors" are not considered errors by the system; they just invoke hitherto unexplained features of the language. PL/I syntax is awkward and in many places inconsistent. PL/I also has a high astonishment factor -- many features just don't work the way you would expect them to. (For example, who would guess that 6E0 * 6E0 is 3E1?) We have restricted attention to a small subset of PL/I called SP/k that was developed specifically for introductory programming in PL/I. The University of Toronto SP/k compiler described in Appendix A restricts students to exactly the SP/k subset.

This book can be used with either or SP/k. The Appendices give a fairly complete definition of PL/I syntax and detail the differences between PL/I and SP/k.

This approach to programming is equally applicable to both "scientific computing" and "business data processing", and this book could be used for an introductory course for students in either area. The subset of PL/I used is common to both fields and the examples and exercises have been carefully chosen so as not to require substantial prior knowledge of either mathematics or accounting. Parts VIII and IX give very brief introductions to the two major areas of computer application and include suggestions for further reading.

The material in Part X on languages and translators is not essential to programming. But many students become curious about such matters, and since we are also interested in the subject, we are happy to encourage their curiosity.

It is a pleasure to acknowledge our indebtedness to our colleagues John Dennis and Jorge More', who contributed Part VIII, to Richard C. Holt who contributed part of Appendix A, and to Steven Worona, who helped to eliminate some of our errors.

This book is an adaptation by the third author of: An Introduction to Programming - A Structured Approach Using PL/I and PL/C-7 (second edition) by Richard Conway and David Gries. The PL/C subset of PL/I has been uniformly replaced by the SP/k subset and all examples have been reprogrammed. The author gratefully acknowledges the assistance of Ms. I. Weber in the text editing of this book.

Ithaca, N. Y.   R. Conway
                                                             D. Gries
Toronto, Ont.   D. Wortman

**An Introduction to Structured Programming
Using PL/I and SP/k**

PART I   FUNDAMENTAL CONCEPTS

Section 1   The Computing Process

We are concerned with the process by which a digital computer can be used to solve problems -- or at least aid in the solution of problems. This involves learning to:

1. Choose problems that are appropriate to the computer's abilities, and describe the problem requirements, conditions, and assumptions clearly and precisely.

2. Design a solution to a problem and describe it in a language intelligible to a computer. This description is called a "program", while the process of producing a program is called "programming". Programming is a systematic, level-by-level process in which the original problem description, usually given in a combination of English and mathematics, is translated into a "programming language". This process must also transform a statement of objectives -- what is required -- into a description of an executable procedure -- how the objectives are to be achieved. A third aspect of the transformation is to make explicit and precise those portions of the problem description that are implicit and rely on the intuition, common sense, or technical knowledge of the reader, since the computer is completely lacking in these virtues.

3. Confirm the correctness of the program. This means demonstrating in as convincing a manner as possible that the program precisely satisfies the problem requirements.

The selection of appropriate problems is as difficult and important as the analysis and programming, but it is impossible to discuss this issue until one has some understanding of the

nature   of computing systems and their special abilities.
However, two initial observations might be helpful.   Firstly,
problems for which computer assistance is sought are generally
of substantial magnitude.   There is non-trivial effort involved
in the mechanics of obtaining computer assistance, and if the
problem is simple, not repetitive, and not likely to recur,
computer assistance may cost more than it is worth. One must
bear this in mind even though the examples that will be used for
instruction will necessarily be short and often trivial.   They
are presumably used to develop a competence which will be useful
for subsequent attack on real and substantial problems.

Secondly, the computer can only assist in the solution of
problems which can be stated very precisely and for which a
detailed and precise method of solution can be given.   Roughly
speaking, one cannot expect a computer to perform a process that
could not be performed by a human--if he lived long enough.   The
digital computer permits a tremendous increase in the quantity
of symbols that may be considered, in the precision and
reliability with which they will be manipulated, and above all
in the speed with which the process will be carried out. But in
principle the computer is only performing operations that could
be carried out by a human being. It is true that the orders-of-
magnitude differences in volume, speed and reliability combine
to produce spectacular capability, but the fundamental process
is simple and not unlike what a human could perform.

For example, a computer can "play chess" only because the
game of chess has been described to the computer as an elaborate
symbol manipulation task. On the other hand, a computer cannot
be requested to "solve the vehicle emission problem" because no
one has as yet figured out how to describe this problem strictly
in terms of symbol manipulation. As another example, a computer
is not infrequently asked to "select a date for a person from a
set of potential candidates" and sometimes produces rather
humorous recommendations. The source of the humor lies not in
the computer's execution of the process but in the fact that no
one really knows how to precisely describe this   complex
selection process.

1.1 An Example of a Program

At this point we present an example of a simple but complete computer program. Although you will not understand all the details at this point, you should get a general idea of what the end product of the programming process is going to be.

Suppose one has to determine the maximum of a set of non-negative numbers which are punched on "IBM cards". The program to do this uses a process that is repeated for each of the numbers. It will cause the computer to "read" a number (by analyzing the pattern of holes punched in the card) and compare it to the greatest number encountered "so far". If the new number is greater than the previous maximum it will be retained as a new maximum. The number of numbers is also counted.

This process is straightforward, once it gets started, but some provision is required to make it work properly on the first repetition. Secondly, so that the end of the list can be recognized we will append a dummy number (in this case a -1, which cannot occur in the actual data). The program will check each value as it is read to see if it is this dummy value.

A program has to be able to store values in the "memory" of the computer and later retrieve these values. Each location for storing a value is called a "variable" and is assigned a name so that the program may refer to it. The names of the variables used in this program are:

    NUMBER -- the current number being processed
    MAXNBR -- the maximum number encountered "so far"
    COUNT -- the number of times the central process has been
              repeated "so far"

The complete program for this problem, written in a programming language called SP/k, is given on the next page. The numbers at the beginning of each line of the program are not part of the program but have been added so that the notes following the program can readily reference each line.

The printed "output" produced by executing this program with the data on line 28 is:

    NUMBER OF VALUES =   5
    MAXIMUM VALUE =   12

This example will often be referred to in later sections. In particular, Section 1.4 discusses its "correctness".

```
1)   $JOBK ID='DAVE WORTMAN'
2)    FINDMAX: PROCEDURE OPTIONS(MAIN);
3)       /* COMPUTE THE MAXIMUM OF NON-NEGATIVE INPUT NUMBERS */
4)       /* DUMMY -1 ADDED AT END OF INPUT FOR STOPPING TEST */
5)
6)       DECLARE (NUMBER,      /* THE CURRENT NUMBER */
7)                MAXNBR,      /* MAXIMUM VALUE SO FAR */
8)                COUNT)       /* NUMBER OF NUMBERS SO FAR */
9)                  FIXED;
10)
11)      MAXNBR = -1;          /* INITIAL VALUE LESS THAN ALL */
12)                            /* POSSIBLE DATA VALUES */
13)      COUNT = 0;
14)      GET LIST(NUMBER);
15)
16)      DO WHILE (NUMBER ¬= -1);
17)         COUNT = COUNT + 1;
18)         IF NUMBER > MAXNBR THEN
19)            MAXNBR = NUMBER;
20)         GET LIST(NUMBER);
21)         END;
22)
23)      PUT SKIP LIST('NUMBER OF VALUES =', COUNT);
24)      PUT SKIP LIST('MAXIMUM VALUE =', MAXNBR);
25)
26)      END /* FINDMAX */;
27)  $DATA
28)  3 7 12 2 6 -1
```

The following remarks attempt to explain some of the less
obvious aspects of the program:

   Line 1 is a control card that tells the computer that the
   program is written in SP/k which is a special form of a
   language   called   PL/I.   Most computing systems accept
   programs in   many   different languages and the user must
   indicate which of these he will use. Line 1 also gives the
   name of the programmer.

   Lines 2 and 26 indicate the beginning and end of this
   program -- which is named FINDMAX.

   Lines 3 and 4 are program comments. These are intended for
   human readers and have no effect on the execution of the
   program. In PL/I comments are denoted by /* preceding and
   */ following the text of the comment. Comments are also
   included in lines 6, 7, 8, 11, 12, and 26.

   Lines 5, 10, 15, 22 and 25 are blank and are inserted to
   visually indicate the separate sections of the program.
   They have no effect on execution.

Lines 6-9 define the variables that will be used in the
program and specify that they may contain integers ("FIXED"
means integer).

Lines 11-14 are "initialization" actions -- special steps
necessary to make the central, repeated section operate
properly on its first execution. GET LIST(NUMBER); means
to "read" the first number on the data card following the
$DATA card (line 27) and store it in variable NUMBER.

Lines 16-21 form the central section, which is repeated for
each number. The symbol "¬=" in line 16 means "not equal".

Lines 23-24 are the final steps that cause the results of
the process to be displayed.

Line 27 indicates that data follows.

Line 28 consists of the data (including a dummy data value
of -1) to be processed by this program.

1.2 Analysis of a Problem and Design of a Program

The starting point of the analysis process is a problem
statement. This is usually given in English or in a hyprid
combination of English and the symbols used in that problem area
(mathematical symbols, for example). It generally deals with
things -- temperatures, automobiles, colors, voters, dollars,
etc. -- that cannot themselves be stored and manipulated by a
computer. It is also usually stated in terms of commands that
are not intelligible to a computer -- words like "solve",
"find", "choose", etc. Typically a problem statement is at
least initially somewhat vague and imprecise. This is partly
because of a tacit reliance on the knowledge and common sense of
the human reader, but also partly because the originator has
often not completely formulated the exact requirements.

The end point of the process is a program -- a procedure that
can be executed on a computer and that represents a solution to
the initial problem. This process of transforming a problem
description into a program has several different aspects:

1. A translation of language -- from English/mathematics
to a programming language (PL/I, FORTRAN, COBOL, etc.)

2. A conversion from a statement of objectives -- what is
to be done -- to an executable procedure -- how the task is
to be accomplished.

3. The definition of symbols (variables) in a program to
represent the real-world objects of the problem. For
example, a variable in one problem might represent the

status of one of the squares of a chess board; in another problem, the number of dollars in a bank account; in another, the temperature at a particular point on a rocket nozzle.

4. The elimination of all vagueness, imprecision and ambiguity in the description. There is never any vagueness in a computer program -- every program always tells the computer precisely what to do. The trick is to construct a program whose execution exactly solves the particular problem in question.

Only on very simple problems (such as those found in programming textbooks) is there much chance of success if one starts immediately to write the program -- no matter how experienced one might be at programming. On problems of any size and complexity a systematic analysis of requirements, and design of the overall structure of the program, should precede any attempt to write program statements. It is convenient to view this process as a "top down" or "level by level" analysis of the problem. The top level is the initial problem statement; the bottom level is a complete program; the number of intervening levels depends on the complexity of the problem.

Generally the second level is just an elaboration of the problem statement -- an attempt to make complete and precise exactly what is required. This is often achieved by a dialog between the programmer and the "customer" -- the owner of the problem. This dialog can involve questions like the following:

1. In what form will the data be supplied?

2. Are there reasonable limits on the values of data that may be expected?

3. How will the end of the data be recognized?

4. What errors in the data should be anticipated? What action should be taken?

5. What form should the output take? What labelling and titling should be provided?

6. What precision (number of significant figures) of results is required?

7. What changes in problem statement are likely (or possible) to occur during the lifetime of the program?

There may also be questions and discussion of alternative strategies of solution. There might be two approaches -- one more costly to design and program, and the other more costly to execute. The customer must provide information to guide such a choice.

While the objective of this dialog is ostensibly to convey
information to the programmer, to help him to understand exactly
what has to be done, very often the customer discovers that the
problem is not yet well-formulated, and that he himself is not
sure, in detail, what he wants done.

The levels occurring after this refinement of the problem
statement are generally designed to accomplish two tasks:

1.To break up big problems into little problems -- which
in turn are attacked by this same approach.

2.   To reduce the commands from English to programming
terms. That is, "find", "solve", etc. must be reduced to
"read", "print", "assign", "repeat", and then eventually
to GET, PUT, DO -- the statements of a programming
language.

1.2.1 An Example of Initial Problem Analysis

Suppose a problem statement (level 1) is given in the
following way:

Given a list of numbers, print the first, second, third
numbers, etc., but stop printing when the largest number in
the list has been printed.

After some discussion this statement of the problem might be
refined to something like the following (level 2):

A set of not more than 100 integers, each greater than
zero, is given on punched cards. A dummy value of zero
will be added to denote the end. The ordering with respect
to value is unknown. Print a column of numbers
corresponding to these numbers in the order given. Begin
printing with the first and terminate when the last number
printed is the maximum of the entire set. For example, if
1, 7, 3, 9, 5, 0 are given, the output should be:

            1
            7
            3
            9

It should be evident that it is not known how much printing is
to be done until the position of the maximum value is
determined, and this cannot be done until the last number of the
input data has been examined (since the last could be the
maximum). Therefore either the numbers will have to be read
twice (once to determine the position of the maximum, and a
second time to print the values) or the numbers will have to be
read once and stored in the computer memory for later use. Card

reading is a relatively slow and often irreversible operation
for a computer, so the second strategy is preferable. This
could lead to a third level of description:

   3.1 Read a sequence of 100 or fewer positive integers from
   cards until a zero value is encountered; store these
   integers in memory, preserving order.

   3.2 Find the position of the integer with maximum value in
   this sequence.

   3.3 Print the early values of the sequence, from the first
   to the maximum value, one per line.

One would then attack each of these subproblems to reduce the
commands -- "read from cards" and "store in memory" in the first
subproblem -- to the corresponding statements in the target
programming language. We have carried this analysis far enough
here to give the general idea -- the program is completed in
Section 5.4.

1.3 Translation to a Programming Language

   The level-by-level transformation of the problem description
is complete when the entire description is in a language that is
intelligible to a computer. However, there is no single,
universal programming language into which all problem
descriptions are translated; there are literally hundreds of
programming languages in use today. The choice of language will
have some influence on the manner in which a problem is solved,
and may have considerable influence on the difficulty
experienced in obtaining a solution. Some programming languages
have been designed to facilitate solution of certain classes of
problems; they exchange generality for convenience for a
particular type of problem. Some exist to serve different makes
and models of computers, and many exist just because there are
wide differences of opinion as to what a programming language
should look like. Opinions on the subject are strongly held,
and debated with a fervor normally reserved for politics or
religion.

   Although there are hundreds of languages in use, a relative
handful dominate the field. The most widely used programming
language today is COBOL, which was designed for business data
processing problems. (The name comes from the first letters of
the words: COmmon Business Oriented Language.) The most widely
used language for engineering and scientific computation is
called FORTRAN (from FORmula TRANslation). Both of these
languages were developed in the 1950s -- a long time ago in this
field. Other important languages are ALGOL, APL, BASIC, LISP,
PL/I, PASCAL, and SNOBOL.

PL/I was developed in the mid-60s in an attempt to serve both the scientific and data processing areas with a single language. The price of this flexibility is complexity. Fortunately one does not have to learn the entire language in order to use part of it. One can learn a small subset of the language initially and then add topics as required to meet new and more challenging tasks. Unfortunately this partitioning of the language is not at all clean, and the unused and unseen portions sometimes intrude upon the initial subset, causing surprising results and forcing one to do things in ways that are not easily explained. One critic compared PL/I to a Swiss Army knife with 100 blades -- there is unquestionably a blade for whatever one might want to do, but there is some risk that in using one blade you will cut yourself with another.

For most students, the first programming language learned will be only the first of several. This is true both because there are many specialized languages available for various different areas of application, and because progress in the field of computer science should eventually lead to languages that will replace all those in use today. PL/I's generality makes it attractive in this regard, for many of the concepts that are emphasized in special-purpose languages are present in some form in PL/I. It is easier for a student who initially learned PL/I to later learn FORTRAN or COBOL on his own than it would be to proceed in the opposite order.

In this book we use SP/k, a specially designed subset of the full PL/I language. SP/k was developed by restricting PL/I to those constructs that are easy to learn and easy to use. (A detailed comparison of SP/k and PL/I is given in Appendix A.) Because SP/k is a subset of PL/I, statements which are true about PL/I may be true only in some restricted form when applied to SP/k. In writing this book we adopted the convention that a statement qualified by "in SP/k" refers to some characteristics of the programming language that are more restricted in SP/k than in PL/I.

The idea of subsetting a language to make it easier for beginning programmers to use is not a new one. Previous versions of this book were based on a larger dialect of PL/I called PL/C that was developed at Cornell University.

It often seems that learning the programming language itself is the major goal of the course. This is not the case. Our primary goal is to teach programming principles; to teach problem solving and programming methodologies which can be used no matter what programming language is being used.

1.4 Confirmation of Program Correctness

    Confirming correctness of a program requires a convincing
demonstration that the program actually satisfies the precise
requirements of the problem.   This phase of the computing
process is typically so badly neglected by writers and teachers
that it seems as if they regard the possibility of mistakes as
somewhat remote and distinctly embarrassing.   In any but the
most trivial task many errors will be made in each phase.
Anyone who intends to use a computer might as well accept this
unfortunate fact and make plans to systematically track down the
inevitable errors. Very typically more than half of the total
time, effort, and cost of the computing process is devoted to
testing and "debugging" the program -- and yet in spite of
this effort the process is not often completely successful.   An
embarrassingly large fraction of programs that are declared to
be complete and correct by their authors still contain latent
flaws. This situation is so prevalent and serious that a large
proportion of society today has diminishing confidence in the
computing process. Computers are increasingly thought to be
somehow inherently unreliable, but in almost all cases the
true fault lies in a program that was ill-designed and/or
inadequately tested.

    The program in Section 1.1 was deliberately constructed to
illustrate this point. It works perfectly for the data given,
and also for many other sets of data, but line 9 restricts this
program so that it can only successfully handle integer values.
However, there is nothing in the problem statement that suggests
that the program will only be used for integer values.   As a
consequence any time this program is used for data that are not
all integers (that is, values like 17.3), it is likely to
produce incorrect results without even warning the user that he
is in trouble. The program "works" for some sets of data but it
is not a correct program for the given problem.

    Many people seem to regard testing in a negative sense -- as
an extra phase of the computing process that must be performed
only if there appear to be errors. In fact, it is an essential
part of programming. One must take positive action to try and
force latent errors into revealing themselves -- so that one can
reasonably infer correctness if no errors are exposed by
determined and persistent testing. This must be done not just
for a few simple test cases, but for maliciously contrived test
cases that exercise a program more strenuously than is likely to
occur in actual use. Contriving sufficiently difficult test
cases is something of an art in itself. While testing is listed
as a separate phase of the programming process it actually
pervades the entire process, and if all consideration of
determining correctness is postponed to the final phase it will
almost surely be unsuccessful.   It is essential that the
necessity of demonstrating correctness be considered at the time
that the overall structure of the program is chosen and that
provision for testing be incorporated in the program as it is
written, rather than as an afterthought.

1.5 Loading, Translation and Execution of a Program

When the program is complete and data have been prepared, both must be transmitted to the computer. The usual means of communication is the "punched card" or "IBM card". A machine called a "keypunch" is used to encode information in a card by punching holes in it. Each different character has a different pattern of holes; each character in the program and data is represented by the pattern in one vertical column of the card.

The key point in understanding the loading and execution of a program is the timing of the reading of the cards. the card deck consists of two parts -- the program (lines 1 to 26 of the example in Section 1.1) and the data (lines 27 and 28). The cards for the entire program are read initially -- before any execution of the program begins; the cards for the data are not read until specifically called for during execution of the program. The computer does not read a card and execute the statement on it, read the next card and execute, etc. Instead it reads the entire program, creates a copy of the program in "memory", and then begins execution with the first statement of the program. In the course of execution the "card read" statements (such as lines 14 and 20 of 1.1) will cause the data cards to be read.

The initial loading of the cards of the user's program is controlled by execution of another program called a "compiler" (or sometimes a "translator" or "interpreter"). As the user-program cards are read a translation is performed by the compiler with the result that the "copy" of the program in memory, while functionally equivalent to the initial program, is very different in appearance. During this translation the compiler checks the program statements for "syntactical" (grammatical) errors and reports these to the user. If any errors are discovered during this loading-translation process most compilers will halt after loading and refuse to initiate execution of the user-program; a few compilers will effect some repair of minor errors and permit execution to begin. Most users will become aware of the existence of a compiler only through this error checking and will never have occasion to see the strange form their program has assumed in memory. Part X contains a more detailed discussion of program translation.

The printed output for a program can also be divided into two parts, corresponding to the loading and execution phases described above. During loading, a copy of the user-program is printed, including announcement of any errors discovered. This much of the printing is automatic -- a service performed by the compiler. Further printing will be done only as called for by the "output" statements (such as lines 23 and 24 of 1.1) of the program. If the user fails to include any such statements there will be no output during execution and the results of the computation will never be known.

Section 1 <u>Exercises</u>

The following all refer to the programming example given   in
Section   1.1. You cannot   be   expected to   answer   all   of   these
questions at this point, but   attempting   to   do   so   should   be
interesting and educational.

1. What would have to be done to cause this program   to   obtain
the maximum of the following eight numbers:
     2 4 6 15 3 9 7 9

2. What would happen if the   program   were   used   to   find   the
maximum of the following nine numbers:
     6 45 -3 14 0 2 -1 52 143

3. What would happen if line 28 looked like the following:
     5 5 5 -1 -1 -1

4.What   would   happen   if the order   of   lines   17   and   18-19
were reversed? Lines 13 and 14?   Lines 18-19 and 20?

5.Suppose the problem definition were broadened to require the
program to work for negative as well as positive numbers.   What
changes would have to be made?

6.How   could   the   program   be   changed   to obtain the <u>minimum</u>
rather than the maximum of the numbers?

7. How could the program be changed to produce both the <u>maximum</u>
and the <u>minimum</u> of the numbers?

8. What would happen if line 17 were accidentally left out (say
the card was dropped) before the program was submitted   to   the
computer? Line 20? Line 24?

9. What would happen if line 23 were replaced by the   following
line?

     /* PUT SKIP LIST('NUMBER OF VALUES =', COUNT); */

10. How could the program be changed to produce the sum of   the
numbers in addition to the maximum?

11. What would happen if line 3 were replaced by the   following
line:

     /* COMPUTE THE PRETTIEST OF THE GREEN NUMBERS */

and no other change were made in the program?

12. Construct a set of test data (a replacement   for   line   28)
that would cause the program to produce incorrect results.

Section 2   Variables

A program describes how a set of values is to be manipulated. However, the description deals not directly with these values, but with entities called "variables". For example, instead of writing

                2 + 3   one could write   X + Y

and make arrangements so that "X had the value 2" and "Y had the value 3". The difference is essentially the same as that between arithmetic and algebra, and yields roughly the same advantage. One gains the ability to specify a procedure which may be applied, without change in the written form, to many different sets of values.

A variable is a place or location in the memory of a computer which can hold a value, and to which a name may be attached. The following line pictorially represents three variables:

A ---> 20   TOTAL ---> 456.003   ACCOUNT ---> -20.7

The first variable is named A and has the value 20 in its location (on its line). The second variable is named TOTAL and has the value 456.003. Variable ACCOUNT has the value -20.7.

We often omit the arrow in the pictorial representation, if the name and location are close enough so that no misunderstanding can take place:

    A 20   TOTAL 456.003   ACCOUNT -20.7

A variable is relatively permanent -- it is created when execution of a program begins and lasts until execution is completed. The value is generally more transient, and may change often during execution. At any given instant, a variable contains a single, specific value, which is referred to as the current value of the variable. The current value of the variable named A above is 20. The phrase "current value of the variable named A" is long, and is often shortened to "value of A". A's value changes whenever a different value is placed in the location named A.

It is important to clearly distinguish between creating a variable and assigning a value to a variable. A variable is

created only once -- when a physical location in the memory of
the computer is set aside to hold its value. The creation
process is also referred to as "declaring" or "defining" a
variable. Once a variable has been created it may have a value
assigned to it, and that value may be frequently changed.
This "assignment process" is the topic of Section 3.

In SP/k, declarations give the name to be attached to each
variable and describe the kinds of values each variable can
contain. The actual assignment of memory locations is performed
automatically by the computing system and the programmer need
not be concerned with it. He must only give a declaration for
each variable. For example,

        DECLARE (MINVALUE, CUM_SUM) FIXED;

defines two different variables named MINVALUE and CUM_SUM, each
of which can contain a decimal integer between -999999999
and +999999999. The declaration does not automatically
assign an initial value to the newly created variables; hence
they exist, they have a location ready to receive a value, but
have not as yet received one. Variables that have not yet
been assigned a value are said to have the value "undefined".

In SP/k it is an error if you attempt to use a variable that
has the value undefined; this always indicates an error in the
logic of your program.

Variables play an important role in programs. Each variable
contains a value with a specific meaning -- for example, the
minimum value of a list of numbers, or the cumulative sum of a
list of numbers. Knowledge of the variables and their meaning
is essential for any person trying to understand a program. In
order to help the reader, declarations for all variables must
be placed at the beginning of the program, before any statement
which uses the variables.

It is a good practice to describe the use of each variable
with a "comment". In PL/I, "/*" marks the beginning of a
comment and "*/" marks the end. The comment may contain any
characters on the keypunch -- except the sequence "*/" which
would be interpreted as the end of the comment. For example:

        DECLARE (MINVALUE,   /* MIN. VALUE OF X'S SO FAR; >= 0*/
                  CUM_SUM)   /* SUM OF X'S PROCESSED SO FAR*/
                  FIXED;

Clarity and precision in defining the role of each variable
in a program is of vital importance in producing a correct and
understandable program. Many programming difficulties can be
traced to fuzziness in the meaning of key variables. We find it
useful, when asked to help "debug" (find the mistakes in) a
program, to start by asking such questions as:

"What does this variable represent?"
"Does it have the same meaning everywhere in the program?"
"What are the extreme limits on the values it may contain?"

This approach is aided by following a consistent practice of supplementing the declaration of each variable with comments.

2.1 Identifiers

The sequence of characters that forms the name of a variable is called an "identifier". Each programming language has a set of rules that control the choice or construction of identifiers. These rules sometimes seem arbitrary, and at this stage it is best just to accept and learn them. Among the most widely used programming languages -- FORTRAN, COBOL, PL/I and ALGOL -- the rules are quite similar, but just enough different to be a nuisance to the unwary programmer. In almost any language, however, an identifier can consist of a letter, followed by a sequence of other letters and digits, and this is the kind of identifier you will use most often. PL/I also allows the underscore " _ " to be used anywhere after the first letter. The complete PL/I rules for forming identifiers are given in Appendix B.2.

You should choose variable names that suggest the role the variables play in the program. While it may seem clever to name variables after girls or flowers, it doesn't help to make a program understandable. For example, although SUSAN is a legal identifier, using SUSAN as the name of a variable which holds the average of 10 numbers is not helpful. AVERAGE or AVG would be better since it would help to indicate the role of the variable.

The SP/k keywords (such as GET, PUT, LIST, SKIP, DO, END, DECLARE) may not be used as identifiers. Using these words for the names of variables makes a program hopelessly hard to understand. A list of keywords that cannot be used as identifiers is given in Appendix A.5.2.

2.2 Values

Programming languages allow a variety of different types of values to be stored in variables. The most important types for ordinary numeric computation are signed integers (..., -2, -1, 0, 1, 2, ...) and real numbers -- such as 20.3, -463.2, .000043, and 4.3×10^{-5}. (Note that the last two real numbers look different but represent the same quantity.) Since each value is placed in a physical location in the computer's memory, there must obviously be a limit on the number of digits allowed. One must be aware of such limits, but they are not germane to this discussion; they are listed in Appendix A.5. We assume

here that all numerical values will be represented in the
computer in conventional decimal notation, and that a reasonably
adequate number of digits is permitted in each value.

Constant values are often written in a program. In general,
integers can be written in their usual form:

-20   10365   23   1471   -1943

In SP/k constants that are real numbers must be written in
"scientific" or "exponential" form:

-20E0   1.0365E+4   4E-1   0.15E0   -4.3E-4

The exponent "E0" following the number specifies that the
fractional number is to be multiplied by 10^0, which is 1. In
general, one can put any positive or negative integer after the
"E" to represent a power of 10. Thus, the following are all
equivalent:

4.3E-5   .43E-4   .000043E0   .00000043E+2

This is often called "floating point format", since the position
of the decimal point "floats" depending on the exponent
following "E".

Some programming languages allow other types of values. A
value may also be a string (or sequence) of characters, such as
'TORONTO'. Variables with such "character" values are discussed
in Section 9. The values "true" and "false" are important in
certain contexts and we will discuss them in Sections 4 and 10.
For the moment we will consider only values that are integers
and real numbers.

2.3 Type Attributes

In PL/I each variable is restricted to one particular type of
value. The value may change, but the type of value (like the
name) is permanent for the life of the variable. For example,
if variable COUNT is defined to hold only integer values it
might at different times have values such as 2, 1501, -3 and 0,
but it could never have values such as 20.3E+1 or 'HOLT'.

The properties that determine the type of value that can be
stored in a variable are called "attributes" of the variable.
We describe the attributes by putting them in brackets [and
] after the variable. The following examples illustrate how
the names, values and attributes of variables will be indicated
in the text:

         MAX   20 [fixed]   MAX may only contain integers
                                       (e.g. -3, 0, 1, +5)

         TB42 -2.0E-3 [float]   TB42 may contain real numbers
                                       (e.g. 2.03E+1, 2.00E+1, -8.2E-1)

         Z4 -2.00E+1 [float]   Z4 may contain real numbers

"FIXED" and "FLOAT' are PL/I's way of saying "integer" and
"real", respectively. In SP/k programs, integer and real number
constants are represented in the decimal number system.

    A variable always has some particular type attribute.
When we neglect to mention them it is only because the type of
value is not relevant to the point under discussion -- not
because attributes do not exist for that variable.

    In PL/I type attributes are specified by listing them in the
declaration of the variable. For example:

    DECLARE (MAX) FIXED;

    DECLARE (TB42) FLOAT,
       (Z4) FLOAT;

When several variables have the same set of attributes, a
list of names of the variables may be given in parentheses, and
the attributes given only once. For example, the following
declarations are equivalent:

    DECLARE (TB42, Z4) FLOAT;

    DECLARE (TB42) FLOAT,
       (Z4) FLOAT;

Section 2 <u>Summary</u>

1.A variable is a named location in computer memory into which
a value may be placed.

2.All variables to be used in a program should be defined
(created) by specifying their names and type attributes in
declarations placed at the beginning of the program.   The name
should be chosen to reflect the role the variable plays in the
program, and the declaration should be supplemented by a comment
that describes the role exactly and clearly.

3.We will use the type attributes FIXED for integer values and
FLOAT for real values.

4.Integer   constants may be written   in   a   program   in
conventional form: 32, -61, 43, 198.   Real number constants
must be written in exponential form: 3.2E1, -61E0, 4.3E0,
198E-3.

Section 2 <u>Exercises</u>

Exercises 1 to 4 concern the following variables:

      LAST_ONE <u>-20 [fixed]</u>

      ANSWER   <u>-3.02E+1 [float]</u>

      BAD20   <u>0 [fixed]</u>

      COSINE   <u>-3.02E+1 [float]</u>

      TEXT   <u>3.00E+1 [float]</u>

      MINIMUM   <u>+3.02E+1 [float]</u>

1.   a) What is the current value of variable ANSWER?
      b) What is the current value of variable COSINE?
      c) What is the current value of variable TEXT?
      d) Which variables have the value -3.02E+1
      e) Which variables have the value 20?

2. Which of the following values:

        -30, -30.1E+0, 0, 5E-3 43891, 4.38915E+2, 4.3891E4

    can be stored in variable:

      a) LAST_ONE ?
      b) BAD20 ?
      c) MINIMUM ?

3. Define the term "variable".

4. Write a PL/I declaration for the variables given above.

5. Consider the following declaration:

    DECLARE (POSTOT) FLOAT,   /* TOTAL OF X'S > 0 */
        (SUM, COUNT) FIXED; /* SUM OF Y'S, NO. OF PTS */

Write three separate declarations (one for each variable)
that are exactly equivalent to the single declaration given.

Section 3   Assignment of Value

The computing process involves the assignment of values to variables. The basic assignment process, in any programming language, has two distinct stages:

1. The production of a new value.
2. The assignment of that new value to a variable.

The construction for specifying a new value is called an "expression". Examples are:

    26   X   Y+1   (X3+ABC)/ZZZ

where X, Y, D3, ABC, and ZZZ are variable names. In the evaluation of an expression the current value of each variable referenced is used, but this does not change the values of those variables. Regardless of the length and complexity of an expression the result of its evaluation is a <u>single</u> <u>value</u>.

The second stage of the assignment process is the assignment of the new value. A logical form for describing this would be:

    X + Y -> Z

A precise description of the execution of this process is:

> Evaluate the expression X + Y, by adding a <u>copy</u> of the current value of the variable named X to a <u>copy</u> of the current value of the variable named Y. Store this sum as the new value of variable Z (replacing and destroying whatever previous value Z may have had).

Note that the values of X and Y are only copied and are not changed in the process. Typical values of X, Y and Z before and after such an assignment are:

    before: X 1   Y 3   Z 2
    after: X 1   Y 3   Z 4

3.1 <u>The</u> <u>PL/I</u> <u>Assignment</u> <u>Statement</u>

The syntax for an "assignment statement" in PL/I is:

        variable name = expression;

The expression on the right gives the formula to obtain a new
value; the variable on the left receives this new value.   The
"=" denotes the assignment process (instead of the arrow used on
the previous page) and the ";" denotes the end of the statement.
The following are examples of PL/I assignment statements:

        A = 4.3E+0;
        Z = X + 1;
        I = I + 1;
        LOW = CTR - 1.43E-1;
        SUM = 0;
        SUM = SUM + NUMBER;
        RATIO = (A+B) / (C+D);
        SUP = Z3 + P / (A + B/4E0);

Unfortunately, most programming languages use this syntax,
which does not suggest the order in which the actions are
performed. For example,

        X = Y;

should be read "get a copy of the value of Y, and store it in
X". It might seem that this is equivalent to saying "let X take
on the value of Y", but consider the following statement:

        X = X + Y;

It is clearer to read this as "add together the current values
of X and Y, and store the result in X", than it would be to say
"let X take on the value of X plus the value of Y".

Furthermore, the use of "=" improperly suggests a similarity
to an algebraic equation.   The assignment statement is a
<u>command</u> to perform a sequence of actions, whereas an equation is
a statement of <u>fact</u>. If equality between the left and right
sides already existed, there would be no point in writing the
statement at all, since no action would be required.   One might
try to salvage this "equation interpretation" by suggesting that
it is a command to "make the equation become true".   However,
this interpretation just cannot explain examples such as:

        X = X + Y;   and   W = W + 2;

The assignment statement <u>must</u> be considered a command to perform
two distinct actions: first, produce a value from the expression
on the right; second, assign this value to the variable on the
left.

Note that the two sides of an assignment statement are not symmetric in role. The following two statements have different meanings, although as equations they would be equivalent:

    X = Y;   and   Y = X;

Assignment statements are executed in the order in which they appear (reading from left to right, and top to bottom). Consider the two statements

    X = Y + Z;   and   Z = X + Y;

Assuming a set of initial values, the effect of executing these statements in one order would be:

before		X 3	Y 5	Z 2
after	X = Y + Z;	X 7	Y 5	Z 2
after	Z = X + Y;	X 7	Y 5	Z 12

With the same initial values the effect of executing these same statements in the opposite order would be:

before		X 3	Y 5	Z 2
after	Z = X + Y;	X 3	Y 5	Z 8
after	X = Y + Z;	X 13	Y 5	Z 8

As a further example, consider the task of interchanging, or "swapping", the values of two variables. Suppose we want to

change	A 3	B 5
to	A 5	B 3

Since there is no single statement in PL/I to perform this, it must be done with a sequence of assignment statements. Let T be a variable not used in the program so far. The following uses T as a "temporary" variable to accomplish the swap:

```
/* SWAP VALUES OF A AND B */
T = A;
A = B;
B = T;
```

Given the initial values of the variables as shown below, we show the contents of the variables after execution of each statement. Question marks ??? are used as the value of a variable that has not yet been assigned a value (i.e. has the value "undefined").

before	A 3	B 5	T ???
after T = A;	A 3	B 5	T 3
after A = B;	A 5	B 5	T 3
after B = T;	A 5	B 3	T 3

The comment /* SWAP VALUES OF A AND B */ summarizes the actions of the group of statements that follow it. When reading a program that includes this segment, to find out what is being performed we read the comment instead of the statements underneath it. The detailed statements under the comment need be read only to find out how the swap is being performed. Comments are entirely for the benefit of human readers; they have no effect on the execution of the program by the computer. When used properly, comments make it significantly easier for us to read and understand a program, but when badly used they obscure rather than clarify.

3.2 Arithmetic Expressions

Expressions are used in many different contexts in programs. Wherever they occur they always have the same basic purpose -- to provide a formula by which a value can be obtained. The simplest expressions are constants, like 3 or 20.6E0, or variables, like I or TOTAL. In general, an expression can include a number of terms or "operands", and "operations" by which the operand values are to be combined to yield a single value. Examples of expressions are shown in the right side of the assignment statements of Section 3.1. (The semi-colon ends the assignment statement and is not part of the expression.)

3.2.1 Symbols for Operations

The SP/k symbols for arithmetic operations are:

    +   for addition
    -       for subtraction, or to indicate negation
    /   for division
    *   for multiplication

The symbol for an operation is often called an "operator". The * operator is used for multiplication in most programming languages, because all the familiar means of indicating multiplication lead to confusion and ambiguity. (For example, a period could get confused with a decimal point -- would 2.34.5 mean 2.34 times 5 or 2 times 34.5?)

Other operations operate on non-numeric values. For example, the operations performed on string-valued variables are described in Section 9.

3.2.2 Precedence of Operations

Some concern must be given to the order in which arithmetic operations are performed. For example, should the expression

    A + B * C

be evaluated as A+(B*C) or (A+B)*C? In any expression, however complicated, a lavish enough use of parentheses will remove any possible ambiguity. However, to avoid too many parentheses, PL/I has conventions corresponding to normal algebra to indicate, for example, that:

	a + bc,	a - b + c,	a / b - c
means	a + (bc),	(a - b) + c,	(a / b)- c
and not	(a + b)c,	a - (b + c),	a / (b - c)

The PL/I rules for evaluation of an expression are:

1. Expressions in parentheses are evaluated first, from the innermost set of parentheses to the outer.

2. Subject to rule 1, the order of operations is:
   first: negation (-)
   next: multiplication (*) and division (/)
   last: addition (+) and subtraction (-)

3. Sequences of operations in the same category under rule 2 are evaluated:
   negations: right to left
   multiplications and divisions: left to right
   additions and subtractions: left to right

   For example:

   -X*Y   is equivalent to (-X)*Y

   X/Y*Z   is equivalent to (X/Y)*Z

   X-Y+Z   is equivalent to (X-Y)+Z

It is not necessary to memorize these rules; just use enough parentheses to specify the desired order, and keep a programming language manual handy to look the rules up if necessary. The important thing to note is that PL/I does remember these rules and will always follow them in determining the order of execution.

3.2.3 Conversion of Values

PL/I is usually quite accommodating with regard to the conversion of values between FIXED and FLOAT forms. FIXED and FLOAT variables, and conventional and exponential constants can all be used in the same expression. When the operands of an arithmetic operator are of different type (one FIXED and the other FLOAT) the non-FLOAT operand will be converted to FLOAT form. (Actually, a copy of the value is converted.) For this

purpose, a conventional constant is considered to be in FIXED
form and an exponential constant is in FLOAT form.

However, there are some surprises. One that causes trouble
is the fact that a FIXED variable will only accept an integer
value no matter what kind of value is produced by the expression
on the right side of the assignment statement. For example, if
variable INDEX is FIXED, the statement

        INDEX = -17.3E+0;

is legal (no error warning) but upon executionINDEXreceives
the value -17. The value -17.3E+0 has been "truncated" to -17
by dropping the digits to the right of the decimal point. This
truncation may be intended by the programmer, but if not, it is
a particularly insidious kind of error. The program could be
tested on data which are all integers, and work satisfactorily.
Then later, if it is used for data that are not all integers,
this supposedly correct program could give incorrect results.

Surprises may occur with multiplication and division when
constants alone appear as operands. For example, the expression
25 + 1/3 yields the value 5.33333 in PL/I, and 25.0000E+00 in
SP/k The reasons for this are complicated, and we will not go
into them here; they have to do with PL/I's unconventional way
of dealing with precision of arithmetic values. Avoid the
problem by making sure that at least one operand of a division
is a variable or constant in FLOAT form.

3.3 Built-in Functions

Some common "functions" are used so often in programming that
they have been included in the language. (This is only a
convenience since the task of each of these functions could be
accomplished by explicitly writing all the statements needed to
evaluate the function.) For example, to obtain the square root
of the value of variable X or of an expression X+Y/Z, write

        SQRT(X)   or   SQRT(X+Y/Z)

The expression whose square root is sought is called the
"argument" of the function.

This functional form can be used as an operand in an
expression, just as one would use a variable:

        X + SQRT(Y)
        SQRT(TEMP - SQRT(T4K/PRESSURE))
        B4 * (SQRT(SQRT(J3) + R2PEAK) + SIDE4)

Another function gives the maximum of a set of values:

        MAX(A,B)

yields a value equal to the greater of the values of A and B.
Similarly the MIN function obtains the minimum of its arguments.

The built-in functions included in a language depend heavily
on the problem area for which the language is designed.   PL/I
has a particularly large collection of built-in functions.   A
complete list is given in Appendix B.8. Take a minute to scan
this list to see what is available. When you encounter a built-
in function in one of our examples, refer again to B.8 for a
definition of its action. Note that the SP/k subset includes
only a few of the PL/I built-in functions. See Appendix A.4 for
a list of built-in functions included in SP/k.

In PL/I problems can arise in distinguishing between a
function name and a variable name. One could prohibit the use
of the function names as variable names, but this would force
the programmer to memorize a list of about 90 names he could not
use for variables, including such useful ones as HIGH, INDEX,
LOW, LENGTH, ALL, SUM, MAX, MIN, COUNT, DATE, and TIME.   To
avoid this, PL/I requires only that the same name not be used as
a variable and a function in the same part of the program. That
is, if you are using the SQRT built-in function you cannot use
SQRT as a variable name, but if you are not using the COUNT
function (and perhaps had forgotten that it even existed) you
can use COUNT as a variable name. The declaration of such a
name as a variable indicates that it will not be used as a
built-in function. Since SP/k allows only a short list of
built-in functions, it is good programming practice to not use
SP/k built-in function names as variable names.

3.4 Assignment from External Data

Evaluation of an expression generates a new value in terms of
values that are already in the computer memory. One also needs
a mechanism to enter values from outside the computer.
Execution of an "input" statement causes an auxiliary device --
such as a punched card reader, a magnetic tape reader, or a
typewriter terminal -- to deliver one or more values to the
memory of the computer. The form of the simplest input
statement is

        GET LIST(variable names, separated by commas);

An example is:

        GET LIST(AMOUNT);

Its execution causes the next value to be read from the data
list which is given on cards after the program, and assigned to
variable AMOUNT.   The value is assigned using the same rules
as in an assignment statement; if AMOUNT is a FIXED variable
the value is truncated to an integer.   Execution of the
statement

```
        GET LIST(X, Y);
```

would cause the next two values to be read (from the data list)
and assigned to X and Y, respectively.

    Recall (from Section 1.5) that the cards bearing data at the
end of the program are not read automatically into memory as the
program is being loaded. Loading ends with the last card of the
program body, and the cards bearing data wait in the card
reader, to read if and when the program calls for them by
executing GET statements.   The cards supply a list of values;
the reading process moves through this list from left-to-right,
one card to the next, as demanded by the execution of GET
statements. Each value is read only once from this list.
Suppose there are three GET statements in a program, where all
variables are FLOAT:

```
        ...
        GET LIST(BASE, HEIGHT);
        ...
        GET LIST(WIDTH, TEMP, TIME);
        ...
        GET LIST(LIMIT);
        ...
```

and the data list for this program is:

```
(3.4a)     $DATA
             17.5E+0
             8.372E+1
             .2305E+2
             76E+0
             2.314E+3
             964.122E+0
```

When the first GET statement is executed the first two values
are read from the data list (two values because there are two
variables listed in the statement) and 17.5E+0 becomes the value
of BASE and 8.372E+1 becomes the value of HEIGHT.   When the next
GET statement is executed the next three values are read;
.2305E+2 assigned to WIDTH, 76E+0 to TEMP and 2.314E+3 to TIME.
When the third GET is executed 964.122E+0 is read and assigned
to LIMIT.

    A total of six values are read in by the three GET statements
and exactly six values are provided in the data list. If more
than six had been provided, the extra values would simply have
been ignored since the program never calls for them to be read.
This could be intentional -- the amount of data processed might
depend upon some test the program performs upon the early
values. This could also happen by accident if the programmer
did not properly coordinate his input statements and data list.

    The opposite condition is more common; a GET statement is
executed and an inadequate number of data values remain on the

list to satisfy all of the variables in the GET. Different
languages react to this situation in different ways. It is
essentially an error, but is often considered a legitimate way
to stop execution. In order to detect the end of the data from
within the program, we often add some marker value at the end of
the actual data. This should be a value that is clearly
recognizable -- it cannot be a possible data value -- so that
the program can test for it after each GET statement. This
technique was used in the example of Section 1.1.

The variables listed in the GET statement and the values on
the data list must be synchronized with respect to order as
well as quantity. The variable to which each value is
assigned is entirely determined by the order in which the
variable names appear in the GET statements. (For this purpose
the order of the GET statements is the order in which they are
executed, and not the order in which they are written.
This distinction is the topic of Section 4.) Hence the
programmer must know exactly what the order of the variables in
the "GET lists" will be and arrange the data values accordingly.
This is not always easy and is a common source of errors. For
example, in the data list above there is nothing in the list
that suggests that 17.5E+0 is intended to be assigned to BASE
and 8.372E+1 to HEIGHT. If the position of these two values
had been reversed the computer would have uncomplainingly
assigned 8.372E+1 to BASE and 17.5E+0 to HEIGHT.

3.4.1 Data Format

The data associated with the GET LIST statement is a list of
values. No blanks may separate adjacent characters of a value,
while adjacent values must be separated by one or more blanks.
The entire card may be used, with column 1 considered to come
immediately after column 80 of the previous card. (SP/k does
not allow splitting a single value onto two cards -- for
example, avoid punching the value 23 with the 2 in column 80 of
one card and the 3 in column 1 of the next.) Values can be given
in either conventional or exponential form.

In example (3.4a) the values were given on six different
cards. Each of the following forms is equivalent to (3.4a),
although (3.4.1d) is best for humans since the arrangement
suggests which values will be read by each GET statement.

(3.4.1a) $DATA
            17.5E0   83.72E0   76E0   2314E0   964.122E0

(3.4.1b) $DATA
            17.5E0   83.72E0   23.05E0   76E0   2314E0   964.122E0

(3.4.1c) $DATA
            1.75E1   8.372E1   2.305E1   7.6E1   2.314E3   9.64122E2

(3.4.1d) $DATA
            .175E2   .8372E2
            .2305E2   .76E2   .2314E4
            .964122E3

   Only values can be given as data. It would not make sense to
give a variable as a datum -- each datum will be assigned as the
value of a variable, and variables of the kind we are using
cannot have another variable as value. Arithmetic operations
are not allowed in the data -- 5E-1 cannot be given as 1/2.

Section 3 <u>Summary</u>

1. The form of an assignment statement is:

        variable = expression ;

To execute an assignment statement, evaluate the expression and
assign the result to the variable on the left of the =.

2. +, -, / denote   addition,   subtraction   and   division.   *
denotes multiplication. In every division at least one of the
operands should be in FLOAT form.

3. Parenthesized   subexpressions are evaluated from inside out.

4. When not overruled by parentheses the   order   of   operations
is:
     a.   Negation
     b.   Multiplication and division
     c.   Addition and subtraction

Within these categories a sequence of negations   proceeds   from
right to left; the others from left to right.

5.   When   a   value   is   assigned   to   an   integer   variable any
fractional part of the value is dropped.

6. A library of built-in functions such as SQRT(...)   is
provided.

7. The form of the simplest input statement is:

        GET LIST(variable names, separated by commas);

8. The order of data values on cards is crucial, but format is
immaterial. The entire card may be used; adjacent values should
be separated by one or more blanks.

Section 3 Exercises

1. In each of the following assignment statements delete all "redundant" parentheses -- that is, parentheses whose deletion does not change the result of the statement:

a) ALT = ALT + (BASE + COL4) + DIV;

b) PRESSURE = (TEMP + ENTROPY) * SPEC22;

c) GRADIENT = (GRADIENT - (HGT-SLOPE));

d) EFF = (EFF + (FULL * (LOSS*H3)));

e) X = -B + SQRT((B*B -(4*(A*C))));

2. Suppose the following were the values of four variables at a certain point in a program:

BASE	4.0E+0	[float]
HGT	3.0E+1	[float]
SIDE	0.0E+0	[float]
TOP	1.42E+1	[float]

Starting at that point, the following four assignment statements are executed in the order shown below:

```
SIDE = SIDE + BASE/HGT;
SIDE = SIDE + BASE/HGT;
TOP = BASE + HGT + SIDE + TOP;
TOP = TOP/HGT;
```

What are the resulting values of the four variables?

3. The following are all intended to be assignment statements. Which ones contain at least one syntax error?

a) A = B + C

b) A = B, C;

c) A = (B + C);

d) A + B = C;

e) (A = B + C);

f) A = (B) + C;

g) A = B (+) C;

h) A = (B + C;)

4. Write a GET statement and a data list that will assign the
same values as the following pair of assignment statements:

    XPLUS = 93.17E+0;
    XMINUS = -4.593E+1;

5. Suppose the data given after a program are the following:

    $DATA
    2 4 6 8 10 12 14

What would be the values of the variables T4, LOW and VAL after
execution of the following statement (assuming that it is the
first GET statement to be executed in the program):

    GET LIST(VAL, LOW, LOW, T4, LOW, VAL);

Give a different data list and GET statement that will produce
exactly the same result (but are shorter and more reasonable
than the example shown).

Section 4   Flow of Control

The essential work of a computer program is performed by the assignment statements. Other statements are used to specify the order in which different statements are to be executed; they specify the "flow of control" in the execution of a program.

4.1 General Program Structure; Executing Programs

A complete "job" to be processed by a computer consists of a program and data, in that order. In SP/k, the form of a job is:

```
$JOBK ID='name of programmer'
 procedure-name : PROCEDURE OPTIONS(MAIN);        ⌐
     /* Comment summarizing program function */   |  main
     Declarations                                 |  proc-
     Body of procedure (imperative statements)     |  edure
     END /* procedure-name */;                     ⌐
$DATA
       Data cards
```

The program consists of a "main procedure". The "procedure name" that appears before PROCEDURE is also called an "entry-name" of the procedure, and can be used to refer to the program as a whole. Procedure-names are chosen subject to the same rules as variable identifiers (Appendix B.2) and should be chosen to suggest the action the procedure performs.

A procedure consists of declarations and imperative statements. The declarations describe the variables (giving their names and attributes) to be created before execution of the procedure body begins. They are written immediately after the procedure heading and are effectively part of that heading.

The body of the procedure consists of imperative statements that direct the computer to perform certain actions -- such as assign a new value to a variable, read new data values from cards, and print results. Normal execution order of the statements is like the normal order of reading English text -- from left to right, top to bottom, from the beginning to the end of a procedure.

The $JOBK and $DATA cards are not part of the SP/k program, but serve to tell the computer where the SP/k program and its data begin.

4.1.1 <u>Writing</u> <u>Simple</u> <u>Programs</u>

At this point you have seen almost enough of PL/I to be able to write simple programs; we need only explain how to get "output" -- how to cause the computer to write numbers out in a readable form.

The simplest form of output statement is

PUT SKIP LIST(list of expressions, separated by commas) ;

Thus, execution of a statement

PUT SKIP LIST(X, Y, Z);

causes the values of variables X, Y and Z to be printed in a readable form, on one line. The output resulting from execution of such PUT LIST statements will accompany the "listing" of the program you receive after your program has been executed on the computer. Output is discussed further in Sections 6 and 7.

We now show two examples of complete programs -- the kind you should be able to write, keypunch and submit for execution.

```
          $JOBK ID='RIC HOLT'
            ADDER: PROCEDURE OPTIONS(MAIN);
               /* READ TWO VALUES AND PRINT THEM, AND THEIR SUM */
               DECLARE(X,Y,              /* INPUT NUMBERS */
                       Z) FLOAT;         /* SUM OF X AND Y */
(4.1.1a)  GET LIST(X,Y);
               Z = X + Y;
               PUT SKIP LIST(X,Y,Z);
               END /* ADDER */;
          $DATA
          1.55E+1   10.2E+0
```

The second example is:

```
          $JOBK ID='JIM CORDY'
            SROOT: PROCEDURE OPTIONS(MAIN);
               /* PRINT INPUT VALUE AND ITS SQUARE ROOT */
                    /* ASSUMES INPUT VALUE IS >=0.0 */
               DECLARE (ARG) FLOAT;      /* INPUT VALUE */
               DECLARE (SRARG) FLOAT;    /* SQUARE ROOT OF ARG */
               GET LIST(ARG);
               SRARG = SQRT(ARG);
               PUT SKIP LIST(ARG,SRARG);
               END /* SROOT */;
          $DATA
             2.501E+1
```

4.1.2 <u>Tracing</u> <u>Execution</u>

You should understand both the meaning of each PL/I statement
and the manner in which they are executed, well enough to be
able to follow the execution of a program on a statement-by
statement basis. In fact, you should be able to <u>simulate</u> <u>the</u>
<u>action</u> <u>of</u> <u>the</u> <u>computer</u> and "trace" the execution of a program on
paper. Your action should differ from the computer's only in
speed (by a factor of 10^6 or more).

For example, a detailed trace of the loading and execution of
(4.1.1a) is given below:

1. The cards, from $JOBK through $DATA are read; a copy of
the program (in translated form) is created in memory.

2. Execution begins by entering the main procedure ADDER.

3. As ADDER is entered three variables are created (recall
that ??? is used to indicate an undefined value):

    X ??? [float]
    Y ??? [float]
    Z ??? [float]

4. The first statement in the body of ADDER is GET
LIST(X, Y);. Execution of this statement reads the two
numbers on the first (and only) data card and assigns them
to variables X and Y. At this point, the variables are:

    X 1.55E+1 [float]
    Y 1.02E+1 [float]
    Z ???   [float]

5. Execution of the next statement, Z = X + Y;, changes
the value of Z. The variables now are:

    X 1.55E+1 [float]
    Y 1.02E+1 [float]
    Z 2.57E+1 [float]

6. Execution of the next statement, PUT LIST(Z);, causes
an output line to be printed:

    2.57000E+01

(The actual number printed is 2.56999E+01. The reason for
the difference is given in Section VIII.1.)

7. The end of ADDER is reached; execution of the program
is finished.

Having completed ADDER, the computer begins execution of some
other program. The next program "overwrites" and destroys the
ADDER program, and its variables X, Y and Z.

4.2 Repetitive Execution

Most programs require statements to be executed repeatedly, so it is essential to have convenient mechanisms to control repetition. In PL/I a sequence of consecutive statements whose execution is to be repeated, or "iterated", may be formed into the "body" of a "DO group" or "loop", which has the general form:

```
DO control phase;
    Body of loop(sequence of statements)
    END;
```

Types of control phrases that may be used in a DO statement are considered in Sections 4.2.1 and 4.2.2.

The complete loop is a single unit -- a single complex statement. It can appear wherever any other statement can appear.

4.2.1 Conditional Repetition

The basic PL/I loop has the form

```
DO WHILE(condition);
    Body of loop(sequences of statements)
    END;
```

The "WHILE loop" is executed as follows:

1. Evaluate the condition. If the result of evaluation is "false", execution of the loop is completed; if "true", proceed to step 2.

2. Execute the body of the loop. Upon completion, return to step 1.

The action is suggested by the English meaning of the keywords -- the body is iterated while the condition remains true. The action can be shown graphically by a "flow-diagram":

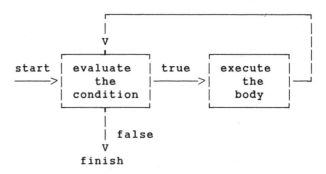

A WHILE loop was used in the example in Section 1.1. As another example, suppose one wished to sum the integers from 14 through 728. (There is a simple formula to sum consecutive integers so this program would not actually be used, but it provides a simple and clear example of the control of repetition.) The following program segment could be used:

```
            DECLARE (I,SUM) FIXED;
            /* SUM INTEGERS FROM 14 THRU 728 */
            I = 14;
            SUM = 14;
(4.2.1a)    DO WHILE(I < 728);
                I = I + 1;
                SUM = SUM + I;
                END;
```

The first two assignment statements establish initial values for the variables I and SUM. Then the WHILE loop is executed. Since the condition I < 728 is true (I=14) the loop body is executed. This changes I to 15 and SUM to 14+15=29. Then the condition is re-evaluated. It is still true (since the value of I is now 15) so the body is again executed. This repetition continues until finally the value of I becomes 728. At this point the condition is found to be false, and the execution of the WHILE loop is finished. The required task has been accomplished -- the variable SUM contains the sum of the integers from 14 to 728.

We can "prove" that (4.2.1a) performs the desired task by showing that, just before and after each execution of the loop body,

(4.2.1b) SUM contains the sum of the numbers from 14 to I.

Before executing the loop I=14 and SUM=14, so that (4.2.1b) holds. The body of the loop always increases I by 1 and then adds the new I to SUM, so that the relation (4.2.1b) does indeed hold <u>after</u> <u>every</u> execution of the body. Hence after the last <u>execution</u> we have I=728, and SUM contains the sum of the integers from 14 to 728.

A more detailed analysis of WHILE loops is given in Section VII.2.

Execution of the body of a WHILE loop must provide some action that affects the condition, so that <u>it</u> <u>eventually</u> <u>becomes</u> <u>false</u>. In the example above an assignment statement increases the value of I to serve this role. If the body never affects the condition, then if it is initially true it will remain true and the body of the WHILE loop will be iterated indefinitely. This is a classic program error called an "infinite iterative loop" and every programmer produces one once in a while. In practice, of course, each program is subject to a time limit so that repetition does not continue forever.

The condition may be false when the WHILE loop is first encountered.   In this case the body is not executed -- not even once -- so the statements of the body have no effect upon the condition or upon anything else.

It is important to understanding the action of a WHILE loop to know <u>when</u> the condition is evaluated.   This is done before the body itself is executed.   If the condition is true then the <u>entire</u> <u>body</u> <u>is</u> <u>executed</u>. Even if statements within the body change the values of variables to make the condition false, the <u>condition</u> <u>is</u> <u>not</u> <u>under</u> <u>continuous</u> <u>review</u> <u>during</u> <u>execution</u> <u>of</u> <u>the</u> <u>body</u>.   The condition is not re-evaluated until after execution of the body is completed.

As a final example, we present a program segment which reads input numbers from the data cards behind the program, until a number less than zero has been read.

```
/* READ UNTIL A NEGATIVE NUMBER IS READ */
GET LIST(N);
DO WHILE(N >= 0);
   GET LIST(N);
   END;
```

4.2.1.1 <u>Simple</u> <u>Conditions</u>

A simple "condition" or "relational expression" is a special type of expression that involves a "relation".   The symbols for the SP/k relations are the following:

<u>symbol</u>	<u>meaning</u>
=	is equal to
¬=	is not equal to
>	is greater than
>=	is greater than or equal to
<	is less than
<=	is less than or equal to

(The double-character symbols cannot have a blank between characters.)   A condition consists of two arithmetic expressions (as described in Section 3.2) separated by a relation:

arith-expr   relation   arith-expr

A condition describes a relationship that is either <u>true</u> or <u>false</u>.   For example, 2<3 is a condition that is always true; 2=3, a condition that is always false; J=K, a condition that may be either true or false depending upon the values of the variables J and K at the instant the condition is evaluated.

Other examples are:

```
TEST = 0
J+2 < K
TEMP*(PRESSURE - 4*PI) <= BASE_PRESSURE
```

4.2.1.2 Compound Conditions

Conditions can be made more complex by the use of "Boolean operators". These are "and", "or" and "not". "And" and "or" are used to combine two conditions to form a "compound condition". "Not" is used to reverse the truth of a condition. Letting A and B represent conditions which are true or false, we describe the symbols and meanings of the three operations:

English	symbol	meaning		
"and"	&	A & B	is true if both A and B are true
"or"	|	A | B	is true if either A or B is true
"not"	¬	¬ A	is true only if A is not true

The following table gives the values of these compound conditions for different values of the conditions A and B.

A	B	A & B	A | B	¬ A
true	true	true	true	false
true	false	false	true	false
false	true	false	true	true
false	false	false	false	true

WHILE loop conditions can be simple or compound:

```
DO WHILE ((I>56) & (I<729));
DO WHILE ((PRESSURE > PRESSMIN) & (TEMP < TEMPMAX));
DO WHILE ((REG_GAP <= 15.2E+0*GAP) | (FLAG = 2));
```

Precedence rules for these operators are analogous to those for arithmetic operations given in Section 3.2.2. "And" is considered before "or", so that

    A=B & C=D | E=F   is equivalent to   (A=B & C=D) | E=F

It is a good idea to use parentheses in compound conditions to be certain that the order of consideration is what you intended.

"Not" should be used sparingly, since it tends to make programs harder to understand. When "¬" must be used, parentheses should always be given to enclose the condition to which it applies. In simple cases, "¬" can often be avoided by choosing the opposite relation:

    ¬(A=B) is equivalent to A¬=B
    ¬(A<=B) is equivalent to A>B

Note also the following rules (DeMorgan's Rules):

    ¬A & ¬B is equivalent to ¬(A | B)
    ¬A | ¬B is equivalent to ¬(A & B)

We have used the terms "true" and "false" quite often in this section. Actually, any condition evaluates to a value which is '1'B if it is true, and '0'B if the condition is false. '1'B and '0'B are <u>bit</u> <u>constants</u>, which mean true and false respectively in SP/k.

These constants can be used as values in conditions, just the way arithmetic constants can be used in arithmetic expressions. Thus, the condition ¬('0'B) yields the value true, or '1'B; while '1'B & '0'B yields false, or '0'B.

4.2.2 <u>Repetition</u> <u>with</u> <u>Different</u> Values

An alternative form of loop is used to specify that execution of the body is to be repeated with different values of a key variable, called the "index" variable. Example (4.2.1a) could be rewritten in this form as

```
            /* SUM INTEGERS FROM 14 THRU 728 */
            SUM = 0;
(4.2.2.a) DO I = 14 TO 728 BY 1;
              SUM = SUM + I;
            END;
```

The index variable I is set to 14 and the body is executed; then I is set to 15 and the body is executed; etc. The final execution of the body has I equal to 728. The loop ends with I=729.

The general form of this type of DO group is:

```
            DO index-var = exp¹ TO exp² BY exp³;
(4.2.2b)        Body of loop (sequence of statements)
                END;
```

where "exp^1", "exp^2", and "exp^3" are arithmetic expressions. "exp^1" gives the value of the index variable for the first repetition; "exp^3" gives the "increment" to be added to the index variable after each iteration; and "exp^2" gives the termination test value. Iteration continues until the value of the index variable "passes" this test value. If the increment is positive iteration continues until the index variable is greater than the test value; if the increment is negative, until the index variable is less than the test value. In SP/k the index variable must be a FIXED variable.

Execution of such a loop can be explained in terms of an equivalent WHILE loop. Let IVAL, INCR and TERM be three new variables that are not used in the body of (4.2.2b). If the initial value of $\exp^3$ is positive, then (4.2.2b) is exactly equivalent to:

```
          IVAL = exp ;
                    1
          TERM = exp ;
                    2
          INCR = exp ;
                    3
          index-var = IVAL;
          DO WHILE(index-var <= TERM);
(4.2.2c)      Body of 4.2.2b
              index-var = index-var + INCR;
          END;
```

If the initial value of $\exp^3$ is negative then the equivalent WHILE loop would be written with the condition

```
          (index-var >= TERM).
```

Studied carefully, the equivalent WHILE loop reveals some interesting properties of the new form of loop;

1. A form of assignment is embedded in the control phrase; the index variable is changed just as if it were the left-side variable of an ordinary assignment statement.

2. Since the index variable is incremented and tested after the last execution of the body, the final value of the index variable is not the same as the value during the last execution of the body.

3. It is not necessary to use the index variable in the body. Frequently it serves only as a "counter" to determine the number of iterations of the body.

4. Alteration of the index variable within the body affects the control of iteration. This dangerous practice usually leads to confusion. Therefore it is good programming practice to never assign a new value to index-var in the body of a DO group.

5. Assignment within the body to a variable that appears in a control expression $\exp^1$, $\exp^2$ or $\exp^3$ has no effect on the control of iteration; these expressions are only evaluated before the first iteration of the body.

This second form of repetition can be quite useful. However, you should recognize that it is just a special case of the more general WHILE loop. When iteration is of this special form it is certainly easier to write "I = 14 TO 728 BY 1" than to write the statements necessary to initialize and increment the index variable in a WHILE loop. However, not all iteration has this form and one should not try to force it to do work for which it of consecutive statements. The two basic forms of a loop was

not intended. The WHILE loop is the general form always to be
used except when this special form of iteration is required.

To illustrate the use of a negative increment, (4.2.2a) could
be rewritten:

```
          /* SUM INTEGERS FROM 728 DOWN THRU 14 */
          SUM = 0;
          DO I = 728 TO 14 BY -1;
(4.2.2d)     SUM = SUM + I;
          END;
```

The DO groups in (4.2.2a) and (4.2.2d) produce the same final
value of SUM, but different final values of I. After executing
(4.2.2a) the value of I is 729; after (4.2.2d) it is 13.

4.2.3 Nesting of Loops

Since the body of a loop is a sequence of statements, and
since an entire loop is itself effectively a statement, one loop
can be included in the body of another. Suppose the input data
consists of a list of pairs of numbers, and for each pair (LOW,
HIGH) we want to print the sum of the integers from LOW to HIGH.
We always have LOW <= HIGH, and the last pair is followed by the
pair (1,0). For example, for the input "1 2 2 3 1 0" we
should print "3, 5". The following segment, which includes an
English statement, performs this service.

```
          /* READ INPUT PAIRS (LOW,HIGH) UNTIL LOW > HIGH. */
          /* FOR EACH PAIR PRINT LOW + (LOW+1) +...+ HIGH. */
          GET LIST(LOW,HIGH);
          DO WHILE (LOW <= HIGH);
(4.2.3a)     Set SUM to LOW + (LOW+1) + (LOW+2) +...+ HIGH;
          PUT LIST(SUM);
          GET LIST(LOW,HIGH);
          END;
```

Using the integer summing example (4.2.2a), we "refine" the
English statement into PL/I:

```
          /* SET SUM TO LOW + (LOW+1) + (LOW+2) +...+ HIGH */
          SUM = 0;
          DO I = LOW TO HIGH BY 1;
             SUM = SUM + I;
          END;
```

Substituting in (4.2.3a) we end up with the following segment:

```
/* READ INPUT PAIRS (LOW,HIGH) UNTIL LOW > HIGH.*/
/* FOR EACH PAIR PRINT LOW + (LOW+1) + ... + HIGH.*/
GET LIST(LOW,HIGH);
DO WHILE(LOW <= HIGH);
   /* SET SUM TO LOW + (LOW+1) + ... + HIGH */
   SUM = 0;
   DO I = LOW TO HIGH BY 1;
      SUM = SUM + I;
      END;
   PUT LIST(SUM);
   GET LIST(LOW,HIGH);
   END;
```

As a final example, consider the program segment

```
OUTSUM = 0;
INNERSUM = 0;
DO OUTINDEX = 1 TO 5 BY 1;
   OUTSUM = OUTSUM + 1;
   DO ININDEX = 1 TO 4 BY 1;
      INNERSUM = INNERSUM + 1;
      END;
   END;
```

Both index variables OUTINDEX and ININDEX are counters that
control the number of iterations but are not used within the
body. The segment does nothing useful, but study it until you
understand very clearly why after its execution the values of
the variables are:

    OUTSUM 5   INNERSUM 20   OUTINDEX 6   ININDEX 5

   Note that each segment in these examples could be presented
and discussed out of context -- it was not necessary to specify
whether it was part of some larger, unseen loop. Each segment
could in fact be buried in the interior of a nest of loops
several layers deep, so that its execution would be repeated
many times.

4.3 Conditional Execution

   It is often necessary to execute a statement conditionally.
For example, this was done in the program in Section 1.1 to find
the maximum of a set of values:

```
IF NUMBER > MAXNBR THEN
   MAXNBR = NUMBER;
```

The candidate number in NUMBER was compared to the largest that
had been encountered up to that point. If the new candidate was
larger, then execution of the assignment statement recorded it
as the largest encountered. If the new number was not larger,
then that assignment statement had to be skipped.

In PL/I the conditional statement has two forms. The simpler
one, used in the example above, is

    IF condition THEN
      statement[1]

The interpretation is suggested by the English meaning of the
keywords "IF" and "THEN":

    If the condition is true then execute statement[1].   If
    the condition is false, do not execute statement[1].

This flow-of-control is as follows:

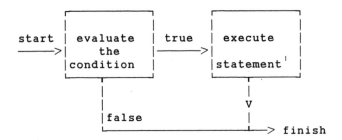

The second form of the IF statement is very similar:

    IF condition THEN
      statement[1]
    ELSE
      statement[2]

The interpretation is:

    If the condition is true then execute statement[1].   If the
    condition is false execute statement[2].

That is, one or the other of statement[1] and statement[2], but not
both, will be executed, depending upon the truth or falsity of
the condition. The flow-of-control is:

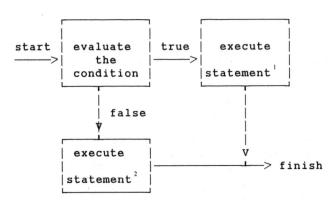

Either simple or compound conditions can be used, as described in Sections 4.2.1.1 and 4.2.1.2. The condition need not be enclosed in parentheses, unlike the condition in the WHILE loop where parentheses are required. (A programming language should not have such inconsistencies, but PL/I does, and you will just have to learn to live with them.)

Examples of conditional statements are given below. None of the parentheses in the conditions in these examples is required; they have been added only to make the meaning clearer to a human reader.

```
IF (NEWVALUE > MAXVALUE) THEN
    MAXVALUE = NEWVALUE

IF QTY < 0 THEN
    NEGCOUNT = NEGCOUNT + 1;
ELSE
    POSCOUNT = POXCOUNT + 1;

IF (B*B - 4*A*C) < 0 THEN
    PUT SKIP LIST('IMAGINARY ROOTS');

IF (CONTROL = J+1) | (VALUE = 0) THEN
    GET LIST(VALUE);
```

The "THEN statement" following the condition is mandatory; the "ELSE statement" is optional, since it is only present in the second form. Situations arise where it seems useful to have only an "ELSE statement" -- that is, a statement to be executed only if a condition is false. Since this is not possible (except by the clumsy artifice of using a "dummy THEN statement") one should reverse the sense of the condition. For example:

    replace A>B with A <= B

    replace (A=B) | (C<D) with ¬((A=B) | (C<D))
                        or with (A ¬= B) & (C >= D)

The required statement can then be given as the "THEN statement" -- to be executed when the reversed condition is true.

4.3.1 Compound Statements

Any single statement may follow the THEN or ELSE in a conditional statement. Thus an assignment statement, a GET statement, a loop, or another conditional statement may appear in this position. Sometimes one wants to execute a sequence of statements conditionally. To do this, a "compound statement" of the following form is used:

```
DO;
   Body (sequence of statements)
   END;
```

This form of DO group is not repetitive -- the body is executed
only once. The "delimiters" DO and END serve only to indicate
that the enclosed statements are to be considered as a single
unit. Examples are:

```
/* TEST  FOR NEGATIVE VALUE, RECORD ERROR, CORRECT TO +1 */
IF VALUE < 0 THEN
    DO;
        ERRORCOUNT = ERRORCOUNT + 1;
        PUT SKIP LIST('IMPROPER VALUE', VALUE);
        VALUE = 1;
        END;

/* SUM AND COUNT NEGATIVE AND NON-NEGATIVE VALUES */
IF NEWVAL < 0 THEN
    DO;
        NEGCOUNT = NEGCOUNT + 1;
        NEGSUM = NEGSUM + NEWVAL;
        END;
ELSE
    DO;
        POSCOUNT = POSCOUNT + 1;
        POSSUM = POSSUM + NEWVAL;
        END;
```

4.3.2 Nesting of Conditional Statements

The statement following THEN or ELSE in a conditional
statement can be another conditional statement. When this
occurs they are said to be "nested". For example, the form of a
complete, symmetric nest of three conditional statements, each
with both THEN and ELSE statements, is:

```
            IF condition¹ THEN
                IF condition² THEN
                    statement¹
                ELSE
(4.3.2a)            statement²
            ELSE
                IF condition³ THEN
                    statement³
                ELSE
                    statement⁴
```

The flow-of-control in this nest is:

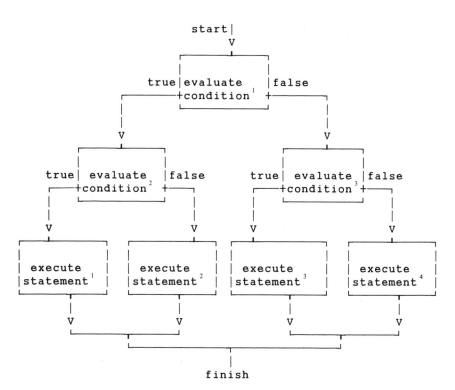

Great care is required in using nested conditional statements since it is very easy to write nests that are syntactically correct (hence do not receive any warning messages) but do not do exactly what was intended. For example, suppose in (4.3.2a) the second conditional statement did not have an ELSE statement. If the fourth line were simply removed from (4.3.2a) the program would look like:

```
            IF condition¹ THEN
                IF condition² THEN
(4.3.2b)            statement¹
            ELSE
                IF condition³ THEN
                    statement³
                ELSE
                    statement⁴
```

The indenting in (4.3.2b) is deceptive and does not accurately show the program structure. The lines should be indented as:

```
IF condition¹ THEN
    IF condition² THEN
        statement¹
    ELSE
        IF condition³ THEN
            statement³
        ELSE
            statement⁴
```

This is because <u>an</u> <u>ELSE</u> <u>belongs</u> <u>with</u> <u>the</u> <u>last</u> <u>preceding</u> <u>conditional</u> <u>statement</u> <u>that</u> <u>lacks</u> <u>an</u> <u>ELSE</u>. To achieve the intended flow-of-control a null ELSE statement could be provided for the second conditional statement:

```
IF condition¹ THEN
    IF condition² THEN
        statement¹
    ELSE
        ;
ELSE
    IF condition³ THEN
        statement³
    ELSE
        statement⁴
```

A preferable way of writing this to avoid the clumsiness of the null statement is:

```
IF condition¹ THEN
    DO;
        IF condition² THEN
            statement¹
        END;
ELSE
    IF condition³ THEN
        statement³
    ELSE
        statement⁴
```

If the reader finds the schematic nests above hard to follow he may well believe that when written with actual conditions and statements (including compound statements), and even deeper nesting this construction becomes very difficult to understand.

Fortunately the most obvious and common type of nested conditional statements can usually be replaced by a single conditional statement with a compound condition. The following examples are effectively equivalent:

```
IF condition¹ THEN          IF condition¹ & condition² THEN
    IF condition² THEN          statement¹
        statement¹
```

Note that the entire condition is evaluated, even if its value could be determined with less work. For example, the condition

    (I ¬= 0) & (A < B/I)

is obviously false if I has the value zero. Unfortunately PL/I will also attempt to calculate A<B/I and will produce an error message when an attempt is made to divide B by zero. Therefore, in writing compound conditions, one should always be sure that it is safe to evaluate all the parts of the condition.

4.4 Tracing Execution

Tracing was introduced in Section 4.1.2. To trace execution of a loop, construct a table with a row for each variable, and a column for the execution of each statement that changes the value of at least one variable. For example, consider the following program:

```
$JOBK ID='DAVID BARNARD'
WILL_SUM: PROCEDURE OPTIONS(MAIN);
        /* INPUT CONSISTS OF AN INTEGER N FOLLOWED BY */
        /* N FLOAT NUMBERS. SUM THE FLOAT NUMBERS */
        DECLARE (N) FIXED; /* NUMBER OF DATA ITEMS */
        DECLARE (I) FIXED; /* LOOP COUNTER */
        DECLARE (X) FLOAT; /* NEW DATUM */
        DECLARE (SUM) FLOAT; /* SUM OF DATA */

        GET LIST(N);
        SUM = 0;
        DO I = 1 TO N BY 1;
           GET LIST(X);
           SUM = SUM + X;
           END;
        PUT SKIP LIST('SUM IS:', SUM);
        END;
    $DATA
        3  5.6E+0   42.1E+0   31.7E+0
```

The first part of the trace table for this program is:

Variable	Values as execution proceeds -->									
N	???	3	3	3	3	3	3	3	3	3	3
I	???	???	???	1	1	1	2	2	2	3	3
X	???	???	???	???	5.6	5.6	5.6	42.1	42.1	42.1	31.7
SUM	???	???	0	0	0	5.6	5.6	5.6	47.7	47.7	47.7

Tracing execution is for the programmer's benefit -- to help him understand a program or to help him detect an error in it. Thus, tracing occurs mainly when he is in difficulty of one sort or another. It must be done with care, one step at a time. While tracing, the programmer must execute the program the way the machine does, without thinking about the task being performed. Too often, a programmer executes what he thinks is there, and not what really is there, which of course doesn't help at all.

It is not necessary to write down each value in each column, but only that value that is being changed. The trace table shown above would then be

Vari-able	Values as execution proceeds -->							
N	???	3						
I	???		1			2		3
X	???			5.6			42.1	31.7
SUM	???	0			5.6		47.7	

Often, the trace table becomes complicated and messy, and it is difficult to go back and analyze it. To aid in studying it, one often uses an extra row to indicate which statement is being executed, or to indicate the result of evaluating a condition. For example, consider the program segment

```
SUM = 0; /* START */
GET LIST(X);
DO WHILE (X ¬= 0);
   IF X<0 THEN /* L */
      SUM = SUM - X;
   ELSE
      SUM = SUM + X;
   GET LIST(X);
   END;
SUM = SUM+1;
...
$DATA
   8  -5  0
```

In the trace table below, the top row indicates either the statement executed (by giving its identifying comment) or the result of evaluating a condition of a loop or conditional statement.

Vari-able	/*STA-ART*/	loop true	/*L*/ X>0				loop true	/*L*/ X<0	
SUM	???	0	0	0	0	8	8	8	13	13
X	???	???	8	8	8	8	-5	-5	-5	0

The amount of information needed in the trace table varies from program to program, depending on how difficult it is and how much trouble the programmer is having. But get in the habit of putting in as much information as possible.

4.5 Initialization and Exit Problems

Most problems with iteration involve starting and stopping the iteration, or equivalently, entering and exiting the program segment that performs the iteration. If one can get the first and last iterations to work properly, the iterations in between generally pose much less of a problem. Developing correct loops is one of the hardest parts of programming. We give some direction in this matter here; the subject is discussed again in Section II.1.5.

4.5.1 Exit Problems in Loops

Exit problems seem to have two principal sources:

   1) Design of the stopping condition -- in particular, treatment of the "=" case.

   2) Position of the "increment step" relative to the rest of the body.

These problems are more often associated with the DO WHILE form since these tasks are handled more or less automatically in the DO index-var form. However, since the DO WHILE is the more general and important form these questions can neither be ignored nor avoided.

We use an integer summing example, similar to (4.2.1a):

```
               /* SUM INTEGERS FROM 14 THRU 728 */
               I = 14;
               SUM = 0;
(4.5.1a)       DO WHILE (I<729);
                    SUM = SUM + I;
                    I = I + 1;
                    END;
```

The condition in this segment could just as well have been written (I<=728). That is, it could be written to include the case of equality, and with a test value that is to be used in the body. Either form is equally correct -- they result in exactly the same execution -- and there are no general grounds for preferring one form to the other. However, there are two other possibilities that are likely to occur:

condition   result in (4.5.1a)

(I< 728)   one iteration too few
(I<=728)   correct number
(I< 729)   correct number
(I<=729)   one iteration too many

As indicated, the improper matching of the stopping value and
the condition will cause improper timing of the exit. This is
an exceedingly common type of error, even among experienced
programmers.

   Similarly, the position of the increment step can be
critical. Changing its position, (4.5.1a) could be written as
below. The comment notwithstanding, (4.5.1b) sums the integers
from 15 through 729.

```
            /* SUM INTEGERS FROM 14 THRU 728 */
            I = 14;
            SUM = 0;
(4.5.1b)    DO WHILE (I<729);
                I = I + 1;
                SUM = SUM + I;
                END;
```

   If it is important to have the increment step in the position
used in (4.5.1b) other parts of the segment could be changed.
For example, (4.5.1c) is a corrected version of (4.5.1b):

```
            /* SUM INTEGERS FROM 14 THRU 728 */
            I = 13;
            SUM = 0;
(4.5.1c)    DO WHILE (I<728);
                I = I + 1;
                SUM = SUM + I;
                END;
```

To the beginner, whether one increments at the beginning of the
body of the loop or at the end seems to be a matter of taste.
More insight into the problem is given in Sections II.1.5 and
VII.2.

4.5.2 Initialization and Entry Problems

   Typically, one or more variables must be "initialized" prior
to entry of a loop, as for example, SUM in (4.5.1a). This is
obvious, and logically straightforward, but nevertheless it is
overlooked surprisingly often.

   The benign form of error, in this regard, is to accidentally
place the initialization within the body of the loop, as in
(4.5.2a). This form of error is annoying but is usually
revealed during testing, since it makes the loop ineffective.

```
              /* SUM INTEGERS FROM 14 THRU 728 */
              I = 14;
(4.5.2a)      DO WHILE (I<729);
                  SUM = 0;
                  SUM = SUM + I;
                  I = I + 1;
              END;
```

The malignant form of error is to omit initialization
altogether. For example, if the SUM = 0; statement were omitted
from (4.5.1a), the result of execution would depend upon what
value SUM happened to have when this segment was encountered.
If this happened to be zero throughout testing the error would
not be detected and this faulty program would be proclaimed
"correct". Later, in production use, different initial values
for SUM might arise, and this latent error would affect the
results of the program. If the user is fortunate, the effect
will be so dramatic that it is obvious that something is wrong.
If he is less fortunate the error will remain hidden, and it
will intermittently injure the results by varying amounts.

Initialization problems can be much more subtle than the
previous example might suggest. For example, consider the
following task:

Read data from cards and sum the values, until a value of
-1 is encountered. Do not include the -1 in the sum.

Execution of a program for this task will involve the following
sequence of actions:

                   Read a value
                   Add the value just read to a running sum
                   Read a value
                   Add the value just read to a running sum
                   ...
                   Read a value and discover it is -1

Obviously this will involve a loop whose body includes a GET
and an assignment statement, but the entry and exit from the
loop are not as obvious. Note that the sequence must both begin
and end with a read. That is, at least one value must be read,
and when the last value (the -1) is read, it must not be
followed by an addition.

If one thinks of this program in terms of iteration of a pair
of actions

                   Read a value
                   Add the value just read to a running sum

then the simple DO WHILE loop cannot be used, since it is unable
to prevent the addition following the last read. One could use
the conditional statement of Section 4.3 to build a solution.

```
          /* READ AND SUM DATA UNTIL FIRST -1 */
          SUM=0;
          VAL=0;
          DO WHILE(VAL¬= -1);
(4.5.2b)     GET LIST(VAL);
             IF VAL ¬= -1 THEN
                SUM = SUM + VAL;
          END;
```

Alternatively, one can think of the program in terms of iteration of the pair

          Add the value just read to a running sum
          Read another value

This simplifies the exit problem considerably, and a normal WHILE loop can be used:

```
          DO WHILE (VAL ¬= -1);
             SUM = SUM + VAL;
             GET LIST(VAL);
          END;
```

However, now the problem is to get the loop started properly. One method would be to read the first value as an initialization action, outside of the DO group:

```
          /* READ AND SUM DATA UNTIL FIRST -1 */
          SUM = 0;
          GET LIST(VAL);
(4.5.2c)  DO WHILE (VAL ¬= -1);
             SUM = SUM + VAL;
             GET LIST(VAL);
          END;
```

It is not very clean to have to rewrite a portion of the body of the loop as initialization, but all things considered, for most simple tasks the style of (4.5.2c) is preferable to that of (4.5.2b). Since at least one number must be read, having the first number read outside of the loop makes sense.

The style of (4.5.2c) begins to become burdensome as the size and complexity of the initialization action grows. If an appreciable number of statements in the body must be rewritten outside, the risk increases that they will not be exactly the same. They might start out identical, but subsequent changes in one location might not be faithfully repeated in the other. In such cases, one sometimes contrives a way to get the iteration started, with minimal initialization. For example:

```
            /* READ AND SUM DATA UNTIL FIRST -1 */
            SUM = 0;
            VAL = 0;
(4.5.2d)    DO WHILE (VAL ¬= -1);
                SUM = SUM + VAL;
                GET LIST(VAL);
                END;
```

(4.5.2d) differs from (4.5.2c) only in the replacement of GET
LIST(VAL); with VAL = 0; but the difference in philosophy is
quite significant. A dummy value has been contrived to force
execution of the loop body; and the first statement in the body
is executed pointlessly but harmlessly. This was done just to
avoid having to write a duplicate of a portion of the body
outside the loop.   It should be obvious that this is a tricky
and dangerous practice.

The previous examples illustrate three unattractive ways of
performing a very common kind of task: (4.5.2b) requires an
extra conditional statement; (4.5.2c) requires rewriting of a
portion of the body outside the loop; and (4.5.2d) requires a
devious contrivance to get the loop started. The least
unattractive of these will vary, depending upon context and
other circumstances. Basically, the problem is that PL/I (as
well as most other programming languages) does not offer a
natural and convenient way to perform this task.

Section 4 <u>Summary</u>

1.   A PL/I job consists of a "main procedure", optionally
followed by data. The execution of a program consists of a
single execution of the main procedure.

2.   The normal order of statement execution is the order in
which the statements are written.

3.   A loop is a control mechanism to provide iteration of a
group are:

        DO WHILE (condition);
           sequence of statements
           END;

        DO index-var = expr^1 TO expr^2 BY expr^3;
           sequence of statements
           END;

4. A   condition   is an expression involving a relational
operator, and possibly Boolean operators. Its evaluation yields
either "true" or "false".   In PL/I, "true" and "false" are
represented by the constants '1'B and '0'B, respectively.

5.   There are two forms of conditional execution of a statement:

        IF condition THEN
           statement^1

        IF condition THEN
           statement^1
        ELSE
           statement^2

Statement^1 and statement^2 can be either simple or compound
statements.

Section 4 <u>Exercises</u>

1. Write a separate, complete program (similar to the examples
in Section 4.1.1) to perform each of the following tasks:

  a)Read   five data values, compute their sum and print the
    sum.

  b)Read   three data values, compute the first times the sum
    of the second and third, and print the result.

  c)Without reading any data (no GET statements) compute the
    sum of the integers from 1 to 8 and print the result.

  d)Read four data values, print the maximum of the four
    values.

2.   Write a single program to perform all four of the tasks
listed in Exercise 1, one after another.

3. Trace the execution of the programs in Exercise 1.

4. Keypunch and run the programs in Exercise 1.

5. Trace the execution of the following program segments:

```
  a) TOTAL = 0;
     DO WHILE (TOTAL < 5);
        TOTAL = TOTAL + 1;
        END;

  b) R1 = 0;
     R2 = 0;
     R3 = 0;
     DO I = 1 TO 3 BY 1;
        R1 = R1 + 1;
        DO J = 3 TO -1 BY -1;
           R2 = R2 + 1;
           DO K = 3 TO 5 BY 2;
              R3 = R3 + 1;
              END;
           END;
        END;
```

```
c)      A = 2;
        B = 5;
        /* COMPUTE Z=A**B, ASSUMING A > 0 AND B > 0 ARE */
        /* INTEGERS */
        Z = 1;
        X = A;
        Y = B;
        DO WHILE(Y ¬= 0);
            DO WHILE(MOD(Y,2)=0); /* WHILE Y EVEN */
                Y = Y/2E0;
                X = X*X;
                END;
            Y = Y - 1;
            Z = Z*X;
            END;
```

d) Same as c), but with "A=2; B=5;" replaced by "A=1; B=1;".

```
e) /* PRINT THE FIRST 7 FIBONACCI NUMBERS */
   N = 7;
   FIRST = 0;
   PUT LIST(FIRST);
   SECOND = 1;
   PUT LIST(SECOND);
   DO I = 3 TO N BY 1;
       THIRD = FIRST + SECOND;
       PUT LIST(THIRD);
       FIRST = SECOND;
       SECOND = THIRD;
       END;
```

```
f)   GET LIST(N);
     DO I = 1 TO N BY 1;
       GET LIST(X);
       IF X < 0 THEN
          PUT LIST(X+1);
       END;
       ...
     $DATA
         0    8    8    9    8    3
```

g) Same as f), but with the data

```
     $DATA
         5   -30   40   50   -60   -70   -80
```

6. The following exercises are to be written using only
conditional statements, assignment statements, and GET and PUT.

   a) Write   a   single   conditional   statement   with   only   an
      assignment statement as a substatement, for the following:

```
        IF X < 0 THEN
           IF Y < 0 THEN
              IF Z = 5 THEN
                 A = X + Y + Z;
```

b) Rewrite the following using a single conditional statement:

```
        IF X < 0 THEN
           DO;
              IF Y < 0 THEN
                 A = X+Y+Z;
              END;
        ELSE
           IF X = 5 THEN
              A = X+Y+Z;
```

c) Given are three variables A, B, and C. Write a program segment to interchange the values of A, B and C so that the largest is in A and the smallest is in C.

d) Given three variables X, Y, and Z, write a program to determine if they are the sides of a triangle. (X, Y, and Z are the lengths of the sides of a triangle if all are greater than 0 and if X+Y>Z, X+Z>Y, and Y+Z>X.)

e) Write a program segment to print '1' if X, Y, and Z are the lengths of the sides of an equilateral triangle, and '2' if they are the sides of a non-equilateral triangle. A triangle is equilateral if all its sides are the same.

f) A, B and C are three variables with different values. One of these variables has the "middle value" -- one other is greater, one smaller. Write a program segment that will set variable D to this middle value. Compare this to the program for c).

7. Exercises with loops.

a) Write a WHILE loop with initialization that is equivalent to:

```
FACT = 1;
DO I = 2 TO N BY 1;
   FACT = FACT*I;
   END;
```

b) Write a program segment to read in a sequence of 50 numbers and print out those numbers that are > 0.

c) Given variables N and M, both with values > 0, write a segment to print all powers of N that are less than M.

d) The <u>Fibonacci numbers</u> are the numbers 0, 1, 1, 2, 3, 5, 8, 13, 21, ... The first one is 0, the second is 1, and each succesive one is the sum of the two preceding ones.   The segment of Exercise 1 e) calculates the first 7 Fibonacci numbers and prints them out.   Given a   variable N≥2, write   a program segment to print out   all   Fibonacci numbers which are   less   than   N   (not the first N Fibonacci numbers).

8.   Write complete programs for the following problems.   Most of these use the program segments written in earlier exercises.

a) The input consists of groups of three   numbers.   The   last group   is an   end-of-list   signal consisting of three   zero values.   Write a program to read each group   in,   print   it out, and print an indication of whether the   three   numbers represent the sides of a triangle.   (See Exercise 6d.)

b) The input consists of an integer   N ≥ 0,   followed by N groups   of   three   numbers.   Write   a   program to read the groups of numbers in, print them out, and   then   print   the middle value of the three.   Each group and its middle value should appear on a separate line.

c) The input consists of a single integer N.   Write a   program to   read in N and print the first N Fibonacci numbers.   (If N < 1, don't print any out.)

d) The input consists of two positive integers M and N, with M ≥ N.   Write a program to print all Fibonacci numbers which lie between M and N.

e) The input consists of a positive integer N. Write a program to read N and to print out the   first,   second,   third and fourth   powers   of the integers 2, 3, ..., N. The beginning of your output should look like

2	4	8	16
3	9	27	81

9.   What   is the effect on the correctness of program 4.5.2b if the   assignment   statement   VAL=0;   were   omitted?   Under   what conditions might this program fail to execute correctly?

Section 5   Multiple-Valued Variables

5.1 Arrays of Subscripted Variables

Suppose it is necessary to store and process a large amount
of data at the same time.   For example, we might want to
calculate a set of numbers, then sort them into increasing
order, and finally print them in sorted order.   If there were 50
different numbers, using 50 different variables with different
names would be cumbersome.   In order to handle such situations,
most programming languages use a "data structure" called an
array.

An array is a set of variables, each having a separate value
just like an ordinary simple variable, but with all the
variables of the set sharing a common identifier. A "subscript"
is added to this common identifier to produce a unique name for
each individual element of the set.   For this reason these are
often called subscripted variables.   For example, an identifier
X could refer to a set of five variables:

	X(1)	20
	X(2)	-2
(5.1a)	X(3)	6
	X(4)	217
	X(5)	8

Programming languages are unable to use conventional subscripts
because the keypunch (and most other input devices) lack the
capability of depressing a character below the normal printing
line.   As a consequence subscripts are generally identified by
being enclosed in parentheses.

In the example above, X is called an array of subscripted
variables. Each of the variables named X(1), X(2), X(3), X(4)
and X(5) is itself called a subscripted variable.
(Unsubscripted variables -- those discussed before this section,
whose names are just simple identifiers -- will now be called
simple variables.) The "name" of a subscripted variable has the
form:

        identifier(signed or unsigned integer)

Thus X(1), X(0), X(+1), and X(-1) are all valid subscripted variable names. X(1) and X(+1) refer to the same variable. Note that the parentheses are necessary: X(2) is a subscripted variable, while X2 is just a simple variable with no relation whatever to the array X of subscripted variables.

Subscripted variables usually have positive subscripts, but zero and negative subscripts can also be used when convenient.

For example, suppose we need a table whose values represent the number of minutes in a day that the temperature is between i and i+1 degrees Fahrenheit. For each integer i, we can store the number of minutes that the temperature is between i and i+1 in the appropriate element of an array named MINUTES. Thus, the value of MINUTES(2) represents the number of minutes the temperature is between 2 and 3 degrees; MINUTES(47) represents the number of minutes between 47 and 48 degrees, MINUTES(-3) the number of minutes between -3 and -2, etc.

The name of a subscripted variable can be used exactly as the name of a simple variable is used. For example, execution of

        A = X(3) * X(1);

causes the current value of X(3) (which is given as 6 in (5.1a)) to be multiplied by X(1) (which is 20), and the result 120 to be stored in simple variable A. Similarly, a subscripted variable can be given as the target of an assignment process:

        X(2) = X(4) * 5;

The value of X(4) (which is 217) is multiplied by 5 and the result (1085) is stored in X(2). At this point, then, there seems to be little difference between a simple and subscripted variable, except that the name of the latter has a somewhat more complicated form. The real power of subscripted variables is shown in the next section.

5.1.1 Referencing Subscripted Variables

Suppose we wish to write a program to obtain the sum of the values of 50 different variables. We could use 50 simple variables named V1, V2, V3, ..., V50, and obtain their sum using a single, long assignment statement:

```
        /* COMPUTE SUM OF V1 TO V50 */
        SUM = V1 + V2 + V3 + ...  + V50;
```

(The three dots ... commonly used in algebra to indicate repetition are not valid in PL/I, so the statement shown above is not really complete. It would have to be written out with all fifty variables in the expression.) Alternatively the sum could be obtained using a sequence of 51 assignment statements:

```
/* COMPUTE SUM OF V1 TO V50 */
SUM = 0;
SUM = SUM + V1;
SUM = SUM + V2;
SUM = SUM + V3;
   ...
SUM = SUM + V50;
```

A slight modification of this second method would be to use an array U of subscripted variables:

(5.1.1a)
```
/* COMPUTE SUM OF ALL VARIABLES IN U */
SUM = 0;
SUM = SUM + U(1);
SUM = SUM + U(2);
SUM = SUM + U(3);
   ...
SUM = SUM + U(50);
```

Now suppose there is a simple variable I with value 2:

I $\underline{2}$

and suppose we execute the following assignment statement:

```
SUM = SUM + U(I);
```

This is interpreted as follows:

Add a copy of the current value of variable SUM to a copy of the current value of one of the subscripted variables of the array U. The subscripted variable to be used is determined by the value of the variable I. Since I's value is currently 2, the term U(I) refers to U(2). Hence a copy of the value of U(2) is added to the value of SUM. The result is stored as a new value for SUM.

Note that the assignment process remains the same <u>except that a preliminary evaluation of variable I is required to determine which of the subscripted variables of U is to be used</u>. This may not seem significant on first encounter, but it is, in fact, exceedingly powerful. Using this method of referencing subscripted variables and the means of controlling repetition introduced in Section 4.2, (5.1.1a) can be written as

(5.1.1b)
```
/* COMPUTE SUM OF ALL VARIABLES OF U */
I = 0;
SUM = 0;
DO WHILE(I < 50);
  I = I + 1;
  SUM = SUM + U(I);
  END;
```

Assuming a set of values for the array U, after execution of the first two assignment statements of this program the values might be the following:

$$
\begin{array}{llll}
U(1) & \underline{5} & I & \underline{0} \\
U(2) & \underline{7} & SUM & \underline{0} \\
U(3) & \underline{1} & &
\end{array}
$$

Execution of the WHILE loop starts with the evaluation of the condition. The condition is true, since the current value of I, 0, is less than 50, and the body of the loop is executed. First I is increased to 1. The second assignment statement in the body involves a subscripted variable. The current value of I, which appears as the subscript, is 1 so the current value of U(1), which is 5, is added to the value of SUM. Thus 5 is stored as the new value of SUM. At this point the values of the variables are:

$$
\begin{array}{llll}
U(1) & \underline{5} & I & \underline{1} \\
U(2) & \underline{7} & SUM & \underline{5} \\
U(3) & \underline{1} & &
\end{array}
$$

The condition is then evaluated. I is still less than 50 so the body is again executed. The first assignment statement increases I to 2. Since I is now 2, the value of the subscripted variable U(2) is added to SUM to give 12. This is stored as the new value of SUM.

The reader should continue this exercise until convinced that the result is the same as that obtained by (5.1.1a). Of particular interest is the last execution of the loop body, when I is 49. At this time I is increased to 50, and the value of U(50) is added to SUM (which by then contains the sum of the first 49 elements of the array U). Evaluation of the condition now yields false and execution of the loop is finished.

(5.1.1b) could also be written using the second loop form:

```
/* COMPUTE SUM OF ALL VARIABLES OF U */
SUM = 0;
DO I = 1 TO 50 BY 1;
    SUM = SUM + U(I);
    END;
```

As a further example, suppose the problem required the sum of the variables U(1), U(2), ..., up to the first variable with zero value. A program segment for this task would be:

```
/* COMPUTE SUM OF U VARIABLES THRU FIRST 0 */
I = 1;
SUM = U(1);
DO WHILE ((U(I) ¬= 0) & (I < 50));
    I = I + 1;
    SUM = SUM + U(I);
    END;
```

An expression may be given for a subscript -- the constants and variables in the examples so far are just special cases of expressions. The only restriction is that when evaluated the expression must yield an appropriate integer value. Expression subscripts can be very useful. For example, suppose there were two arrays, LEFT and RIGHT, each consisting of 15 variables. The following segment of program would copy the values of LEFT into RIGHT in inverted order:

```
/* REVERSE COPY 'LEFT' INTO 'RIGHT' */
DO I = 1 TO 15 BY 1;
   RIGHT(I) = LEFT(16-I);
   END;
```

5.2 Variables with Multiple Subscripts

It is sometimes convenient to use more than one subscript to designate a particular variable from an array. This is done when there is more than one natural pattern for referencing variables from the array. For example, suppose one had grades in nine courses for fifty students. We store these grades in an array GRADE of doubly-subscripted variables so that GRADE(I,J) represents the grade of the jth student in the ith course. That is, GRADE(3,17) is the grade of the 17th student in the 3rd course. Then to obtain the average grade in a certain course one could write:

```
/* COMPUTE AVERAGE GRADE IN ITH COURSE */
TOTGRADE = 0;
DO J = 1 TO 50 BY 1;
   TOTGRADE = TOTGRADE + GRADE(I,J);
   END;
AVGGRADE = TOTGRADE/50E0;
```

To obtain the average for a particular student for his nine courses one could write:

```
/* COMPUTE AVERAGE GRADE FOR JTH STUDENT */
SUMGRADE = 0;
DO I = 1 TO 9 BY 1;
   SUMGRADE = SUMGRADE + GRADE(I,J);
   END;
STUDAVG = SUMGRADE/9E0;
```

The overall average (all students in all courses) could be obtained by executing

```
/* COMPUTE OVERALL AVERAGE GRADE */
GSUM = 0;
DO I = 1 TO 9 BY 1;
   DO J = 1 TO 50 BY 1;
       GSUM = GSUM + GRADE(I,J);
       END;
   END;
OVAVG + GSUM/(9*50E0);
```

An array of singly-subscripted variables is a <u>list</u> of variables -- with the subscript specifying the position on the list. The analogous interpretation of an array of doubly-subscripted variables is a <u>table</u> or <u>matrix</u>. The first subscript specifies the <u>row</u> position and the second specifies the <u>column</u>:

GRADE(1,1)   GRADE(1,2)   GRADE(1,3)   GRADE(1,4)   ...

GRADE(2,1)   GRADE(2,2)   GRADE(2,3)   GRADE(2,4)

GRADE(3,1)   GRADE(3,2)   GRADE(3,3)   GRADE(3,4)

  ...

It is also common to visualize the variables of an array as being distributed in a geometric space. An array of singly subscripted variables is said to be a <u>one-dimensional array</u> or <u>vector</u>. The values are considered to be positioned along a line, with the subscript giving the position on the line. An array of doubly-subscripted variables is called a <u>two-dimensional array</u> or <u>matrix</u> and the pair of subscripts specifies a position in the plane of values. Although singly and doubly-subscripted variables are the most common, three or more subscripts can be used if required.

5.3 <u>Declaration of Arrays</u>

An array declaration specifies the number of subscripted variables to be created and the number of subscripts to be used for referencing each variable, as well as the type of value each variable can contain. The most common form for a one-dimensional array is

DECLARE (identifier(bound)) attribute ;

An example is:

DECLARE (TEMP(50)) FLOAT;

This defines an array of 50 variables named TEMP(1), TEMP(2), ..., TEMP(50), each capable of holding one FLOAT number.

If subscript values are to start anywhere except 1, then a lower bound must also be given. For example, to define an array of 22 variables named POP(-1), POP(0), ..., POP(20), use

    DECLARE (POP(-1:20)) FLOAT;

Multiple subscripts are indicated by two or more bounds, separated by commas. For example, to define an array of 450 doubly-subscripted variables with the values of the first subscript ranging from 1 to 9, and the second from 1 to 50, use

    DECLARE (GRADE(9,50)) FLOAT;

As a final example, the following declaration defines a three-dimensional array of 60 integer variables, each with three subscripts. The values of the first subscript range from -5 to -2; the second from 1 to 3; and the third from 0 to 4.

    DECLARE (POINT(-5:-2,3,0:4)) FIXED;

In referring to arrays in the text we will generally use the same form as the declaration. That is, MAT(1:5,1:9) refers to the array defined by the declaration

    DECLARE (MAT(1:5,1:9)) FLOAT;

We use the complete form of the declaration in these references -- MAT(1:5,1:9) rather than MAT(5,9) -- since this distinguishes between a reference to the complete array and a reference to the particular subscripted variable with maximum subscript values. We also use the notation to refer to an array segment -- a part of the array. For example, if A(1:100) is an array, we might discuss the segment A(1:50), or A(1:N) where N contains the subscript value. A(1:1) refers to the single element A(1), while A(1:0) refers to the array segment containing no elements, the empty segment.

5.4 Program for the Example of 1.2.1

In Section 1.2.1 the analysis of a problem description was carried through several levels, but the programming was postponed until subscripted variables could be employed. The analysis in Section 1.2.1 had reached the following stage:

    3.1 Read a sequence of 100 or fewer positive integers from cards until a zero value is encountered; store these integers in memory, preserving order.

    3.2 Find the position of the integer with maximum value in this sequence.

3.3 Print the early values of the sequence, from the first
to the maximum value, one per line.

Each of these subtasks is well defined and detailed program
design can begin. The next step is to specify the data
structures that will be used.

The principal data structure will be an array, say
INTEGER(1:100).   It needs 100 variables since there may be that
many data values, and should be FIXED. There should be a
variable TOP (say) to indicate the number of values currently in
the array, and a variable MAXP (say) to mark the position of
the maximum value. Later, as we design the different subtasks,
we may find that other variables will be needed.

Now the problem statement can be rewritten in terms of the
variables that will be used:

4.1 Read data into INTEGER(1:TOP) until a zero value is
encountered (keeping the value of TOP as defined above).

4.2 Set MAXP to mark the position of the maximum value in
INTEGER(1:TOP).

4.3 Print the values in INTEGER(1:MAXP), one per line.

This description is now very close to programming language
terms.   Although it may not seem so to one who is just learning
the language, the hardest part of the programming process is
bringing the problem description to this level.   The analysis
and design have been completed -- from here on it is just a
matter of translating into the proper form.

We will program the sub-tasks one at a time, taking them in
reverse order just to demonstrate their relative independence.
The program for 4.3 is obviously a loop:

```
DO I = 1 TO MAXP BY 1;
   PUT SKIP LIST(INTEGER(I));
   END;
```

Problems concerning extreme values of MAXP might arise in this
subtask. If MAXP<1 no values will be printed. This makes sense
since MAXP<1 means that <u>no</u> values appeared in the input -- only
the end signal 0. If MAXP>100 an invalid subscript will be
used, so prior statements must ensure that MAXP<=100.

The program for 4.2 must take into account that no values may
be supplied in the data -- only the end-of-list signal may
appear. We set MAXP to zero initially, to indicate that no
maximum has been found yet. We also find it advantageous to
introduce a variable MAXVAL to contain the maximum value
encountered so far; we initialize it to -1, which is less than
any possible value. If there is actually no list then the body

of the loop labeled FINDMAX will never be executed and MAX will remain at zero.

```
MAXVAL = -1;
MAXP = 0;
DO I = 1 TO TOP BY 1;
    IF INTEGER(I) > MAXVAL THEN
        DO;
            MAXVAL = INTEGER(I);
            MAXP = I;
            END;
    END;
```

This routine has potential problems if TOP>100. However, note that if 0≤TOP≤100, this segment automatically guarantees a value for MAXP that will be acceptable to the routine for 4.3.

The program for 4.1 is less obvious and could be done in several different ways. It must make provision for a number of extreme conditions with respect to the input data:

1. It must work properly for every valid quantity of data -- as little as none, to as much as 100 values.

2. It must provide adequate warning when it encounters improper data -- no data at all, too much data, data without the proper end signal, or improper values as described in 3 below.

3. The problem statement specifies that the data will be positive integers. A fundamental decision must be made as to whether the program will <u>trust</u> that it will only be presented with such proper data, or whether it will <u>test</u> to make sure that this is the case. As a general philosophy, programs should be <u>suspicious</u> <u>and</u> <u>trust</u> <u>no</u> <u>one</u>.

Reading each value directly into a FIXED variable would cause it to be truncated without warning. So that we can test for non-integers, each value will instead be read into a temporary variable TFLOAT which is FLOAT. The following segment (which still includes English statements) contains a loop which reads and processes the data until the endmarker 0 is read or until 100 values have been processed. The last statement prints an error if the endmarker has not been read. The segment also relies on PL/I to provide a warning if it runs out of data unexpectedly; this would occur if the endmarker was missing and there were 100 or fewer proper values. By "process TFLOAT" we mean to check for errors in TFLOAT and store it in the array. Remember, TOP always indicates the number of values in the array.

```
    TOP = 0;
    GET LIST (TFLOAT);
    DO WHILE ((TOP<100) & (TFLOAT¬=0));
        Process TFLOAT;
        GET LIST(TFLOAT);
        END;
    IF TFLOAT ¬= 0.00E+0 THEN
        Print error;
```

The complete program, after further refinement, is

```
LISTTOMAX: PROCEDURE OPTIONS(MAIN);
    /* PROGRAM TO LIST POSITIVE VALUES FROM FIRST TO MAXIMUM */
    DECLARE (INTEGER(1:100), /* THE POSITIVE VALUES READ*/
             TOP,            /* ARE IN INTEGER(1:TOP).  */
             MAXVAL,         /* MAXVAL = MAX(INTEGER(1:TOP)) */
             MAXP,           /* MAXVAL = INTEGER(MAXP) OR MAXP=0 */
             I)FIXED;        /* LOOP INDEX */
    DECLARE (TFLOAT) FLOAT ; /* LAST VALUE READ IN */
    DECLARE (IFLOAT) FIXED;  /* INTEGER VALUE OF TFLOAT */

    /* READ DATA, CHECK, AND STORE IN "INTEGER", UNTIL */
    /* 0 IS FOUND.  */
    TOP = 0;
    GET LIST(TFLOAT);
    DO WHILE((TOP<100) & (TFLOAT¬=0.0E0));
        IFLOAT = TFLOAT;   /* CONVERT TO INTEGER */
        IF (TFLOAT>0.00E0) & (IFLOAT = TFLOAT) THEN
            DO;
                TOP = TOP + 1;
                INTEGER(TOP) = IFLOAT;
                END;
        ELSE
            PUT SKIP LIST('IMPROPER DATA:',TFLOAT);
        GET LIST(TFLOAT);
        END;

    IF TFLOAT¬=0 THEN
        PUT SKIP LIST('MORE THAN 100 VALUES');
    /* SET MAXP TO MARK POSITION OF MAXIMUM VALUE */
    MAXVAL = -1;
    MAXP = 0;
    DO I = 1 TO TOP BY 1;
        IF INTEGER(I) > MAXVAL THEN
            DO;
                MAXVAL = INTEGER(I);
                MAXP = I;
                END;
        END;

    /* PRINT NUMBERS IN INTEGER(1:MAXP) */
    DO I = 1 TO MAXP BY 1;
        PUT SKIP LIST(INTEGER(I));
        END;
    END /* LISTTOMAX */;
```

Section 5 <u>Summary</u>

1. An array is a set of subscripted variables. These are
distinct variables but all have the same identifier and contain
the same type of value.

2. A subscripted variable reference consists of an identifier
with a subscript -- an expression enclosed in parentheses. Upon
evaluation the subscript expression must yield an appropriate
integer value. Multiple subscripts are expressions separated by
commas.

3. An identifier is declared to be an array by giving the upper
bound on the subscript:

        DECLARE (identifier(bound)) attributes ;

A lower bound other than 1 must be specified:

        DECLARE (ident(lower-bound : upper-bound)) attribute;

For multiple subscripts the bounds are separated by commas.

4. References to an array in the text will generally be in the
same form as a declaration, including explicit lower bounds on
subscript values. For example, MATRIX(1:5,1:10), SET(0:4).

Section 5 **Exercises**

1. The following are values of certain arrays and simple variables: (??? means no value has been assigned yet.)

B(-3)	20	AGE(1)	1	I	1
B(-2)	25	AGE(2)	13	J	2
B(-1)	42	AGE(3)	21	K	3
B(0)	9	AGE(4)	6	M	4
B(1)	8	AGE(5)	7	SUM	???
B(2)	13	AGE(6)	12	C	???
B(3)	-20	AGE(7)	8	MAX	???
B(4)	-40	AGE(8)	0	MIN	???
B(5)	50				

a) Give the values of B(-2), AGE(5), B(I), AGE(I+J).

b) Give the name of the variable containing the largest value in array B(-3:5); in array AGE(1:8).

c) Evaluate the following expressions:

```
B(1) + AGE(4)
B(3) * AGE(1)
5 + B(5) + AGE(5)
AGE(6)/6E0
```

d) Give the value of B(1), B(I+1), B(I+J).

e) Which of the following refer to existing variables?

```
AGE(I-M)    B(I-M)    AGE(I+M)    B(I+M)
```

f) Give the values of:

```
B(AGE(1))    B(AGE(M)-1)    AGE(AGE(4))    AGE(AGE(M+I)-2)
```

g) Evaluate the following expressions:

```
M + AGE(M)
M + AGE(K)
B(3)*3 - AGE(3)
AGE(J+J)/AGE(J)
B(M-I)
```

h) Give declarations for all of the arrays and variables shown. (Assume FIXED values for I, J, K and M; FLOAT for the others.)

i) Write assignment statements to assign the values to the variables as shown.

j) Write GET statements and a data list to assign the values to the variables as shown.

k) Write GET statements, using arrays rather than subscripted
   variables, and a data list that would assign the values to
   the variables as shown.

2. Assuming variables with initial values as in Exercise 1,
   trace the execution of the following program segments and
   show the values that result from their execution.

a) /* PUT IN SUM THE SUM OF AGE(J),...,AGE(M) */

```
   C = J;
   SUM = 0;
   DO WHILE (C <= M);
     SUM = SUM + AGE(C);
     C = C + 1;
     END;
```

b) /* PUT IN MAX THE MAXIMUM OF AGE(I),...,AGE(M) */
   /* I IS NEVER GREATER THAN M */

```
   MAX = AGE(I);
   C = I + 1;
   DO WHILE (C <= M);
     IF MAX < AGE(C) THEN
        MAX = AGE(C);
     C = C + 1;
     END;
```

c) /* ADD THE SUBSCRIPT VALUE I TO EACH VARIABLE B(I) */

```
   C = -3;
   DO WHILE (C <= 5);
     B(C) = B(C) + C;
     C = C + 1;
     END;
```

d) /* STORE INTO AGE(1) THE VALUE 0, INTO AGE(2) 1, */
   /* AND INTO AGE(I) THE VALUE A(I-2) + AGE(I-1) FOR I>2 */
   /* THESE NUMBERS FORM THE "FIBONACCI SEQUENCE" */

```
   AGE(1) = 0;
   AGE(2) = 1;
   C = 3;
   DO WHILE (C <= 8);
     AGE(C) = AGE(C-1) + AGE(C-2);
     C = C + 1;
     END;
```

e) /* PUT THE ABSOLUTE VALUE OF EACH B) IN B(-3:5) INTO B(I) */

```
   C = 5;
   DO WHILE (C >= -3);
     IF B(C) < 0 THEN
        B(C) = -B(C);
     C = C - 1;
     END;
```

```
f)/* MOVE EACH VALUE IN B [-3:4] "UP" ONE POSITION */
   /* STORE 0 IN B(-3), DISCARD B(5) */
   C = 5;
   DO WHILE (C > -3);
      B(C) = B(C-1);
      C = C - 1;
      END;
   B(-3) = 0;
```

3. Draw lines (locations) as shown in Exercise 1 for variables declared as follows:

a) DECLARE (A, B) FIXED;

b) DECLARE AGE(3,4) FIXED;

c) DECLARE COST(-3:0) FLOAT;

d) DECLARE (PAY(0:10),AMOUNT(0:10),I) FLOAT;

4. Write program segments to accomplish each of the following tasks, using the variables declared in Exercise 3:

a) Set all of the variables in the array AGE(1:3,1:4) to zero.

b) Set each variable in the array AGE(1:3,1:4) equal to the sum of its own subscripts -- that is, AGE(I,J) equal to I + J.

c) Set each variable in the array COST(-3:0) equal to whatever is the minimum of the initial values of the variables in COST.

d) Subtract the value of each variable in the array AMOUNT(0:10) from the variable in the corresponding position in the array PAY(0:10).

e) Compute the sum of the values of all of the variables in the array PAY(0:10).

f) Swap the values of PAY(1:10) to put the largest in PAY(10). Thus if initially PAY is

PAY	10	9	8	7	6	5	4	3	2	1

then after execution, the array might be

PAY	9	8	7	6	5	4	3	2	1	10
or PAY	1	9	8	7	6	5	4	3	2	10

5. Suppose array B(1:N) contains a sequence of values, some of which appear more than once. Write a program segment to "delete" duplicates, moving the unique values towards the beginning of the array. Assign to variable M the number of unique values. The order of the values should be preserved. For example, if we have

          N 7   B 1 6 1 8 3 7 6

after execution the variables should be as   follows   (where   "−"
indicates that the value is immaterial):

          N 7   M 5   B 1 6 8 3 7 − −

6.   The following segment searches array segment   B(1:N)   for   a
value equal to X.   When it finds it, it sets J to the index of X
in B so that B(J) = X.   This is a <u>linear</u> <u>search</u> algorithm.

```
     J = 1;
     DO WHILE (B(J) ¬= X);
        J = J+1;
        END;
```

a) What value is in J after execution if X is not in the array?

b) Change   the program to set 0 in J   if X   is not in the array.

c) What happens if N = 0?   Change the program segment to   store
     0 in J if this is the case. (Such a case actually arises
     in programming, and is not always a mistake.)

7.   The following questions refer to the program in Section 5.5.

a) Suppose there is a tie for maximum −− several input   numbers
     are   the   same   and   are   greater   than   all   others.   What
     <u>should</u> the program do in this case; what <u>does</u> the program
     do?

b) What does the program do if several improper data values are
     included?

c) Precisely what happens if 110 data values   followed   by   the
     end-of-input signal appear in the input?

d) What would the output look like if the following   data   were
     presented?

          $DATA
            14 13 −3 15 2 7 15 12 0 23

Section 6   Display of Results

Printed output from a PL/I program is produced by execution of "output" statements. The detailed discussion of these statements is prefaced by two general comments on output.

First, _output_ _during_ _execution_ of a program is entirely the _programmer's_ _responsibility_. A copy of the program, called a "source listing", is produced automatically, but once execution begins, the only further printing is the result of executing output statements of the program. All values produced during execution are lost unless specifically printed.

Second, the statements that control output are typically the most complex statements in a programming language. If not the most difficult in concept they are at least the richest in detail and the most tedious to learn to use. This seems to be required in order to give the programmer flexible control over what information is to be displayed and the format in which it is to appear. PL/I is certainly not an exception in this regard, and the following paragraphs offer a brief introduction to only the simplest type of PL/I output statement.

6.1 Display of Values of Variables

The simplest output statement in PL/I has the form

    PUT LIST(expressions, separated by commas);

The expressions may of course, be simple or subscripted variables. For example:

(6.1a)   PUT LIST(TOTAL, I+1, PLACE(I), 2*MAXPLACE-7);

The standard output format divides the printed page horizontally into five "fields" of 24 columns each. (This is somewhat analogous to the "tab stops" on a typewriter.) Each column is one "print position" and will contain one character. Each field is used to display the value of one expression from the list given in the PUT statement. In example (6.1a) the value of TOTAL will be printed in the first (leftmost) field; I in the second; PLACE(I) in the third; and MAXPLACE in the fourth. (The particular variable from the array PLACE to appear in the third field will of course depend upon the value of the subscript I at the time the statement is executed.) Each value begins at the left of the field and uses as many columns as required. Any unused columns of the field are left blank and the next value begins in the leftmost column of the next field.

FIXED expressions are printed in integer form, FLOAT variables in exponential form. The decimal point is always given after the first digit and the power of ten required to properly position the point is given after the digits of the number. For example, if the variables contain:

TOTAL	-.0036	[float]
I	2	[fixed]
PLACE(1)	-124.3	[float]
PLACE(2)	63.7	[float]
MAXPLACE	806	[float]

the values displayed by PUT statement (6.1a) would be as below (the full number of blanks between values is not shown here since the print line in this book is not a full 120 positions):

```
-3.60000E-03   2       6.37000E+01   8.06000E+02
```

A PUT LIST statement does not automatically begin a new line. It begins with the next unused field, wherever that may be. For example, if PUT LIST(J); places J's value in the third field of a line, then the next executed PUT statement will place its first value in the fourth field on that same line. Thus, (6.1a) is exactly equivalent to the sequence

```
PUT LIST(TOTAL,I+1);
PUT LIST(PLACE(I), 2*MAXPLACE-7);
```

In other words, the expressions in consecutively executed PUT statements form one continuous list -- to be assigned to the continuous sequence of fields on the printed page. After the fifth field of one line comes the first field of the next line.

The programmer can control the placement of values on a line by using the "SKIP option". The keyword SKIP causes the statement to begin placement with the first field of a new line, regardless of where the last PUT statement left off. Hence

```
PUT SKIP LIST(TOTAL, I);
PUT SKIP LIST(PLACE(I), MAXPLACE);
```

will cause two new lines to be printed, with values in the first two fields of each line. Note, however, that unless the next PUT statement also specifies SKIP it will begin placing values in the third field of this second line.

A number of lines may be skipped by giving an integer in parentheses after the keyword SKIP. For example:

```
PUT SKIP(3) LIST(TOTAL);
```

will leave two lines blank and place the value of TOTAL in the
first field of the third line. SKIP is equivalent to SKIP(1).

    As a further example

    /* TABULATE 'HEIGHT' AND 'WIDTH' */
    DO I = 1 TO 10 BY 1;
        PUT SKIP(2) LIST(I, HEIGHT(I), WIDTH(I));
        END;

will produced ten double-spaced lines with values in the first
three fields of each print line.

    The PUT statement can be used with the SKIP option alone to
terminate a logical section of printed output. For example, the
PUT SKIP(4); below ensures that this section of output will be
separated by at least three blank lines from what follows,
regardless of the form of the next PUT:

        . . .
        PUT SKIP LIST(X, Y, Z);
        PUT SKIP LIST(R, S, T);
        PUT SKIP(4);
        . . .

6.2 Titling and Labeling Results

    The appearance of printed results can be improved by adding
appropriate titles and labels. To a limited extent this can be
done with LIST format output by placing a "literal" instead of a
variable in the list of the PUT statement. A literal is a
string of characters enclosed in single quotes. For example:

        'TOTAL'
        'TEMPERATURE ='
        'RESULTS FOR 9/23/72 ARE:'
        '*-*-*-*-*-*-*'
        ' '   (blank is a valid character)

The character string is printed exactly as given -- without the
quotes. The printing begins in the leftmost column of the
"next" field. For example, if TOTAL and SUM have values

        TOTAL 642.17E+0 [float]
        SUM   -10.437E+2 [float]

then execution of the statements

        PUT SKIP LIST('TOTAL =', TOTAL);
        PUT SKIP LIST('SUM =', SUM);

would produce the output

```
TOTAL =                 6.42170E+02
SUM =                  -1.04370E+03
```

The appearance of these lines can be improved by including blanks in the literals to displace the words toward the right in the 24 position print field:

```
PUT SKIP LIST('             TOTAL =', TOTAL);
PUT SKIP LIST('              SUM =',SUM);
```

These statements will produce:

```
TOTAL =  6.42170E+02
SUM   = -1.04370E+03
```

Literals are often used to identify different values, using their variable names. For example,

```
PUT SKIP LIST('X', X);
```

will print the name X, in the first field of a line, and the value of X in the second field. Whatever is included in the literal is printed; the content of the literal has no significance to PL/I. For example, execution of the following would cause the deceptive label to be printed, without complaint:

```
PUT SKIP LIST('THE VALUE OF Y IS:', X);
```

Blank literals can be used to control the placement of other values on the printed line. For example, the following PUT statement causes the value of X to be printed in the second field of a new line, and the value of Y in the fourth field.

```
PUT SKIP LIST(' ', X, ' ', Y);
```

PUT statements whose list consists of a single literal are frequently used. For example:

```
PUT SKIP LIST('IMPROPER DATA ENCOUNTERED');
PUT SKIP LIST('UNEXPECTED NEGATIVE VALUE');
```

Another example is shown in the sample program in Section 5.4. Such statements announce to the programmer that the flow-of-control has reached a certain point in the program or that an exceptional condition has occurred. One often includes such statements to help test a new program; they are removed after the correctness of the program has been established. This technique is discussed in Section V.4.

If a literal of more than 24 characters is given it will simply continue into the next field on the line. (A literal of exactly 24 characters completely fills one field and causes the next to be skipped.) If a literal reaches the end of a line it will continue in the first field of the next line. This applies

to the printed output line -- a different rule applies to the
cards on which the PUT statement itself is punched.

SP/k normally forbids a "symbol" to be split between two
cards -- to be started on one card and continued on the next.
Keywords, variables and constants are all symbols. A literal or
a comment, however long, is also considered a single symbol. A
statement may be continued onto as many cards as necessary, but
an individual symbol cannot be split over a card boundary.
Hence, the following would not be valid in SP/k:

```
PUT SKIP LIST(TOTAL,SUM,AVERAGE,MEDIAN,'THESE STATISTICS
ARE OBTAINED FROM 9/23/72 DATA');
```

This same statement would be valid if it were divided between
symbols instead of in the middle of the literal:

```
PUT SKIP LIST(TOTAL, SUM, AVERAGE, MEDIAN,
       'THESE STATISTICS ARE OBTAINED FROM 9/23/72 DATA');
```

Although the statement is now acceptable, the format of the
printed output is likely to be disappointing since the long
literal will begin in the fifth field of the line and spill over
into the first field of the following line. The following
sequence would produce more attractive and readable output:

```
PUT SKIP LIST('STATISTICS FROM 9/23/72 DATA:');
PUT SKIP LIST('               TOTAL =', TOTAL);
PUT SKIP LIST('               SUM =', SUM);
PUT SKIP LIST('               AVERAGE =', AVERAGE);
PUT SKIP LIST('               MEDIAN =', MEDIAN);
```

6.3 Display of Arrays

DO groups can be used to print all the variables of an array.
For example, if TAB(1:8) is an array, the program segment:

```
PUT SKIP;
DO I = 1 TO 8 BY 1;
   PUT LIST(TAB(I));
   END;
```

will print all the variables in the array TAB.

As another example, for array M(1:3,1:15) the nested loops
below place the variables in this array in the next 45 fields.

```
DO I = 1 TO 3 BY 1;
   DO J = 1 TO 15 BY 1;
      PUT LIST(M(I,J));
      END;
   END;
```

6.4 <u>Control</u> <u>of</u> <u>Display</u> <u>Format</u>

More flexible control over the format of output is provided
by the "PUT EDIT statement". This statement can be very
complex; we give here only a brief introduction. Nevertheless,
this will permit substantial control of printing format in the
most common situations. The general form of the statement is:

PUT SKIP(i) EDIT(element list)(format list);

SKIP(i) is optional and has the same effect as with PUT LIST.
The "element list" is the list of variables, literals and
expressions (separated by commas) to be printed, as with PUT
LIST. But with PUT EDIT they are printed under control of the
"format list".

The format list is a list of "items", separated by commas.
Items are "data-items" (the items A, A(w), B(w), F(w,d) and
E(w,d) below) or "control-items" (X(i) and COLUMN below). The
element list and format list are processed concurrently,
from beginning to end. The first data-item controls the
printing of the first value, the second data-item controls
printing of the second value, and so on. Control-items are
"executed" as they are passed over when looking for the next
data-item to use to control printing. (Thus, SP/k does not
permit control-items to appear after the last data-item). The
values denoted by i, w, and d must be constants or expressions
of type FIXED.

The following format items are available in SP/k. (Appendix
B.9 has a discussion of other items available in PL/I.)

A -- print a character string. This can be a literal (or a
string-valued variable -- see Section 9). The width of the
printing field is the length of the string.

A(w) -- print a character string left-justified in a field
w positions wide (truncating the string if necessary).

B(w) -- Print a logical value. 1 or 0 is printed depending
on whether the value is true or false. If w>1, the value
will be followed by w-1 blanks.

COLUMN(i) -- This control item causes columns to be skipped
until column i of the current line is reached. Skipped
columns are filled with blanks. If the current line is
already positioned <u>after</u> column i, the current line is
completed and a new one started in column 1.

X(i) -- skip i spaces.

F(w) -- print an integer right-justified in a field w
positions wide.

F(w,d) -- print a decimal number with d digits to the right
of the decimal point, right-justified in a field w
positions wide. The width w must include a position for
the decimal point and a position for a minus sign, if that
can occur. The number is rounded to fit, if necessary.

E(w,d) -- print a number in exponential form, with d digits
to the right of the decimal point, right-justified in a
field w positions wide. The width w must include positions
for the decimal point, the sign, and the exponent
(e.g., w cannot be less than d+6). The number is rounded to
fit, if necessary.

The F and E format-items can be used for either FIXED or FLOAT
values; necessary conversions will be performed automatically.

In EDIT format, fields are not pre-defined (as in LIST
format). Each format-item defines its own field-length, which
begins immediately after the termination of the preceding field.

We give examples, assuming the following values:

TOTAL 14.3 [float]   COUNT 25 [fixed]

The output produced by various PUT EDIT statements is shown
below. (Print position numbers are shown to indicate exact
placement. They would not appear on actual output.)

```
PUT SKIP EDIT(COUNT)(F(5));
output:        25
positions: 12345

PUT SKIP EDIT(COUNT)(F(5,1));
output:      25.0
positions: 12345

PUT SKIP EDIT(COUNT)(E(10,2));
output:      2.50E+01
positions: 1234567890

PUT SKIP EDIT(COUNT)(X(4),F(5));
output:           25
positions: 123456789

PUT SKIP EDIT(COUNT, COUNT)(F(5),F(5,2));
output:        2525.00
positions: 1234567890

PUT SKIP EDIT (COUNT, COUNT) (F(5), X(3), F(5,2));
output:        25   25.00
positions: 1234567890123

PUT SKIP EDIT(TOTAL)(E(10,2));
output:      1.43E+01
positions: 1234567890
```

```
PUT SKIP EDIT(TOTAL)(F(6,2));
output:      14.30
positions: 123456

PUT SKIP EDIT(TOTAL)(F(5));
output:         14
positions: 12345

PUT SKIP EDIT('IMPROPER DATA')(A);
output:    IMPROPER DATA
positions: 1234567890123

PUT SKIP EDIT('IMPROPER DATA')(A(8));
output:    IMPROPER
positions: 12345678

PUT SKIP EDIT('COUNT IS:',COUNT,'TOTAL IS:',TOTAL)
          (A,F(4),X(3),A,E(10,2));
output:    COUNT IS:  25    TOTAL IS:  1.43E+01
positions: 12345678901234567890123456789012345
```

Expressions can be given for the parameters w, d, and i in the format-items described above. These expressions are evaluated during execution of the PUT statement to determine the field width or number of digits. This allows the output format to depend on computational results, but this capability is not often used. Generally, the format is predetermined, and w, d, and i are given as constants, as shown in the examples.

Section 6 <u>Summary</u>

1. The form of the simplest PL/I output statement is:

PUT LIST(expressions, separated by commas);

2. The "LIST format" print line consists of five fields of 24
characters each.   Fields are filled from left to right, top to
bottom, starting wherever the last PUT statement left off.   Each
element on the PUT list starts a new field, and continues
through as many fields as are required to display its value.

3. The SKIP(i) option will cause a PUT statement to skip down i
lines.   SKIP(1), or SKIP, will skip to the beginning of the next
line; SKIP(2) will skip to the second line, etc.

4.   A <u>literal</u> is a quoted string of characters; it will be
printed <u>exactly</u> as given. Literals can be used to title and
label results, and to print messages.

5. The PUT EDIT statement gives control over output format:

PUT EDIT(element list) (format list) ;

Section 6 Exercises

1. Write a single PUT statement to produce the same printed output as the following sequence:

```
PUT SKIP LIST(TOTAL);
PUT LIST(MAX);
PUT LIST(MINIMUM, AVG);
```

2. What would the output from the following segment look like?

```
DO I = 1 TO 5 BY 1;
   PUT SKIP LIST(I,I,I,I,I,);
   END;
```

3. What is the result of executing the following statement?

```
PUT LIST(' ',' ');
```

4. What is printed by execution of the following statement?

```
PUT SKIP LIST('PUT SKIP LIST(X);');
```

5. Write a sequence of PUT statements to print the pattern shown below (where ƀ indicates a blank):

```
ƀOƀ
OƀO
ƀOƀ
```

6. Write a PUT EDIT statement that will repeatedly display the value of a FIXED variable named K, whose value is 2, yielding exactly the same output as the following statement:

```
PUT SKIP LIST('22222222');
```

7. Assuming that X and Y are FLOAT variables, write a PUT EDIT statement that will produce the same output as:

```
PUT SKIP LIST(X, Y);
```

8. TABLE(1:5,1:5) is a square array of FIXED variables, all of whose values are integers greater than 0 and less than 10. Print the values of this array in rectangular form, on five consecutive lines, with a single blank between the values on each line. For example, if all of the values are 9, the array would be displayed as:

```
9 9 9 9 9
9 9 9 9 9
9 9 9 9 9
9 9 9 9 9
9 9 9 9 9
```

Section 7   The Execution of Programs

After a program has been written, and painstakingly checked
for errors in logic and syntax, it must be transmitted to a
computer for execution. This is usually done by "punching" both
the program statements and suitable test data onto cards. Each
card generally contains one line of the program as it was
written on paper, and columns should be skipped at the left of
the card to reflect the indentation of the program lines.

"Keypunching" is a major source of errors. Many programs,
correct on paper, reach the computer in garbled form simply
because the lines are not exactly represented by the information
actually punched in the cards. Much time and effort is saved if
the cards are checked against the written form, with great care,
before the deck is submitted for processing. If at all
possible, you should get a "listing" of the cards and check this
listing, rather than attempt to read the cards directly.

When cards containing keypunch errors have been replaced, the
deck is arranged as follows for presentation to the computer:

```
$JOBK ID='name of programmer'  options
 procedure-name: PROCEDURE OPTIONS(MAIN);
    /* comment summarizing program function */
    cards containing declarations
    cards containing imperative statements
    END /* procedure-name */;
$DATA
    cards containing data
```

The $JOBK and $DATA cards must begin in column 1. Program and
comment cards must not begin in column 1. Data cards may begin
in column 1. (See Appendix B.3 for further information on card
formats.)

7.1 Loading, Translation and Execution

Processing a program takes place in two distinct stages.
First, the program is "loaded" into the memory of the computer;
second, it is executed. In order to load a program, the deck of
cards is placed in a device called a "card reader". The card
reader examines the cards one at a time, in the order presented,
detects the position of holes in the cards, and transmits this
information to the computer. The card-reading operation appears

to proceed very rapidly (300 to 1000 cards per minute) but it is
in fact very slow compared to the speed with which statements
are executed once the program is loaded.

    The loading of a program for processing is actually performed
by another program, called a "compiler", which is already in the
computer. During loading, the compiler scans the program for
errors and translates the SP/k statements into an internal form
that the computer can understand and execute. This translation
is a complicated, but not fundamentally mysterious process; it
is described briefly in Part X.

    A crucial point is that the program is <u>not executed as it is
loaded</u>. Only after the complete program has been loaded, does
the second stage -- execution -- begin. <u>Execution of a PL/I
program</u> consists of <u>one execution of the</u> "main procedure".

    At the moment that execution begins only the cards containing
the program statements have been read. Cards containing data
remain in the card reader -- ready to be read when called for by
the execution of GET statements in the program.

7.2 Analysis of Printed Output

    The amount and type of printed output produced during the
processing of a program can vary considerably. Certain portions
are always provided, some portions depend upon the choice of
"options" for the particular program, and some depend upon the
execution of output statements in the program.

    Each computing facility has predetermined a set of standard
or "default" choices for the various options. These are
presumably chosen to be the most appropriate for the greatest
number of users of the computer. The default options are
automatically assigned to each program -- but you can <u>override
the defaults</u> by specifying your own choice of options. In SP/k,
options are specified on the $JOBK card -- the first card of
the program. The options are described in the following
section:

    The complete printed output produced during loading,
translation and execution of a SP/k program can be divided into
the following sections, to be described in more detail
subsequently:

    Header Box: a rectangular box surrounded by asterisks. It
    identifies the version of SP/k being used and contains the
    programmers name copied from the ID= parameter on the $JOBK
    card. If the programmer has overridden default parameters
    using the $JOBK card, the values of these parameters used
    for this run will be printed in the header box.

Source Listing: A copy of the program, with additional
information such as statement numbers and error messages,
and a summary of source program characteristics.

Execution Output: The result of executing PUT statements
(with error messages, if necessary). Followed by a summary
of execution activity.

7.2.1 Source Listing

The column headed STMT gives "statement numbers" that are
assigned by SP/k. Statements are numbered in the order that
they are loaded. One minor difficulty is that SP/k is very
generous in what it considers a "statement". Declarations are
numbered as if they were statements, as are PROCEDURE, DO and
END. When a single statement takes more than one line, the
statement number will be printed only once.

These STMT numbers are used throughout the printed output to
refer to individual statements -- in error messages produced
during loading and in error messages produced during execution.

When errors are detected during the initial scanning of a
program, an error message is printed directly following the
offending statement. The SP/k processor attempts to repair the
error so that the program can be executed; this correction is
printed below the error message. For example:

```
    8      X = Y*(X+Z;
 ****      SYNTAX ERROR IN PREVIOUS LINE. LINE IS REPLACED BY:
    8      X = Y*(X+Z);
```

Unfortunately, the repair is not always successful. Sometimes,
in its efforts to construct a syntactically correct program,
SP/k constructs statements that are very unlike what the
programmer intended. The proper attitude is to be appreciative
when the correction is helpful; amused when it is not; and try
to give SP/k as few opportunities to make corrections as
possible. Note that even though a particular correction does not
recreate what you intended, it still permits execution of the
program. This execution may yield information that will help
expose other faults in the program.

Certain errors are easily detected only after the complete
program has been scanned. Since the listing of the program
statements is printed as the program is loaded and scanned,
these additional error messages cannot be printed immediately
after the offending statement. Instead they are collected, and

printed in a group after the end of the program statement
listing.

These messages are especially confusing when they describe an
improper meaning that is a direct consequence of an earlier SP/k
"correction". When one of these errors is completely
mystifying, see if there has been a previous error message and
correction for the same statement.

7.2.2 Execution Output

The output generated by the actual execution of a program is
completely dependent upon execution of PUT statements in the
program. If no PUT statements are executed, there is no
execution output. PL/I intrudes in this output only if an error
is committed during execution. For example, suppose

        BASE_VALUE = SQRT(LEFT_PT);

is executed at a point where LEFT_PT < 0. Since the SQRT built-
in function requires a non-negative value as argument, an error
message is inserted at that point in the execution output.

This section of output is not automatically titled in any
way, nor are the pages numbered. It normally begins a few lines
after the end of the source listing and error messages (if any).
The end of execution output is denoted by a line that announces
the completion of execution of the program:

        END OF EXECUTION.   n1 BYTES OF DATA AREA USED.
            n2 STMTS EXECUTED.   n3 LINES OUTPUT. n4 ERRORS.

Where n1...n4 are integers that describe what happened during
the execution of your program.

        n1 - the amount of storage used for variables, constants
             and arrays
        n2 - the number of statements executed
        n3 - the number of lines printed by the program
        n4 - the number of error messages printed during execution

Section 8   The Declaration of Variables

Declarations have been mentioned in several earlier sections. These are so crucial that their consideration could not be entirely postponed to this point, but the previous fragmented presentation is not sufficient. Section 8 provides a general discussion of declarations, repeating much of what has been mentioned previously. The following is a summary of the previous references to the declaration of variables:

1. Variables are defined by listing their names in a declaration. Section 2.

2. Declarations are part of the heading of a procedure, and are placed at the beginning. Creation of the variables takes place as the procedure is entered -- before execution of any statement in the procedure.

3. The type of value that a variable can contain is determined by the type attributes given in the declaration of that variable. Section 2.3. PL/I is very generous in allowing the programmer to specify many aspects of how variables are to be represented. In SP/k many of these choices have been made for the programmer so that the major choice left is between the FIXED and FLOAT attributes.

4. A variable can be declared to be an array by specifying the bounds on its subscript values in its declaration. Section 5.3.

8.1 The Form of a Declaration

The declaration of an unsubscripted variable has the form

     DECLARE (identifier) attribute;

Examples are:

     DECLARE (POLYPHASE) FLOAT;
     DECLARE (K_BOUND) FIXED;

Note the following:

     1. The attribute follows the identifier.

2. No comma is given after the identifier.

Several variables may be included in the same declaration, separated by commas. For example, the following are equivalent:

```
DECLARE(J) FIXED;
DECLARE(SUM) FLOAT;

DECLARE(J) FIXED,
    (SUM) FLOAT;
```

Two or more variables having exactly the same attributes can be grouped in parentheses, so that the attribute list need not be repeated. The attributes are said to be "factored".   For example, the following declarations are equivalent:

```
DECLARE (I) FIXED,
    (J) FIXED,
    (K) FIXED;

DECLARE (I, J, K) FIXED;
```

8.1.1 Declaration of Arrays

An array is declared by specifying bounds on its subscript values immediately after the identifier. The general form is:

```
DECLARE (identifier(lb1:ub1, lb2:ub2, ... )) attribute ;
```

where lb1, ub1, lb2, ub2, ... are integer constants giving the lower bound and upper bound for the first subscript; the lower bound and upper bound for the second subscript, etc. If only an upper-bound-constant is given, a lower bound of 1 is assumed. For example:

```
DECLARE (X(5), MAT(0:6,5)) FLOAT;
```

creates two arrays of FLOAT variables. X consists of five singly-subscripted variables. MAT is doubly-subscripted -- the first subscript ranging from 0 to 6; the second from 1 to 5.

8.2 Implicit Declaration and Default Attributes

The PL/I language is very liberal with respect to declaration of variables. Variables that are not explicitly declared by the programmer are given an implicit declaration by the compiler; if the programmer does not specify all the attributes of a variable, default attributes are automatically provided.

Implicit declaration and default attributes have turned out in practice to be very error-prone. For example if a programmer

makes a keypunch mistake, misspelling the name of a variable;
rather than recognize the error, in most contexts PL/I accepts
the misspelling as a new identifier and considers it the
"implicit declaration" of a different variable with default
attribute. Normally no warning message is given and such errors
may be difficult to detect.

    To prevent such errors, SP/k requires that all variables must
be explicitly declared and all type attributes must be specified
by the programmer. Further, SP/k requires that all variables be
declared at the start of a procedure; therefore the declarations
in each procedure must precede all other statements in the
procedure.

8.3 Initial Values

    The creation of a variable and the assignment of value are
distinctly different actions and initial values are not
automatically supplied when a variable is created. In fact, in
SP/k, all variables are automatically given the initial value
"undefined". It is such a common mistake to assume that an
initial value is automatically supplied that a few
languages, including SP/k, supply a value if a variable with
undefined value is used in a program. But this is a correction
of an error and a warning message is printed.

Section 8 Summary

1. Variables are created, and have their type attributes
    assigned by a declaration: assigned by a declaration:

    DECLARE (identifier) attribute ;

2. Declarations must be placed at the beginning of a
    procedure. Variables are created immediately upon entry to
    the procedure -- before the execution of any statement in
    that procedure.

3. Several variables can be given in the same declaration:

    DECLARE (ident) attribute, (ident) attribute, ... ;

4. Variables with identical attributes can be grouped in
    parentheses:

    DECLARE (ident, ident, ...) attribute ;

5. The only attributes discussed so far for SP/k are:
    FIXED to declare integer variables
    FLOAT to declare real variables

6. The form for declaration of an array is:

    DECLARE (identifier(lb1:ub1, lb2:ub2, ...)) attribute ;

    If only an upper-bound-constant is given, a lower bound of
    1 is assumed.

7. The initial value undefined is automatically assigned to a
    variable when it is created.   A different value must be
    assigned before the variable can be used.

Section 8 Exercises

1. Write a declaration to create a variable named TOTAL that
will hold values such as -1.2379E+02 and 6.200E-4.

2. What type of variables are created by the declaration

    DECLARE (COL(0:1), TABLE(4:10,14)) FLOAT;

Section 9   Character-Valued Variables

Up to this point we have considered numeric-valued variables. We have used non-numeric "strings" of characters as literals in a PUT statement (Section 6.2), but not as values to assign to variables. Some languages are only capable of processing numeric values, and are considered useful primarily for scientific and engineering applications. However, in many types of applications it is useful to be able to store, manipulate, and display values that include characters that are not digits. Values that include letters and special symbols as well as digits are called "character data", or "strings".

For example, programs called "text editors" take a sequence of words, punctuation marks, and format commands, and format the words and punctuation marks into lines, paragraphs, and pages. This book was produced by such a program.

More important applications involve both numeric and character data. Consider a program to maintain a customer charge account system for a retail store. Each account includes numeric information on charges, payments, balance due, arrears, finance charges, etc. It also contains character information giving the name of the customer, his address, credit references, etc. A brief introduction to such "file processing" programs is given in Part IX. A majority of the world's computers are used primarily for file processing, and computers, in the aggregate, process more character data than numeric data.

Since PL/I was designed to serve both scientific and file processing applications it includes facilities for processing strings.

The characters that may appear in a string are those that occur on the keypunch. They are the following, with "ƀ" representing the underline blank character:

ƀ¢.<(+|&!$*);¬-/,%_>?:#ə'="ABCDEFGHIJKLMNOPQRSTUVWXYZ0123456789

String processing is in a sense more fun than numeric processing. After learning a few details, you will find it easy to format output nicely, to write programs to print out graphs and pictures, and to perform other interesting tasks.

9.1 Declaration of Character Variables

The declaration of a character-valued variable has the form:

    DECLARE (identifier) CHARACTER(length) VARYING;

"length" specifies the maximum number of characters in the value. VARYING indicates that the character variables can have as a value any string of characters ranging from zero characters up to the number of characters given by "length".

The CHARACTER attribute is incompatible with the numeric attributes FIXED and FLOAT; they cannot be given to the same variable. They can appear in the same declaration:

    DECLARE (LINE) CHARACTER(50) VARYING,
        (LINE_COUNT) FIXED;

An array can consist of string-valued subscripted variables. The following declaration describes an array of fifty, singly-subscripted variables, each of whose values is a string of 20 characters:

    DECLARE (WORD(50)) CHARACTER(20)VARYING;

Multiple subscripts and lower bounds other than 1, are declared in the same way as for numeric-valued arrays.

9.1.1 Initial Character Values

As with all other variables in SP/k, string variables are given an initial value of "undefined" when they are created during program execution. A warning message will be printed if an attempt is made to use a string variable that has the value undefined.

9.2 String Assignments and Expressions

9.2.1 String Assignment

The string assignment statement has the same form as a numeric assignment:

    variable = expression ;

The string variable denoted by the left side is first determined, the expression is evaluated to yield a string value, and this value is assigned to the variable.

The simplest form of string expression is a literal -- a quoted string of characters. Literals, discussed in Section 6.2, are used as string constants, in the same way that numeric constants are used. For example, if WORD has been declared CHARACTER(5)VARYING, then

    WORD = 'ABCDE';

would assign the value ABCDE to variable WORD. The quotes around ABCDE are crucial -- without them, ABCDE would be interpreted as the name of a variable, rather than as a value. To further illustrate the point, consider

    WORD = 'A + B';

Like the previous example, the right side of this assignment statement is just a five-character literal. Without the quotes the right side would be interpreted as an arithmetic expression consisting of two variables and an addition. Note that the quotes enclose the value, but are not part of the value. The value consists of the five characters between the quotes:

    WORD A + B [character(5)varying]

In SP/k a string variable always has the length of the last value assigned to it, up to its declared maximum. If a value longer than the declared maximum is assigned it will be automatically truncated on the right to the maximum length. For example, consider the following:

    DECLARE (A) CHARACTER(3) VARYING;
    A = '';

The literal on the right side of each statement is the empty string (since no characters are given between the quotes). Since A has the attribute VARYING after execution of these statements the values are:

    A [character(3)varying]   (length is 0)

9.2.2 Expressions

A string expression yields a string of characters as a result. The only string operator is concatenation. Operands may be literals, string variables, and functions which return strings as values.

Concatenation

Strings are built by combining two smaller strings end to end. The operation is called "concatenation"; the PL/I symbol

for it is "||". (These two adjacent vertical strokes have no
intervening blanks; the vertical stroke is the character above
the Y on the keypunch.) For example, suppose that the following
variables exist:

```
    STR(1) ABC [character(4)varying]
    STR(2) DEF [character(4)varying]
    CHR(1)     [character(10)varying]
    CHR(2) 1234567890 [character(10)varying]
    SVAR   1234567890 [character(10)varying]
```

After execution of the assignment statements

```
    CHR(1) = STR(1) || STR(2);
    CHR(2) = STR(1) || ' ' || STR(2);
    SVAR = ' ' || STR(1) || STR(2);
```

the values would be

```
    STR(1) ABC [character(4)varying]
    STR(2) DEF [character(4)varying]
    CHR(1) ABCDEF [character(10)varying]
    CHR(2) ABC DEF [character(10)varying]
    SVAR    ABCDEF [character(10)varying]
```

SUBSTR and LENGTH Built-in Functions

The substring function is used to refer to a portion of a
string. The form of the function is

```
    SUBSTR(char-expr, start-pos, length)
```

where char-expr is an expression which yields a string value,
start-pos is the position number (counting from 1, left to
right) of the leftmost position of the desired substring, and
length is the number of positions in the substring. Start-pos
and length are expressions that must evaluate to integers.
Their values must be reasonable; they must specify a substring
that really exists in the string referred to. For example:

```
    SUBSTR('ABCDEF',2,3) is 'BCD'
    SUBSTR('ABCDEF',1,1) is 'A'
    SUBSTR('ABCDEF',1,6) is 'ABCDEF'
    SUBSTR('ABC'||'DEF',2,5) is 'BCDEF'
```

As further examples, if variables and values are

```
    SA ABC [character(3) varying]
    SB DEF [character(3) varying]
    J  2   [fixed]
    K  3   [fixed]
```

then SUBSTR(SA,1,2) is 'AB'
     SUBSTR(SA||'ABC',2,4) is 'BCAB'

```
SUBSTR(SA||' '||SB,J,K+2) is 'BC␣DE'
SA||SUBSTR(SB,3,1) is 'ABCF'
SUBSTR(SUBSTR(SB,1,2),2,1) is 'E'
```

The SUBSTR function can be given without specifying "length". In this case, the value of the function is the right portion of the string, starting with the position specified. For example,

```
SUBSTR(SA,2) is 'BC'
SUBSTR(SA||SB,3) is 'CDEF'
```

The LENGTH built-in function has the form

```
LENGTH(char-expr)
```

Its value is the <u>actual</u> length of the string expression given as argument. For example, if the value of WORD is:

```
WORD HOPE [character(10) varying]
```

then LENGTH(WORD) is 4
     LENGTH(WORD||'XY') is 6
     LENGTH(SUBSTR(WORD,2)) is 3

<u>String</u> <u>Values</u> <u>in</u> <u>Conditions</u>

String expressions can be used in conditions. The form is:

```
character-expr   relation   character-expr
```

The relations are the same as those used for arithmetic-expression conditions (listed in Section 4.2.1.1.) Compound conditions can be used as described in Section 4.2.1.2.

The relationship between two string values depends upon an ordering that has been defined over all of the valid characters that might be included in such a value. This ordering is called the "collating sequence". In PL/I it is defined to be:

␣¢.<(+|&!$*);¬-/,%_>?:#@'="ABCDEFGHIJKLMNOPQRSTUVWXYZ0123456789

This is an extension of "alphabetical order" with the digits higher than Z, and the special characters lower than A. The blank is lowest of all. Any character in this sequence is said to be "less than" a character to its right in the sequence.

If two strings being compared have different lengths, the shorter one is extended on the right with blanks until it is the same length as the longer. Both this length equalization, and the effect of the collating sequence are illustrated by the following conditions -- <u>all</u> <u>of</u> <u>which</u> <u>are</u> <u>true</u>:

```
'A' = 'A'
'A' = 'Aʹ'
'A' ¬= 'ʹA'
'A' ¬= 'AB'
'A' < 'B'
'/' < 'A'
'Z' < '3'
'AA' < 'AB'
'A' < 'AB'
'ʹB' < 'AB'
'ZZ' < '1.'
```

9.3 String Assignment from External Data

String variables may appear in the list of a GET statement. The value assigned from the data may be truncated exactly as discussed under "String Assignment".

The data format is similar to that described in Section 3.4.1, except that any value on a data card to be assigned to a string variable must be enclosed in quotes. For example, if X and Y are FIXED, and SA and SB are CHARACTER(1) VARYING, then values could be read from data cards as follows:

```
    GET LIST(X, SA, Y, SB);
    ...
$DATA
    ...
    5 'P' 7 '9'
```

9.3.1 EDIT Format Character Data

Placing quotes around each string on a data card is a nuisance. If only string values are to appear on a card, the use of quotes can be avoided by reading the entire card as a single string value. For example, if CARD is CHARACTER(80) VARYING values can be assigned to CARD from data with the statement

```
    GET EDIT(CARD)(COLUMN(1),A(80));
```

The COLUMN(1) phrase causes reading to start at column 1 of the card, no matter where reading for the previous GET left off. The character positions in CARD correspond to the columns of the card, so the SUBSTR function can be used to extract individual strings from CARD. For example, SUBSTR(CARD,1,8) gives the first eight columns of the card.

9.4 Display of Character Values

String expressions may be included in a PUT LIST stAtement.
Values are displayed in the standard format, as described in
Section 6.1. The value begins in the left-most print position of
the "next" field. If the length of the value is greater than
24, it simply continues into the following field.

More flexible control of output format can be achieved by use
of the PUT EDIT statement, as described in Section 6.4. The "A"
data-item should be matched with a string expression. If the
data-item is given as "A" alone, without a field width
specification, the field width is determined by the length of
the expression. If a width is specified in the data-item, the
value is either truncated or extended on the right with blanks
to fit the specified field.

9.5 An Example

Consider the following problem. The input contains the names
of 50 people, each consisting of a first name followed by a last
name, all enclosed in quotes. A name may be at most 20
characters long. One blank separates the last from the first
name. For example, the first two names in the list might be

     'TOM HULL'   'PAT HUME'

The program should read in these 50 names, and print out all the
last names which begin with 'H'. For the two names shown above,
the program should select and print both names.

Our program first reads all the names into an array, then
selects and prints. In this case, the array is not necessary,
since the names could be examined as they are read. Note that
the selection criterion is a search for the sequence 'H'
which signifies the beginning of a last name starting with H.
This program illustrates the topics of Section 9, but is highly
vulnerable to errors in the data. For example, both of the
following names would be selected for printing:

    ' HARRY BROWN'   'ROBERT H JONES'

```
PRINT_NAMES: PROCEDURE OPTIONS(MAIN);
    /* PROGRAM TO PRINT LAST NAMES BEGINNING WITH H */
    DECLARE (NAME(50),  /* LIST OF NAMES */
             NM)        /* NAME CURRENTLY BEING PROCESSED */
             CHARACTER(20) VARYING;
    DECLARE (I, J,NOT_PRESENT) FIXED;

    /* READ NAMES INTO NAME ARRAY */
    DO I = 1 TO 50 BY 1;
       GET LIST(NAME(I));
       END;

    /* PRINT THOSE LAST NAMES WHICH BEGIN WITH H */
    DO I = 1 TO 50 BY 1;
       NM = NAME(I);
       /* PRINT LAST NAME IN NM IF IT BEGINS WITH H */
       NOT_PRESENT = 1;
       J = 1;
       DO WHILE((J < LENGTH(NM)) & (NOT_PRESENT = 1));
          IF SUBSTR(NM,J,2) = ' H' THEN
             DO;
                PUT SKIP LIST(SUBSTR(NM,J));
                NOT_PRESENT = 0;
                END;
          J = J + 1;
          END;
       END;
    END /* PRINT_NAMES */;
```

Section 9 <u>Summary</u>

1. A string variable is declared in the following way:

    DECLARE (identifier) CHARACTER(length) VARYING;

All of the forms of declarations described in Section 8 can be used for string variables except that CHARACTER(...) VARYING is used in place of FIXED or FLOAT). Declarations for string variables can be interspersed with declarations for numeric variables.

2. The length of a string variable is the same as the length of the value most recently assigned to it (but not more than the declared maximum length).

3. String variables <u>do not</u> have an automatic initial value.

4. A string constant is a literal -- a sequence of characters enclosed in single quotes.

5. In SP/k, string variables cannot be subject to arithmetic operations, even if their values happen to be numbers.

6. The only operation that can be performed on string values is "concatenation". The symbol is "||" the action is to join two string values, end to end.

7. The SUBSTR built-in function extracts a portion of the value of a string expression. The form is:

    SUBSTR(char-expr,start-pos,length)

If the length is not specified, the entire right portion of the value is assumed.

8. The LENGTH built-in function gives the length of a string expression. The form is: LENGTH(char-expr)

Section 9 <u>Exercises</u>

Write programs for the following problems.

1. Read a string of up to 40 characters, reverse the order of
the characters, and print it out. For example, 'EVIL' becomes
'LIVE'. You may determine the input form.

2. Read a string of up to 40 characters, using GET LIST; delete
all blanks up to the first non-blank; print the result.

3. Read a string of up to 40 characters, delete all characters
'A', and print the result. You may determine the input form.

4. Read in three strings, call them A, PATTERN, and REPLACEBY.
Replace every occurrence of PATTERN in A by the string
REPLACEBY. Print the result. For example, if we have

    A <u>BIG</u>, <u>BIGGER</u>, <u>BIGGEST</u>PATTERNBIG<u>RE</u>PLACEBY SMALL   _____

the program should print the string

    'SMALL, SMALLGER, SMALLGEST'.

Be careful. If we have

    A <u>LASTPATTERNAREPLAC</u>EBYEA   __

A should not be changed to 'LEAST', then to 'LEEAST', and then
to 'LEEEAST', etc. Stop with 'LEAST'.

5. Write a program to perform the equivalent of the functions
below (see Appendix B.8 for their definition).

    INDEX, VERIFY, TRANSLATE (assume p is always given)

6. Read a three-digit integer and print it in English. For
example, print 182 as ONE HUNDRED AND EIGHTY TWO. You will need
string arrays to hold the English equivalents of the digits.

7. The input consists of three two-digit numbers representing a
date. The first is the day, the second the month, and the third
the last two digits of the year. For example: 25, 12, 75. Read
the number and print it in English, using the PUT EDIT
statement. For example, DECEMBER 25, 1975. Use an array for
the names of the months.

8. Read in a list of words and print out (1) the number of
words made up of 1 to 6 characters, (2) the number with 6 to 12
characters, and (3) the number of times the word 'THE' appears.
The words appear on one card each, left-justified in columns 1
through 12, with no surrounding quotes.

Section 10   Bit-Valued Variables

The conditions described in Section 4.2 are a powerful tool for controlling the sequence of statements executed in programs. PL/I also allows the programmer to declare and use variables that take on the values _true_ and _false_. These _bit_ _variables_ are the subject of this section.

10.1 Declaration of Bit Variables

The declaration of a bit-valued variable in SP/k has the form:

    DECLARE (identifier) BIT;

(Some older versions of PL/I require the programmer to use BIT(1) instead of BIT.)

The BIT attribute is incompatible with the numeric attributes FIXED and FLOAT, and with the CHARACTER attribute; they cannot be given to the same variable. Bit-valued variables can appear in a declaration with other types of variables:

    DECLARE (I) FIXED,
       (P,Q) BIT,
       (S(20)) CHARACTER(10) VARYING;

An array can consist of bit-valued subscripted variables. In this case, the declaration has the form:

    DECLARE (identifier (lb1:ub1, lb2:ub2,...)) BIT;

The rules for array bounds were described in Section 8.

10.2 Bit Assignments and Expressions

10.2.1 Bit Assignment

The bit assignment statement has the same form as a numeric or string assignment:

    variable = expression;

The bit variable denoted by the left side is first determined, the expression is evaluated to yield a bit-value, and this value is assigned to the variable. The expression on the right side of the assignment statement must have the value <u>true</u> ('1'B) or <u>false</u> ('0'B). Bit valued expressions were called conditions in Section 4.2. For example:

```
DECLARE (P,Q,R)BIT;

P = '0'B;
Q = P;
```

10.2.2 <u>Bit</u> <u>Expressions</u>

The essential properties of bit-expressions (conditions) were described in Section 4.2. The main extension introduced by this section is that now a simple condition may be a bit-valued variable as well as a relation. The important properties of bit expressions are summarized below.

1.   There are two bit-constants, '1'B is <u>true</u> and '0'B is <u>false</u>.

2.   There are six relation operators
        =   means "is equal to"
        ¬= means "is not equal to"
        <   means "is less than"
        <= means "is less than or equal to"
        >   means "is greater than"
        >= means "is greater than or equal to"

3.   The relational operators can be used in comparisons to create simple bit-expressions

        expression^1 relation expression^2

   where expression^1 and expression^2 must evaluate to the same type (numeric, character or bit) value. The only relations that are allowed between bit-expressions are = and ¬=.

4.   The Boolean operators & (and), | (or) and ¬ (not) can be used to create compound conditions as described in Section 4.2.1.2.

The following assignment statements illustrate some possible bit expressions.

```
P = (I < 25);
Q = (¬P) & (I ¬= J);
R = (S = 'A') | (LENGTH(S)=0)
Q = ¬(P & R);
```

10.3 Bit Assignment from External Data

Bit variables may appear in the list of a GET statement. For GET list statements the data to be read in must be written as the constants '0'B and '1'B. For example, three bit variables P, Q and R could be given values from external data as follows:

```
        GET SKIP LIST(P,Q,R);
        ...
    $DATA
        ...
        '0'B    '1'B    '0'B
```

10.3.1 EDIT Format BIT Data

Use of the GET EDIT statement permits a much more compact representation of bit-valued data. The B(w) format item (usually B(1) is used) allows bits data to be represented as 0 and 1 rather than '0'B and '1'B respectively. Using EDIT input, the input in the example above could also be read as shown below:

```
        GET SKIP EDIT(P,Q,R)(B(1),B(1),B(1));
        ...
    $DATA
        ...
        010
```

10.4 Display of Bit Values

Bit expressions may be included in a PUT LIST statement. Values are displayed in the standard format as described in Section 6.1. The constant '0'B or '1'B is printed, right justified in the print field.

The format item B(w) allows explicit control of the print spacing in PUT EDIT output. Bit values are printed as 0 or 1 followed by enough blanks to fill out the field to w characters.

10.5 An Example

Consider the problem of finding all prime numbers less than some given number. One could obviously test each number by trying all possible divisors to determine whether a number is prime or not as in the program in Section VI.2.5. The ancient algorithm called the Sieve of Eratosthenes is more efficient. It operates on the principle that a number cannot be prime if it is a multiple of some smaller number. A list of all possible numbers is set up. The sieve algorithm consists of going through this list and sucessively crossing out all numbers that are a multiple of 2,3,5,7..., that is, all numbers which have some prime number as a factor. If one were interested in all prime numbers less than or equal to 50, the final list would look like:

	2	3	~~4~~	5	~~6~~	7	~~8~~	9	~~10~~
11	~~12~~	13	~~14~~	~~15~~	~~16~~	17	~~18~~	19	~~20~~
~~21~~	~~22~~	23	~~24~~	~~25~~	~~26~~	~~27~~	~~28~~	29	~~30~~
31	~~32~~	~~33~~	~~34~~	~~35~~	~~36~~	37	~~38~~	~~39~~	~~40~~
41	~~42~~	43	~~44~~	~~45~~	~~46~~	47	~~48~~	~~49~~	~~50~~

A program that prints out all prime numbers less than or equal to 500 is given below.

```
PRIMES:PROCEDURE OPTIONS(MAIN);
   /* PRINT OUT PRIME NUMBERS <= 500 */
   DECLARE (IS_PRIME(2:500)) BIT,  /* SIEVE */
      (I,LIMIT) FIXED;

   /* INITIALIZE IS_PRIME ARRAY */
   DO I = 2 TO 500;
      IS_PRIME(I) ='1'B;
      END;

   /* CROSS OUT ALL NUMBERS THAT ARE SOME MULTIPLE OF A PRIME */
   I = 2;  /* FIRST PRIME */
   LIMIT = SQRT(500); /* LARGEST POSSIBLE PRIME FACTOR */
   DO WHILE (I <= LIMIT);
      IF IS_PRIME(I) THEN
         /* CROSS OUT REMAINING MULTIPLES OF PRIME NUMBER I */
         DO J = I*I TO 500 BY I;
            IS_PRIME(J) = '0'B;
            END;
      I = I + 1;
      END;

   /* PRINT ALL PRIME NUMBERS */
   PUT SKIP LIST('LIST OF PRIME NUMBERS <= 500');
   PUT SKIP;
   DO I = 2 TO 500;
      IF IS_PRIME(I) THEN
         PUT LIST(I);
      END;
END /* PRIMES */;
```

PART II   PROGRAM STRUCTURE

This part introduces no new PL/I or SP/k features. It is entirely concerned with ways in which the statements presented in Part I should be used to enhance the clarity, readability and understandability of programs.

We assume not only that you can now write PL/I statements to perform simple tasks, but also that you realize that there are various different ways of performing the same task. Once you pass the first threshold of being happy to find any way at all of programming a given task, you should become concerned with which of several possible ways is better.

A program to solve a particular problem is not unique -- many different programs could solve the same problem. But although different programs may produce the same final answers, there may still be significant differences between them and hence strong reasons to prefer one form of program over another. Some of the possible reasons for prefering one program over another are:

1. One is easier to write than the other.

2. One is easier to test and show correctness than the other.

3. One is easier to change, if problem requirements are later altered.

4. One takes less computer time to execute than the other.

5. One is shorter and requires fewer variables -- hence requires less computer memory space during execution.

In Part II we are concerned with the first three of these reasons, which are generally involved with a form of programming that is _easy_ _to_ _read_ _and_ _understand_. This form does not necessarily produce programs that are efficient as far as the computer is concerned (reasons 4 and 5), but neither are they obviously inefficient. At this point _human_ _efficiency_ is more important to us than computer efficiency and we will concentrate on a type of programming that is oriented to human understanding.

Programs are <u>not</u> <u>only</u> meant to convey information to a computer; programs are written by people <u>to</u> <u>be</u> <u>read</u> by people, and for many reasons:

1. Except for trivial problems, programs are rarely completed at a single sitting. Programs take several days to over a year to complete, and you must often review what you have done before.

2. Programs are rarely entirely correct on the first try, and the testing process requires that the program be read.

3. A programming task is often divided among several people who must read and understand portions of each other's work, so that their sections communicate properly.

4. Program segments are often reused in contexts other than the one for which originally written. To do so it is necessary to understand exactly what the segment does.

5. Programs often need to be modified to meet changes in problem requirements.

Most people read programs not for enjoyment, but in order to <u>understand</u> <u>what</u> <u>the</u> <u>program</u> <u>does</u> <u>when</u> <u>executed</u> <u>by</u> <u>a</u> <u>computer</u>. This does not just mean what it will do in one particular execution with one particular set of input data, but what it will do in general, for any possible set of data, any choice of execution options, and any other conditions of context or environment. This is a difficult task at best, and the reader needs all the help he can get.

We must of course understand the precise meaning of each statement type in the programming language so that we can, if necessary, trace or simulate the action of the computer. In theory, we can simulate the entire execution and thereby understand the meaning of any program. In practice this just isn't reasonable. Even for programs of modest size we lack the time or patience to read them as if we were a computer. So we are forced to try to read programs in a way that is quite different from a computer. For example, consider the simple program segment:

```
TOTAL = 0;
DO I = 1 TO N BY 1;
    TOTAL = TOTAL + ARR(I);
    END;
```

Depending upon the value of N, the computer may execute hundreds or even thousands of statements from this segment. Regardless of the value of N, the human reader sees this as a single task: compute the sum of the values of ARR(1:N). Instead of making

the reader figure this out for himself, the writer can help by
describing the task just this way in a heading comment:

```
/* SET TOTAL TO SUM OF VALUES OF ARR(1:N) */
TOTAL = 0;
DO I = 1 TO N BY 1;
    TOTAL = TOTAL + ARR(I);
    END;
```

As far as the computer is concerned the program is unchanged --
the presence or absence of comments, and the contents of
comments are immaterial. But the human reader now has a choice
as to what to read: either the heading comment or the program
under the comment. He can read the comment to find out what the
segment does, or the program statements to find out how the task
is performed.

In general, being able to understand substantial programs
depends on our being able to understand them at a level higher
than that of the individual PL/I statement. To facilitate
reading a program in this way the programmer should structure
the program in terms of higher-level units, and organize and
present the program so that its structure is clear and obvious.
If this is carefully done it is much easier to view the program
in terms of larger units and to understand its action without a
statement-by-statement trace of execution.

For example, consider the two program segments given below.
These segments give identical results; they include exactly
the same PL/I statements. They differ only in that in the
second the statements have been slightly reordered into a more
logical grouping, indentation has been used to show the
relationship between various statements, and comments have been
added to summarize the purpose of various subsections. These
two segments are equivalent as far as the computer is concerned,
but the second is much clearer and easier for us to
understand. If the program required several hundred statements
the form illustrated by (IIa) would be very difficult to
understand -- and yet several hundred statements is not
really a large program. The larger the program, the more
important it is to use an understandable style.

(IIa)

```
    TOTAL = 0; DO I = 1 TO T BY 1;
    M(I) = 0; END; I = 0;
    GET LIST(A);
    DO WHILE(I<N & A¬=0);
    TOTAL = TOTAL + A; I = I + 1;
    M(I) = A;
    GET LIST(A); END;
```

(IIb)
```
    /* SET M(1:T) TO ZEROES */
    DO I = 1 TO T BY 1;
       M(I) = 0;
       END;

    /* READ VALUES UNTIL N HAVE BEEN READ OR UNTIL 0 IS READ */
    /* STORE POSITIVE VALUES IN M(1:I) AND THEIR TOTAL IN SUM*/
    I = 0;
    TOTAL = 0;
    GET LIST(A);
    DO WHILE((I<N) & (A¬=0));
       TOTAL = TOTAL + A;
       I = I + 1;
       M(I) = A;
       GET LIST(A);
       END;
```

Consider the ways in which the writer of (IIb) has undertaken
to help the reader. Most importantly, he shows with comments
that the program consists of two subtasks that are relatively
independent. The first sets M to zeroes; the second loads and
sums. The same two subtasks are present in (IIa), but the
reader must discover this for himself. Not only does he not
have comments to aid him; the statement order does not
suggest this logical division. (IIa) starts with two statements
that are part of the initialization of the second subtask. As
far as the computer is concerned these can just as well be
first, but it diverts the human reader to find these
statements that are not related to or needed by their immediate
successors. The point is that (IIa) must be studied as a
single entity, while (IIb) can be studied as a sequence of
smaller, simpler subtasks.

Even the task of understanding the individual statements is
easier in (IIb). To understand the extent of a DO loop in (IIa)
the reader must scan the entire program and count ENDs very
carefully. In (IIb) the extent of each loop is indicated by
indentation.

The style of (IIb) is recommended, not as a matter of
consideration for some hypothetical reader of your program, but
simply as a matter of self-interest. You will repeatedly have
to read and understand your own programs. The process of
completing later parts requires re-reading earlier parts; the
process of testing requires frequent re-reading. The time spent
in carefully organizing and presenting a program is handsomely
repaid before you have finished with the program.

Section 1   Basic Program Units

The previous section stated our objective of making programs
more readily <u>understandable</u> <u>to</u> <u>a</u> <u>human</u> <u>reader</u>. Now we propose a
systematic method by which this can be done.

The easiest program construction to understand is a <u>sequence</u>
of actions that has <u>no</u> <u>loops</u> <u>or</u> <u>branches</u>. That is, given a
sequence

        S1 S2 S3

we know that S1 will be executed first, then S2, and finally S3.
However, it must be obvious from the examples of Part I, and
even from the statement types of PL/I, that programs must have
loops and branches. In a sense, what we are going to do is try
to hide that fact. We will try to write programs that actually
contain loops and branches in such a way that they can be read
and understood as if they were a simple sequence of actions. In
effect, we will say that it is useful to be able to regard the
execution of a program as "first S1, then S2, and finally S3",
even though we know that internally S2 involves a loop.

We are interested in identifying patterns of statements that
can be usefully regarded as a single unit for purposes of
reading and understanding the action of a program. The three
patterns that dominate are called "the compound statement", "the
repetition unit" and "the alternate selection unit". Each of
these basic units behaves as if it were a single "statement" in
some language that is at a higher level than PL/I. The key
point is that, as a statement, each of these units has a <u>single</u>
<u>entry</u> <u>point</u> and a <u>single</u> <u>exit</u> <u>point</u>. The only control of flow
between such units is the normal sequential order -- the order
in which they are written. Note that the simple statements
of PL/I -- the assignment, input and output statements -- have
this single-entry single-exit property.

1.1 <u>The</u> <u>Compound</u> <u>Statement</u>

Any simple sequence of statements that follow one after
another can be considered a "compound statement". For example,
a sequence of three assignment statements could be considered a

compound statement, or unit, to interchange the values of two
variables:

```
        /* INTERCHANGE VALUES OF A AND B */
        T = A;
        A = B;
        B = T;
```

We require only that the statements perform some logically
related task and that the statements follow one another in
normal sequential order. Other examples are:

```
        /* PRINT TITLE AND HEADING FOR TABLE */
        PUT SKIP LIST
            (' ', 'TEMPERATURE-PRESSURE EQUIVALENTS');
(1.1a)  PUT SKIP LIST
            ('STANDARD CONCENTRATION WITHOUT CATALYST');
        PUT SKIP LIST
            ('TEMPERATURE', 'PRESSURE', 'REACTION TIME');


        /* INITIALIZE TABLE LINE GENERATION */
(1.1b)  LINE_COUNT = 0;
        COLUMN_SUM = 0;
        TIME_BASE = TEMP_BASE/EQUIL_CONST;
```

   We want to be able to regard an entire sequence of PL/I
statements as if they were a single statement in some even-
higher-level language than PL/I. A single statement has a
single entry point and a single exit point:

```
                    ┌──────┐
    enter-->│ S1 │-->exit
                    └──────┘
```

So if a sequence is to behave as a single statement we require
that the <u>entire</u> <u>sequence</u> <u>has</u> <u>a</u> <u>single</u> <u>entry</u> <u>point</u> <u>and</u> <u>a</u> <u>single</u>
<u>exit</u> <u>point</u>:

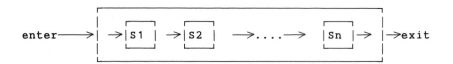

Figure 1. A Compound Statement

   In some contexts it is necessary to identify a compound
statement to PL/I. That is, if you want PL/I to treat several
statements as a single unit you mark the beginning and end with
DO;...END;. For example:

```
IF N > NMAX THEN
    DO;
        PUT SKIP LIST('TOO MUCH DATA.   USE ONLY',NMAX);
        N = NMAX;
        END;
```

If the grouping is entirely for the benefit of the human
reader and not the computer then the grouping is better shown
with comments as   in (1.1a) and (1.1b). The general rule
for format of a compound statement is:

> Write a comment to summarize the purpose (or action) of the
> compound statement and indent the comment so it is left-
> aligned with the preceding unit. The individual components
> of the unit are left-aligned with respect to each other and
> with respect to the heading comment.

> If DO-END delimiters are needed   use   the   following
> indentation convention:

```
                    DO;
                        S1
                        S2
                        ...
                        Sn
                    END;
```

Note finally that we can see from Figure 1 above that the
compound statement itself has the single-entry single-exit
property, and can thus be used as a substatement of another
compound statement.

1.2 The Repetition Unit

Repetition is a common task in programs, and it is relatively
difficult for a human reader to comprehend. With the other
types of units the execution sequence is at least similar to the
sequence that appears on the program listing; with repetition it
is very different. It is crucial that it be carefully organized
and clearly presented.

Repetition is always accomplished with some type of loop.
The loop may be preceded by initialization statements and it may
be followed by termination statements. The idea of the
"repetition unit" is to regard this entire sequence as a single
entity:

```
(1.2a)    /* Description of what the unit does */
          Sequence of statements to initialize for loop
          DO...
              Body of loop
              END;
          Sequence of statements to terminate the task
```

The general form of a loop is shown in Figure 2. The "cond" represents the condition of a DO WHILE loop and indicates by becoming false when the loop should terminate. The statements S1 through Sn form the <u>body</u> of the loop. This loop was discussed in Section I.4.2.

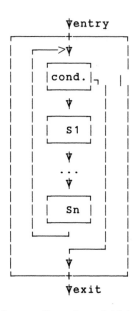

Figure 2. Repetition

Now note that if the statements S1 through Sn each have the single-entry single-exit property, then <u>the</u> <u>whole</u> <u>loop</u> <u>has</u> the <u>single-entry</u> <u>single-exit</u> property. In effect, we consider the loop as a single statement, which can be used as a substatement in a compound statement.

Although the individual statements in a loop may be repeated, and the condition causes a branch, <u>taken</u> <u>as</u> <u>a</u> <u>whole</u>, <u>the</u> <u>loop</u> <u>has</u> <u>a</u> <u>single</u> <u>entry</u> <u>point</u> <u>and</u> <u>a</u> <u>single</u> <u>exit</u> <u>point</u>. It can be regarded as a single statement, so that with the initializing and terminating statements (1.2a) is a single-entry, single-exit compound statement. But because of the presence of the loop we recognize it as a special type of statement and call it a "repetition unit".

Look again at the examples given in I.4.2 and I.4.5. Although they perform very different tasks their similarity in structure is apparent. Additional examples are:

```
          /* SET M TO MAXIMUM OF A(J:K), ASSUMING J <= K */
          I = J;
          M = A(J);
(1.2b)    DO WHILE (I < K);
              I = I + 1;
              M = MAX(A(I),M);
              END;

          /* N>3 AND ODD.  SET DIVISORFOUND TO "N IS PRIME" */
          J = 3;
          DIVISORFOUND = '0'B;
          DO WHILE((¬DIVISORFOUND) & (J <= SQRT(N)));
              IF MOD(N,J) = 0 THEN
                  DIVISORFOUND = '1'B;
(1.2c)        J = J + 2;
              END;
```

A "repetition unit" is a compound statement built around a single loop. As such, its format will be the same as any other compound statement as shown in the examples above. The loop statement itself must be indented to show its structure:

```
     DO WHILE( condition );
         S1
         ...
         Sm
         END;
```

If the loop body is particularly long or detailed, it should be preceded by a comment stating what the body does on each repetition. The body itself is a compound statement and this is its heading comment. This lets us understand the loop without having to understand how the body works, but just what it does.

```
     /* comment describing what the entire loop does */
     DO WHILE( condition );
         /* comment describing what the body does each time */
         S1
         ...
         Sm
         END;
```

The general rules for the format of a repetition unit are:

1. Write a heading comment that summarizes what the entire unit does. Indent this comment so it is left-aligned with the heading of the preceding unit.

2. The individual components of the unit -- initialization, loop and termination -- are left-aligned

with respect to each other, and indented to line up with
the heading comment.

3. The statements that constitute the body of the loop
should be indented with respect to the DO statement that
controls the loop. The END is left-aligned with the
statements of the body of the loop.

4. If the loop body is long or complex it should be
treated as a compound statement (or as several compound
statements), with a heading comment that describes what the
body does on each repetition.

1.3 The Alternate Selection Unit

1.3.1 The Single Alternative Unit

   The third basic type of unit occurs when one of several
alternative tasks is to be selected for execution. The simplest
and most common case is when there are two alternatives, but one
of the two is null. That is, there is one statement that may or
may not be executed. This is of course the "conditional
execution" described in Section I.4.3 and programmed with the IF
construction. However, now we want to make the IF construction
conform to our single-entry, single-exit requirement. We do
this simply by regarding the entire construction as a
single unit, as shown in Figure 3.

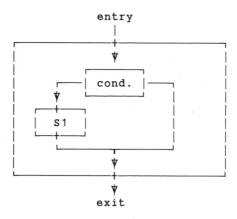

Figure 3. The Single Alternative Unit

There is a single entry point and a common exit point whether or
not the conditional statement is executed. The following are
examples of single alternative or conditional units:

```
(1.3.1a)    /* REPLACE NEGATIVE X BY 0 */
            IF X(I) < 0 THEN
                X(I) = 0;

(1.3.1b)    /* DISCARD NEGATIVE DATUM */
            IF DATUM < 0 THEN
                GET LIST(DATUM);

(1.3.1c)    /* DISCARD AND REPORT NEGATIVE DATUM */
            IF DATUM < 0 THEN
                DO;
                    ERRORCOUNT = ERRORCOUNT + 1;
                    PUT SKIP(2)LIST('ERROR NUMBER',ERRORCOUNT);
                    PUT SKIP LIST('NEGATIVE DATUM', DATUM);
                    GET LIST(DATUM);
                END;

(1.3.1d)    /* SAVE NEW MAXIMUM VAL */
            IF VAL < MAXVAL THEN
                MAXVAL = VAL;

(1.3.1e)    /* SAVE VAL AND POINTER IF NEW MAXIMUM */
            IF VAL(I) > MAXVAL THEN
                DO;
                    MAXVAL = VAL(I);
                    MAXLOC = I;
                END;
```

Since single$_{alternative}$ units are often short and obvious, as
in these examples, we often shortcut the full$_{blown}$ unit format
shown above. The criteria, as always, are readability and
clarity. If the actual PL/I statements are clear and obvious
then a summary comment is not needed. In fact, being redundant,
the comment then tends to clutter and obscure the program rather
than clarify it. Some judgement is required. In the examples
above (1.3.1a), (1.3.1b) and (1.3.1d) probably do not need a
heading comment and perhaps are clearer without it. On
the other hand, (1.3.1c) is probably large enough that the
heading comment is useful, and (1.3.1e) could be written either
way.

Note that if the conditional statement is itself a compound
statement the DO and END delimiters must be used. The extent of
the conditional statement must be conveyed to PL/I as well as
the human reader, and PL/I does not consider comments and
indentation.

The general rules for the format of a single$_{alternative}$ unit
are:

    1. If the unit is long or complex it should be treated
    formally as a distinct unit, with a heading comment left-
    aligned with the heading of the preceding unit. The IF
    should be aligned with respect to the heading, and the
    alternative should be indented with respect to the IF.

2. If the unit is short and obvious it should just be
written as a simple statement i.e., there should be no
heading comment.

1.3.2 The Two-Alternative Unit

The case with two non-null alternatives is obviously
programmed with the IF-THEN-ELSE construction (see Section
I.4.3).   It can still be viewed as a unit with a single exit
point, as shown in Figure 4.

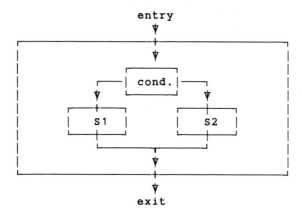

Figure 4.   The Two-Alternative Unit

Examples of two-alternative units are the following:

```
IF A < B THEN
   X = B;
ELSE
   X = A;

/* SET VAL FROM A OR DATA LIST */
IF A(I) ¬= 0 THEN
   VAL = A(I);
ELSE
   GET LIST(VAL);

IF NEWVAL >= 0 THEN
   POSCOUNT = POSCOUNT + 1;
ELSE
   NEGCOUNT = NEGCOUNT + 1;
```

```
/* READ NEXT VALUE INTO NUMBER OR LETTER */
IF TYPEFLAG = 1 THEN
    DO;
        GET LIST(NUMBER(I));
        I = I + 1;
        END;
ELSE
    DO;
        GET LIST(LETTER(J));
        J = J + 1;
        END;
```

The two-alternative unit should <u>not</u> <u>be</u> <u>used</u> <u>to</u> <u>combine</u> <u>two</u> <u>unrelated</u> <u>tasks</u>. The following is an example of <u>poor</u> <u>usage</u>:

```
/* PRINT TITLE OR ERROR MESSAGE */
IF N > 50 THEN
    DO;
        PUT SKIP LIST('EXCESSIVE DATA');
        DONE = '1'B;
        END;
ELSE
    DO;
        PUT SKIP LIST('LIST OF INPUT DATA');
        PUT SKIP;
        END;
```

The title in this example should not be viewed as an alternative to the error message. It would be clearer when presented in the following way:

```
/* TEST FOR EXCESSIVE DATA */
IF N > 50 THEN
    DO;
        PUT SKIP LIST('EXCESSIVE DATA');
        DONE = '1'B;
        END;
```

The general rules for the format of a two-alternative unit are:

1. If the unit is long or complex it should be treated formally as a distinct unit, with a heading comment left-aligned with the heading of the preceding unit. The IF should be left aligned with the heading, and the two alternatives should be indented with respect to the IF.

2. The THEN should follow the conditional on the same line as the IF; The ELSE should be on a separate line between the two alternatives, left aligned with the IF. If the body of the alternative cannot be completed on one line its continuation lines should be indented.

1.3.3 The Multiple-Alternative Unit

The general case, with more than two alternatives, is shown in Figure 5. S1 to Sn are the alternatives, one of which is to be executed; "cond" is the condition by which selection of one alternative is made.

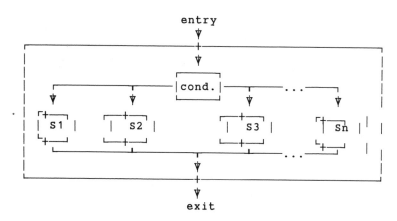

Figure 5.   An Alternate Selection Unit

The entire construction has a single entry-point and a single exit and can be treated as a single unit. Unfortunately, there is no really clear way of programming this unit in PL/I. Some programming languages have a "case statement" for this purpose, but PL/I does not, and we must make do with a combination of IF statements.

When there are three or more alternatives things get more complicated. The most natural way to handle this with a "case statement" but unfortunately it is not available in PL/I. "Label variables" can be used in PL/I, as explained in Appendix B.10.

There are two possible constructions in SP/k using only the IF statement.   Suppose we have four alternatives, one of which is to be executed depending upon the value of a variable CLASS. (1.3.2a) shows a possible construction. It has the desirable single entry and single exit.

```
        /* EXECUTE APPROPRIATE REDUCTION ALGORITHM */
        IF CLASS = 1 THEN
            DO;
(1.3.2a)        ...
            END;
        ELSE
          IF CLASS=2 THEN
              DO;
                ...
                END;
          ELSE
            IF CLASS=3 THEN
                DO;
                  ...
                  END;
            ELSE
                DO; /*ALGORITHM FOR GENERAL CASE */
                    ...
                    END;
```

(1.3.2b) shows a second construction that looks like a minor
variation of (1.3.2a) but in fact it is dangerous and should be
used only with extreme caution:

```
        /* EXECUTE APPROPRIATE REDUCTION ALGORITHM */
        IF CLASS = 1 THEN
            DO;
              ...
              END;
        IF CLASS = 2 THEN
            DO;
              ...
              END;
(1.3.2b) IF CLASS = 3 THEN
            DO;
              ...
              END;
        IF (CLASS¬=1)&(CLASS¬=2)&(CLASS¬=3) THEN
            DO; /* ALGORITHM FOR GENERAL CASE */
                ...
                END;
```

(1.3.2b) avoids the use of deeply nested IF statements but it is
no longer a strictly alternate construction. The possibility
now exists that more than one of the alternatives could be
executed (if the value of CLASS is changed in the body of one
of the alternatives). The construction illustrated in (1.3.2a)
executes at most one of the alternatives, regardless of the
action performed by that alternative.   (1.3.2b) executes
exactly one alternative only if the alternatives refrain from
doing certain things. Therefore, (1.3.2b) should be used if and
only if great care is taken to insure that none of the
alternatives can modify the variable CLASS.

The general rules for the format of an alternate selection unit with more than two alternatives are:

1. Write a heading comment that summarizes what the entire unit does, emphasizing that one of many alternatives is to be executed. Indent this comment so it is left-aligned with the heading of the preceding unit.

2. The individual alternatives are left-aligned with respect to each other. Their alignment should show their parallel role. either event the body of the alternatives should be indented with respect to the IF or ELSE so that the beginning of each alternative is emphasized.

3. If an individual alternative is long or complex it should be treated as a compound statement with its own heading comment, etc.

1.4 Units and Levels

In the preceding sections the basic units were generally described as if their components were simple PL/I statements. Actually the components can just as well be units, since units have a single entry and exit point and in that regard behave as if they were single statements. An entire compound statement (Figure 1), a repetition unit (Figure 2) or an alternate unit (Figures 3 and 4) could be inserted in the position of any one of the Si blocks in any of these figures. The properties of the units, and the rules for their presentation, remain the same whether their components are simple statements, or program units -- which in turn can have units as their components.

There is a hierarchy of these units. At the highest level there will be a compound statement -- a simple sequence of units. Each of these can be a unit of any type, whose components are in turn also units, etc. At some lowest level the components will be single PL/I statements. Since there is no limit either to the size of an individual unit or to the number of levels in the structure, there is no limit to the size or complexity of program that can be organized and presented in this manner.

Some judgement must be used in organizing the program. For example, there are two IF constructions in (1.2c) and you could treat these as units. We have not done so because they are short and obvious, and their formal identification as units with heading comments and extra levels of indentation would not enhance the clarity of the program.

For example, consider a program to read 100 numbers, sort them into ascending order, and print the sorted list:

```
S:PROCEDURE OPTIONS(MAIN);
   /* READ IN 100 NUMBERS,SORT,PRINT OUT */
   DECLARE (A(1:100),T)FLOAT,
      (I,J) FIXED;

   /* READ IN NUMBERS */
   DO I=1 TO 100 BY 1;
      GET LIST(A(I));
      END;

   /* SORT A(1:100) */
   DO J=1 TO 99 BY 1;
      /* INTERCHANGE VALUES OF A(J:100) TO PUT */
      /* SMALLEST IN A(J) */
      DO I=100 TO J+1 BY -1;
         IF A(I) < A(J)THEN
            DO;
               T=A(I);
               A(I)=A(J);
               A(J)=T;
               END;
         END;
      END;

   /* PRINT THE SORTED LIST */
   DO I=1 TO 100 BY 1;
      PUT LIST(A(I));
      END;
   END /* S */;
```

The main program is a compound statement consisting of the three statements

```
Read in numbers
Sort A(1:100)
Print the sorted list
```

Consider the statement Sort A(1:100); the indentation lets us read this as

```
DO J = 1 TO 99 BY 1;
   Interchange values of A(J:100) to put smallest in A(J);
   END;
```

That is, we can understand the algorithm without having to understand <u>how</u> the body works; we need to know only <u>what</u> it does. First the smallest value is put into A(1), then the next is put into A(2), and so on.

1.5 The Well-Structured Program

A program is said to be "well-structured" if it is organized
so that the entire program is itself a unit of one of the types
described above. The components of this unit are themselves
units, etc., to however many levels are required. This means
that the program consists of segments that are readily
understandable at a level higher than individual PL/I
statements, and that the control paths between segments are few
in number and simple in form.

Structure and format are actually two different issues,
although the preceding sections have treated both together. A
program is well-presented if its structure is clearly and
quickly apparent to the reader. This means grouping statements
in a logical way, and providing heading comments so the purpose
of each group is apparent without having to figure it out from
the individual PL/I statements. It also means using indentation
in a clear and consistent way to emphasize the grouping, and to
indicate the flow-of-control during execution.

A program that is both well-structured and well-presented has
a high degree of predictability, and this is useful to the
reader. For example, suppose you encounter the following line
in reading a program:

    /* FIND THE MINIMUM OF THE PN FUNCTION */

If, at the moment, you are looking for something else in the
program and don't need to know how the program actually finds
that minimum, you can confidently skip over the following lines
of program. The next following comment at the same level of
indentation will be the next line to consider. Note that it is
the commenting and indenting convention that helps you find this
next line quickly, but it is the unit structure convention that
allows you to go directly to that line. Knowing that the FIND
MINIMUM unit has a single exit point you know that it will
reach that next line, without having to trace through the detail
of FIND MINIMUM to make sure.

In a well-structured program the different PL/I statements
will always be used in a consistent manner. Repetition is
always controlled as a DO loop. You can read and understand a
program more quickly, simply because you actually have less
to learn about the program. You know in advance how the program
will be organized, how it will be presented, and how each PL/I
statement type will be used. If a program doesn't use these
conventions, then you must approach it with much less of a
headstart. All you have is your knowledge of the meaning of
each individual PL/I statement.

Variation in program style is not desirable. A given
programmer, when confronted with similar tasks at different
points in a program, should solve those tasks in a similar way.
From the point of view of the reader, when he encounters

apparently similar tasks that are handled in different ways, he
should take this as a warning that he does not fully understand
the tasks -- and not just that the programmer got bored with one
approach and decided to try another. For example, suppose that
in the process of reading a program you encounter the following
three segments at three different points:

```
/* MOVE A(1:N) TO B(1:N) */
DO I = 1 TO N BY 1;
   B(I) = A(I);
   END;

/* REPLACE X(1:N) WITH Y(1:N) */
DO I = N TO 1 BY -1;
   Y(I) = X(I);
   END;

/* COPY R(1:N) INTO S(1:N) */
I = 0;
DO WHILE (I < N);
   I = I + 1;
   S(I) = R(I);
   END;
```

First you might wonder whether "move", "replace", and "copy"
mean exactly the same thing to the writer, or whether there are
subtle differences in objective. You should certainly wonder if
there is something peculiar about X and Y that makes it
necessary to index backward (that is, from N to 1) over their
elements.   Finally, you should be concerned with why the writer
chose to use a WHILE loop for R and S when he has used a DO-
index loop in other cases. If it turns out that these are in
fact exactly comparable tasks, and the writer simply amused
himself by seeing how many different ways he could find to write
the same task, you will have wasted time looking for differences
that don't exist and are entitled to be annoyed -- especially if
you were the writer at some earlier time.

    Effectively, you are asked to yield some of your freedom of
choice in writing a program. But this compromise is for your
own benefit. It is in your best interest to do this, since you
the programmer are the most frequent reader of the program.
You must find the errors in it; you must be sure of its
correctness.

    Another major virtue of the structure recommended above is
the limitation of context. This structure makes it possible to
understand a particular unit with relatively little knowledge
about its context.   Without this type of discipline it may be
necessary to examine and understand an entire program before one
can understand much about a particular small segment. This same
characteristic allows units of a program to be written, and
later modified or replaced, while only considering a carefully
circumscribed local environment of that unit.   This makes it
possible to produce relatively large programs and achieve the

same confidence in their correctness as is possible for small
programs.

   If it were possible for a unit to branch arbitrarily to other
sections of the program its successor is no longer unique or
apparent. The sequence of statements executed is very different
from the sequence as written. Similarly, if other units have
the privilege of unrestricted branching then the entry point and
entry conditions of the unit under consideration are not easily
determined.

   This structure is not always the most obvious or natural for
a problem.   But it is the most desirable structure for a
program, and it is worth trying to organize a problem so that it
takes this form. It is not always easy to do so and it takes a
good deal of practice. For non-trivial programs the effort is
clearly worthwhile.   The additional time spent in initial
planning is more than recovered by a reduction in testing time,
and the overall result is a significant improvement in clarity
and reliability.

   For very small programs a less structured organization may
suffice, and a well-structured program requires extra work.
While an experienced programmer who knows how to produce a good
program might be permitted to "shortcut" under special
circumstances, a beginner trying to learn the art of programming
should practice using the proper style at every opportunity.
Even for the professional a casual approach is risky since very
often little programs reappear later as pieces of big programs.

   If there is a "break-even point" with regard to these
practices it occurs at a surprisingly small size of program.
The extra effort pays off for programs as small as 10 statements
just in a reduction in the time required to adequately test the
program. This means it will be valuable even for exercises that
are encountered in a first programming course.

1.5.1 The Art of Writing Comments

   It is comparatively difficult to learn to write good, useful
comments in a program, and many programmers refuse to learn. The
difficulty lies in the complete freedom that is allowed. A
programming language specifies precisely the form of the
statements that are allowed, and the translator enforces those
rules, but for comments the language and translator require only
that they be properly identified. Thus the programmer must
develop his own rules, and there is no mechanism to remind him
when he departs from his rules. We have tried to use comments in
a consistent manner throughout the book, but there are
undoubtedly lapses where we should have done better. Ours is
admittedly an extreme position among programmers with regard to
comments and you will encounter much skepticism among
knowledgeable programmers. Ultimately, you will have to decide
for yourself whether our comments help you to understand our

examples, and more importantly, whether your comments help you
to write and test your own programs.

The rules that we are trying to observe, and that we
recommend to you, are the following:

1. In many contexts and for many purposes _comments_ _should_ _be_
read _as_ _an_ _alternative_ _to_ _a_ _group_ _of_ _program_ _statements_. To be
able to read comments in this way the reader must have complete
confidence that a comment is a valid alternative -- that it says
the same thing as the program statements, but in a different
form. To maintain this confidence, comments must be precise and
accurate. For example, compare the following possible heading
comments for a segment to read data:

          /* LOAD AR(1:50) FROM DATA. STOP ON FIRST -1 */

          /* READ DATA */

          /* LOAD AR */

The first example specifies fairly precisely what is going to be
done, and for many purposes it would be unnecessary to read the
corresponding program statements. The second and third
possibilities just generally describe the purpose of the
statements, but with these comments you would be more likely to
have to read the statements to understand the action of that
part of the program.

   Use _specific_ _variable_ _names_ _in_ _comments_. For example,
compare the following alternatives:

          /* SET MINA TO MIN OF A(J:K) */

          /* FIND MINIMUM */

   Keep _your_ _comments_ _up-to-date_. When you change program
statements, adjust the comments accordingly. No matter how
well-written the comments were initially, unless they are kept
current the reader can have no confidence in them. This
confidence is a fragile thing -- once the reader has discovered
one inaccurate or obsolete comment in a program he must be
suspicious of all other comments.

   There must be some convention (usually indentation) to
indicate the precise scope of each comment -- that is, the
program statements to which it is an alternative. Our
convention in SP/k is that _program_ _statements_ _are_ _lined_ _up_ _with_
respect _to_ _the_ _corresponding_ _comment_. For example:

```
/* LOAD X(1:N) FROM DATA */
GET LIST(N);
DO I = 1 TO N BY 1;
   GET LIST(X(I));
   END;
SUM = 0;
COUNT = 0;

/* WRITE TITLE AND COLUMN HEADINGS */
PUT SKIP(3) LIST(' ', ' ', 'DEMOGRAPHIC PROFILE');
PUT SKIP LIST('YORK COUNTY, 1970 CENSUS');
PUT SKIP(2) LIST
   ('SIZE','NUMBER','SOURCE','INCOME','LOCATION');
PUT SKIP(2);
```

2. The reason for having comments as an alternative description
for a human reader is to provide a form that is more efficient
for him -- that is, a form that is both _more_ _concise_ and _more_
comprehensible. The comments should be written in a semi-formal
higher-level _language_. They should _never_ _simply_ _duplicate_ the
program statements. For example, the following are examples of
poor _comments_ -- in each case the program would be at least as
clear without them so there is no reward for the effort of
writing them.

```
SUM = 0; /* INITIALIZE SUM TO 0 */

/* GET NEW VALUE OF N */
GET LIST(N);

/* PUT TWO WORDS TOGETHER */
LONGWORD = LEFT || RIGHT;
```

The purpose of a comment is _not_ to explain the action of a
program statement to a reader who does not understand the
programming language. Start with the assumption that the reader
could read and understand the program statements, if necessary,
but your job is to make it unnecessary for him to do so in many
cases. Remember that you are going to be the most frequent
reader, and hence the principal beneficiary of this kindness.

In summary, comments can be useful, but only _if_ _you_ _take_ _them_
seriously. Time spent in writing comments that are precise,
concise alternatives to program segments is generously repaid
later in the programming and testing process. Comments that are
casually written -- and inserted more because of compulsion than
conviction -- are probably not worth the bother. Evaluate our
examples critically in this regard and decide what your own
"comment conventions" should be.

1.5.2 On Programming Style

The reader should be aware that all programming styles are in
some sense arbitrary. It is important to develop a readable

style and to use it consistently but the conventions adopted for the placement of comments and program units is somewhat a matter of taste. In writing this book we have used the commenting and indentation style that is automatically provided by the SP/k compiler developed at the University of Toronto. (See Part X and Appendix A). An earlier version of this book, An Introduction to Programming - A Structured Approach Using PL/1 and PL/C-7 by Richard Conway and David Gries used a somewhat different style that emphasized the hierarchical structure of the program. In the style recommended in that book, comments served as headings for major sections of programs and the statements described by the comment were indented with respect to the comment. That book's version of the body of the procedure in Section 1.4 is:

```
/* READ IN NUMBERS */
   DO I = 1 TO 100 BY 1;
      GET LIST (A(I)); END;
/* SORT A(1:100) */
   DO J = 1 TO 99 BY 1;
      /* INTERCHANGE VALUES OF A(J:100) TO PUT */
      /* SMALLEST IN A(J) */
         DO I = 100 TO J+1 BY -1;
            IF A(I) < A(J) THEN
               DO; T = A(I); A(I) = A(J);
                  A(J) = T; END;
            END;
      END;
```

The reader should select a style that makes programs easy to read. The major reason for developing a consistent style is to make the physical appearance of a program an aid to understanding the logical structure of the program.

1.5.3 A Comparative Example

With this discussion as background we now give another example, presenting the same program in both "well-structured" and "conventional" form, as we did in (IIa) and (IIb).

Consider a program which is to read in a 2 dimensional array of integers A(N,N), and then determine the following three values:

1. The largest element on the principal diagonal -- the maximum A(I,I) for I=1,2,...,N. Call this maximum DMAX.

2. The largest element in row I, the row in which DMAX occurs. Call this RMAX.

3. The largest element in column I, the column in which DMAX occurs. Call this CMAX.

The input consists of a number N, less than 25, followed by the N^2 numbers of the array in row-major order. The required output is a display of the array and the values of DMAX, RMAX and CMAX.

(1.5.3a) and (1.5.3b) are alternative programs which are both correct and solve the problem. (1.5.3a) could be written by a programmer who has not studied and understood the values of structure. (We have tried not to make it deliberately obscure.) (1.5.3b) follows the recommendations of the preceding sections. (1.5.3b) is written following the recommendations of the preceding sections. As you consider these two programs, realize that they <u>are</u> <u>identical</u>, <u>as</u> <u>far</u> <u>as</u> <u>the</u> <u>computer</u> <u>is</u> <u>concerned</u>. They differ only in the manner in which they are <u>organized</u> <u>and</u> <u>presented</u> <u>for</u> <u>a</u> <u>human</u> <u>reader</u>.

(1.5.3a)

```
    MAXELMT: PROCEDURE OPTIONS(MAIN);
    DECLARE (A(24,24),N,LD,LR,LC,I,J) FIXED;
    GET LIST(N); LD=1; LR=1; LC=1;
    IF (N<1)|(N>24) THEN DO; PUT SKIP LIST('WRONG SIZE',N);
    RETURN;END;
    DO I = 1 TO N BY 1; PUT SKIP(' ');
    DO J = 1 TO N BY 1;
    GET LIST(A(I,J)); PUT LIST(A(I,J));
    END; END;
    DO I = 2 TO N BY 1;
    IF A(I,I) > A(LD,LD) THEN LD = I; END;
    PUT SKIP LIST('DMAX IS:',A(LD,LD),'IN ROW,COL',LD);
    DO I = 2 TO N BY 1;
    IF A(LD,I) > A(LD,LR) THEN LR=I;
    IF A(I,LD) > A(LC,LD) THEN LC=I; END;
    PUT SKIP LIST('RMAX IS:',A(LD,LR),'IN COL',LR);
    PUT SKIP LIST('CMAX IS:',A(LC,LD),'IN ROW',LC);
    END;
```

(1.5.3b)

```
    MAXELMT: PROCEDURE OPTIONS(MAIN);
        /* FIND DMAX, RMAX AND CMAX IN A(N,N). */
        DECLARE (A(24,24),
             N,
             LD,          /* ROW, COL OF DMAX */
             LR,          /* COL OF RMAX */
             LC,          /* ROW OF CMAX */
             I,J) FIXED;

        /* READ IN ARRAY A, STOP IF IMPROPER SIZE */
        GET LIST(N);
        IF (N < 1) | (N > 24) THEN
            DO;
                PUT SKIP LIST('SIZE OF ARRAY WRONG:',N);
                RETURN; /* TERMINATES PROGRAM EXECUTION */
            END;
        DO I = 1 TO N BY 1;
            DO J = 1 TO N BY 1;
                GET LIST(A(I,J));
                END;
            END;

        /* PRINT ARRAY A */
        DO I = 1 TO N BY 1;
            PUT SKIP(' ');
            DO J = 1 TO N BY 1;
                PUT LIST(A(I,J));
                END;
            END;

        /* FIND INDEX LD OF DMAX */
        LD = 1;
        DO I = 2 TO N BY 1;
            IF A(I,I) > A(LD,LD) THEN
                LD = I;
            END;

        /* FIND INDEX LR OF RMAX, LC OF CMAX */
        LR = 1;
        LC = 1;
        DO I = 2 TO N BY 1;
            IF A(LD,I) > A(LD,LR) THEN
                LR = I;
            IF A(I,LD) > A(LC,LD) THEN
                LC = I;
            END;

        /* PRINT RESULTS */
        PUT SKIP LIST('DMAX IS:',A(LD,LD),
                'IN ROW,COL',LD);
        PUT SKIP LIST('RMAX IS:',A(LD,LR),'IN COL',LR);
        PUT SKIP LIST('CMAX IS:',A(LC,LD),'IN ROW',LC);
        END /* MAXELMT */;
```

We claim that (1.5.3b) is more readily understandable than (1.5.3a) even though it has more lines to read. (1.5.3b) makes it obvious that the program is a compound statement -- a simple sequence of five subtasks:

       Read in array A
       Print array A
       Find index LD of DMAX
       Find index LR of RMAX and LC of CMAX
       Print results.

Each of these subtasks is itself a compound statement, and four of them involve looping, but that does not obscure the fact that there are essentially five steps in executing the program. Within each of the subtasks the extent and purpose of each loop are made clear by labelling and indentation.

It is probably not obvious at this stage of your programming development, but real programs are often modified. That is, after a program is completed and tested, and has been used for awhile, it is not unusual for problem requirements to be slightly changed. Then someone -- not always the original author -- must go back and re-read the program and find the appropriate points at which to make changes. Consider (1.5.3b) from the point of view of making changes. It is easier to find the place to make the change, easier to write the new statements, and we have greater confidence that the change is correct and does not disturb other sections of the program. In effect, we really have to study (1.5.3a) in order to find out information that is readily apparent in (1.5.3b). For example, consider the relative ease and confidence with which (1.5.3a) and (1.5.3b) could be modified to make one or more of the following changes:

1. The program is to be run only on "sparse" arrays -- arrays where most of the elements are 0. To make it easier to keypunch the input data, change the program to accept input of the following form, where the user need only specify the non-zero elements:
        a) card 1 contains the integer N
        b) each successive card describes one non-zero array element by giving its row number, its column number and its value
        c) the last card contains three zero values.

2. The output is difficult to read if N>5 because a row of the array will be printed on several successive lines. Use EDIT format output to reduce the size allowed to each value and make the output more readable.

3. Change the output format so the array is printed with 2 stars "**" on either side of the values DMAX, RMAX and CMAX.

4. Change the program so that DMAX is the largest value on
the lower-left-to-upper-right diagonal.

Section 1 <u>Summary</u>

1. A well-structured program is a hierarchy of program units.
The highest level is a unit, whose components are also units,
etc. The lowest level consists of simple PL/I statements.

2. A program unit is a group of statements that are logically
related to each other in that they perform some well-defined
task.   There are three principal kinds of units: "compound
statement", "repetition" and "alternate selection".

3. In SP/k a unit should begin with a comment that is left-
aligned with the start of the statements in the unit.
Indentation should be used to indicate the structure of units.

4. A unit has a single entry point and a single normal exit
point.

Section 2   Program Schemata

When we introduced the IF construction in Section I.4.3 we gave the model of the construction as

```
IF condition THEN
    statement.
```

This gave the form or _schema_ of that conditional statement in PL/I. The symbol "statement" in the schema stands for any simple or compound PL/I statement. Written in this form, before some particular statement is specified, the schema is said to be _uninterpreted_. We defined the action of the IF construction in terms of an uninterpreted schema; that is, we described its action independent of what particular statement might be given as the body.

This seems like a complicated way of explaining something that was fairly obvious on first encounter, but we would like to extend this argument to larger program constructions. For example:

```
     I = 0;
     DO WHILE ( I < N );
         I = I+1;
(2a)     Body
         END;
```

This is a schema uninterpreted with respect to the body, the index variable i, the stopping value n, the loop-name and the heading comment -- the elements given in lower-case letters. A particular example or interpretation of this schema would have these lower-case elements replaced by specific PL/I elements. For example, the following are specific interpretations of (2a):

```
        /* MOVE A(1:K) TO B(1:K) */
        J = 0;
        DO WHILE (J < K);
           J = J + 1;
           B(J) = A(J);
           END;

        /* PRINT 12 LINES OF 10 *'S EACH */
        I = 0;
        DO WHILE (I < 12);
           I = I + 1;
           PUT SKIP LIST('**********');
           END;
```

```
/* CLEAR X(1:K) TO ZERO */
M = 0;
DO WHILE (M < K);
   M = M + 1;
   X(M) = 0;
   END;

/* CLEAR A(1:K,2:M) IF LESS THAN A(1:K,1) */
I = 0;
DO WHILE (I < K);
   I = I + 1;
   /* CLEAR ITH ROW */
   DO J = 2 TO M BY 1;
      IF A (I,J) < A(I,1) THEN
         A(I,J) = 0;
      END;
   END;
```

Although these examples perform very different tasks, in each
case the basic structure is the same -- some task is repeated a
definite number of times. That subtask may be a single
statement or a substantial program segment, but the statements
that control its repetition are the same (except for the
particular names used). Each of these examples follows the
pattern shown in (2a) with the lower-case elements of (2a)
replaced by particular PL/I elements. These different
interpretations of (2a) <u>differ</u> from each other <u>only in the
choices of specific elements to replace the lower-case elements
of (2a).</u>

Definite repetition is a common task, and (2a) can be
regarded as a schema for a "statement" to accomplish this task.
You can learn this schema and use it more-or-less automatically
each time that you need to repeat some action a definite number
of times. It means that you will not have to "re-invent" a
mechanism for definite repetition each time it is required.

There are many other common tasks and corresponding schemata.
For example, suppose a program is to perform some task for each
item of a list of data, where the end of the list is recognized
by the presence of some distinctive value. An appropriate
schema is:

```
       Initialize
       GET LIST(item);
       DO WHILE(item ¬= stopping flag);
(2b)      Perform the task for the item
          GET LIST(item);
          END;
```

This schema is uninterpreted with respect to the nature of the
task, the stopping value, and the name of the item. One
particular interpretation of this schema is the example of

Section I.1.1 where the task is to find the maximum. Another
interpretation where the task is to find the sum is given as
example (I.4.5.2c).

Further examples of schemata are given in (2c) and (2d). An
especially common task in programs is to perform some action
on each element of an array, or on some portion of an array.
(2c) gives a schema for this task.

```
         /* Perform action on each element of a(j:k) */
         Initialize
         DO i = j TO k BY 1;
(2c)         Perform action on a(i)
             END;
```

The following are examples of interpretations of (2c):

```
         /* DISPLAY VALUES OF AR(A:B) */
         PUT SKIP(3) LIST('VALUES OF AR(A:B)');
         PUT SKIP LIST('A =', A, 'B =', B);
         PUT SKIP;
         DO I = A TO B BY 1;
            PUT SKIP LIST(AR(I));
            END;


         /* LOAD X(1:N) FROM DATA */
         DO I = 1 TO N BY 1;
            GET LIST(X(I));
            END;


         /* MOVE X(1:N) TO Y(1:N) */
         DO J = 1 TO N BY 1;
            Y(J) = X(J);
            END;
```

Another common task is to perform some operation on each element
of a data list, when the list is preceded by an integer
specifying the number of items on the list. One possible schema
is:

```
     Initialize
     GET LIST(N);
     DO WHILE ( N > 0 );
        GET LIST(item);
(2d)    Process item
        N = N - 1;
        END;
```

An interpretation of (2d) is the following:

```
/* PRINT TABLE OF SQUARES AND SQUARE ROOTS */
PUT SKIP LIST('X','X*X','SQRT(X)');
GET LIST(N);
DO WHILE (N > 0);
   GET LIST(X);
   PUT SKIP LIST(X,X*X,SQRT(X));
   N = N - 1;
   END;
```

We cannot catalog all common program tasks for you and give schemata for them. We are just trying to make you aware that there are certain patterns that recur frequently, and that you should learn to recognize them. You should develop your own repertoire of schemata, and apply them whenever a familiar task appears. This will save you the time and effort of re-inventing solutions to these problems, and make your programs more consistent and predictable.

Notice that it is the control structure of the segment that recurs more often than the specific action. The action will vary from problem to problem, but the manner in which it is repeated is often familiar. There are infinitely many different problems to be solved -- you will rarely meet one that is identical to one you have solved before. But any problem can be broken down into sections, and many of the sections may be recognizable as some action to be repeated in some familiar way. Viewed in this way, even large problems are not quite so formidable.

We have several objectives in this discussion. First, many programs that perform quite different tasks are, in fact, very similar in structure. Once we become familiar with certain common structures we can reuse them with confidence, rather than approach every new problem as if it were going to be completely different from what we have done before. Second, if we make an effort to cleanly separate control structures from controlled actions it will help to make the true nature of the program apparent.

Finally, and most importantly, it is useful to be able to make some definite statements about the action of a program while considering only some of its statements. That is, we would like to be able to make positive statements about uninterpreted schemata. For example, we would like to say of schema (2a) that it repeats the body N times regardless of what is given as the body. Unfortunately this is not true, in general, because actions could appear in the body to interfere with the control structure. However, the statement is true if the body is restricted in the following ways:

1. It does not alter the values of either I or N.
2. It does not execute a RETURN statement.
    (RETURN will be introduced in Part IV.)

Schema (2b) performs some task upon each item of data, assuming the task is a program segment subject to the following restrictions:

1. It does not alter the value of the stopping flag.
2. It does not execute a RETURN statement.
3. It does not execute a GET statement.

Such restrictions are not arbitrary infringements of the programmer's freedom of expression, but are necessary limitations to allow the control structure and the controlled task to be cleanly separated. When handled in this way the task or body is very usefully isolated from its environment. For example, in (2b) the task is to be performed on some "item". The task can be studied and programmed without knowing that that item came from a data list, how many more might follow it, what its disposition will be, etc. It is simply an object upon which some action is to be performed. Not knowing that the item came from external data, the task would have no reason to include another GET statement. The task might require hundreds of PL/I statements, but as long as it observes these simple restrictions it is a logically simple task, wholly independent of the controlling structure.

A very useful consequence of this type of disciplined structure is that it makes it possible to prove certain properties of real programs. For example, given a segment of a real program, one could prove that its action was to repeat a certain sub-segment a certain number of times, just by showing that the overall segment is an interpretation of (2a) and that the repeated sub-segment avoids the interfering actions. This property of the sub-segment can be shown to be true regardless of the length and complexity of its statements. It is a consequence of demonstrating the <u>absence</u> of certain actions, rather than requiring an analysis of what the subsegment actually accomplishes.

Someday programming languages may be more suitable for this disciplined style of programming. For example, a language might provide control structures such as:

```
REPEAT count TIMES;
    Body
    END;

REPEAT FOR EACH DATA item UNTIL item = stopping flag;
    Body
    END;
```

```
REPEAT FOR EACH ELEMENT OF array(1:m,1:n);
    Body
    END;
```

These constructions are the obvious counterparts to (2a), (2b)
and (2c). They might be more convenient to use, but more
importantly, the language could suitably restrict the contents
of the body of each construction. For example it would be
illegal, rather than just unwise, to write the restricted
statements described above these bodies. There is no technical
reason why such a language could not be produced, but no one has
yet done so. Making do with languages that are available
today we write the natural control phrase in English as a
comment, translate it as well as possible into whatever
control structures the language offers, and try to teach
programmers to avoid statements in the body that will
destroy the structural quality of their program. (This
issue of separation of action and control is discussed
further in Section IV.2.3.)

2.1 A Classification of Very Simple Programs

For many of the very simple problems used as examples and
exercises in introductory programming courses one can give
schemata for the entire program, rather than just for segments
of it. Many of these simple problems consist of some repetition
of three actions:

1. Read an item of data;
2. Perform some action upon the item;
3. Print some results.

The problem requirements will detail the action to be performed,
and the result to be printed. This will dictate which of two
basic strategies must be used.

The simplest strategy consists of dealing with the data items
one at a time. There is never any need to have more than one
item available at any point in execution of the program. The
entire program is just an interpretation of schema (2b) or (2d).
For example, (2.1a) gives a schema for the entire program based
upon (2b).

```
$JOBK ID='programmer name'
program-name:PROCEDURE OPTIONS(MAIN);
    /* read, process and print, one item at a time */
    Declarations
    Initialize
    GET LIST(item);
    DO WHILE(item ¬= stopping flag);
        Perform action on item
(2.1a)      PUT SKIP LIST(item result);
        GET LIST(item);
        END;
    Write out results
    END /* program-name */;
$DATA
data list
```

A simple interpretation of (2.1a) is a program to print a copy of the data list:

```
$JOBK ID='I.WEBER'
PRINTDATA:PROCEDURE OPTIONS(MAIN);
    /* PRINT LIST OF DATA, UP TO FIRST NEGATIVE VALUE */
    DECLARE (VALUE) FLOAT;
    PUT LIST('WEBER DATA LIST:');
    PUT SKIP;
    GET LIST (VALUE);
    DO WHILE (VALUE >= 0);
        PUT SKIP LIST (VALUE);
        GET LIST (VALUE);
        END;
    PUT SKIP(2) LIST('END OF LIST');
    END /* PRINTDATA */;
$DATA
14E0    23.56E0    23E2    -1.0E0
```

Another example of an interpretation of (2.1a) would be to print running sums of the values on a data list, stopping when -999 is encountered:

```
$JOBK ID='JAN STURGIS'
JANSUM:PROCEDURE OPTIONS(MAIN);
   /* SUM VALUES ON DATA LIST, UP TO -999 */
   DECLARE (ITEM, SUM) FLOAT;
   DECLARE (COUNT) FIXED;
   COUNT = 0;
   SUM = 0;
   GET LIST (ITEM);
   DO WHILE (ITEM ¬= -999);
      SUM = SUM + ITEM;
      COUNT = COUNT + 1;
      GET LIST (ITEM);
      END;
   IF COUNT = 0 THEN
      PUT LIST('NO DATA GIVEN');
         ELSE
      PUT LIST('SUM OF', COUNT, ' ITEMS IS', SUM);
   END /* JANSUM */;
$DATA
4.5E1    0.0E0    27E-1    2.3E+1    -1.000E0    5.61E+1    -999
```

Now suppose the problem requirements were changed just enough to make it necessary to retain <u>many data values at the same time</u>. Schema (2.1a) can no longer be used since it is limited to a single data value at a time. The program will now require an array to hold the data list, and will likely involve two principal steps, each one being a loop over the elements of the array. A schema such as (2.1b) would be required. The "load-loop" in (2.1b) could be of the form of either schema (2b) or (2d). The "process-loop" is likely to be of the form of schema (2c).

```
$JOBK ID='programmer name'
PROGRAM-NAME:PROCEDURE OPTIONS(MAIN);
   /* summary of program action */
   Declaration of array to hold data
   Declarations of other variables

   /* LOAD ARRAY FROM DATA-LIST */
   Load-loop

   /* PROCESS ELEMENTS OF ARRAY */
   Process-loop
   END /* PROGRAM NAME */;
$DATA
data-list
```
(2.1b)

A simple example of an interpretation of (2.1b) would be a problem requiring printing some summary results <u>before</u> printing a copy of the data list. For example:

```
$JOBK ID='SARAH HOLT'
CTPDATA:PROCEDURE OPTIONS(MAIN);
   /* COUNT, TITLE, AND PRINT DATA, UP TO 1ST NEG VALUE */
   DECLARE (DLIST(50)) FLOAT;
   DECLARE (DTEMP) FLOAT;
   DECLARE (I,J) FIXED;
   PUT LIST('HOLT DATA LIST');

   /* LOAD DLIST (50) FROM DATA, UP TO 1ST NEG VAL */
   I = 0;
   GET LIST (DTEMP);
   DO WHILE ((DTEMP >= 0) & (I < 50));
      I = I + 1;
      DLIST(I) = DTEMP;
      GET LIST(DTEMP);
      END;

   /* COMPLETE TITLE */
   PUT SKIP (2) LIST(I, 'ITEMS BEFORE 1ST NEG VALUE');
   PUT SKIP(2);
   /* PRINT DLIST(1:I) */
   DO J = 1 TO I BY 1;
      PUT SKIP LIST(DLIST(J));
      END;
   END /* CTPDATA */;
 $DATA
 1.2E+1   2.4E+1   3.648E+1   2.9001E+1
 3.000E-2   1.0E+0   -1
```

A good way to get started on your first programming exercise is to study the problem requirements to see whether it is a "one at a time" problem or an "all at once" problem. Then view your program, not as an entirely original creation, but just as an interpretation of either (2.1a) or (2.1b). This prescription won't handle all of your assigned problems, but it should help with many of them.

PART III   PROGRAM DEVELOPMENT

Section 1   The Phases of Development

Our task is to write a program to solve some problem.   Given
the problem description in English, we have to figure out a way
in which a computer can be used to solve the problem, and then
describe this plan very precisely in some programming language.
This process has four distinct phases:

1. Clarify the problem requirements.

2. Design a program strategy.

3. Specify critical data structures.

4. Write the program statements.

Although the phases should occur roughly in the order listed,
there is a good deal of overlap and backtracking, and
particularly for small problems they are difficult to separate.
Nevertheless they each represent a distinct function that must
be performed in every programming process. At least initially,
while struggling to learn the details of a programming language,
phase four may look the most formidable. With practice and
experience you will discover that if the other three phases are
properly done then phase four is quite straightforward. It may
still be time-consuming and error-prone, but it will not be the
critical phase.

In this section we give a brief introduction to each of these
phases. In Section 2 we illustrate the complete process for
several simple programs. In Section 3 we elaborate upon general
problems and considerations that arise in various phases of the
process.

1.1 Clarification of the Problem

Surprisingly, clarification of the problem is a major phase
of the process. It would   seem reasonable that a clear and
precise statement of the problem would be given, but in fact

this is rarely the case and more programming disasters can be blamed on failure in this regard than any other. It is very easy to misunderstand the precise requirements of a problem and proceed to write a program that solves the wrong problem. This phase is hard enough even in an programming course where the problem is stated by someone who (presumably) understands what can be programmed, and chooses problems to be only interestingly difficult. Real problems are usually posed by someone who isn't sure exactly what he wants done, much less how the computer is going to contribute to a solution, and the problem definition often becomes precise only in response to persistent and pointed questions on the part of the programmer.

A substantial fraction of the clarification dialog is concentrated on three key issues:

   1. <u>Input</u>. What is its format and order? What are the limits of volume that may occur and how will the end of the input be recognized? What are the limits on values that will be encountered?

   2. <u>Output</u>. What is the content, format and order of output? What titling is appropriate? What limits on volume may be expected?

   3. <u>Errors</u>. What types of errors (both in input and in processing) must the program guard against, and what action should be taken when they are encountered? Which problem specifications can be taken as guaranteed, and which only as good intentions -- to be checked by the program?

For example, suppose you are given the following problem:

(1.1a) Write a program to compute the sum of a list of numbers.

This statement gives only a general idea of the objective of the program; much more detailed information is required before you could begin to design the program. For example:

   1a. Can the data be presented on punched cards in a format
        acceptable to the PL/I GET LIST statement?
   b.   How many values can there be? How can the end of the
        list of values be recognized?
   c.   What types and sizes of values might be expected?
   2a. In what form should the sum be displayed?
   b.   What identifying title should be provided?
   3a. What action should be taken for values on the list
        that violate the specifications of 1c?
   b.   What action should be taken if the quantity of values
        violates instructions given in 1b?

After obtaining specific answers to these questions you might have the following refinement of (1.1a):

(1.1b)Write a program to compute the sum of a list of positive
     integers, given in PL/I LIST format. The end of the data
     list will be denoted by two consecutive values of -999.
     Improper values on the list should be rejected (excluded
     from the sum) and printed on a list titled "REJECTED
     VALUES":. Any irregularity in termination should result in
     a warning message.   The result should be given in three
     lines, after the list of rejects (if any).

          SUM OF POSITIVE INTEGERS
            n VALUES INCLUDED
            SUM IS s

   As a second example, consider a simple text-processing
problem:

(1.1c)Write a program to delete duplicates from a word list.

Clarification of (1.1c) might result in something like the
following:

(1.1d)Write a program to print a list of words, one per line,
     in the order given, but excluding any word that has
     appeared earlier in the list. The data will be given as an
     integer n (not more than 100), followed by n words, each a
     quoted character string in LIST format. These words may
     vary in length from one to twenty characters.   Each word
     should consist of a compact sequence of letters A-Z; no
     digits, blanks or special characters are allowed. The
     output should be given as follows:

          WORD LIST WITHOUT DUPLICATES:
            m ENTRIES
            first word
            second word
            ...

   m given in the title indicates the length of the final
list, after duplicates and improper words have been
rejected.   Report any difficulties with the length of the
list, but produce some list if at all possible.

   (1.1b) and (1.1d) have obviously been written by someone who
understands programming, and is anticipating many of   the
difficulties the program must face. Given a description in this
form and this much detail, the program is well-specified and not
very difficult to write. But, in general, (1.1a) and (1.1c) are
samples of what you can expect to be given as an initial problem
statement.   (1.1b) and (1.1d) are the corresponding samples of
what you must produce by asking the right questions.   In   a
programming course your assignments may look more like (1.1b)
and (1.1d), but someday you will face problems like (1.1a) and
(1.1c).

Whenever possible obtain samples of input and corresponding output. English is a disappointingly ambiguous descriptive tool, and a concrete example often clarifies (or obviates) a voluminous description.

Initially, don't even think about the program; <u>concentrate</u> on the <u>problem</u> until it becomes absolutely clear. Make up several sets of input data, and figure out the corresponding output results. This sample data should be designed to test and increase your understanding of the <u>details</u> of the problem, and not just its general nature. It might seem a waste of time to make up input data and perform hand calculations, but in doing so you are actually executing an algorithm to solve the problem. Thus while concentrating on understanding the problem, you are also working toward designing the solution.

While studying the problem you should ask questions like "What is to be done if the input number is incorrect?", "What happens if this particular number is 0? Is it correct or incorrect and what should I do with it?", and "What should I do here -- the problem statement seems to be ambiguous?" It is important that these questions be raised and answered <u>before</u> any programming is done. Proper understanding of the problem before you begin programming is crucial. Without this understanding, the program can never be correct.

The first step, clarification, is rarely completely successful. In general you will discover the omission of some necessary detail in the problem requirements only after you are engaged in the detailed execution of a later phase. For example, you will discover the lack of some detail about the volume of data only when you are attempting to specify the data structures and need a specific value to give as the size of an array. Or you will discover that you don't know how to process a particular error when you are actually writing the conditional unit to check for that error. In either case, you have discovered that the first phase is not quite completed and you must return and work on it further.

1.2 <u>Design</u> <u>of</u> <u>a</u> <u>Solution</u> <u>Strategy</u>

This is certainly the hardest part of the process for which to give general advice as to how to proceed. Whatever creativity exists in programming is concentrated in this phase. We will give some vague suggestions as to where you may get ideas, and will give some helpful procedures for developing ideas once you have them -- but we recognize that we are helping you least just where you need it most. We recommend you read Polya's classic book <u>How</u> <u>to</u> <u>Solve</u> <u>It</u>.

A useful device is to initially ignore the computer and its programming language, and try to figure out how you would <u>solve</u> <u>the</u> <u>problem</u> <u>by</u> <u>hand</u>, if you were presented with the data on

cards in such a way that you could see each item only once, and
only in the order given. Assume further that the only "scratch
paper" available to you is a number of very small cards (one
number apiece) on which you can write, erase and rewrite
numbers. If you can figure out some way to solve the problem by
hand under these restrictions, then you can generally figure out
how to describe that method in a program.

The important thing is to separate the process of planning a
solution from the task of describing that solution in a
programming language. Once you learn to make this separation,
the challenging and difficult part of the process will be the
planning. For example, if you are unable to write a program to
"sort" a list of numbers into increasing order, it is likely
because you cannot figure out how to do it by hand in a
systematic manner, and not because you don't know PL/I.
Conversely, if your sorting program is particularly efficient it
is because you devised a clever plan, and not because a mediocre
plan was cleverly described in PL/I statements.

1.2.1 Algorithms

An algorithm is a sequence of statements to be executed in
order, to produce some desired result. It may also contain
comments or descriptions to aid us in "executing" or
understanding it. A cooking recipe, instructions to put a FM
tuner together, or instructions to build a model airplane are
all good examples of algorithms.

Algorithms should be written in whatever language and
notation will make them most understandable to the reader.
Often we assume a certain background and knowledge on the part
of the reader and adopt some technical vocabulary that makes the
algorithm more precise and compact. Algorithms are written for
people to read, rather than for computers and are therefore
generally not written in a programming language. We adopt or
invent whatever language seems best for the particular problem.
Often this is a combination of English, mathematics and whatever
technical vocabulary is peculiar to the problem area.

A program is an algorithm that has been translated into a
programming language. We regard a program as a specific
implementation of an algorithm. The point is that the algorithm
comes first, and it is written in an informal (but still
precise) English-like language. The program comes later, and
its preparation is a process of translation rather than
creation.

An algorithm can be translated into different programming
languages. However, since we often know in advance what
language we will use, we tend to bias the algorithm toward
convenient operations of that language. In our case, knowing
that we are headed for a PL/I program, we start with a mixture

of English and PL/I, using PL/I terms where convenient but
inventing terms whenever that seems more convenient. Generally
the terms we invent are at a "higher level" than PL/I
statements. For example, we say "Swap A and B". PL/I has no
single statement to "Swap" and this will later be translated
into three assignment statements:

```
T = A;
A = B;
B = T;
```

We can use terms like "find", "solve", and "search" that are at
a much higher level and will eventually be expressed as a
substantial segment of program.   In our examples, as   we
illustrate the gradual and systematic conversion of an algorithm
into a program, we use upper case (capital) letters for phrases
in PL/I and lower case letters for phrases that have   not   yet
been translated into PL/I.   For example, we used this convention
in Section II.2 to present program schemata:

```
Initialize
GET LIST(item);
DO WHILE(item ¬= stopping flag);
    Body
    GET LIST(item);
    END;
```

We will sometimes simply <u>replace</u> the English phrase with its
PL/I equivalent, but often we will <u>carry</u> <u>the</u> <u>English</u> <u>phrase</u> <u>over</u>
<u>into</u> <u>the</u> <u>program</u> <u>as</u> <u>a</u> <u>heading</u> <u>comment</u>, to be followed by the
PL/I implementation of the function described in the
comment.

1.2.2 Top-<u>Down</u> Development

   The general plan of attack is called "top-down development"
or "successive refinement". We try to decompose a problem into
a simple sequence of sub-problems. Given a problem P, try to
discover a set of smaller problems P1, P2, P3, ... such that
solving P1 first, then P2, etc, will be equivalent to solving
the original P. Then apply the same approach to each of these
sub-problems in turn -- determine a set of sub-sub-problems P11,
P12, P13, ... whose solutions in sequence constitute a solution
to P1. This leads quite naturally to a well-structured program
as described in Section II.1.

   Each time we find a sequence of sub-problems that correspond
to a given problem we are, in effect, <u>refining</u> the statement of
that problem into one with more detail and more indication as
to <u>how</u> the problem is to be solved. This process continues
until we have refined all of the high-level English phrases into
PL/I statements. At this point we have completely specified how

the problem is to be solved, and have a program ready for
testing.

The top-down analysis of a problem can usefully be guided by
constructing a "development tree":

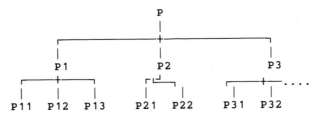

Such a tree is not a "flow-chart". A flow-chart shows
alternative paths of flow-of-control; a tree shows the structure
of a program. Each horizontal level of the tree is a
complete description of the problem; each lower level refines
that description to give more detail. All the sub-problems on
any horizontal level are to be executed, in left to right order.

1.2.3 A Comment Outline

A convenient way to preserve the information contained in the
development tree and at the same time initiate the actual
preparation of the program is to transform the tree into a
"comment outline". Each phrase in the tree becomes a separate
PL/I comment. Left-to-right order in the tree becomes normal
sequential order (top-to-bottom) in the outline. These comments
serve as headings for program units and describe the function
performed by the statements beneath them. For example, the tree
in 1.2.2 might become:

```
P: PROCEDURE OPTIONS(MAIN);
        /* P       */
          /* P1        */
             /* P11     */
             /* P12     */
             /* P13     */
          /* P2        */
             /* P21     */
             /* P22     */
          /* P3        */
             /* P31     */
             /* P32     */
        END /* P */;
```


1.3 Choice of Data Structures

Key decisions must be made with regard to what elements of
the problem will require storage. Variables have to be

specified to accomplish this storage, including names,
dimensions, type attributes, and the logical relationship
between variables. Much of this information obviously comes
from the clarification of the problem with respect to the volume
and form of the input data, but the choice of data structures
depends equally importantly on the program strategy.

Although we treat them here as separate phases, in general
data structure and program strategy are inextricably related.
For example, consider the programs classified in Section II.2.1.
The strategy represented by (2.1a) needs only one datum at a
time, while strategy (2.1b) requires an array to hold all the
data at once.

The choice of data structures takes place after the program
strategy has been chosen, and sometimes the final choice can be
delayed until after most of the actual program statements are
written. In general, postpone the final specification of data
structures as long as possible. This will reduce the
backtracking that is required. There are often details that
don't become clear until much of the program has been written.

Relationships between variables are important, and you should
emphasize these relationships to the reader by the order in
which you give declarations. For example:

```
(1.3a)     DECLARE (PR(50),TP(50),MAX,MIN) FLOAT;
           /* TABLES OF PRESSURE AND TEMPERATURE */
           DECLARE (N,M,POSMAX) FIXED;
           /* LENGTHS AND POSITION OF MAX */


(1.3b)     DECLARE (PR(50)) FLOAT, /* TABLE OF PRESSURES IS */
              (PRTOP) FIXED,       /* PR (1:PRTOP) */
              (PRMAX) FLOAT,       /* MAX VALUE IN PR(1:PRTOP) */
              (PRMIN) FLOAT;       /* MIN VALUE IN PR(1:PRTOP) */
           DECLARE (TP(50)) FLOAT, /* TABLE OF TEMPERATURES IS */
              (TPTOP) FIXED,       /* TP(1:TPTOP) */
              (TPPOSMAX) FIXED;    /* POSITION OF MAX(TP(1:TPTOP))*/
```

It takes a little longer to write declarations like (1.3b) but
they are much clearer to the reader. Both the names and the
grouping emphasize the relationships between variables. Grouping
variables just to avoid repeating attributes is false economy.
(1.3b) also avoids names such as MAX and MIN which would
prevent the use of the built-in functions with those names.

1.4 Writing the Actual Program Statements

Relatively little needs to be said about the detailed
programming phase. If phase two has been adequately done you
have a detailed comment outline describing the action of each
unit of the program. Phase three has defined the objects upon

which those units must act. All that remains is to translate
these detailed English-like specifications into statements of
PL/I (or whatever programming language is being employed).

However, as suggested earlier, as you write the detailed
program statements you often discover that the data structures
are not quite right, so you have to return to phase three. You
may also find it necessary to return to phase two to alter the
organization of the program. Rarely can you complete the
detailed translation without having to return at least once to
phase one to clarify some aspect of the problem definition,
which in turn may require changes in the program organization or
data structures. Backing up and making changes can be a tricky
business. The difficulty lies in making sure that you have
identified all the implications of the change and have made all
the necessary adjustments. The development tree is particularly
helpful in indicating what program sections are affected.

Few people compose well at a keypunch. The usual practice is
to write the program statements by hand, and then keypunch (or
enter on a typewriter terminal) from this handwritten copy. The
accuracy of the keypunching depends, to a considerable extent,
upon the legibility of the handwritten copy. We often see
students punching from copy that is at best only semi-legible.
This inevitably introduces errors into the program. I's get
mistaken for 1's; 2's for Z's; O's for zeros; inserts get
inserted in the wrong place; and the indentation is generally
fouled up. Considering how hard it is to detect and remove
errors once they are in a program it is worth spending some time
and effort keeping them out in the first place.

The initial writing of a program can be a pretty messy
process. Statements have to be added, or deleted, or changed.
They sometimes have to be shifted left or right to reflect
changes in the nesting level. (An optimist has been defined as
someone who programs in ink.) It is usually worthwhile copying a
program over to have a clear, readable copy before attempting to
keypunch it. This makes keypunching a simple transcription
process, rather than a decyphering problem. The time spent in
producing the extra initial copy will be more than offset by a
reduction in testing time.

Section 2   Examples of Program Development

The following sections present the development of five different examples in varying degrees of completeness. Although we are primarily concerned with the development process rather than the particular problems, three of these examples -- searching, sorting and scanning for symbols -- are in fact important problems with which you should become familiar.

We try to describe the development process in some detail, identifying each phase and presenting some of the alternatives from which one must choose. For short examples this may seem laborious since one obviously can produce a satisfactory program by a much less studied and formal process. However, the process described here is indispensable for larger and more complicated problems. It is not entirely natural or intuitively obvious, so if you are to use this technique when it is needed, you must learn and practice it in situations where it may not be absolutely necessary.

2.1 The Example of I.1.2.1

In Section I.1.2.1 the following problem is posed:

> Given a list of integers, print the first, second, third integers, etc., but stop printing when the largest integer in the list has been printed.

The development begun in I.1.2.1 is later completed in Section I.5.4. You should now reread these sections and try to identify the various phases of the development.

A development tree was not given for this problem. It would be something like the following:

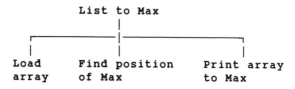

The data structures consist of an array INTEGER of sufficient size to hold all the data, and two variables TOP and MAX to point to the last position used in INTEGER and to the position of the maximum.

The development tree can be converted to a comment outline:

```
/* PROGRAM TO LIST VALUES FROM FIRST TO MAXIMUM */
/* READ DATA INTO "INTEGER" UNTIL ZERO IS FOUND */
/* SET "MAX" TO MARK POSITION OF MAXIMUM VALUE */
/* PRINT "INTEGER" FROM 1 TO "MAX", 1 PER LINE */
```

Now analyzing the subproblems presented by these headings, the
first subproblem is an example of the basic program schema (2b)
given in Section II.2. A list of data is to be read, with a
specified stopping flag. The task to be performed on each datum
is a test, with "good" values to be preserved in an array. The
second subproblem is a variation of the program given in Section
I.1.1, differing only in that the data whose maximum is sought
is already in an array, rather than in an external data list.
The third subproblem is a straightforward printing task such as
the examples given in Section I.6.1 and I.6.3. Although this
problem may have looked formidable when you first read Section
I.5.4, it is apparent now that it actually consists of a simple
sequence of three subproblems, each of which is some variation
of a task that you have seen previously.

Of course, you are entitled to be suspicious of examples in
textbooks, where everything works out neatly and the authors
obviously had every opportunity to rig things to make their
point. Nevertheless this is not an atypical experience. You
will discover that each new problem can be broken down into
subproblems, most of which are variations of things you have
done before. There are a relatively small number of basic tasks
-- perhaps several dozen -- that recur very often in problems
that seem entirely different.

2.2 The Problem of Searching a List

Consider the following "list-searching" problem:

Given is a "list" of integers, in a particular order, and
a set of "inquiries" -- integers which may or may not
be duplicates of those included in the list. For each
inquiry determine whether or not it is on the list. If
it is on the list, indicate what position it occupies; if
it is not on the list report that fact.

For example, if a list consists of the numbers 9, -4, 16 and 5,
in that order, then the inquiry "16" should result in the report
that this number is in third position on the list; the
inquiries "12" and "4" should result in a report that they are
not on the list.

Clarifying the problem will lead to detail about the quantity
and the form of the input. This might result in the following
specification:

The input will consist of: a) an integer specifying the
length of the list; b) the list values, in order; c) an
integer specifying the number of inquiries; d) the
inquiries. The list will have not more than 100 values,
which can be positive, negative or zero, and in integer
form only.

This means that the example above would be given in the form:

```
$DATA
4 9  -4  16   5
3 16   12   4
```

Detailed specifcation of required output might be the following:

For each inquiry print a line that gives the value, and
either its position on the list or the fact that it does
not appear on the list.

With this specification the exact format and wording of the
output line is left to the programmer's discretion. Presumably
lines such as the following would be acceptable (but it is worth
checking in advance to make sure):

```
16 IS IN POSITION 3
12 IS NOT ON THE LIST
 4 IS NOT ON THE LIST
```

The only data errors that can occur in this problem are in the
control values that specify the length of the list and the
number of inquiries. Error processing might be specified as
follows:

The list length may be anything from 0 to 100; if not,
terminate execution with an appropriate warning. The
number of inquiries is arbitrary.

This method of specifying list length with a control value is
not a particularly good idea. It is easy to handle in the
program, but the program cannot check for certain obvious and
ruinous errors. For example, if the list length is specified as
90, but 91 values are actually given, then the 91st will be
interpreted as the number of inquiries. If only 89 values are
given then the number of inquiries will become the last item on
the list, and the first inquiry will be taken to be the number
of inquiries. Such miscounting is a common error, and the
program can do little against it. On the other hand, the
specification that the program should work for a list of length
zero, or for no inquiries is not unreasonable. Posed as a
separate problem, it would be foolish for anyone to run the
program with no list or no inquiries, but such programs are
often later incorporated into a larger program. The ability to
operate properly for extreme values -- in particular, the
ability to do nothing gracefully -- is very valuable.

Obviously, the entire list must be available for processing
each inquiry. This is the reason the list is placed before the
inquiries in the input data. On the other hand, each inquiry is
processed separately and there is no need to retain an inquiry
value after it is processed. Hence the problem does not quite
fall in any of the simple categories described in Section
II.2.1. But it can be divided into two sub-problems:

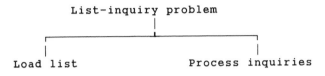

"Load list" is an interpretation of program schema (2d) given in
Section II.2. The body of the schema in this case is simply to
insert each datum in an array. "Process inquiries" is another
interpretation of the same schema. The body in this case is
more complex, involving searching the list and reporting
results. The second level of development would be:

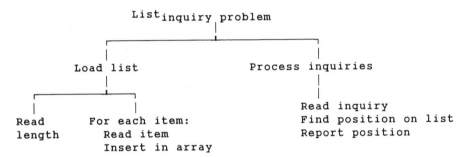

The principal data structure is an array to hold the list,
together with a variable to indicate its length. The array must
have at least 100 elements since the given list may be that
long, and can consist of FIXED variables since we know
the values will be integers. We will call the list "GLIST",
for "given list", avoiding the obvious name "LIST" since this
happens to be a reserved word in SP/k.

No array is necessary to store the inquiries since they can
be processed one at a time. A simple FIXED variable "INQ"
will suffice to hold the current inquiry value. You could <u>not</u>
elect to read all the inquiries into a second array and then
process them one at a time from that array, because you have no
idea how large an array is required. We also need variables
to store the number of inquiries remaining to be processed,
and the position of a particular value in the list. The values
of these variables will always be integers.

The development tree can be converted into a comment outline
as shown below. The declarations of the required data
structures are also included.

```
LISTINQ: PROCEDURE OPTIONS(MAIN);
   /* LIST-INQUIRY PROGRAM */
   DECLARE (GLIST(100)) FLOAT; /* GIVEN LIST IS */
   DECLARE (GLNG) FIXED;       /* GLIST (1:GLNG) */
   DECLARE (GPOS) FIXED;       /* A POSITION IN GLIST */
   DECLARE (INQ) FLOAT;        /* CURRENT INQUIRY VALUE */
   DECLARE (NINQ) FIXED;       /* NUMBER INQUIRIES STILL */
                               /* TO BE PROCESSED */

   /* LOAD LIST, SKIP IF ERROR */
      /* READ LENGTH */
      /* FOR EACH ITEM, READ AND INSERT IN GLIST */

   /* PROCESS INQUIRIES */
      /* FIND POSITION ON LIST */
      /* REPORT POSITION */

   END /* LISTINQ */;
```

Finally we are ready to write PL/I statements to perform the actions. "Read length" can be programmed:

```
/* READ LENGTH */
GET LIST(GLNG);
IF (GLNG<0)|(GLNG>100) THEN
  DO;
     PUT SKIP LIST('IMPROPER LIST LENGTH',GLNG);
     RETURN; /* TERMINATE PROGRAM EXECUTION */
     END;
```

Testing, such as that shown here, should take place any time a control value is read. You should think of such testing as an inherent part of "read". The RETURN statement will be discussed in Section IV.1.2.2. As used here, it will cause execution of the program to be terminated.

The "insert in GLIST" task could be programmed:

```
/* FOR EACH ITEM, INSERT IN GLIST */
DO GPOS = 1 TO GLNG BY 1;
   GET LIST(GLIST(GPOS));
   END;
```

The "process inquiries" task is obviously a repetition unit, modeled after schema (2d) in Section II.2:

```
/* PROCESS INQUIRIES */
GET LIST(NINQ);
DO WHILE (NINQ > 0);
   GET LIST(INQ);
   /* FIND POSITION OF INQ ON LIST */
   /* REPORT POSITION */
   NINQ = NINQ - 1;
   END;
```

Two tasks comprise the principal body of this loop. "Find position" is itself a repetition unit:

```
/* FIND POSITION OF INQ ON LIST */
NOT_FOUND = '1'B;
GPOS = 1;
DO WHILE(NOT_FOUND & (GPOS <= GLING));
    IF INQ = GLIST(GPOS) THEN
        NOT_FOUND = '0'B;
    ELSE
        GPOS = GPOS + 1;
    END;
```

This loop terminates either when a value is found -- in which case it reaches the end of the loop with NOT_FOUND equal to '0'B and GPOS pointing to that value -- or when the loop has indexed past GLNG -- in which case it reaches the end with NOT_FOUND equal to '1'B and GPOS equal to GLNG+1.

"Report position" is a "multiple alternative" unit, with selection depending on the outcome of the list search:

```
/* REPORT POSITION */
IF NOT_FOUND THEN
    PUT SKIP LIST(INQ,'IS NOT ON THE LIST');
ELSE
    PUT SKIP LIST(INQ,'IS IN POSITION',GPOS);
```

The complete program can now be assembled from these segments:

```
LISTINQ: PROCEDURE OPTIONS(MAIN);
    /* LIST-INQUIRY PROGRAM */
    DECLARE (GLIST(100)) FLOAT; /* GIVEN LIST IS */
    DECLARE (GLNG) FIXED;       /* GLIST(1:GLNG) */
    DECLARE (GPOS) FIXED;       /* A POSITION IN GLIST */
    DECLARE (INQ) FLOAT;        /* CURRENT INQUIRY VALUE */
    DECLARE (NINQ) FIXED;       /* NUMBER INQUIRIES STILL */
                                /* TO BE PROCESSED */
    DECLARE (NOT_FOUND) BIT;  /* TRUE IF INQUIRY NOT IN LIST*/

    /* LOAD LIST, SKIP IF ERROR */
    /* READ LENGTH */
    GET LIST(GLNG);
    IF (GLNG < 0) | (GLNG > 100) THEN
    DO;
        PUT SKIP LIST
            ('IMPROPER LIST LENGTH',GLNG);
        RETURN; /* TERMINATE PROGRAM EXECUTION */
        END;

    /* FOR EACH ITEM, READ AND INSERT IN GLIST */
    DO GPOS = 1 TO GLNG BY 1;
        GET LIST(GLIST(GPOS));
        END;
```

```
/* PROCESS INQUIRIES */
GET LIST(NINQ);
DO WHILE (NINQ > 0);
   GET LIST(INQ);
   /* FIND POSITION OF INQ ON LIST */
   NOT_FOUND = '1'B;
   GPOS = 1;
   DO WHILE(NOT_FOUND & (GPOS <= GLING));
      IF INQ = GLIST(GPOS) THEN
         NOT_FOUND = '0'B;
      ELSE
         GPOS = GPOS + 1;
      END;

   /* REPORT POSITION */
   IF NOT_FOUND THEN
      PUT SKIP LIST(INQ,'IS NOT ON THE LIST');
   ELSE
      PUT SKIP LIST(INQ,'IS IN POSITION',GPOS);

   NINQ = NINQ - 1;
   END;

END /* LISTINQ */;
```

Some final observations with regard to this program:

1. The program should check the value read for NINQ to make sure it is reasonable.

2. The program has many comments relative to the number of statements, but this is because the tasks in this case are simple. As problems grow larger it requires more substantial segments to do what each comment heading specifies.

3. The search algorithm used in "find position" is simple, but not efficient for long lists. Alternative algorithms are discussed in Section VI.2.4. Note that the program is structured so the search segment can be easily replaced without requiring a change anywhere else in the program.

4. The RETURN statement, used here to terminate program execution will be explained fully in Section IV.1.2.2.

2.3 The Problem of Ordering a List

A common task is to reorder the elements of a list so that their values are "in order". For numeric variables this is usually "algebraic order", either increasing or decreasing; for character variables it is usually according to the collating sequence given in Section I.9.2.2, which implies both alphabetical and algebraic order. The process of rearranging

values   so   they   satisfy   some   order relationship   is   called
"sorting".   A simple form of sorting problem is:

> Given a list of numbers, sort them so they are in order of
> increasing value. Display the list   before   and   after
> sorting.

For   example, if the list 5, 0, -7, 6.2E+0, 1 is given, the list
-7, 0, 1, 5, 6.2E+0   is to be produced.   One   possible
clarification of the problem is:

> Given data consisting of an integer n (not greater than 50)
> followed by a list of n numbers, sort these n numbers into
> increasing order. Display the list in original order in a
> single column, followed by the sorted list in single
> column. Provide appropriate titles.

Obviously we need to have <u>all</u> <u>the</u> <u>data</u> <u>available</u> <u>at</u> <u>once</u>, so we
cannot use a program like (II.2.1a). We also cannot begin to
print the sorted list until sorting is complete (or at least
until we know which value comes first), so it is probably not
like (II.2.1b).   It is apparently going to be a bit more
complicated. The first level of development might be:

(2.3a)

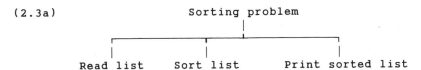

(2.3a) does not indicate when the display of the initial list
will   take   place. There are two possibilities — either before
or after sorting. The most obvious is to display the initial
order before it is changed. This could be done either as part
of the "read" task or as a separate task:

(2.3b)

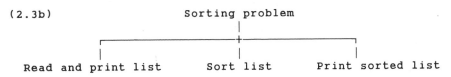

(2.3c)

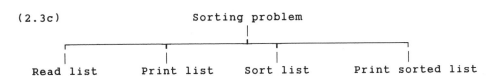

(2.3c) results in two separate loops, and (2.3b) in a single
loop with two statements (GET and PUT) in the body. There seems
to be no advantage in separation and we decide, at least
tentatively, in favor of (2.3b).   If we wanted to have all
printing done in one section of the program we would have to

make an extra copy of the list, so we could sort one copy and keep the other in initial order. The development then would be:

(2.3d)   Sorting problem

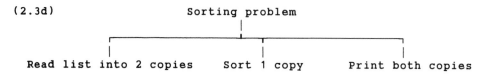

    Read list into 2 copies   Sort 1 copy   Print both copies

(2.3d) is unnecessary in this case and we will use (2.3b), but note that only a slight variation in the original problem statement -- to require the display in side-by-side columns -- would make strategy (2.3d) necessary.

So now we have separated off two minor tasks "read and print" and "print" -- each an interpretation of schema (2b), or an example of a problem like (II.2.1b). By now the programming of tasks like these should be familiar and almost automatic. It is also clear that the principal data structure will be an array to hold the list and a variable to specify how much of the array is used. The elements of the array will have to be FLOAT since no restriction on values is implied by the problem statement. What remains is the following task:

    Given L(1:N), reorder its elements into increasing order.

To figure out a method for reordering, suppose you had n 3 by 5 cards, each bearing a number, laid out in a row. How would you go about rearranging the cards so the numbers were in increasing order? There is the additional restriction that you can only look at and compare <u>two</u> cards at a time (since PL/I has this restriction). One way would be to scan over the cards and find the one with the largest value. This card could be interchanged with the one at the end of the row. Now, ignoring that card (which has been properly positioned), you could repeat the process for the remaining n-1 cards. That is, locate the card with the second largest value (the largest of the remaining n-1) and interchange it with the second from last (the last of the n-1). Now with the last two cards in proper position, work on the remaining n-2 cards in the same way. If this is continued until finally the last two cards are put in order, the entire row will have been sorted. Let us transform this idea into an algorithm:

    Repeat for lists of diminishing length m=n,n-1,n-2,...,2:
        1. Find the maximum value of L(1:m);
        2. Interchange the maximum with L(m).

Interchanging values is a familiar task by now, and finding the maximum is similar to a problem you have seen before. This version differs from I.1.1 only in that the numbers are already in an array (rather than being an external data list) and in that we need to find the <u>position</u> as well as the value of the maximum. A program segment to do this is:

```
    /* FIND POSITION OF MAXIMUM IN L(1:M) */
    MAXVAL = L(1);
    MAXPOS = 1;
    DO I = 2 TO M BY 1;
       IF L(I) > MAXVAL THEN
          DO;
             MAXVAL = L(I);
             MAXPOS = I;
             END;
       END;
```

Given that MAXPOS points to the maximum value in L(1:M) the interchange is simply:

```
    /* INTERCHANGE MAX AND LAST IN L(1:M) */
    TEMP = L(M);
    L(M) = L(MAXPOS);
    L(MAXPOS) = TEMP;
```

These two segments must be repeated for lists whose lengths M vary from N down to 2:

```
    /* SORT L(1:N) */
    DO M = N TO 2 BY -1;
       /* FIND POSITION OF MAXIMUM IN L(1:M) */
       MAXVAL = L(1);
       MAXPOS = 1;
       DO I = 2 TO M BY 1;
          IF L(I) > MAXVAL THEN
             DO;
                MAXVAL = L(I);
                MAXPOS = I;
                END;
          END;

       /* INTERCHANGE MAX AND LAST IN L(1:M) */
       TEMP = L(M);
       L(M) = L(MAXPOS);
       L(MAXPOS) = TEMP;
       END;
```

The complete program would have (2.3e) inserted in the following:

```
    SORT: PROCEDURE OPTIONS(MAIN);
        /* SORT AND DISPLAY A LIST OF NUMBERS */
        DECLARE (L(50)) FLOAT;
        DECLARE (N) FIXED;   /* ACTUAL LENGTH OF LIST IN L */
        DECLARE (M) FIXED;   /* LENGTH OF SUB-LIST */
        DECLARE (I) FIXED;
        DECLARE (TEMP) FLOAT;
```

```
/* READ AND DISPLAY INITIAL LIST */
GET LIST(N);
IF (N < 0) | (N > 50) THEN
   DO;
      PUT SKIP LIST('IMPROPER LENGTH:',N);
      RETURN; /* TERMINATE PROGRAM EXECUTION */
      END;
PUT SKIP LIST('LIST IN INITIAL ORDER');
PUT SKIP;
DO I = 1 TO N BY 1;
   GET LIST(L(I));
   PUT SKIP LIST(L(I));
   END;

/* SORT L(1:N) */
   insert (2.3e)

/* DISPLAY SORTED LIST */
PUT SKIP LIST('SORTED LIST');
PUT SKIP;
DO I = 1 TO N BY 1;
   PUT SKIP LIST(L(I));
   END;
END /* SORT */;
```

Sorting is an important problem in practice, and a very convenient problem to illustrate points in programming. We will refer back to this often in future sections and it will help if you understand this simple version very thoroughly.

2.4 An Accounting Problem

A bank would like to produce records of the transactions during an accounting period in connection with their checking accounts. For each account the bank wants a list showing the balance at the beginning of the period, the number of deposits and withdrawals, and the final balance. This is a simplified version of the type of application described in Part IX.

The accounts and transactions for an accounting period will be given on punched cards as follows:

1) First will be a sequence of cards describing the accounts. Each account is described by two numbers: the account number (greater than 0), and the account balance at the beginning of the period, in cents. The last account is followed by a "dummy" account consisting of two zero values to indicate the end of the list. There will be at most 200 accounts.

2) Following the accounts are the transactions. Each transaction is given by three numbers: the account

number, a 1 or -1 (indicating a deposit or withdrawal,
respectively), and the transaction amount, in cents. The
last real transaction is followed by a dummy transaction
consisting of three zero values.

The following sample input has been supplied, where the words
at the right are not part of the input, but explanatory
notes.

Input numbers			meaning
1025	6150		(account 1025 contains $61.50)
1028	10300		(account 1028 contains $103.00)
1026	10000		(account 1026 contains $100.00)
0	0		(end of accounts)
1025	1	50000	(deposit $500.00 in account 1025)
1028	-1	2000	(withdraw $20.00 from account 1028)
1025	-1	40000	(withdraw $400.00 from account 1025)
1025	+1	5000	(deposit $50.00 in account 1025)
0	0	0	(end of transactions)

For this input, the output should be:

ACCOUNT	PREV BAL	WITHDRAWALS	DEPOSITS	FINAL BAL
1025	61.50	1	2	211.50
1028	103.00	1	0	83.00
1026	100.00	0	0	100.00

Some of the errors that could occur in the data are:
  1) An account is listed two or more times.
  2) The end-of-account signal is missing or incorrect.
  3) A transaction number is not in the list of accounts.
  4) The withdrawal-deposit number is not 1 or -1.
  5) The transaction amount is negative.
  6) The end-of-transaction signal is wrong or missing.

All these errors could be detected by the program. Detecting
other situations such as overdrafts (which are not really input
errors) would probably make the program more valuable. Of
course, not all errors can be detected by the program. For
example, a withdrawal keypunched as a deposit or an error in a
transaction amount can not be detected. To keep our program
development to manageable size we will ignore the question of
data errors. In the real world this is clearly unrealistic, and
the program would have to detect and process these errors.

The following steps give a reasonable chronological record of
the development of a program for this problem.

Step 1. Discovering the overall structure of the algorithm.

Looking at the problem description, note that the account
data precedes the transactions. Thus all accounts must be read
and stored internally, before the transactions can be read and
"processed". Moreover, while processing the transactions we

must be able to access any account at any time, since no
ordering of the transactions by account number is mentioned in
the description of the problem. The sample data confirm this
lack of ordering. Also, since the last transaction may apply to
any account, no result may be printed for an account until all
transactions have been processed. This analysis indicates that
the structure of the program will be:

(2.4a)   2a1: Read in and set up the accounts in a "table";
          2a2: Read in and process the transactions;
          2a3: Print the results;

In tree form this would be:

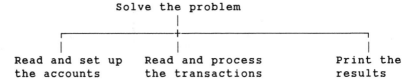

```
                    Solve the problem
                          |
      ┌───────────────────┼────────────────────────────┐
      |                   |                             |
  Read and set up     Read and process          Print the
  the accounts        the transactions          results
```

It should already be apparent that the structure of this
problem is somewhat similar to the list-searching problem of
Section 2.2. Task 2a1 is directly comparable to the first task
of 2.2, except that the table of accounts is a more complex data
structure than the list of values in 2.2. Task 2a2 searches for
a particular entry in the table, but instead of reporting the
position of the entry it modifies the entry. Task 2a3 is added;
it has no counterpart in 2.2.

(2.4a) is an algorithm using the English commands "read",
"set up", "process" and "print". These are not yet precise
enough to specify the action to be taken, and our task is to
refine them so that they are precise and are expressed in PL/I
terms.

There are now three separate, smaller problems, but they are
obviously not entirely independent of each other. All three
share the data structures used to contain the accounts and the
information connected with them. Whenever we split a problem
into several smaller parts, it is important to look at the
"interface" or connections between them. Often, several
strategies exist for implementing each one, but implementing one
in a particular way may reduce the flexibility in designing the
others. We must weigh carefully the benefits and disadvantages,
including effects on other modules, in choosing a strategy for a
given module.

Step 2. The data structures representing the accounts.

We must keep the accounts accessible in a table until all
transactions have been processed and the results have been
reported. This can be done using an array ACCT (say) to hold
the ACCounT numbers and an array IBAL to hold the corresponding

Initial BALances. We also need a variable N (say) to hold the number of accounts. Thus, if i is an integer between 1 and N, ACCT(i) contains an account number and IBAL(i) contains the corresponding initial balance. Other alternatives for storing the data exist of course, but this is probably the simplest and easiest.

Now review the problem statement to make sure the accounts have been described completely and accurately. Certainly this is all we need initially, but look at the sample output. After processing the transactions, in addition to the initial balance we must report the number of deposits and withdrawals and also the final balance. This will require three more arrays; we need two arrays to contain the number of withdrawals and deposits, and a third to contain the balances. The arrays holding the number of withdrawals and deposits will be initially set to 0, and will be increased to count the number of withdrawals and deposits that are processed for each account. Similarly, the array holding the final balances will be initialized to the initial balances and will be updated as transactions are processed.

To summarize, we write down the names of the variables which describe the accounts and define as precisely as possible how they will be used:

1. Variable N contains the number of accounts.

2. Five arrays describe the accounts: ACCT, IBAL, WITH, DEP and CBAL (meaning Current BALance). If i is an integer between 1 and N, then during execution of the program

```
ACCT(i)    is an ACCounT number,
IBAL(i)    is the corresponding Initial BALance,
WITH(i)    is the number of WITHdrawals processed so far,
DEP(i)     is the number of DEPosits processed so far,
CBAL(i)    is the Current BALance in the account.
```

CBAL(i) depends of course on the withdrawals and deposits processed so far. In order to fix these definitions more clearly in our minds, consider some examples. Just after reading in all the accounts in the sample input, the arrays are:

	ACCT	IBAL	WITH	DEP	CBAL
(1)	1025	61.50	0	0	61.50
(2)	1028	103.00	0	0	103.00
(3)	1026	100.00	0	0	100.00

Note that each CBAL(i) is the same as IBAL(i), since no transactions have been processed. After processing the first transaction, the arrays are:

	ACCT	IBAL	WITH	DEP	CBAL
(1)	1025	61.50	0	1	561.50
(2)	1028	103.00	0	0	103.00
(3)	1026	100.00	0	0	100.00

We could at this point write PL/I declarations for these data structures, but it is better to wait. These structures should be considered tentative, and may have to be revised as the detailed design of the program unfolds.

We have looked at the data structures which contain the accounts from the viewpoint of the information that must be available as the program executes. Now consider <u>how</u> this information is accessed and changed -- how the three statements of algorithm (2.4a) use the information. Statement 2a2, "Read in and process the transactions", requires us to locate in the table of accounts the account associated with each transaction. This means a search in the array ACCT of account numbers for each transaction account number. That is, given a transaction like (1028, 1, 100), we have to find an integer i such that ACCT(i) = 1028. Assuming a search algorithm such as the one used in Section 2.2, on the average we must look at half of the accounts in order to find the right one. If there are only a few hundred accounts this may be feasible. But if there are 5000 or more accounts the time to search would be in seconds for each transaction, and we could not afford to structure the table of accounts as we have done.

This search time can be drastically reduced if the accounts are rearranged so that the account numbers are in ascending order: ACCT(1) ≤ ACCT(2) ≤ ... ≤ ACCT(N). (We discuss more efficient searching algorithms in Section VI.2.4.) If we sort the array of accounts as we read them in, we can process the transactions more efficiently. But sorting takes time too, and we must carefully weigh the sorting time against the efficiency gained in processing, before we decide which approach to take. This depends on the number of accounts relative to the number of transactions, and we now realize that we lack such information. The problem description is not complete, and without such information we cannot design the best program.

An even better solution would be for the bank to keep their accounts in ascending order, so that neither sorting nor a slow search would be required.

This discussion should illustrate the need for thinking about the various ways of implementing each succesive statement of an algorithm, and considering the effects of each. For now, assume that the accounts cannot be kept sorted because of other considerations, and that the simple search algorithm of Section 2.2 is adequate.

Step 3.   Refining the statement "Read and set up the accounts."

Statement 2a1 is not yet in PL/I, so it must be refined further. The required action is

    Read and set up the first account;
    Read and set up the second account;
                ...
    (until the account just read has account number 0)

Such a sequence of similar statements can be replaced by a loop which iteratively executes a single statement like "Read and set up the Kth account", where K is of course increased after each execution.   There are several ways of writing this loop.   One method recognizes that the first statement "Read and set up the first account" must always be executed and can therefore be put outside the loop:

              K = 1;
              Read and set up the Kth account;
              DO WHILE (ACCT(K) ¬= 0);
                K = K + 1;
                Read and set up the Kth account;
                END;
              N = K - 1;

The final statement that assigns K-1 instead of K to N is necessary because the last account read is just a dummy account serving as a stopping flag.

An alternative technique uses a dummy account ACCT(0) whose account number is set to 1 so that the loop body is always executed at least once:

              K = 0;
              ACCT(0) = 1;
              DO WHILE (ACCT(K) ¬= 0);
(2.4b)   K = K + 1;
                Read and set up the Kth account;
                END;
              N = K - 1;

Either refinement could be used.   If the refinement of the statement "Read and set up the Kth account" turned out to be long and difficult, we would tend to choose (2.4b) because this difficult statement only appears once. (Recall the discussion of this issue in Section I.4.5.2.) At this point we arbitrarily choose (2.4b) and the development tree is:

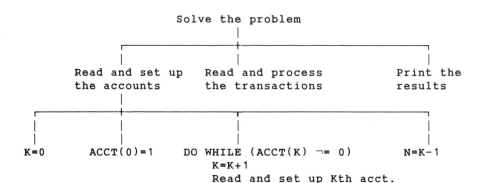

We have introduced a variable K, and should indicate what it means. While executing (2.4b) (and only then), K is the number of accounts read in so far, including the end-of-list signal as an account.

Note that when we declare the array ACCT we must give an upper bound on the number of elements in it. If the input happens to have more than that number of accounts, then (2.4b) will execute incorrectly.

Algorithm (2.4b) still contains an English statement which must be translated into PL/I. To "read and set up account K", we must obtain values from the input data and store the account number and balance in ACCT(K) and IBAL(K), and initialize the other three variables that comprise account K:

```
(2.4c)    GET LIST (ACCT(K), IBAL(K));
          WITH(K)=0;
          DEP(K)=0;
          CBAL(K)=IBAL(K);
```

As a final step, we insert this refinement into (2.4b) to yield the following program segment. Note that the original statement 2a1 becomes a comment of the PL/I program which replaces it:

```
          /* READ AND SET UP THE ACCOUNTS. */
          K=0;
          ACCT(0)=1; /* EXECUTE LOOP BODY A LEAST ONCE */
(2.4d)    DO WHILE( ACCT(K) ¬= 0);
             K = K+1;
             GET LIST( ACCT(K), IBAL(K));
             WITH(K)=0;
             DEP(K)=0;
             CBAL(K)=IBAL(K);
             END;
          N = K - 1;
```

Step 4.   Refining "Read and process the transactions."

Consider statement 2a2, keeping in mind that the table of accounts is not ordered by account number. Two actions are required -- reading and processing the transactions -- and there may be several ways of performing them. Two possibilities come to mind:

1) First read and store all the transactions, then process all the transactions.

2) Read and process the first transaction, read and process the second transaction, etc.

The first possibility requires arrays in which to store all the transactions. How big should the arrays be? We don't know, since we have no idea how many transactions there may be. To use this method, we would have to determine the maximum number of transactions in any one run. This is essentially the same question we faced with inquiries in Section 2.2.

The question with the second method is feasibility. Is it possible to process a single transaction without having access to the others? The answer in this case is yes.

This is not really such a pointless question to ask as it might seem. For example, consider the task "Read in a list of transactions and print them out in order of the account number." We cannot "Read one and print, read one and print, etc.", so we must read all of them before we can begin printing.

With the second method, an array is not needed to hold the transactions, since we need only keep track of one transaction at a time. This second method seems to have no disadvantages compared to the first, and should be used.

Note that without a change in the problem definition, we are forced to use the second method. Since we don't know how many transactions might appear, we cannot assume any maximum and hence cannot use the first method. Quite often, a careful examination of the problem will answer a question for us. We should be continually asking ourselves questions like: "Have I used everything that was given to me?" "Could the problem definition be changed to make the solution easier, clearer, or more efficient?" "Have I assumed something that is not explicitly stated to be true?"

A second point is the question of efficiency. For example, we use the second possibility rather than the first, because it uses less computer storage space but otherwise is essentially the same. We may strive for efficiency with respect to execution time, storage space, or with respect to the time it takes to write the program. There is always a trade-off when trying to gain efficiency; usually what executes faster will take more space, or what is easier to program and understand may

be slower. A programmer must know what the value criterion is
for each program he is to design.

   Our choice, then, for reading and processing transactions is

          Read a transaction;
          Process the transaction just read;
                 . . .
          Read a transaction;
          Process the transaction just read;
          Read a transaction;
               (until transaction acct. number is 0)

This is a sequence of (a pair of) statements which is to be
executed several times, and we can use a loop. Since the first
statement "Read a transaction" must always be executed and the
last transaction is not to be processed, it is easiest to
perform the first "read" outside the loop and to let the loop
body consist of "Process transaction; Read transaction". That
is, we are pairing the statements as indicated by the spacing in
the following algorithm:

          Read a transaction;

          Process the transaction just read;
          Read a transaction;
                 . . .

          Process the transaction just read;
          Read a transaction
               (until transaction acct. number is 0)

The algorithm using a WHILE loop is:

          Read a transaction;
          DO WHILE (transaction account number $\neq$ 0);
(2.4e)   Process the transaction just read;
          Read a transaction;
          END;

   Further refinement requires a decision as to how the
transactions are to be stored. We should question the format of
the input transactions. If we allow a negative amount to
specify a withdrawal, then the withdrawal-deposit code is not
necessary. Let us assume that the bank says the given form is
indeed necessary, and continue with the development.

   Since only one transaction need be accessed at any time, only
three simple variables are needed:

          TACCT   contains the Transaction ACCounT number.
(2.4f)   DEPWITH contains the action code:
                  1 means DEPosit, -1 means WITHdrawal.
          AMT   contains the AMount of the transaction.

This leads to the following refinement of algorithm (2.4e):

```
          GET LIST( TACCT, DEPWITH, AMT);
          DO WHILE( TACCT ¬= 0);
(2.4g)        Process the transaction just read;
              GET LIST( TACCT, DEPWITH, AMT);
          END;
```

The final task is to reduce the phrase "Process the transaction just read" to PL/I. Processing a transaction requires us to find the corresponding account in the array ACCT. Suppose that while searching ACCT we store in a new variable J an integer so that TACCT = ACCT(J). Then account ACCT(J) is to be changed as follows: If DEPWITH(J) = 1 then add 1 to DEP(J) and add AMT to CBAL(J); if DEPWITH(J) = -1 then add 1 to WITH(J) and subtract AMT from CBAL(J).

A search algorithm similar to that of Section 2.2 will be used:

```
          /* PROCESS THE TRANSACTION JUST READ. */
          J = 1;
          /* SEARCH FOR TRANSACTION ACCOUNT. */
          DO WHILE (ACCT(J) ¬= TACCT);
(2.4h)        J = J + 1;
              END;
          IF DEPWITH = 1 THEN
              DO;  /* DEPOSIT */
                 DEP(J) = DEP(J) + 1;
                 CBAL(J) = CBAL(J) + AMT;
                 END;
          ELSE
              DO; /* WITHDRAWAL */
                 WITH(J) = WITH(J) + 1;
                 CBAL(J) = CBAL(J) - AMT;
                 END;
```

Note that we assume that DEPWITH is a 1 or -1, without checking. The program should check for values other than 1 or -1 and print a message if an error has occurred. We also assume that the transaction account number will be valid -- that the account will be found in the table. The program should check for this, as in Section 2.2.

Step 5. Refining "Print the results."

Statement 2a3 is the easiest to translate into PL/I. Since an order was not specified by the problem description, we will print the accounts in the easiest order possible -- the order in which they were read in.

```
              /* PRINT THE RESULTS. */
              PUT SKIP LIST('ACCOUNT', 'PREV BAL', 'WITHDRAWALS',
                 'DEPOSITS', 'FINAL BAL');
(2.4i)        DO I = 1 TO N BY 1;
                 PUT SKIP LIST(ACCT(I), IBAL(I), WITH(I), DEP(I),
                    CBAL(I));
              END;
```

The development tree now has become:

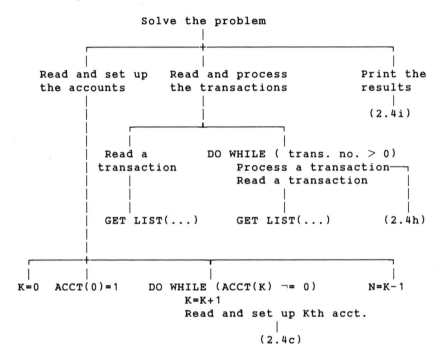

Step 6. Assembling the complete program.

The final task is to gather together the refinements for the
three statements of (2.4a) into a PL/I program. These
refinements are (2.4d), (2.4g) with (2.4h) replacing the single
English statement of (2.4g), and (2.4i). We also produce
declarations from the descriptions of variables written in steps
2 and 4. We end up with the program below. It should be
pointed out that this is not the only possible program. Just
considering the same basic algorithm, there are many minor
variations. For example, the statement "Read and set up the
accounts" could have been written so that the array could be
declared ACCT(1:200) instead of ACCT(0:201). Many possibilities
exist, and one cannot always say which is better.

```
BANK: PROCEDURE OPTIONS(MAIN);
   /* BANK BOOKKEEPING PROGRAM */
   /* THE ACCOUNTS, IN ORDER READ: */
   DECLARE (N,                  /* THERE ARE N ACCOUNTS */
        ACCT(0:201),            /* THE ACCOUNT NUMBERS*/
        WITH(1:201),            /* NUMBER OF WITHDRAWALS*/
        DEP (1:201))FIXED;      /* NUMBER OF DEPOSITS*/
   DECLARE (
        IBAL(1:201),            /* THE INITIAL BALANCES */
        CBAL(1:201))FLOAT;      /* THE CURRENT BALANCES*/
   DECLARE (                    /* CURRENT TRANSACTION:*/
        TACCT,                  /* TRANSACTION ACCOUNT NUMBER*/
        DEPWITH) FIXED,         /* 1=DEPOSIT, -1=WITHDRAWAL*/
        (AMT) FLOAT;            /* TRANSACTION AMOUNT*/
   DECLARE (I, J, K) FIXED;

    /* READ AND SETUP ACCOUNTS */
    K = 0;
    ACCT(0) = 1;
    DO WHILE(ACCT(K) ¬= 0);
       K = K + 1;
       GET LIST(ACCT(K),IBAL(K));
       WITH(K) = 0;
       DEP(K) = 0;
       CBAL(K) = IBAL(K);
       END;
    N = K-1;

    /* READ AND PROCESS THE TRANSACTIONS */
    GET LIST(TACCT,DEPWITH,AMT); /* FIRST TRANSACTION */
    DO WHILE(TACCT ¬= 0);
       /* PROCESS TRANSACTION JUST READ */
       J = 1;

       /* SEARCH FOR TRANSACTION ACCOUNT */
       DO WHILE(ACCT(J) ¬= TACCT);
          J = J + 1;
          END;

       IF DEPWITH = 1 THEN
          DO; /* DEPOSIT */
             DEP(J) = DEP(J) + 1;
             CBAL(J) = CBAL(J) + AMT;
             END;
       ELSE
          DO; /* WITHDRAWAL */
             WITH(J) = WITH(J) + 1;
             CBAL(J) = CBAL(J) - AMT;
             END;

       /* READ NEXT TRANSACTION */
       GET LIST(TACCT,DEPWITH,AMT);
       END;
```

```
/* PRINT THE RESULTS */
PUT SKIP LIST('ACCOUNT','PREV BAL','WITHDRAWALS',
     'DEPOSITS','FINAL BALANCE');
DO I = 1 TO N BY 1;
    PUT SKIP LIST(ACCT(I),IBAL(I),WITH(I),DEP(I),CBAL(I));
    END;
END /* BANK */;
```

2.5 Scanning for Symbols

Many programs process "text". The SP/k translator is such a
program (see Part X); this book was produced by a "text-editing
program" (see Section 3.2.2). Such programs have the common
sub-problem of reading lines of text and dividing them into
separate "symbols". A simplification of this sub-problem may be
stated separately as follows:

> The input consists of a sequence of "symbols" on cards.
> Each symbol consists of 1 to 40 nonblank characters, and
> each adjacent pair of symbols is separated by one or more
> blanks. The last symbol is also followed by at least one
> blank. A symbol may be split onto two cards.

> Write a program segment which, when executed, will store
> the next symbol which has not yet been processed into
> variable SYMBOL. SYMBOL has the attributes CHARACTER(40)
> VARYING. If a symbol is more than 40 characters long, it
> may be split into two or more symbols without giving any
> error message.

Let us assume that a CHARACTER VARYING variable named CARD
will always contain that part of the input that has been read
but not yet "processed". Initially, then, we have CARD = ''.
The process of getting the next symbol into SYMBOL consists of
deleting blanks preceding the next symbol in the input, finding
the end of the symbol, moving it to SYMBOL, and finally,
deleting the symbol from CARD. Thus we write down the following
algorithm:

> S1: Delete blanks preceding the first nonblank in CARD
>   and the rest of the input;
> S2: Find the first blank in CARD and the input;
> S3: Put the symbol into SYMBOL;
> S4: Delete the symbol from CARD;

Step 1. Refinement of S1, Deleting the Blanks

There are two difficulties with S1. First, CARD may contain
nothing but blanks, and secondly it might even contain nothing
(as it does the first time this segment is executed). Either

case should cause us to read in more input. The following
program segment serves the purpose:

```
/* DELETE BLANKS BEFORE SYMBOL */
/* PUT INTO I THE POSITION OF FIRST NONBLANK */
ONLY_BLANKS = '1'B;
DO WHILE(ONLY_BLANKS);
    /* SEARCH CARDS UNTIL NONBLANK CHARACTER IS FOUND */
    DO WHILE((I < LENGTH(CARD)) & ONLY_BLANKS);
        I = I + 1;
        ONLY_BLANKS = (SUBSTR(CARD,I,1) = ' ');
        END;
    IF ONLY_BLANKS THEN
        DO;
            GET EDIT (CARD) (A(80)); /* READ NEXT CARD */
            I = 0;
            END;
    END;

/* DELETE THE BLANKS IN POSITIONS 1:I-1 */
CARD = SUBSTR(CARD,I);
```

Step 2.   Refinement of S2, Finding the End of the Symbol

The only difficulty with S2 is that the symbol may be split
on two cards. We must also watch out for the length of the
symbol. We should stop when the length is 40. The program uses
a CHARACTER(80) VARYING variable named CARD1 as a temporary
location to hold a card just read. Note that the maximum length
of the variable CARD must be large enough so that it can hold 40
characters from CARD plus 80 characters from CARD1. Therefore
CARD must be declared to be CHARACTER(120) VARYING.

```
/* AFTER EXECUTION OF THIS SEGMENT, */
/* THE SYMBOL IS IN SUBSTR(CARD,1,I-1) */
I = 1;
DO WHILE((SUBSTR(CARD,I,1) ¬= ' ') & (I <= 40));
    I = I + 1;
    IF I > LENGTH(CARD) THEN
        DO; /* READ NEXT CARD */
            GET EDIT(CARD1)(A(80));
            CARD = CARD || CARD1;
            END;
    END;
```

Step 3.   The Final Program

Statements S3 and S4 of the original algorithm are simple
statements, so the development is finished. We assemble the
various segments below, adding the necessary declarations. This
is given not as a complete program, but as a segment to be
included in a program that will use the symbols produced by this
segment.

```
DECLARE (CARD) CHARACTER(120) VARYING, /* CONTAINS INPUT READ */
                                       /* BUT NOT YET PROCESSED */
        (CARD1) CHARACTER(80) VARYING, /* USED TO READ IN CARD */
        (SYMBOL) CHARACTER(40) VARYING,/* HOLDS OUTPUT SYMBOL */
        (ONLY_BLANKS) BIT, /* STOPPING FLAG FOR LOOP */
        (I) FIXED;

/* PUT NEXT INPUT SYMBOL INTO "SYMBOL". */
/* DELETE BLANKS BEFORE SYMBOL */
/* PUT INTO I THE POSITION OF FIRST NONBLANK */
ONLY_BLANKS = '1'B;
DO WHILE(ONLY_BLANKS);
   I = 0;
   /* SEARCH CARD AND INPUT UNTIL NONBLANK CHARACTER IS FOUND */
   DO WHILE(I<LENGTH(CARD) & ONLY_BLANKS);
      I = I + 1;
      ONLY_BLANK = (SUBSTR(CARD,I,1) = ' ');
      END;
   IF ONLY_BLANKS THEN
      DO;
         GET EDIT (CARD) (A(80)); /* READ NEXT CARD */
         I = 0;
         END;
   END;

/* DELETE THE BLANKS IN POSITION 1:I-1 */
CARD = SUBSTR(CARD,I);

/* AFTER EXECUTION OF THIS SEGMENT, */
/* THE SYMBOL IS IN SUBSTR(CARD,1,I-1) */
I = 1;
DO WHILE((SUBSTR(CARD,I,1) ¬= ' ') & (I <= 40));
   I = I + 1;
   IF I > LENGTH(CARD) THEN
      DO: /* READ NEXT CARD */
         GET EDIT(CARD1)(A(80));
         CARD = CARD || CARD1;
         END;
   END;

/* PUT SYMBOL INTO "SYMBOL" */
SYMBOL = SUBSTR(CARD,1,I-1);

/* DELETE SYMBOL FROM INPUT */
CARD = SUBSTR(CARD,I);
```

Section 2 Exercises

Exercises 1 to 8 refer to the accounting problem of Section 2.4.

1. Why is ACCT declared as ACCT(0:201) instead of ACCT(0:200)?

2. For each of the 6 errors discussed in the first part of Section 2.4, indicate whether the program should stop or whether it may be reasonable to continue.

3. Change the program to consider these 6 errors. These changes should not be made by trying to revise the final program. Instead, go back to the proper step (3, 4, or 5) and perform the complete analysis and program creation once more, this time with the view of checking and documenting possible input errors.

4. Suppose the signal ending the accounts is a single 0 instead of two 0's. Change the program to reflect this. In making the changes, repeat the program analysis and development from the beginning; don't attempt to just change the final program. Which signal is better and why?

5. Suppose we wish to change the end-of-transaction signal to a single 0 instead of three. Change the program to reflect this.

6. Below are several problem statements. For each, develop an algorithm in English to solve it. This algorithm should contain no details about arrays used, variables used, etc. It should be only the first step toward a final program -- on the same level of detail as algorithm (2.4a). Note that the problem statements do not in fact give you exact details about the input. Compare your algorithms with each other and with (2.4a). Relate your algorithms to the program schemata of Section II.2.

   a) The input consists of two lists X and Y of numbers. Print out the number of times each number in list Y occurs in the first list X.

   b) The input consists of a list of bank accounts and transactions concerning these accounts. Print out the number of transactions for each account.

   c) The input consists of the text of a book, punched on cards, followed by a list of words. Print out the number of times each word on the list is used in the book.

   d) The input consists of a list of student records (name, address, grades in each course, etc.), followed by a list of a few student names. Find and print out the average, highest, and lowest grade point average for the students given in the second list.

7. In developing subalgorithm (2.4e), one problem was preventing the "Process transaction just read" statement from being executed if the transaction just read was the end-of-list signal. Is there another way to write the loop without adding conditional statements? If you produce a different version, with or without conditional statements is it more efficient? Easier to understand? Easier to modify?

8. Suppose the account numbers were limited to three digits. Can you think of a way to sort the accounts efficiently? What modifications would you have to make in the program? What are the relative merits of your solution and the one developed here in terms of time and space?

9. Below are several problem statements. For each, develop an algorithm, which shows the overall structure of the final program. Your algorithm should probably be along the lines of algorithm (2.4e).

   a) The input consists of a list of integers. Print out all those integers which are even.

   b) The input consists of a list of integers. Print out those integers which are prime. (An integer is prime if it is greater than 1 and evenly divisible only by 1 and itself. The integers 2, 3, 5, 7, 11, 59 are prime; the integers -2, 0, 1, 4, 9, 100 are not.)

   c) The input consists of a list of names of people. Print out all the names that contain the letter A.

10. "Comment outlines" for the top level of development of several programs are given below. Complete the programs by adding the actual PL/I statements that will perform what is specified by the heading comments. The problem requirements given in these comments are sketchy; assume whatever detail is necessary to write the programs. Document all such assumptions.

```
10a.   POSROW: PROCEDURE OPTIONS(MAIN);
          /* DETERMINE POSITIVE ROW AVERAGES, AND NBR ZEROS */
          DECLARE (TAB(10,10)) FLOAT, /* GIVEN ARRAY IS */
             (NR, NC) FIXED;          /* TAB(1:NR,1:NC) */
          DECLARE (SUM(10),AVG(10)) FLOAT;
          /* SUM(1:NR) ARE ROW SUMS OF TAB */
          /* AVG(1:ZNR) ARE ROW AVERAGES OF TAB */
          DECLARE (ZEROS(10)) FIXED;
          /* ZEROS(1:NR) ARE NBR OF ZEROS IN ROWS */
          DECLARE (I,J) FIXED;

          /* READ AND TEST: NR AND NC */

          /* LOAD TAB IN ROW MAJOR ORDER */

          /* REPLACE NEGATIVE ENTRIES WITH 0, AND */
          /* COUNT ALL ZEROS IN EACH ROW */

          /* COMPUTE ROW AVERAGES FOR NON-ZERO ENTRIES */

          /* DISPLAY AVG AND NBR ZEROS FOR EACH ROW */

          END /* POSROW */;

10b.   INVMAX: PROCEDURE OPTIONS(MAIN);
          /* READ 7X9 ARRAY, INVERT ODD ROWS, */
          /* FIND COLUMN MAXIMA, AND DISPLAY */
          DECLARE (TAB(7,9)) FLOAT;
          DECLARE (COLMAX(9)) FLOAT; /* COLUMN MAXIMA */
          DECLARE (I,J) FIXED;

          /* LOAD ARRAY (ROW MAJOR ORDER) */

          /* REVERSE ORDER OF ELEMENTS IN ODD-NUMBERED ROWS */

          /* FIND MAXIMUM VALUE IN EACH COLUMN */

          /* DISPLAY COLUMN MAXIMA */

          END /* INVMAX */;
```

```
10c.  REVTEST: PROCEDURE OPTIONS(MAIN);
          /* REVERSE STRINGS AND TEST FOR "A" BEFORE "B" */
          DECLARE (STR(50)) CHARACTER(20)VARYING,
            /* TABLE OF STRINGS IS: */
            (N) FIXED, /* STR(1:N) */
            (L) FIXED, /* L CHARACTERS IN EACH STR */
          DECLARE (I,J) FIXED;

          /* READ NBR AND LENGTH OF STRINGS FROM INITIAL DATA */

          /* LOAD ARRAY OF STRINGS */

          /* INVERT EACH STRING, */
          /* CHARACTER BY CHARACTER, END FOR END */

          /* PRINT A LIST OF INVERTED STRINGS IN WHICH AN "A" */
          /* APPEARS TO THE LEFT OF THE FIRST "B" */

          END /* REVTEST */;

10d.  ROTATE: PROCEDURE OPTIONS(MAIN);
          /* ROTATE SQUARE ARRAY QUARTER-TURN CLOCKWISE */
          DECLARE (AR(40,40),AR2(40,40)) FLOAT, /* ARRAYS ARE */
            (N) FIXED;            /* AR(N,N), AR<(N,N) */
          DECLARE (I,J) FIXED;

          /* READ NBR OF ROWS, AND LOAD AR BY ROWS */

          /* COPY EACH COLUMN OF AR, LEFT TO RIGHT, */
          /* INTO ROW OF AR2, TOP TO BOTTOM */

          /*  DISPLAY ROTATED ARRAY AR2 BY ROWS, TOP TO BOTTOM*/

          END /* ROTATE */;
```

11. For each of the following problems, develop a program to the point of having a "comment outline", such as those illustrated in Exercise 10.

11a. Given a list of non-zero numbers (with zero added to the end as a stopping flag) determine which numbers in the list are not unique (that is, which appear more than once). The list may be long but it will not contain more than 40 different numbers.

11b. Given a list of not more than 100 non-negative numbers (with -1 added as a stopping flag) either:

   1. print a list of the numbers which are greater than the final value on the list and which are not repeated in the list, or

   2. print a list of the numbers which are greater than the average of all the numbers on the original list.

Do 1 if there are more numbers on the list <u>greater</u> than the first value, than there are numbers <u>less</u> than the first value; otherwise do 2. There will be at least one value given. That is, the -1 stopping flag will not be the first value given.

11c. Given three lists of numbers, each n numbers long, produce another list called the "merged list" with the following properties:

1. It contains all the non-zero values from the 3 lists.

2. Values on the merged list are in the same order they appeared in the given lists.

3. If a value was in position i in one of the given lists, it will appear in the merged list before any number that was in a position later than i in any one of the given lists.

The 3 given lists are preceded by an integer n (less than 50) specifying the length of each of the 3 given lists. Print the merged list first, 3 values per line. Then print the given lists in 3 column format. For example, if the data are:

    4   7 0 3 9   0 4 5 0   1 2 0 0

the output would be:

    MERGED LIST
        7   1   4
        2   3   5
        9

    GIVEN LISTS
        7   0   1
        0   4   2
        3   5   0
        9   0   0

Section 3   General Design Considerations

The preceding sections have described the basic idea of program development in several different ways:

1. Break a problem into a sequence of sub-problems.

2. Refine a statement into several finer statements with increasing detail.

3. Expand a statement of what has to be done into a specification of how it is to be done.

4. Expand "high-level" commands such as "solve", "find" or "compute" into lower-level statements of a programming language.

5. Translate a problem description from English to PL/I.

These are different aspects of the same general process: the systematic transformation of a statement of requirements in English to a detailed specification of actions in PL/I.

We outlined the phases of the process in Section 1 and gave examples in Section 2. In Section 3 we review the process and describe several of the key issues in more detail.

3.1 Top-Down Development

In general, development decisions should be made in "outside-in", "top-down" order -- in order of increasing detail. In the bank problem of 2.4, initially there were a number of questions that could have been raised and answered -- how accounts should be stored, how the transactions should be processed, how the transactions should be stored, etc. Out of all these, we chose the one which helped determine the overall structure and which led to a correct program with just more detail: what were the main subproblems and in which order should they be executed?

This is not to say that your thoughts shouldn't skip to various parts of the program in varying amounts of detail. (They will whether you want them to or not.) There is nothing wrong in beginning by looking at various possibilities for the representation of data and subalgorithms to process them. Sometimes this is necessary in order to obtain a better understanding of the problem and possible solutions. Sometimes this is necessary in order to come up with any idea at all. But

this should just be considered a side trip. Any ideas
discovered on it should <u>not</u> be accepted as final, and the main
program development should then proceed <u>top</u>-<u>down</u>. It may be
necessary to develop several alternatives to some depth
before it is clear which one is best.

This top-down process is not as easy and straightforward as
it may seem from the examples given in Section 2. Programming,
like any problem solving, is a trial and error process.
Mistakes will be made, or just the wrong avenue explored, which
will cause the programmer to undo several levels of refinements
(discarding several parts of the tree) and to repeat the process
in a different manner. This "backing up" is discussed in more
detail in Section 3.1.3.

Programming in top-down fashion may seem foreign and
difficult, especially to beginners. Yet for most problems it is
the best approach, because it will lead to efficient,
understandable, and correct programs. Attempt right from the
beginning to develop programs in a top-down, outside-in, general
statement to fine detail, manner.

In programming in this fashion we attempt to make <u>one</u> clear
decision at a time. A decision leads to a refinement of part
of the program. The two types of refinement are:

1. A statement is refined.
2. The method of storing data is refined, by describing
    the variables used to store the data.

We discuss these separately in the next two subsections.

3.1.1 <u>Refining</u> <u>a</u> <u>Statement</u>

<u>Concentrating</u> <u>on</u> <u>"What"</u> <u>rather</u> <u>than</u> <u>"How"</u>

One of the advantages of top-down programming is that it
helps us concentrate initially on <u>what</u> is to be done, and then
systematically becomes concerned with <u>how</u>. For example, in
developing the overall structure of the accounting problem in
2.4, we refined "Solve the problem" into algorithm (2.4a):

    Read in and set up the accounts;
    Read in and process the transactions;
    Print the results

Here, we were not <u>primarily</u> interested in <u>how</u> the accounts and
transactions were to be stored or processed, but only in <u>what</u>
was to be done, so that we could concentrate on the order in
which the various functions were to be performed.

As another example, consider the sorting problem of 2.3.
Sorting is refined in terms of

"move the maximum element to the end of the list".

This states what is to be done, but not how. There are several
methods that could be used. "Move..." is refined into

> find the position of the maximum;
> interchange maximum and last

This suggests what could be done to accomplish "move..." without
specifying how either "find..." or "interchange..." will   be
performed.

Limiting Ourselves to Understandable Refinements

   When refining a statement we replace a statement of what to
do by an algorithm which indicates how to do it. In making such
a refinement it is important to limit ourselves to refinements
we can easily understand, and which we can easily communicate to
others.

   Given a statement, what possibilities exist?   The most
general possibility is a sequence of statements to be executed
in order.   Thus we should   attempt to break the original
statement into successive parts to be executed in order. Other
possibilities for a refinement are:

   1. Use a conditional statement to break the problem into
       two subcases.

   2. Break it into several (instead of two) subcases.

   3. Replace it by a loop (perhaps with initialization
       statements).

Faced with these limited possibilities for refining a statement,
we can focus attention on the following questions:

   1. How can it be broken up into successive parts?
   2. Does it break up easily into two or more subcases?
   3. Is it an iteration problem -- can a loop be used?

These methods of refinement lead naturally to the program units
described in Section II.1.

   The symbol scanning problem of Section 2.5 is a good example.
Given an "unprocessed" string in CARD, we wanted to "process"
the left-most "symbol" of that string into SYMBOL.   We refined
this into a sequence of four steps:

   S1: Delete blanks preceding the first nonblank in CARD
       and the rest of the input;
   S2: Find the first blank in CARD and the input;
   S3: Put the symbol into SYMBOL;
   S4: Delete the symbol from CARD.

We now have four simpler problems to refine. The problems of no word on a card or a word split onto two cards have been postponed -- in fact, we didn't even have to mention them.

Using Suitable Notation for Statements

Whatever language and notation suits the problem at hand should be used in order to aid in an orderly development and to make the final program as lucid as possible. Usually the initial notation consists of English commands like "Sort the list", "Process the transactions" and "Generate a value to ...". any imperative statement can be used, provided its meaning is sufficiently clear.

In particular, it is often convenient to invent control mechanisms that do not exist in PL/I (and perhaps not in any real programming language). As other examples, the meaning of the following two algorithms should be clear without any formal definition of how the "for each" statement is to be executed:

```
For each account in the list
    IF the account balance < 0 THEN
        Print a message.
```

```
For each position of the chessboard
    IF the position is occupied by a white piece THEN
        DO;
            IF the white piece can capture the black king THEN
                Print "check".
            IF the white piece can capture the black queen THEN
                Print "watch out!".
        END;
```

Using such statements helps postpone decisions about the order in which the accounts or positions on the chessboard should be processed. These can wait, and will probably depend on how the list and chessboard are stored as variables. Once we decide on an order, translating the "for each" loops into PL/I WHILE loops will not be difficult.

As another example, consider a program to simulate a baseball game. We have variables which keep track of the inning, number of outs, men on base, etc., and we have a way of generating an integer PITCH to represent what happens next. A partial list of the values of PITCH and the corresponding actions are given below:

value of PITCH	action after pitch
1	ball
2	strike
3	foul ball
4	single
5	double
etc.	

We need a program section that will select one of these
alternatives depending on the value of PITCH. This is the
multiple alternative situation discussed in Section II.1.3 and
it needs the "case statement" which, unfortunately, is lacking
in PL/I. But this doesn't mean that we can't use some form of
case statement as a convenient notation in our development. For
example:

```
Do one of following, depending on value of PITCH:
    ball  : Process ball;
    strike: Process strike;
    foul  : Process foul ball;
    single: Process single;
    double: Process double;
```

Eventually this will have to be expressed in the statements
actually available in the programming language being used (see
(II.1.3a),(II.1.3b) and Appendix B.10), but during development
it is clearer to have it in the form shown here.

3.1.2 <u>Refining</u> <u>a</u> <u>Data</u> <u>Description</u>

   Data refinements are just as important as statement
refinements, but decisions about how to store the data should be
postponed <u>as</u> <u>long</u> <u>as</u> <u>possible</u>, until no further statement
refinements can be made without knowing more about the data
structures used.

   You will gradually learn that there are many different ways
of keeping data in variables. For example, the list of accounts
in the bank problem of 2.4 can be kept in unsorted form in an
array, or sorted in ascending or descending order. There are
also more sophisticated storage structures such as hash tables,
singly linked lists, doubly linked lists, circular lists,
dequeues, stacks and trees. Each method has advantages and
disadvantages, depending on the nature and form of the
operations to be performed. In order to intelligently choose a
method for data representation, it is necessary to wait until
the operations to be performed on the data are well understood.

   The method of storing transactions in the bank problem is a
good illustration. We could have initially decided to use an
array, since there were many transactions. But waiting and
later deciding based on what was to be done with the
transactions led to the discovery that only <u>one</u> transaction had
to be stored at any time.

   Whenever you decide upon variables, <u>write</u> <u>down</u> <u>their</u> <u>names</u>
<u>with</u> <u>their</u> <u>exact</u> <u>meanings</u> <u>immediately</u>. Don't wait until you
write the declaration for them. Every variable is important (or
else it shouldn't be in the program) and you <u>must</u> know exactly

why it is there. Don't trust these exact meanings to your
memory; write them down.

A recent incident will illustrate the importance of this. A
student came in with a two-page program, the relevant parts of
which are given in (3.1.2a). The program was a simplified "text
editor"; it read text -- a sequence of words interspersed with
symbols for commands like "begin a new line" and "begin a new
paragraph" -- and printed out the text as formatted by the
commands. Each output line was "right justified", which means
that not only were the left margins lined up, but also the right
margins. (Right justification is performed by inserting extra
blanks between words, as in the lines you are now reading.)

There was obviously an error, since occasionally a blank at
the end of a word was missing -- "the big black fox" might
come out as "thebig black fox". The problem was found by
examining the exact role of the variables. Looking at the
program, it was surmised that OUTLINE would contain the current
line to be written out and LENGTHLINE would contain its length.
The student was asked what N meant, since its meaning was not
written down. After some uncertainty he said "Oh, it's just the
length of the word being added to the current line OUTLINE."
("It's just" is used often when one doesn't really know. It
seems to belittle the variable, making it all right not to know
exactly why it is there.)

The program was then examined to find if N was always
assigned and used in this way. The error was exposed when it
was discovered that in one place, N was the length of the word,
while in the other it was the length plus one, to take into
account the blank character following it.

```
            ...
            IF ... THEN
                DO;
                      ...
                      WORD = SUBSTR(LINE,M,N);
                      WORD = WORD || ' ';
                      ...
                      END;
(3.1.2a)        ELSE
                    DO;
                          WORD = WORD || ' ';
                          N = LENGTH(WORD);
                          ...
                          END;
            ...
            LENGTHLINE = LENGTH(OUTLINE) + N;
            OUTLINE = ...
            ...
```

The importance of clearly understanding and having an exact
written description of each variable cannot be overemphasized.

Using Suitable Notation for Data

We used notation outside PL/I in Section 2 during development
of the bank program, programming in terms of a "table of
accounts" and a "transaction" as long as possible before
describing how these quantities were to be represented in the
PL/I program. In effect, we talked as if the whole table of
accounts were contained as a value in a variable. Data can
often be represented using variables in many ways, and it is
important to talk in general terms about the "list" or the
"records" until more is known about the operations to be
performed on them. For example, see the "KWIC index"
development in Section VI.2.6.

Some algorithms just cannot be described coherently without
resorting to notation outside of PL/I. A good example of this
is the "heap sort" algorithm developed in Section VI.2.7.

Using high-level notation for data structures is just as
important as for statements. However it is difficult to give
good examples of this until you have more programming experience
and are familiar with a variety of different data structures.
We leave this discussion to another book. (See for example the
book by N. Wirth, Algorithms + Data Structures = Programs).

3.1.3 Backing Up

Program development is a trial and error process. We make
refinements and try some subalgorithms, and if they don't serve
our purpose we redo them. Redoing one subalgorithm may require
us to change other parts of the algorithm, both in data
structures and in statements, and it is important that all these
changes be made in a systematic way. This should usually be
done by "backing up" to a previous level of the algorithm which
the changes don't affect, and then proceeding to redo all the
top-down refinements taking the changes into account.

For example, suppose a top-down analysis has produced the
tree of refinements (3.1.3a), where each Si is a statement and
the lines leading down from a statement represent a sequence of
statements to be executed from left to right, to replace that
statement. Now suppose while attempting to refine statement S19
that we discover a mistake, or recognize that a change in data
structures designed earlier will make S19 more efficient. In
order to make the change, we must back up to a point where the
change has no effect. Suppose this is S2 (see tree (3.1.3b)).
Then we must proceed downward again, redoing all refinements (in
the example, S4-S7, S11-S15, S18 and S19) to make sure that
every refinement leads to a correct program.

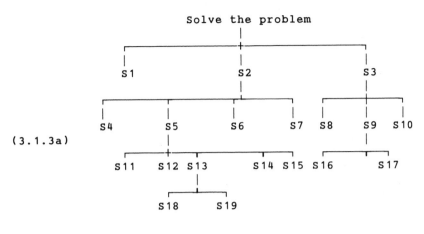

(3.1.3a)

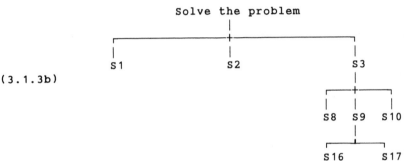

(3.1.3b)

Backing up in this manner is extremely important if a correct program is desired. There is a limit to how much we can keep in our heads, and the only way to extend this limit is to keep things well organized on paper. The more complicated the program, the more important it is to back up systematically.

If instead of using such a systematic procedure, we just "looked around" and tried to figure out what to change, the chances are that we would miss at least one place to change or would change some segment incorrectly. Backing up with a tree as a guide indicates not only what has to be changed, but also what doesn't have to be changed. For example, in the above illustration, once we decide that the change affects only S2 and its refinements, we need not worry about changing anything else in the tree.

To illustrate this process on a real problem, consider again the sorting problem of 2.3. The algorithm used in (2.3e) is:

```
        /* SORT L(1:N) */
        DO M = N TO 2 BY -1;
(3.1.3c)     Find position of maximum in L(1:M)
             Interchange maximum and L(M)
             END;
```

Now consider a different way of performing the same task. Instead of finding the largest value and then making one interchange at the end, compare successive values and interchange immediately if out of order:

```
           /* SWAP VALUES OF L(1-M) TO PUT LARGEST IN L(M) */
           DO I = 2 TO M BY 1;
(3.1.3d)       IF L(I-1) > L(I) THEN
                   Swap L(I-1) and L(I);
           END;
```

This refinement has a property which may be of some use. Note that it looks at successive adjacent pairs of L(1:M) and swaps any pair that is out of order. If no swaps occur during an execution of this subalgorithm, then no adjacent pair is out of order and the array is already sorted. Hence, if no swaps occur the algorithm can be terminated.

How will we stop execution? We have a new idea now, but we must fit it in at the right program level. Part of the change must occur not only in (3.1.3d), but also in the higher level algorithm (3.1.3c) since it must terminate. Thus we should back up to the statement "Sort L(1:N)" and refine anew. This new refinement will be a modification of (3.1.3c).

Looking at (3.1.3c) we see that we now have <u>two</u> stopping conditions: 1) (M < 2), and 2) "no swaps performed during one execution of the loop body". We introduce a new variable SORTED which has the following meaning:

> Whenever the condition of the main loop is evaluated, SORTED = '1'B means the array is definitely known to be sorted, while SORTED = '0'B means we aren't sure.

Now modify (3.1.3c) into (3.1.3e):

```
           /* SORT L(1:N) */
           SORTED = '0'B;
           M = N;
           DO WHILE ((¬SORTED) & (M >= 2));
               Swap values of L(1:M) to put largest in L(M),
(3.1.3e)       and also set SORTED as necessary
               M = M - 1;
           END;
```

Now proceed down again to the next level, redoing the English substatement:

```
/* SWAP L(1:M) TO PUT LARGEST IN L(M) AND SET SORTED */
SORTED = '1'B;              /* ASSUME L(1:M) IS SORTED */
DO I = 2 TO M BY 1;
   IF L(I-1) > L(I) THEN
      DO;
         Swap L(I-1) and L(I);
         SORTED = '0'B;
         END;
   END;
```

This yields the final program known as bubble sort:

```
/* SORT ARRAY(1:N) USING BUBBLE SORT */
SORTED = '0'B;
M = N;
DO WHILE((¬SORTED) & (M >= 2));
   /* SWAP L(1:M) TO PUT LARGEST IN L(M) AND SET SORTED */
   SORTED = '1'B; /* ASSUME L IS SORTED */
   DO I = 2 TO M BY 1;
      IF L(I-1) > L(I) THEN
         DO;
            T = L(I-1);
            L(I-1) = L(I);
            L(I) = T;
            SORTED = '0'B;
            END;
      END;
   M = M - 1;
   END;
```

The important point in the example is to note how we
backed up to a higher program level in order to incorporate
changes in a systematic manner. One can just look around and
try to find all necessary places to change in a haphazard
manner, but doing it in a systematic manner is actually easier
and more reliable.

This systematic backing up process is particularly useful
during testing. If an error is located during testing, it
should be corrected by backing up as we have described here, and
then proceeding down again, taking into account whatever changes
are necessary. The discovery of an error during testing may
well occur several days after that section of the program is
written and your recollection may be less than perfect. Unless
you proceed very systematically in the repair process there is a
good chance you will introduce new errors while trying to
eliminate old ones.

3.2 Sources of Ideas for Refinements

"How to invent something" is difficult to describe, and it is not clear that creativity can be effectively taught. Fortunately, the typical programmer is rarely asked to develop something radically different, and the type of creativity required is modest. Greater amounts of determination, logical thinking, hard work, attention to detail, and patience are involved. We attempt in this section to give some insight into how and where program ideas originate.

3.2.1 Sources of Ideas for Algorithms

A programmer has two main sources of ideas:

1. Programs previously written or studied;
2. Familiar algorithms from everyday life.

For the beginner, the first source is practically non-existent. One obvious way to expand this source is to read and study good programs written by others. Besides expanding the set of algorithms one has at his disposal, it helps teach and emphasize good style and programming practices. Surprisingly, studying other people's programs is not a common practice, even among professional programmers. One good place to look is the book by Kernighan and Plauger listed in the references at the end of this section.

The second source of ideas is almost unlimited. Every day we use algorithms or see others use them. Often, of course, they are informal and not too well defined, and describing them precisely may be difficult. But the ideas are there.

The bank problem is a good example of this. How did we know what to do? Perhaps we imagined what a clerk would do to manually perform this task. In order to write a program for it, we needed only to be able to write down an exact description of the process the clerk performs, taking into account the format of the input (which the clerk need not worry about) and the fact that all data must be stored in variables. The top-down method of development was used only to aid us in writing the algorithm correctly and precisely.

As a second example, suppose we have an array B(1:N) whose values are in ascending order. We want to find the position J of another variable X in the list. That is, search B for X and store in variable J an integer such that B(J) = X. If no such integer exists, store 0 in J. If the list were not sorted we would use a simple search as in 2.2:

```
PRESENT = '0'B;
J = 0;
DO WHILE((¬PRESENT) & (J < N));
    J = J + 1;
    IF B(J) = X THEN
        PRESENT = '1'B;
    END;
IF ¬PRESENT THEN
    J = 0;
```

However, the additional information that B is sorted may permit a more efficient algorithm.

Everyday situations in which something is sought in an ordered list are numerous, and in general a more efficient search method is used. A good example is looking for a name in the telephone book. To find a name, say "Smith", we look at some entry in the book rather randomly, but as near to the S's as we can get. The entry serves to divide the book into two parts -- "before" the entry and "after" the entry. If this entry is less than Smith (alphabetically), then Smith is located in the second part, after the entry. So we "discard" the first part and repeat the process using only the last part. If the entry is greater than Smith, we discard the second part and repeat the process using the first part.

Thus we can repeat a process over and over until we find the desired entry or until we have discarded the whole list (in which case the desired value is not in the list). This repetition suggests the use of a WHILE loop, and after some work we arrive at the following algorithm:

```
Let the list to be searched be B(1:N);
PRESENT = '0'B;
DO WHILE ((the list to be searched is not empty) & (¬PRESENT));
    K = index of some entry B(K) still in list, near X;
    IF B(K) = X THEN
      DO;
          J = K;
          PRESENT = '1'B;
          END;
    IF B(K) < X THEN
      discard first half of list, including B(K);
    ELSE
      discard second half of list, including B(K);
    END;
IF ¬PRESENT THEN
    J = 0; /* X IS NOT IN THE LIST */
```

The statement

    "K = index of some entry B(K) still in list, near X;"

is not precise enough. How do we compute "near"? To simplify this, let us just use

K = index of middle entry of the list;

which is easier to compute. It may not be as good an algorithm as we use with the telephone book, but this change does make it easier to program. When searching the telephone book, we have common sense information which is not ordinarily available to the program. For example, we know there are lots of S's and T's, but few W's and X's. This certainly affects the way we perform the search. The main problem in developing a program based on our experiences is to be able to formalize how we do something, to ferret out the essential details.

This is the beginning of the development of a well-known algorithm called binary search. It is a vast improvement over the algorithm used in 2.2. For example, if there are 256 entries, the 2.2 algorithm may have to look at all the entries, while binary search will never have to look at more than 9 of them! This algorithm is discussed further in Section VI.2.4. The key point here is that the idea for this algorithm comes from the prosaic task of using a directory.

3.2.2 Solving Simpler Problems

Since we have not previously seen every problem we are asked to solve and program, somehow we must be able to find connections between the problems at hand and problems whose solutions we already know (or at least whose solutions are easier). Two obvious methods are to simplify the problem and to find related problems.

It is often useful to explore a problem similar in structure to the one assigned, but is simpler in detail. One can explore alternative strategies and algorithms in this simpler context, and chose which strategy to pursue for the real problem.

To illustrate consider the sorting problem again. We have all done this -- sorted mailing lists, books on shelves, and so on. The problem and its solution are not unfamiliar, but explaining precisely how to sort is not easy if we haven't seen an algorithm for it before. Let us attack the problem as if we had not seen earlier, and look for simpler problems within the sort.

What must happen for the list L(1:N) to be sorted? For one thing, the largest value must eventually appear in L(N). This is a simpler problem which we know how to handle (Section I.5, Exercise 4f).

```
          DO I = 1 TO N-1 BY 1;
(3.2.2a)     IF L(I) > L(N) THEN
                Swap L(I) and L(N);
             END;
```

What else must be done? The second largest value must appear in
L(N-1). If the largest has already been put into L(N) by the
above algorithm, then this means we want to put the largest of
L(1:N-1) into L(N-1). This is roughly the same as (3.2.2a):

```
        DO I = 1 TO N-2 BY 1;
            IF L(I) > L(N-1) THEN
                Swap L(I) and L(N-1);
            END;
```

Continuing, we should recognize that   we   are   performing
essentially the same process a number of times. Getting back to
the original problem, we can write it as

```
    Swap values of L(1:N)    to put largest in L(N);
    Swap values of L(1:N-1) to put largest in L(N-1);
    Swap values of L(1:N-2) to put largest in L(N-2);
                    . . .
    Swap values of L(1:2)    to put larger  in L(2);
```
or
```
            /* SORT L(1:N) BY SUCCESSIVE MAXIMA */
            DO M = N TO 2 BY 1;
(3.2.2b)        Swap values of L(1:M) to put largest in L(M);
            END;
```

One way of refining the English substatement of (3.2.2b) is

```
            /* SWAP VALUES OF L(1:M) TO PUT LARGEST IN L(M) */
            DO I = 1 TO M-1 BY 1;
(3.2.2c)        IF L(I) > L(M) THEN
                    Swap L(I) and L(M);
            END;
```

   Note that we got the idea for the program by tackling smaller
simpler ones and noticing that we had to repeat essentially the
same process many times. We then returned to the original level
and wrote the program (3.2.2b). At this point, we knew how to
write the segment for "Swap values of L(1:M) to put largest in
L(M)", and yet we still wrote this statement in English in
(3.2.2b). This was because we wanted to make one decision at a
time, the decision turning out to be the order in which the
values were placed in their final positions (first L(N), then
L(N-1), and so on). How the values get in their positions is
not a problem of (3.2.2b), but the order in which they get
there is. We can even design different algorithms for
swapping the values, different from the one in (3.2.2a) which
helped us find the solution. Sometimes tackling a simpler
problem or a subproblem is the only way we can proceed. But
once the process of solving the simpler problem has led to an
idea, set the solution to the simpler problem aside, at least
temporarily, and concentrate again on the top-down analysis.

   One way to find a simpler problem is to temporarily make the
problem definition simpler. Set aside all inessential details
(perhaps even some of the essential ones), until a simple,

understandable problem emerges. Once this has been solved, the
original problem can be   attacked   with more understanding.
This deletion of material must of course be done with care to
make   sure   that   the   remaining   problem is instructive and not
trivial.

    To illustrate this, consider the following problem:

(3.2.2d) A Text Editor. Input to the program is to consist of
        normal words, on cards, each adjacent pair being separated
        by one or more blanks. A word may be split onto two cards
        (the end of one and the beginning of the next). The words
        are to be read in and written out in 60-character lines.
        Each line is to be both right and left justified (as are
        the lines of this book). A word may not be split onto two
        lines, unless it is more than 60 characters long or unless
        otherwise there will be only one word on a line (these are
        probably errors, but the program must handle them).

            Interspersed between words (and separated from them by
        one or more blanks) may be commands to be executed by the
        program, at the time they are read. These are:

            command   meaning
)L   Begin a new output line;
)P   Begin a new paragraph (indent 3 spaces);
)E   End of input.

    When processing a command, if a partially filled line must
    be   written out, do not right-justify that line. For
    example, the last line of a paragraph is never right-
    justified.   Commands may not appear as words in the input;
    only as commands.

    Below is some sample input, with the corresponding output
shown at the right, using 14-character instead of 60-character
lines to save space:

    Sample input   Sample output
)P One way to find a simpler | One   way   to
    problem is to make the)L)L |find a simpler
            problem |problem is to
    definition simpler. |make the
    Throw out all |
    inessential details.   )E |problem defini
                                       |tion   simpler.
                                       |Throw out all
                                       |inessential de
                                       |tails.

    This description is full of details, and it is difficult to
know where to start, so begin by temporarily setting details
aside to make it simpler:

1. Any number of blanks may separate a pair of words, and a word can be split on two cards. This may be difficult, so initially consider the input to be just a series of words and commands. That seems to be the essential point.

2. Why are lines 60 characters, and not 61 or 62? Perhaps the line length should be part of the input to the program. For now, since we need some length, use 60.

3. Justifying a line looks relatively complicated, but does not seem important relative to the overall structure of the program. Set it aside.

4. The problem of words of 60 characters or more and the problem of only one word on the line do not seem essential. Set them aside.

5. The commands are essential, and yet probably difficult to work with. Try setting them aside, and if that doesn't work out, bring them back.

This leads to the following problem description:

(3.2.2e) <u>Simplified</u> <u>Text</u> <u>Editor</u>. Read in a sequence of "words" and print them out on 60-character lines. Put as many as possible on one line, but separate each pair by a blank. Don't split words across two lines.

This simpler problem is much easier to understand and work with. A variable L (say) will hold the line currently being built. It will be written out when the next word to be inserted causes it to be longer than 60 characters. The following algorithm could be designed fairly quickly:

```
          L = '';          /* NOTHING IS IN THE CURRENT LINE */
          DO WHILE (there is another input word);
             Read the next word into WORD;
(3.2.2f)     IF LENGTH(L) + LENGTH(WORD) > 60 THEN
               DO;
                  Remove blank from end of L;
                  Print L;
                  L = '';
                  END;
             Add WORD onto L;
             Add 'ƀ' onto L;
             END;
          Remove blank from end of L, if it has one;
          Print L;
```

The most important part of the original problem left out of (3.2.2e) is the commands, so now reinsert them. This will complicate the algorithm (3.2.2f), so we first should hide some of its details. (3.2.2f) can be rewritten as

```
        L = '';          /* NOTHING IS IN THE CURRENT LINE */
        DO WHILE (there is more input);
(3.2.2g)    Read the next word into WORD;
            Process the word in WORD;
            END;
        Remove blank from end of L, if it has one;
        Print L;
```

In adding commands, we see we must process either a word or command. We also know when to stop the loop -- when the command)E is read. Rewriting (3.2.2g) with this information yields

```
        L = '';            /* NOTHING IS IN THE CURRENT LINE */
        WORD = '';     /* NO WORD OR COMMAND READ YET */
        DO WHILE (WORD ¬= ')E');
            Read the next word or command into WORD;
(3.2.2h)    IF WORD is a command THEN
                Process WORD as a command;
            ELSE
                Process WORD as a word:
            END;
        Remove blank from end of L, if it has one;
        Print L;
```

where "process WORD as a word" is

```
        DO;
            /* PROCESS WORD AS A WORD */
            IF LENGTH(L) + LENGTH(WORD) > 60 THEN
                DO;
                    Remove blank from end of L;
                    Print L;
                    L = '';
                    END;
            Add WORD onto L;
            ADD 'Ƅ' onto L;
            END;
```

We now have a reasonable solution to the simpler problem (3.2.2e) plus commands. At this point the original problem should be reread and programmed in top-down fashion, using (3.2.2h) as a model.

On the text editor problem just described, the most common "mistake" is to write the main part of the program as a loop:

```
        DO WHILE (there exists a card);
            Read a card;
            Process the card;
            END;
```

This then requires a second loop in processing the card, and the whole program is unnecessarily complicated because a word could be split across card boundaries. If the problem is first

simplified, we realize that the card boundary problem is just a
detail to be handled at a later time, and is not an essential
point in understanding the general flow of the program.

3.2.3 Solving Related Problems

Consider writing a program segment to sort an array C(1:N) in
descending order: C(1) $\geq$ C(2) $\geq$ ... $\geq$ C(N). You might recall
having developed an <u>ascending</u> sort in the previous section
(program (3.2.2b)). The new sorting program could just be a
modification of the previous one.

Related problems, both in programming and in the everyday
world, are a rich source of ideas. If we can find something
related which we know how to handle, then the problem becomes
much simpler.

In the previous section, we discussed solving simpler
problems, which are of course related to the original problem.
By a "related problem" in this section we mean one which is
roughly the same order of magnitude in size or complexity. One
which, with some work, can be <u>transformed</u> into the desired one.
Everybody uses related problems all the time, and in effect we
are just saying the obvious here. The point is that you should
become <u>aware</u> of the fact that you are using related problems;
this will increase your ability to find solutions and design
programs. Learning consists not only of doing something, but
also of learning why and how one does it.

In programming, related problems occur more often than one
might think. For example, consider the four parts of Exercise 6
of Section 2. Although these look quite different, at the
highest level they all have the same algorithmic solution:

        Read in a list of values;
        Read and process a second list of values;
        Print results.

In fact, they are equivalent at this level to algorithm (2.4a)
of the accounting problem of 2.4 and differ only in the meaning
of "values", "read", "process", and "results". Similarly, all
the problems of Exercise 9 of Section 2 have the solution

        DO WHILE (there exists input);
            Read a value;
            Process the value;
            END;

Each of these is an interpretation of schema (2b) of Section
II.2. In order to <u>see</u> that problems are related, we must be
able to recognize the important elements of a problem. All four
problems in Exercise 6 of Section 2 look different on first
inspection, until we state them in a more general manner.

Most programs include a number of simple subalgorithms, many
of which seem to occur over and over again (with perhaps slight
variations). Examples are algorithms to:

Search a list.
Search a sorted list.
Find the maximum or the average of a set of values.
Delete duplicate values from a list.
Read in a list of values which ends with some signal.

Many of these will become part of your "repertoire of
algorithms" and you will find that programming consists in part
in determining how these standard subalgorithms should be
combined into a larger program. In order to do this, however,
you must be able to recognize familiar problems in the   mass   of
detail of the overall problem, and work on modifying them to fit
the current problem.

3.3 Handling Input Errors

Programs are written to be used in the real world -- which
means that they must not assume that input data will always
conform exactly to the problem specifications.   In general,
programs must check all input for errors, and when errors are
detected provide informative output that will help the user to
find and correct the mistake. When a data error is not
detected, the best that can happen is that the program will
"blow up" -- an infinite loop will be executed, an array
subscript will be out of range, or some similar indication will
be given. The worst that can happen is that the program
processes the erroneous input as if it were correct, giving no
indication that anything is wrong. If and when the error is
eventually detected, it can be embarrassing and costly to
correct.

Once you recognize the possibility that data errors can exist
-- and in most situations are in fact likely to exist, you must
decide what is the most reasonable response. For example, five
alternative program segments are given in (3.3a) to (3.3e)
below. Each is an interpretation of schema II.2d; each is
designed to perform the same task -- compute the sum of a set of
integer data values.   They differ only in the manner in which
they react to a non-integer datum. In each case assume these
segments are run in a program with the following declarations:

DECLARE (SUM) FLOAT;
DECLARE (INTG) FIXED;
DECLARE (N) FIXED;
DECLARE (NBR) FLOAT;

To understand these segments, recall that the FLOOR built-in
function yields the greatest integer not greater than its
argument. That is, FLOOR(3.5) is 3; FLOOR(-4.5) is -5.

```
(3.3a)     /* SUM N INTEGER DATA VALUES */
           SUM = 0;
           GET LIST(N);
           DO WHILE (N>0);
              GET LIST(INTG);
              SUM = SUM + INTG;
              N = N - 1;
              END;


3.3b)      /* SUM N INTEGER DATA VALUES */
           SUM = 0;
           GET LIST(N);
           DO WHILE (N>0);
              GET LIST(NBR);
              SUM = SUM + NBR;
              N = N - 1;
              END;


(3.3c)     /* SUM N INTEGER DATA VALUES */
           SUM = 0;
           GET LIST(N);
           DO WHILE (N>0);
              GET LIST(NBR);
              IF NBR = FLOOR(NBR) THEN
                 SUM = SUM + NBR;
              N = N - 1;
              END;


(3.3d)     /* SUM N INTEGER DATA VALUES */
           SUM = 0;
           GET LIST(N);
           DO WHILE (N>0);
              GET LIST(NBR);
              IF NBR ¬= FLOOR(NBR) THEN
                 PUT SKIP(2) LIST('NON-INTEGER VALUE:',NBR);
              SUM = SUM + NBR;
              N = N - 1;
              END;


(3.3e)     /* SUM N INTEGER DATA VALUES */
           SUM = 0;
           GET LIST(N);
           DO WHILE (N>0);
              GET LIST(NBR);
              IF NBR = FLOOR(NBR)THEN
                 SUM = SUM + NBR;
              ELSE
                 PUT SKIP(2)LIST('NON-INTEGER VALUE:', NBR);
              N = N - 1;
              END;
```

If the data happens to be perfect -- that is, N integers --
these five segments are equivalent. If one or more non-integers
are present the segments behave quite differently:

(3.3a)quietly   "repairs" non-integers by dropping any
fractional part. No indication of their presence is given.

(3.3b)is not restricted to integers at all. It includes
fractional portions of values in the sum. No indication of
the presence of non-integers is given.

(3.3c)only includes integers in the sum. It rejects non-
integers, not including them, but not reporting their
presence.

(3.3d)reports the presence of non-integers, but includes
them in the sum.

(3.3e)reports the presence of non-integers and does not
include them in the sum.

There are several other possibilities but these should serve
to illustrate the point. One cannot say, in general, which of
these responses is best. That depends upon the requirements of
the particular problem. But one can say that it is generally
necessary to admit the possibility of different types of errors,
determine what response is appropriate, and write the program
accordingly.

With some errors the program should stop and print a message.
For example, in the accounting problem of 2.4 if the end-of-
account signal is missing, then all transactions have been read
as accounts, and there is no hope of proceeding usefully. With
other errors the program should just print a message and
continue. For example, if a transaction gives a non-existant
account number, that transaction can be rejected and a message
can be printed.

Many programs process data that actually consists of sections
that are quite independent. For example, in 2.4 the data
pertaining to each account is independent of the data preceding
and following. An error in a particular item of data may well
make processing for that account meaningless until the error is
corrected, but it does not affect processing of the other
accounts. This suggests that a well-designed program would
reject the erroneous data with an informative error message,
skip over that account, but resume processing with the next
account. Error rates of several percent in hand-prepared data
are not unusual and programs that have to process thousands of
data cards are also not unusual. If these programs were to stop
as soon as any error is encountered and insist that it be
repaired before proceding they would be impractical to use.   On
the other hand there are cases where the data are all logically
related and the effects of errors are cumulative. In such cases

it is pointless to continue processing. It requires both knowledge of the problem and good judgement to decide whether an error should terminate processing or whether there is some action that will permit continuation to be useful.

One could conceivably overdo error checking. The programmer must weigh each type of input error and the damage its occurrence might cause against the amount of programming necessary to detect it. But at least the programmer should <u>think</u> of all the possible errors and come to a rational decision on each one. If necessary the manager should be questioned about them. Very often the person in charge may not have thought about all the possibilities and will be delighted to hear they can be detected. On the other hand, he may be able to tell the programmer that a particular error will <u>never</u> occur because, for example, the data is produced by another program of known reliability.

In some cases error processing is so important that it dominates the program. For example, there are programs whose sole purpose is to screen data for errors so that these can be corrected prior to submitting the data for actual processing. In general, error processing should be considered an important and integral part of the problem. Error processing is usually more successful when it is developed along with other requirements rather than being added on after the program is otherwise finished.

Part II and Part III <u>References</u>

Aho, A. V., J. E. Hopcroft and J. D. Ullman, <u>The Design and Analysis of Computer Algorithms</u>, Addison-Wesley, 1974

Dahl, O. J., E. W. Dijkstra and C. A. R. Hoare, <u>Structured Programming</u>, Academic Press, 1972

Dijkstra, E.W., <u>A Short Introduction to the Art of Programming</u>, Eindhoven University, 1971

Kernighan, B.W. and P.J. Plauger, <u>Elements of Programming Style</u>, McGraw Hill, 1974

Kernighan, B.W. and P.J. Plauger, "Programming Style: Examples and Counterexamples", <u>ACM Computing Surveys</u>, December 1974

Knuth, D.E. "Structured Programming with GO TO Statement", <u>ACM Computing Surveys</u>, December 1974

McGowan, C.L. and J.R. Kelly, <u>Top-Down Structured Programming Techniques</u>, Petrocelli/Charter 1975

Mills, H., "Top Down Programming in Large Systems", in Rustin (ed.), <u>Debugging Techniques in Large Systems</u>, Prentice Hall, 1971

Polya, G., <u>How to Solve It</u>, Princeton, 1945 (also excerpted in Newman, <u>The World of Mathematics, Vol. 3</u>, Simon & Schuster, 1956)

Weinberg, G.M., <u>The Psychology of Computer Programming</u>, Van Nostrand, 1971

Wirth, N., "Program Development by Stepwise Refinement", <u>Communications of the ACM</u>, April 1971

Wirth, N., <u>Systematic Programming: An Introduction</u>, Prentice Hall, 1973

Wirth, N., "On the Composition of Well-Structured Programs", <u>ACM Computing Surveys</u>, December 1974

Yohe, J.M. "An Overview of Programming Practices", <u>ACM Computing Surveys</u>, December 1974

PART IV   INDEPENDENT SUBPROGRAMS

Section 1   Block Structured Programs

Up to this point we have considered programs that consisted of one main procedure. The procedure constitutes an independent environment whose variables are separate and distinct from those of other programs. Now we generalize this concept somewhat and introduce two new ideas: <u>internal</u> <u>procedures</u>, and <u>recursion</u>.

The language features presented in Part I are adequate to write small programs, but something more is required if we are to effectively write and test significant programs. We need some means of organizing things so that

1. different sections of the program can be made relatively independent, so they can be written and tested separately;

2. program segments can be written in one place and executed "remotely" from some other point in the program;

3. program segments can be written so that they can be reused in different contexts without having to be rewritten; and

4. large programs can be easily constructed from smaller ones already written and checked out.

These capabilities are provided by "procedures" in PL/I. One defines a procedure -- a subalgorithm -- in one place. This procedure can then by "called" or "invoked" into action from places within other program segments. In executing the procedure, it behaves as if it were copied into each position from which it is invoked. This technique is not peculiar to programming. For instance, when baking a cake we might be instructed to "make chocolate icing, page 56". The icing recipe is a separate procedure, with its own set of instructions. To execute this command, we postpone further action on the cake, turn to the icing recipe, and execute it. When finished, we return to the cake recipe and continue where we left off.

The procedure allows us to extend the programming language
with new operations. Once a procedure has been written, it can
then be used as a new operation, just as we use SUBSTR, SQRT,
etc. without needing to know how they work internally.

Procedures are difficult for new programmers to understand,
but the idea is important and worth the struggle. Perhaps more
than anything else procedures mark the dividing line between
casual programmers and those who have serious work to do. We
will illustrate the idea by example in the next section, and
then explore the definition and use of procedures in more detail
in the following sections.

1.1 A Procedure to Interchange Values

Consider the task of exchanging the values of two variables.
We can do this for two given variables X and Y by using a
temporary variable T:

```
          T = X;
(1.1a)    X = Y;
          Y = T;
```

We can write a procedure to do this:

```
          SWAPXY: PROCEDURE;
             /* SWAP VALUES OF X AND Y */
(1.1b)    T = X;
          X = Y;
          Y = T;
          END /* SWAP */;
```

This procedure definition would be placed in the program. Then,
whenever we wanted to swap the values of X and Y, instead of
writing (1.1a) we would write the procedure call CALL SWAPXY;.
Executing the call means executing the three statements of the
procedure (1.1b). It is analogous to turning to the icing
recipe, making the icing, and then returning to the cake
recipe.

Procedures in programming have another advantage which is
very important. They allow us to "communicate" with the
procedure when we call it, to indicate which variables it should
work with. For example, we can write a single procedure SWAP
which will swap the values of any two fixed variables, not
just X and Y. The CALL statement specifies which variables are
to be used. We write this procedure as

```
          SWAP: PROCEDURE(X,Y);
             /* SWAP VALUES OF X AND Y */
             DECLARE (X,Y) FIXED;
             DECLARE (T) FIXED;
(1.1c)       T = X;
             X = Y;
             Y = T;
             END /* SWAP */;
```

X and Y are no longer variables; they are called <u>parameters</u> of
the procedure. When the procedure is called into action (e.g.
using CALL SWAP(I,J);), the calling statement supplies two
variables (e.g. I and J) to be used in place of X and Y. The
names X and Y are just "templates" or "place-holders" for the
variables, which are not known until the procedure is called.

   The first DECLARE of (1.1c) is a new type of declaration in
which parameters rather than variables are defined. This
specifies that the parameters X and Y are to be replaced by
fixed variables each time the procedure is called. The form
of the parameter declaration is like that used for variables;
PL/I recognizes that the identifiers are parameters because they
were given in the parameter list after the keyword PROCEDURE.
The second DECLARE creates a variable T rather than a parameter
since T did not appear in the parameter list.

   The sequence of three statements T=X; X=Y; Y=T; forms the
<u>body</u> of procedure (1.1c). This body cannot be executed by
itself; it must be called into action by a statement which
supplies two variables to use for X and Y. (1.1c) is really a
declaration in that it declares or defines the name SWAP to be a
procedure.

   To illustrate a call of this procedure (1.1c), suppose we
have variables

A(1)	5 [fixed]	I	1 [fixed]
A(2)	3 [fixed]	J	2 [fixed]
P	8 [fixed]	Q	9 [fixed]

To swap the values of I and J execute the procedure call
CALL SWAP(I, J);. I and J are called the <u>arguments</u> of the
procedure call. In executing this call, the procedure body

```
          T = X;
          X = Y;
          Y = T;
```

is executed as if it had been written

```
(1.1d)    T = I;
          I = J;
          J = T;
```

That is, the first argument I replaces the first parameter X,
and the second argument Y replaces the second parameter J. Note
that this all happens automatically during execution. The
programmer just writes the procedure definition, and places a
calling statement wherever he wants the procedure to be
executed, giving as arguments the variables whose values are to
be interchanged. Writing CALL SWAP(P,Q); would cause the
procedure to be executed as if the body had been written

(1.1e)   T = P;
          P = Q;
          Q = T;

writing CALL SWAP(A(1),A(2)); as if written

(1.1f)   T = A(1);
          A(1) = A(2);
          A(2) = T;

writing CALL SWAP(A(1),A(J)); as if written

(1.1g)   T = A(1);
          A(1) = A(J);
          A(J) = T;

   This example is just to give the general idea. More detailed
explanations of the definition and call of procedures are given
in the following sections.

1.2 Definition of a Procedure

1.2.1 Form of a Procedure Definition

The general form of a procedure definition is

```
procedure-name : PROCEDURE( list of parameters );
    /* comment summarizing what the procedure does */
    Declarations to specify parameters
    Declarations to create variables
    Procedure body
    END /* procedure-name */;
```

The procedure-name is any PL/I identifier; this is the name by which the procedure will be called to be executed. The list of parameters is a sequence of PL/I identifiers, separated by commas. These identifiers are the parameters and not names of variables. The parameter names have absolutely no connection with names used elsewhere in the program.

The first set of declarations specifies the type attributes of the parameters. In SP/k all parameters must be declared and their type attributes given explicitly. The form of parameter declarations is exactly like that of variable declarations except for lengths and dimensions. The attribute CHARACTER(...) VARYING must be written as CHARACTER(*)VARYING, where the "*" means we don't really know (or care at this point) how many characters the corresponding variable will have. Indeed, the number of characters can vary from call to call. If the argument corresponding to a parameter A is to be an array, we use the form A(*) for a one-dimensional array, A(*,*) for a two dimensional array, and so on. Here also the "*" means that the bounds depend on the corresponding argument and can be different for each call of the procedure.

The second set of declarations create variables, just as we have been doing since our first example in Section I.1.1. However, now that we are concerned with more than one procedure we must note that variables are "local" to the procedure in which they are declared. This means that they can be used only in that procedure. Their names are not known outside that procedure. Each procedure has its own set of variables (i.e., those variables declared in the procedure), independent of those of every other procedure, and it is immaterial if some of the names happen to coincide. We also note that the variables of a procedure are created as the procedure is entered, and then destroyed when that execution of the procedure is completed. This is discussed further in Sections 1.3 and 1.5.

The procedure body is a sequence of statements which are executed whenever the procedure is called. Any statement may appear within the procedure body -- an assignment, conditional, GET, PUT, compound statement, a loop, or a call on another procedure (as explained in Section 1.4). Note however that

these statements may contain parameters as well   as   variables.
This means that the body cannot be executed unless it is
properly called, with variables as arguments to replace the
parameters.   We write the procedure as if the parameters were
variables or arrays, knowing that they will be replaced by
actual variables or arrays when the procedure is called.   For
example:

```
          SEARCH: PROCEDURE(A,N,X,J);
              /* SEARCH ARRAY A(1:N) FOR X.  STORE A VALUE IN */
              /* J SO THAT A(J)=X. IF NOT POSSIBLE, SET J=0 */
              DECLARE (A(*),X) CHARACTER(*) VARYING;
              DECLARE (J,N) FIXED;
(1.2.1a)      DECLARE (K) FIXED,
              K = 0;
              J = 0;
              DO WHILE ((J = 0) & (K < N));
                 K = K+1;
                 IF A(K) = X THEN
                    DO;
                         J = K;
                         END;
                 END;
          END /* SEARCH */;
```

SEARCH has four parameters A, N, X and J.   Whenever SEARCH is
called, A must be replaced by a one-dimensional array of string
variables, X by a string variable, and N and J by fixed
variables.   The number of elements in the array may vary from
call to call, as may the length of the array elements and the
length of X. One time the procedure may be asked to search an
array B(1:20), the next time an array C(1:1000).

   The comment /* procedure-name */ after the end of the
procedure serves as a reminder to the programmer that the
preceding END is the end of a procedure body. It is not
strictly necessary but we strongly recommend its use as a matter
of good programming style.

1.2.2 The RETURN Statement

   Execution of a procedure ends when the last statement of the
procedure body has been executed.   However, PL/I provides a
RETURN   statement to explicitly terminate execution of a
procedure. When RETURN is executed the procedure terminates
immediately and returns to the calling procedure to continue
execution with the statement immediately following the   CALL.
Using this, (1.2.1a) could have been written

```
         SEARCH: PROCEDURE(A, N, X, J);
                 /* SEARCH ARRAY A(1:N) FOR X.  STORE A VALUE IN */
                 /* J SO THAT A(J)=X.  IF NOT POSSIBLE, SET J=0 */
                 DECLARE (A(*), X) CHARACTER(*) VARYING;
                 DECLARE (J,N) FIXED;
                 DO J = 1 TO N BY 1;
(1.2.2a)             IF A(J) = X THEN
                         RETURN;
                 END;
                 J = 0;
                 END /* SEARCH */;
```

If X is found in array A the RETURN is executed and the
procedure terminates immediately. If X is not in the array,
then the procedure terminates in the normal fashion after
executing the last statement of the body, J=0;.

The use of RETURN makes (1.2.2a) clearer than (1.2.1a).

1.2.3 Placement of Procedures

A procedure is called "internal" when its definition is
positioned so that it is within the body of any other
procedure. For example, suppose a main procedure RASP will call
the two procedures SWAP and SEARCH given in (1.1c) and (1.2.2a).
The deck of cards to be submitted to the computer looks like

```
  $JOBK ID='R. REID'
  RASP: PROCEDURE OPTIONS(MAIN);
       /* comment describing main procedure */
       SWAP: PROCEDURE(X, Y);
         /* SWAP VALUES OF X AND Y */
         ...
         END /* SWAP */;

       SEARCH: PROCEDURE(A,N,X,J);
         /* SEARCH A(1:N) FOR X... */
         ...
         END /* SEARCH */;
       ...
       CALL SWAP(A,B);
         ...
       CALL SEARCH(C,A,D,B);
         ...
       END /* RASP */;
  $DATA
  ...
```

Execution of a PL/I program consists of one execution of the
main procedure. In effect, PL/I executes a single implied call
(without arguments) of the main procedure. Execution of the
program is finished whenever that single execution of the main

procedure is completed. Procedures are executed only if they are called; you cannot "run into" a procedure and execute it as you might with a DO loop. Procedures other than the main procedure will <u>not be executed unless called</u> from the main procedure (or from a procedure called by the main procedure, as explained in Section 1.4).

1.3 <u>Procedure Calls</u>

1.3.1 <u>Calls and Arguments</u>

A procedure call is a PL/I statement, and can be placed anywhere within a program that a PL/I statement may appear. The form of a procedure call is

    CALL procedure-name (list of arguments);

The procedure-name must be the name of a procedure. The arguments are separated by commas. Each argument may be a reference to a variable, a constant, an expression, or the name of an array. The first argument corresponds to (replaces) the first parameter of the procedure, the second argument corresponds to the second parameter, and so on. Examples are:

    CALL SWAP(B(1), A(2));

    CALL SEARCH(A, 20, X||Y, I);

Execution of a procedure call includes replacing parameters by arguments. We have described this replacement as a sort of "textual" substitution of one name for another. However, this replacement can be interpreted in several different ways, and we must therefore define more carefully what we mean by replacement, or parameter-argument correspondence. In order to do this, we must adopt a notation for describing which variables can be referenced at each point in a program.

Let us draw the parameters and variables of a procedure in a box. Thus from (1.3.1a) we can assume that the main procedure has declared in it an array A(1:2) and four simple variables I, J, X and T, while procedure SWAP uses names X, Y and T. Note that we have drawn an arrow from each variable name to the line to which it is attached. Recall from Section I.2 that a name is attached by means of an arrow to a line; we omit the arrows only when the two are close enough. We will see that parameters are also attached to lines at the time parameter-argument correspondence is made. But in (1.3.1a) no arrows are attached to parameters X and Y because the procedure has not been called yet.

When executing a statement, to determine which variable a name references, we look <u>only</u> in the box of variables for the procedure in which that statement occurs. Although both the

main procedure and SWAP have a variable T, these two variables
are completely separate and distinct. Names declared in
one internal procedure have absolutely no effect on the names
used in another.

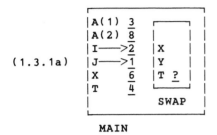

(1.3.1a)

                        MAIN

1.3.2 Calls with Matching Arguments

    Assume for the moment that each argument refers to a
variable, and that the type attributes of each argument match
the attributes of the corresponding parameter.   That is, they
are both fixed, or both float, or both character strings, etc.
With these assumptions, we now explain in detail   exactly how a
procedure call is executed in the computer in terms   of boxes
containing the names defined within a procedure.   In   doing
so, we will illustrate using the call CALL SWAP(I,J); where
the variables in the main procedure are given in Fig. 1a on
the next page, and procedure SWAP is

```
        SWAP: PROCEDURE(X,Y);
               /* EXCHANGE VALUES OF X AND Y */
               DECLARE (X, Y) FIXED ;
(1.3.2a)       DECLARE (T) FIXED;
               T = X;
               X = Y;
               Y = T;
               END /* SWAP */;
```

    Execution of a procedure call takes place as follows:

    1. Draw a box to contain the variables and parameters of
    the procedure (Fig. 1b).

    2. Within the box write the parameters (Fig. 1c).

    3. Make the parameter-argument correspondence as follows:
    Each argument name has an arrow leading from it. For each
    parameter, draw an arrow from it to the same line to which
    the corresponding argument points (Fig. 1d).

    4. Within the box, write the variables declared locally
    within the procedure, using "?" to indicate that a value
    has not yet been assigned (Fig. 1e).

5. Execute the procedure body. Whenever a parameter is referenced, use the line to which it is attached. (The results of executing statements T=X; X=Y; Y=T; are shown in Figs. 1f, 1g, and 1h.)

6. Erase the procedure's box and any arrows leading from it; execution of the procedure call is now finished (Fig. 1i). Study these steps carefully. Understanding this simple case of parameter-argument correspondence is necessary for understanding the more complicated situations that will arise later.

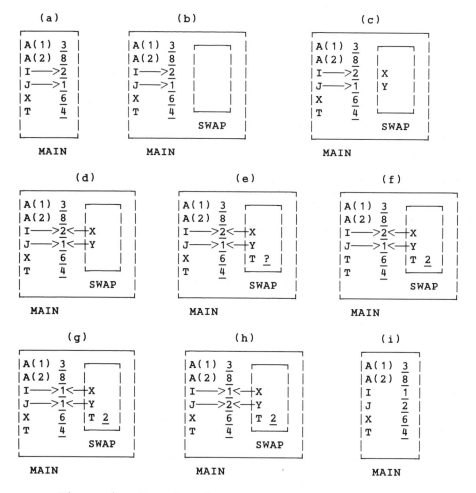

Figure 1.   Example of Execution of a Procedure Call

Figure 1 illustrates several important points. First, the names declared in one internal procedure have nothing to do with names used in others. The name of a parameter and corresponding argument may happen to be the same (as in CALL

SWAP(X,I);) but only then do they refer to the same variable. Arguments and parameters are matched strictly according to the order in which they appear in their respective lists -- their names are irrelevant in this matching.

Secondly, a parameter refers to a line only while the procedure is executing. Thirdly, whenever an assignment X=... is executed where X is a parameter, the corresponding argument variable has its value changed <u>immediately</u>. The change does not occur after the procedure is finished executing, but at the time the assignment statement is executed. Note also that the arrow from parameter to argument is drawn before execution of the procedure body begins. This means that if a subscripted variable A(I) is used as an argument, the variable to which this refers is determined <u>before</u> the body is executed, and is not changed if I happens to be changed during execution of the body (as in CALL SWAP(I,A(I));).

During execution of a program, the equivalent of these boxes and arrows are actually "drawn" as we have depicted. Storage locations are set aside to hold the variables and the "arrows" of a procedure. The arrow locations contain references to the locations where the arguments reside.

Thus far, we have assumed that each argument was a variable, with the same type attributes as the corresponding parameter. In the next few sections, we relax this restriction, and also discuss arrays as arguments. The only difference in executing a procedure call will be in step 3 where we draw the arrows to show the parameter-argument correspondence; otherwise execution of the procedure call is exactly the same.

1.3.3 <u>Arguments</u> <u>with</u> <u>Different</u> <u>Types</u>

The rule for parameter-argument correspondence is this:

(1.3.3a)   During execution, the arrow leading from a parameter X
            (say) which is not an array must point to a <u>variable</u>
            <u>with</u> <u>exactly</u> <u>the</u> <u>same</u> <u>attributes</u> as specified for X.

If the argument is a variable whose attributes differ from those of the parameter, then the argument is <u>automatically</u> evaluated to yield a value; a new variable, called a <u>dummy</u> <u>argument</u>, is generated and initialized to this value; and the parameter arrow is drawn to this dummy argument. This dummy argument will never be referenced by name, so it doesn't matter what name we give it. We indicate such automatically generated variables by using lower case letters for their names.

Consider CALL SWAP(B,J); of the procedure defined in (1.3.2a), where B is float and J is fixed . The values of B and J are given by Fig. 2a. Since B is float and the corresponding parameter is fixed, the value 2E0 of B is

converted to 2 and stored in a new dummy argument which we have
arbitrarily named "d".   Parameter X corresponds to this dummy
argument as shown in Fig. 2b.   Fig. 2c shows the state of
affairs after execution of the procedure body, while Fig. 2d
shows the situation after the call has been completed. Note
that the dummy argument was deleted since it couldn't be
referred to any more.

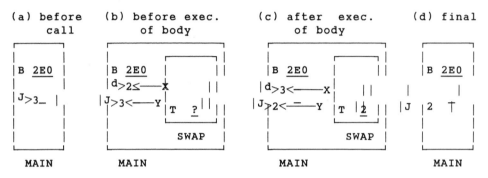

Figure 2.   Execution of CALL SWAP(B,J);

    This example illustrates an important implication of rule
(1.3.3a).   If we want an argument to be used as an "output"
argument -- that is, if we want the procedure to store a value
in it -- then the type attributes of the argument must match
those of the parameter exactly. Procedure SWAP could not store
a value in B because it had no way of referencing B.   In this
example, the effect of the procedure call was to store B's value
in J, but not J's value in B. This almost certainly indicates
an error in program design.

    Because of the hidden effects that may occur, as in the above
example, SP/k gives a warning message before program execution
for each argument which doesn't match its parameter. Look at
these warnings carefully. For input arguments they probably
don't matter. For output arguments they indicate an error on
your part.   Actually, some versions of PL/I don't allow
nonmatching arguments unless an extra "entry declaration" is
also given   (see Appendix B.5).   In general, it is good
programming practice to always make the type attributes of
arguments exactly match the type attributes of the corresponding
parameters.

1.3.4 <u>Expressions</u> <u>and</u> <u>Constants</u> <u>as</u> <u>Arguments</u>

Consider the following procedure:

```
           LARGE: PROCEDURE (A, B, ANS);
               /* STORE IN ANS THE LARGER OF A AND B */
(1.3.4a)       DECLARE (A, B, ANS) FIXED ;
               IF A > B THEN
                   ANS = A;
               ELSE
                   ANS = B;
               END /* LARGE */;
```

Suppose we wish to store in L the larger of 3 and F+G, where F,
G, and L are fixed variables. We can do this using

(1.3.4b) CALL LARGE (3, F+G, L);

This is equivalent to using the following sequence of statements
(where T1 and T2 are FIXED variables not used elsewhere):

```
(1.3.4c) T1 = 3;
         T2 = F+G;
         CALL LARGE(T1, T2, L);
```

Expressions and constants as arguments thus do not add "power"
to the language, they just provide convenience and readability.

When an expression or constant is used as an argument, the
parameter-argument correspondence is performed in three steps:

1. Create a new dummy argument with attributes of the
   parameter.
2. Evaluate the expression or constant and assign the
   result to the dummy argument.
3. Draw the arrow from the parameter to the dummy argument.

Fig. 3 illustrates this for (1.3.4b). The dummy variables are
designated as p and q, but these names are wholly for the
purpose of explanation -- they cannot be used in the program.

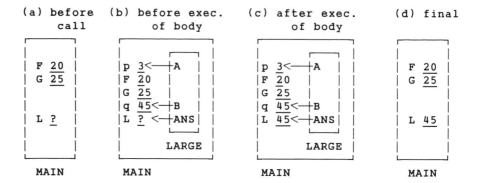

(a) before   (b) before exec.   (c) after exec.   (d) final
    call   of body   of body

Figure 3. Execution of CALL LARGE(3, F+G, L);

1.3.5 <u>Array</u> <u>Names</u> <u>as</u> <u>Arguments</u>

An n-dimensional array B can be an argument only if the
corresponding parameter A (say) is so specified, by using
A(*,*,...,*) in its declaration (with n asterisks). Suppose the
type attributes of B and A match.   Then during parameter-
argument correspondence, an arrow is drawn from the parameter A
to the whole array B.   For example

```
SEARCH: PROCEDURE(A, N, X, J);
    /* SEARCH A(1:N) FOR VALUE X, SET J SO THAT A(J)=X */
    /* STORE 0 IN J IF NO SUCH INTEGER EXISTS */
    DECLARE (A(*), X) FIXED;
    DECLARE (N, J) FIXED;
    DO J = 1 TO N BY 1;
        IF A(J) = X THEN
            RETURN;
        END;
    J = 0;
    END /* SEARCH */;
```

Consider execution of CALL SEARCH(B,M,X,K); where the array B
and variables M, X and K are as described in Fig. 4a.   The
parameter-argument   correspondence   is depicted in Fig. 4b. Note
that parameter A refers to the whole array B(0:4), even though
the procedure does not reference every element. Since M is 2,
only B(1:2) is referenced and the result of execution is a 0 in
K.

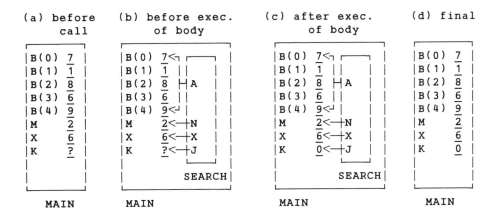

Figure 4.   Execution of CALL SEARCH(B, M, X, K);

The type matching considerations of Section 1.3.3 also apply
to array arguments. In PL/I, if the type attributes of the
argument do not match those of the parameter, then the whole
array is copied into a new "dummy" array, and the arrow is drawn
to this new array. Since creating a dummy array is inherently
an inefficient operation, SP/k enforces the stricter rule that
the type attributes of array arguments and corresponding array
parameters must match exactly.

1.4 Nested Procedure Calls

Thus far we have been considering only procedure calls in the
main procedure. Actually, a procedure call may appear anywhere
that a statement may appear, and this includes the body of any
procedure. A call is simply placed wherever the action of the
procedure is required, with the call designating the
particular arguments upon which the procedure is to be executed.

(1.4a) illustrates a complete program consisting of a main
program and three internal procedures. The main procedure,
reads in a list of integers, calls procedure SORT to sort the
list, and then prints the list. This SORT uses a successive
minima algorithm, a fairly obvious variation of the one used in
Section III.2.3. It calls two other procedures: FINDMIN to
determine the array element with minimum value, and SWAP to
interchange the value of two variables. The ordering of the
four procedure definitions in (1.4a) is significant; SP/k
requires that a procedure be declared before it is used.

The program consists of four separate sections, each of which
performs some logically independent task. Each can be
understood by itself, without having to understand how the

others   work.   In actual   practice one would rarely   write   such
short procedures as are shown here; this program would have been
just   as readable had we written just a main program and a   SORT
procedure, performing the FINDMIN and SWAP commands   within   the
sort   procedure itself. We have written (1.4a) this way just   to
illustrate the use of nested calls.

```
        SORTING: PROCEDURE OPTIONS(MAIN);
          /* READ IN 3 INTEGERS, PRINT IN SORTED ORDER */
          DECLARE (A(3),I)FIXED;

          SORT: PROCEDURE(X,N);
            /* SORT ARRAY X(1:N) USING SUCCESSIVE MINIMA */
            DECLARE (X(*),N) FIXED;
            DECLARE (I,J) FIXED;

            FINDMIN: PROCEDURE(X,I,N,J);
              /* STORE IN J THE INDEX OF MINIMUM VALUE OF X(I:N) */
              DECLARE (X(*),I,N,J) FIXED;
              DECLARE (K) FIXED;
              J = I;
(1.4a)        DO K = I+1 TO N BY 1;
                IF X(K) < X(J)THEN
                   J = K;
                END;
              END /* FINDMIN */;

            SWAP: PROCEDURE(X,Y);
              /* SWAP VALUES OF X AND Y */
              DECLARE (X,Y) FIXED;
              DECLARE (T) FIXED;
              T = X;
              X = Y;
              Y = T;
              END /* SWAP */;

            DO I = 1 TO N-1 BY 1;
              /* PUT MINIMUM OF X(I:N) IN X(I) */
              CALL FINDMIN(X,I,N,J);
              CALL SWAP(X(I),X(J));
              END;
            END /* SORT */;

          /* READ INTEGERS, CALL SORT, PRINT INTEGERS */
          DO I = 1 TO 3 BY 1;
            GET LIST(A(I));
            END;
          CALL SORT(A,3);
          DO I = 1 TO 3 BY 1;
            PUT LIST(A(I));
            END;
          END /* SORTING */;
    $DATA
      2  8  1
```

Let us now execute program (1.4a). Fig. 6a shows the variables after the list of values has been read, and just before execution of CALL SORT(A,3). Note that I is 4 because of the way the preceding loop is executed. Fig. 6b shows the state of affairs after the SORT procedure body execution has begun, and just before CALL FINDMIN(X,I,N,J) executed for the first time. Thus I (within SORT) has the value 1. J still has no value.

The call of FINDMIN is now executed. A box for procedure FINDMIN is drawn, the parameter correspondences are made, and the local variable K is created. Fig. 6c shows the boxes at this stage, just before execution of the procedure body. Note that the arrow for argument X of SORT has been copied over to parameter X of FINDMIN. Similarly parameter N of FINDMIN points where parameter N of SORT does.

Now procedure body FINDMIN executes and terminates. We show the boxes just after the completion of the call on FINDMIN and before execution of CALL SWAP(X(I),X(J)) in Fig. 6d. J is now 3 since A(3) contains the minimum value of A(1:3). We now execute the call. Fig. 6e shows the state of affairs just before execution of the body of SWAP. <u>Note</u> <u>carefully</u> <u>where</u> <u>parameters</u> <u>X</u> <u>and</u> <u>Y</u> <u>point</u>. The parameter X corresponds to the argument X(I) in SORT. Since X in SORT is A and I has the value 1, this is A(1). Similarly, Y refers to A(3). Thus SWAP will exchange the values of A(1) and A(3).

When SWAP finishes, its box will be deleted and we will return to the point following the call of SWAP in SORT. The values of A(1) and A(3) will be interchanged.

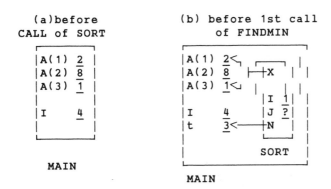

Figure 6. Partial Execution of Program (1.4a)

(c) before exec. of
body of FINDMIN

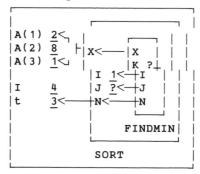

MAIN

(d) before call of SWAP

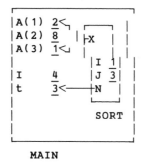

(e)Before exec. of body of SWAP

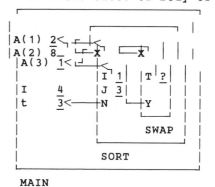

Figure 6. continued

1.5 Dynamic Storage

Section 1.3.2 described the execution of a procedure call. The creation and erasure of the boxes in Figure 1 accurately reflect what actually takes place during each execution of a call. In particular the local variables, such as T in Figure 1, are created as the procedure is entered and destroyed on return from the procedure. This happens each time that the procedure is executed; during the intervals between executions the local variables simply do not exist. This process is called "dynamic storage management" and in PL/I variables that are treated in this way are said to be in "automatic" storage.

Dynamic storage management permits efficient use of storage space. Since variables are assigned space only when their procedures are being executed, the same space can be used at

different times for different variables. It also permits
"recursive" use of procedures, to be described in Section 3.
However, it also means that with automatic variables information
cannot be preserved from one execution of a procedure to the
next. For example, a procedure could not even keep a cumulative
count of the number of times it had been called.

To permit retention of information a variable can be placed
as a local variable in a containing procedure. For example if
we were desirable to count the number of times FINDMIN and SWAP
were called in (1.4a) then variables COUNT#FIMDMIN and
COUNT#SWAP could be declared in SORT. If the information needed
to be retained for an even longer time, the variables could be
declared in the main procedure.

An array takes space proportional to the number of variables
in it. The programmer can control the use of memory to some
extent by using procedures. Suppose that in two _different_ parts
of a program, two arrays A(1:1000) and B(-500:0,1:20) are to
be used. First the array A is used, and then later on the array
B, but not both together. The programmer could structure his
program as shown in (3.1c). The two arrays would be able to
share the same space, since neither exists when the other does.
This reduces the total amount of storage space needed by the
program.

```
        X: PROCEDURE OPTIONS(MAIN);
            . . .
            Y: PROCEDURE;
                DECLARE A(1:1000) FIXED;
                . . .
                END /* Y */;
(5.1)
            Z: PROCEDURE;
                DECLARE B(-500:0,1:20) FLOAT DECIMAL;
                . . .
                END /* Z */;
            . . .
            END /* X */;
```

One could perform the same task for simple variables, but the
memory space saved is generally not worth the effort.

1.6 Function Procedures

Suppose we have a procedure to calculate the average of an array of elements:

```
        AVERAGE: PROCEDURE(A, N, ANS);
            /* STORE IN ANS THE AVERAGE OF A(1:N) */
            DECLARE (A(*), ANS) FLOAT;
            DECLARE (N) FIXED;
            DECLARE (SUM) FLOAT,
                    (I) FIXED;
(1.6a)      SUM = 0;
            DO I = 1 TO N BY 1;
                SUM = SUM + A(I);
                END;
            ANS = SUM/N;
            END /* AVERAGE */;
```

In order to use (1.6a), say to find the average of B(1:M), we must write

```
        CALL AVERAGE(B,M,ANSWER);
```

It would be convenient to be able to use _functional_ notation, as we do when we use SIN(Y) or MOD(X,Y) or SQRT(X+Y). For example, if we wanted to find the sum of the averages of arrays B(1:M) and C(1:L), we would like to write

```
(1.6b)   SUM = AVERAGE(B,M) + AVERAGE(C,L);
```

instead of

```
         CALL AVERAGE(B,M,ANS1);
(1.6c)   CALL AVERAGE(C,L,ANS2);
         SUM = ANS1 + ANS2;
```

We can use (1.6b) if we define AVERAGE to be a _function procedure_:

```
        AVERAGE: PROCEDURE(A, N) RETURNS(FLOAT);
            /* FUNCTION RETURNS THE AVERAGE OF ARRAY A(1:N) */
            DECLARE (A(*)) FLOAT;
            DECLARE (N) FIXED;
            DECLARE (SUM) FLOAT,
                    (I) FIXED;
(1.6d)      SUM = 0;
            DO I = 1 TO N BY 1;
                SUM = SUM + A(I);
                END;
            RETURN(SUM/N);
            END /* AVERAGE */;
```

Function procedures differ from called procedures in three respects:

1. A function must describe the type of value it returns. This is done in (1.6d) by the RETURNS(FLOAT) phrase in the procedure heading.

2. When it returns, a function must indicate what value is to be returned as the value of the function. In (1.6d) this is indicated by <u>executing</u> the statement RETURN(SUM/N); at the end of the procedure body; the value of SUM/N is returned in FLOAT form.

3. A function is invoked using functional form rather than by the CALL statement.

The format of a function definition is:

```
function-name: PROCEDURE( list of parameters )
               RETURNS( attribute );
      /* comment summarizing what the function does */
      Declarations to specify parameters
      Declarations to create local variables
      Function body (including RETURN(expr);)
      END /* function-name */;
```

The phrase "RETURNS(attributes)" specifies the attributes of the value being returned by the function. The only allowable attributes are FIXED, FLOAT, CHARACTER(constant) VARYING, and BIT. An array cannot be returned as the value of a function. (Note that the phrase in the heading uses the keyword "RETURNS", while the statement keyword is "RETURN".)

The list of parameters, declarations, function body, and the function-name are exactly as described for procedures, <u>except</u> that to terminate the body, a statement of the form

```
              RETURN( expression );
```

must be <u>executed</u>. The value returned is the value of the expression.

As a final example, we write a program to read in two values and print their maximum. The first program uses procedural notation, the second functional notation for a function MAXI which returns the maximum of its two parameters.

```
$JOBK ID='KEN SEVCIK'
  M: PROCEDURE OPTIONS(MAIN);
     /* READ TWO VALUES AND PRINT THEIR MAXIMUM */
     DECLARE (A, B, C) FLOAT ;
     MAXI: PROCEDURE(A, B, C);
        /* STORE IN C THE MAXIMUM OF A AND B */
        DECLARE (A, B, C) FLOAT;
        IF A > B THEN
           C = A;
        ELSE
           C = B;
        END /* MAXI */;

     GET LIST(A, B);
     CALL MAXI(A, B, C);
     PUT LIST(A, B, C);
     END /* M */;

$JOBK ID='KEN SEVCIK'
  M: PROCEDURE OPTIONS(MAIN);
     /* READ TWO VALUES AND PRINT THEIR MAXIMUM */
     DECLARE (A, B) FLOAT;
     MAXI: PROCEDURE(A,B) RETURNS(FLOAT);
        /* RETURN MAXIMUM OF A AND B */
        DECLARE (A, B) FLOAT;
        IF A > B then
           RETURN(A);
        ELSE
           RETURN(B);
        END /* MAXI */;

     GET LIST (A, B);
     PUT LIST(A, B, MAXI(A,B));
     END /* M */;
```

1.7 Procedures and Variables

Basic to all procedures is the concept of an independent
environment, which in PL/I is called a "block". Procedures are
one type of block.   The significance of a block is largely in
relation to the ownership, creation and deletion of variables.
Each variable belongs to one particular procedure, the one in
which it was declared, but we are about to discuss
arrangements in which a variable can be used in other procedures
in addition to the owning block.

In SP/k a variable is what PL/I calls "automatic". An
automatic variable is created each time an execution of its
owning procedure is initiated, and destroyed when that execution
is completed. Note that this is not the same thing as saying
"created as a procedure is entered" and "destroyed when the

procedure is left" since we often temporarily leave a procedure
before its execution is completed, and then later return to
resume its execution. For example, when we call another
procedure from the main procedure we temporarily leave the main
procedure, but its execution is not completed.

During the interval between the initiation and completion of
execution of a procedure we say that that procedure is
"active". At some instant we may not be executing that
procedure, having left temporarily to execute some other
procedure, but if the execution has not been completed the
procedure is considered active. Now we can say that an
automatic variable is created as execution of a procedure is
initiated and exists as long as that procedure is active.

1.7.1 Nested Procedures

In Section 1.4 we described the nesting of calls of
procedures. Now we consider the nesting of their definitions --
the positioning of the statements that define the
procedure. Suppose there are five procedures, A, B, C, D and
T, defined as shown in Figure 7.

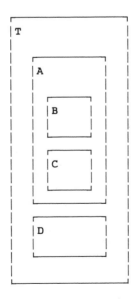

Figure 7. Nested Procedures

T is the main procedure; in PL/I it is called an external
procedure. Procedures A and D are internal; their defining
statements are completely contained in the procedure T. Nesting
can continue to any required depth. For example, procedures B
and C are internal to procedure A, further there could be a
procedure E defined internal to B, a procedure F internal to E,

etc. Procedures must either be external or entirely internal to
some other procedure. They are not allowed to overlap -- one
procedure cannot be partially internal to another.

The significance of the position of a procedure is that it
determines the names of variables and procedures that are
accessible to the procedure. This controls which procedures
can be executed from a given procedure, and also the means of
communication between procedures. This is discussed in the next
section.

1.8 The Scope of Variables

The "scope" of a variable consists of all the procedures
that have access to it. When we were dealing only with main
procedures and had no nesting of procedures the scope rules
were very simple: the scope of a variable was the single
procedure in which it was declared. This simplicity was the
principal reason we limited our initial consideration to main
procedures. With nested procedures the scope rules become more
complicated.

(1.8a)   The scope of a name in PL/I is the procedure b in
           which it is defined, including any procedures internal
           to procedure b that are not explicitly excluded.

For example, if procedures are nested as in Figure 7 and a
variable N is declared in procedure A, the scope of N is A, and
also B and C (assuming that B and C are not specifically
excluded), but not D. This means that D has no access to N --
it cannot use that particular variable N in any way. This is
true regardless of what might be declared in D. D cannot get
access to N unless it is deliberately passed to D as an
argument of a call from some procedure that is within the scope
of N. Another variable N could be declared in procedure D, but
this variable would have nothing to do with the variable in
procedure A that happens to have the same name.

Procedures B and C are within the scope of N unless they are
specifically excluded by declaring an N of their own. Suppose
there is an assignment statement

          N = 5;

somewhere in procedure B. If there is no declaration of an N
in B then this assignment refers to A's N and its
execution will assign a value to A's N. On the other hand,
if there is a declaration of N in B, then B is no longer in
the scope of A's N. The assignment statement refers to B's
N, an entirely different variable from the one in A that
happens to have the same name.

The scope of a variable N declared in B is B and any procedure internal to B that does not use the name N for some other purpose. Note that neither A, C nor D is within the scope of B's N -- regardless of what declarations may or may not be in those procedures.

Suppose there is a procedure E internal to B. Assuming there is no declaration of an N within E any use of the name N in E will refer to B's N. Now suppose that the program were changed to remove the declaration of an N in block B. Uses of the name N in B would now refer to A's N (since B no longer has an N of its own). Furthermore, any use of the name N in procedure E also refers to A's N. The point is that the meaning of a name in procedure E has been changed without any line in the definition of E being changed. The meaning of an internal procedure can be altered by a change in a containing procedure. Since the change may be several pages away the result can be very mystifying. A common dialog goes something like this:

> student: "The computer is fouled up. This program worked last time, but now it won't and I didn't change a thing."

> tutor: "Nothing?"

> student: "Well, nothing in the part we're talking about."

The use of internal procedures is more complicated than the use of main programs, and therefore riskier. If you are not willing to study the scope rules until you really understand them -- then stay away from internal procedures.

1.8.1 Local and Global Names

Within the single procedure in which it is defined a name is said to be "local". Referring again to Figure 7, if a variable N is declared in procedure A then "N is local to A". N may be accessible to other procedures (perhaps B and C) but it is local only to A. When a name is used in a procedure other than the one in which it is defined it is said to be "global". If the scope of N defined in A includes procedure B then "N is global to B".

PL/I allows many different objects to use the same name in a single program, but the language is designed so that no two objects of the same name ever exist within the same procedure. Hence there is never any ambiguity in the use of a name -- each use of a name refers to exactly one object, no matter how many things in the program may happen to have the same name. The trick is to understand which object is referred to by each usage. It should be obvious by now that in a block-structured language (like PL/I) the meaning of a statement can depend critically upon context. That is, exactly the same statement could be written in A and B (of Figure 7) and have two quite different meanings.

The resolution of names -- deciding which object is referred to by a particular usage -- is by the following rules:

(1.8.1a)   A <u>local</u> object always takes <u>precedence</u> over a global object. If there is a local N in B, no global N can ever be referred to in B.

(1.8.1b)   Each procedure inherits global objects from the procedure in which it is defined.

1.8.2 <u>The Scope of Procedure-Names</u>

The rules for the scope of procedure-names are exactly the same as those for variables -- that is, (1.8a) applies to all names. The definition of a procedure-name is accomplished when it is attached to a particular procedure. Writing PA: PROCEDURE... defines a procedure-name PA; CALL PA... references that name.

A procedure-name can only be referenced from procedures that are within the scope of that procedure-name. Consider, for example, Figure 7. Since procedure B is defined in A the name B is considered to belong to A and not to B. Hence the scope of B, according to (1.2a), is procedure A and procedures internal to A that are not specifically excluded. This means that the statement CALL B can be used in procedure A, but not in procedure D since D is not within the scope of name B.

Procedure C is within the scope of B only if it does not exclude itself by declaring its own use of the name B. Assuming it is not excluded, CALL B can be executed from within C. The same thing holds for procedure B itself. If the name B is not defined for some other use within procedure B, then procedure B is within the scope of procedure-name B (since procedure-name B belongs to A, and procedure B is just like C with respect to A). This means that a procedure is <u>allowed</u> <u>to</u> <u>call</u> <u>itself</u>; a useful feature that is described in Section 3.

To summarize, with respect to Figure 7, assuming that the names A, B, C and D are not otherwise defined:

A, B, C, D can be called from A

A, B, C, D can be called from B

A, B, C, D can be called from C

A   and   D can be called from D

A   and   D can be called from T.

1.8.3 Placement of Internal Procedures

The SP/k rules for the placement of internal procedures are as follows:

1. The definition of an internal procedure is positioned within another procedure, as for example, B or C in Figure 7. The definition of any internal procedures must immediately follow the declaration of local variables (if any), and must precede any other statements in the procedure.

2. An internal procedure may be called only from procedures that are within the scope of the procedure-name. That is, in Figure 7 neither B nor C can be called from within D.

3. Communication with an internal procedure, in addition to the arguments of the call, includes variables of the containing procedure (as long as the names have not been declared for another purpose in the internal procedure).

4. SP/k requires that the definition of a procedure must precede any use of the procedure. Thus if one internal procedure calls another internal procedure, the called procedure must be placed before the calling procedure.

Since the definition of an internal procedure is placed within another procedure you should wonder what happens when one "runs into" the definition of a procedure in the course of executing the containing procedure. The answer is that the procedure definition is invisible to normal execution of the containing procedure. You cannot "run into" a procedure to execute it; the only way to execute it is to invoke it with the CALL statement (or functionally, if it is a function procedure). For example, if A, B and C of Figure 7 are all procedures their definitions should be positioned as follows:

```
A: PROCEDURE;
   B: PROCEDURE;
      ...
      END /* B */;
   C: PROCEDURE;
      ...
      END /* C */;
   ...
   END /* A */;
```

Program (8a) below is a nonsense program which illustrates the key points concerning internal procedures. You should be sure you understand why the first execution of CALL P1; produces the following output:

```
          P2  8      9      7     4
          P1  8      7      5
          P2  9     10      8     4
          P1  9      8      5
```

```
    P1: PROCEDURE;
            DECLARE (I,J,K) FIXED;
            P2: PROCEDURE(H);
                DECLARE (H) FIXED;
                DECLARE (I,K) FIXED;
                I = H+1;
                K = 4;
                J = J+1;
                PUT SKIP LIST('P2',H,I,J,K);
                RETURN;
                END /* P2 */;
```

(8a)
```
            J = 6;
            K = 5;
            DO I = 8 TO 9 BY 1;
              CALL P2(I);
              PUT SKIP LIST('P1',I,J,K);
              END;
            RETURN;
            END /* P1 */;
```

1.9 Tracing Execution of Procedures

Suppose that the definitions of procedures A, B and C are nested and that procedures E and F are internal to B. Suppose variables were declared in these four procedures as follows:

```
    A: PROCEDURE OPTIONS(MAIN);
    DECLARE (X,Y) FIXED;
    B: PROCEDURE;
            DECLARE (X,Z) FIXED;
            E: PROCEDURE;
                DECLARE (Y,W) FIXED;
                ...
                END /* E */;
(1.9a)      F: PROCEDURE;
                DECLARE (X,Z) FIXED;
                ...
                END /* F */;
            ...
            END /* B */;
    C: PROCEDURE;
            DECLARE (X,W) FIXED;
            ...
            END /* C */;
      ...
    END /* A */;
```

The meaning of the variable names in the different procedures
is shown in (1.9b):

	In procedure:	Name:	
	A	X	X local to A
		Y	Y local to A
	B	X	X local to B
		Y	Y declared in A
		Z	Z local to B
(1.9b)			
	E	X	X declared in B
		Y	Y local to E
		Z	Z declared in B
		W	W local to E
	F	X	X local to F
		Y	Y declared in A
		Z	Z local to F
	C	X	X local to C
		Y	Y declared in A
		W	W local to C

During execution of (1.9a) variables will be created as the
procedure in which they are declared becomes active, and
then destroyed when it becomes inactive. We can trace this
process by drawing boxes for each procedure showing the
variables that are created as that procedure becomes active. If
a procedure is internal we draw its box inside that of the
containing procedure.

Figure 8 illustrates this for various points in the execution
of (1.9a). Fig. 8a shows the variables just after entering
execution of the procedure A. During execution of procedure B,
Figure 8b is in force. Note that there are two variables named
X. While executing in procedure B, we look first in B's box for
a variable. If we don't find it there we look in the
surrounding box, and then the box surrounding that one, and so
on. Thus while in B, X refers to the local variable of B.
Figure 2c shows the variables while executing in procedure E.
When procedure E is finished executing, its box is deleted and
we return to the state shown in Fig. 8b. When procedure F is
entered, a box for it is drawn as in Fig. 8d. When execution of
both F and B is finished, we are back to Fig. 8a.

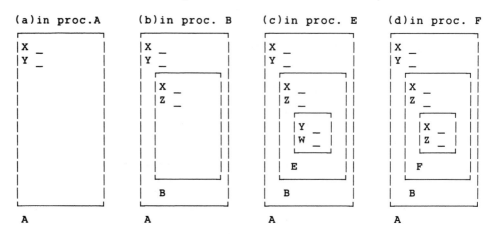

Figure 8.   Various Stages of Execution of (1.3a)

Section 1 <u>Exercises</u>

1. For each sequence of statements below, write a procedure
with that sequence as the body, complete with declarations. The
parameters are those variables and arrays described in the
comment. Other variables should be local to the procedure. All
variables are fixed.

```
a)      /* STORE THE MINIMUM OF A AND B IN C */
        IF A >= B THEN
            C = B;
        ELSE
            C = A;

b)      /* STORE THE SUM OF THE ELEMENTS OF A(1:N) IN SUM */
        SUM = 0;
        DO I = 1 TO N BY 1;
            SUM = SUM+A(I);
            END;

c)      /* REVERSE THE ELEMENTS OF ARRAY X(1:N) */
        FIRST = 1;
        LAST = N;
        DO WHILE (FIRST < LAST);
            T = X(FIRST);
            X(FIRST) = X(LAST);
            X(LAST) = T;
            FIRST = FIRST+1;
            LAST = LAST-1;
            END;
```

2. Make the program segments of Exercise 2, Section I.5, into
procedures. Only the variables described in the comment of each
program segment should be parameters.

3. Execute the following procedure calls by hand, drawing all
necessary boxes. Procedure SWAP is given in (1.1c). Assume all
variables are fixed.

```
a) CALL SWAP(A,B); where      A 5      B 6
b) CALL SWAP(T,X); where      T 3      X 4
c) CALL SWAP(Y,X); where      Y 1      X 8
d) CALL SWAP(V,V); where      V 3
```

4. Write procedures for the program segments of Exercises 4, 5
and 6 of Section I.5.

5. Write a procedure MEAN which, given an array segment X(1:N)
calculates the mean of the values. The mean is the sum of the
elements divided by N.

6. Execute the following procedure calls by hand, drawing all
the boxes. Procedure SEARCH is given in (1.2.1a). The
variables used are given below.

T(0) '6'	N0 0	F '8'
T(1) '8'	N1 1	G '5'
T(2) '4'	N2 2	H '6'
T(3) '9'	N3 3	I 3

    a) CALL SEARCH(T, N0, H, I);
    b) CALL SEARCH(T, N1, H, I);
    c) CALL SEARCH(T, N3, H, I);
    d) CALL SEARCH(T, N3, G, 3);
    e) CALL SEARCH(T, N3, F, I);

7. Execute the following procedure calls by hand, drawing all
the boxes. Be careful to construct dummy arguments if
necessary. Procedures SWAP and SEARCH are given in (1.1c) and
(1.2.1a). The variables used are:

SF(1)	AB [character(2) varying]	SV(1)	AB [character(2) varying]
SF(2)	CD [character(2) varying]	SV(2)	CD [character(2) varying]
SF(3)	EF [character(2) varying]	SV(3)	AB [character(2) varying]
ANS	?? [fixed]	ANT	?? [float]
A	3 [fixed]	B	4 [fixed]
C	5 [float]	D	6 [float]

    a) CALL SWAP(A,B);
    b) CALL SWAP(C,A);
    c) CALL SWAP(C,D);
    d) CALL SEARCH(SF, 0, SV(1), ANS);
    e) CALL SEARCH(SF, 0, SV(1), ANT);
    f) CALL SEARCH(SV, 1, SV(1), ANS);
    g) CALL SEARCH(SF, 1, SV(1), ANT);
    h) CALL SEARCH(SF, D-A, SV(1), ANS);
    i) CALL SEARCH(SF, D-A, SV(D-A), ANS);

8. Write a procedure MEDIAN which, given an array segment
X(1:N) calculates the median of the values. The median is the
value such that half the numbers are greater than that value and
half are less. One way to do this is to first sort the array
and then pick the middle value. If you use this method, use a
previously written sort procedure to do the sorting. But be
careful; MEDIAN should not change the order of the values in its
argument array -- a procedure should never modify the arguments
unless its specific task is to modify them. You may assume
N<=200.

9. Write a program to read a list of values and to print out
the mean and the median. Your program should use the procedures
written in Exercises 5 and 8.

10. Write a procedure which calculates sin(x) using the formula

$$sin(x) = x/1! \; - \; x^3/3! \; + \; x^5/5! \; - \; x^7/7! \; + \; ...$$

The number of terms of the series to be used should be a
parameter of the procedure. Next, write a program to compare
the values of sin(x) calculated using the built-in SIN function

against those values calculated by your procedure. Run the
program with various values of x and various values of the
number of terms used in the series.

11. Write a procedure to calculate the product of two N by N
matrices A(1:N,1:N) and B(1:N,1:N). Each element C(i,k) of the
resulting matrix C(1:N,1:N) is defined as the sum of the values

    A(i,j) * B(j,k)   for j = 1, ..., N.

12. Assume you are given the subroutine FLP shown below and
told only that IN is an input parameter, OUT is an output
parameter, and that the routine neither reads any data nor
prints any lines. Write a program that will allow FLP to be
tested by repeatedly calling it with different input values and
displaying the results. Your program will include FLP but not
change it in any way.

```
FLP: PROCEDURE(IN, OUT);
     DECLARE (IN) CHARACTER(*) VARYING,
        (OUT) FIXED;
     ...
     END /* FLP */;
```

13. What is the <u>execution</u> output from the program shown below:

```
LST: PROCEDURE OPTIONS(MAIN);
     DECLARE (L) CHARACTER(8) VARYING,
        (N,J,K) FIXED;

     EDITOR: PROCEDURE(NBR,CHR);
        DECLARE (NBR) FIXED;
        DECLARE (CHR) CHARACTER(*) VARYING;
        DUP: PROCEDURE(STRING);
           DECLARE (STRING) CHARACTER(*)VARYING;
           STRING = SUBSTR(STRING,1,1) || STRING;
           END /* DUP */;

        COMP: PROCEDURE(VALUE);
           DECLARE (VALUE) FIXED;
           VALUE = VALUE * VALUE;
           END /* COMP */;

        /* RETURN; */
        IF NBR ¬= 0 THEN
           CALL COMP(NBR);
        IF CHR ¬= ' ' THEN
           CALL DUP(CHR);
        END /* EDITOR */;
```

```
         GET LIST(J);
         DO K = 1 TO J BY 1;
             GET LIST(L,N);
             CALL EDITOR(N,L);
             PUT SKIP LIST(L,N);
             END;
         END /* LST */;
     $DATA
     4 'X' 4 'YY' -3 'XYX' 0 '4'
     4 'ABC' 567.9032
```

14. What would the <u>execution</u> output be for the program of exercise 13 if the comment /* RETURN; */ were replaced by the statement RETURN; ?

15. Write the body of the following procedure.

```
     REPTEST: PROCEDURE(WORD);
         /* REPLACE ALL REPEATED OCCURRENCES (EXCEPT THE FIRST)*/
         /* OF ANY CHARACTERS IN WORD BY '*' */
         DECLARE WORD CHARACTER(*) VARYING;
```

16. What is the <u>execution</u> output from the following program?

```
     PROB: PROCEDURE OPTIONS(MAIN);
             DECLARE (M) FIXED,
                (N) FIXED;
             N = 4;
             SUB: PROCEDURE(N);
                 DECLARE (N) FIXED,
                   (M) FIXED;
                 N = 5;
                 M = M + 2;
                 PUT SKIP LIST('INSIDE',M,N);
                 RETURN;
                 PUT SKIP LIST('STILL INSIDE',M,N);
                 END /* SUB */;

             DO M = 1 TO 3 BY 1;
                 CALL SUB(M);
                 PUT SKIP LIST('RESULT IS:',M,N);
                 END;
             PUT SKIP LIST('AFTER LAST CALL',M,N);
             END /* PROB */;
```

17. Write a procedure DEBLANK to serve as a subroutine to eliminate all blanks from a varying character string given as argument.

18. Modify the subroutine DEBLANK of Exercise 17 so that it has a second parameter, which is fixed. If the second argument has a non-zero value then DEBLANK is to return as the value of the second argument the <u>cumulative</u> number of blanks that have been eliminated in all calls so far (including the

current call). If the value of the second argument is zero then
it is to remain unchanged·by DEBLANK.

19. Complete the procedure FINDMAX started below. This is a
procedure to receive positive numbers and report the greatest of
the numbers received. Its action when called is the following:

> -if ACT=1 the value given in VAL is to be saved -- that is,
> it is to be stored in some available slot in the array
> VALS. If this can be done indicate success by returning
> with RES=1; if no space is available indicate failure by
> returning with RES=0.

> -if ACT=2 then the maximum of the values currently in VALS
> is to be returned in VAL. This maximum value is to be
> removed from VALS and the space it occupied made available
> for a new arrival. Indicate success by returning with
> RES=1 and failure (if VALS is empty) by returning with
> RES=0.

```
FINDMAX: PROC(VAL,ACT,RES);
    DECLARE VAL FLOAT,
       (ACT,RES) FIXED;
```

20. Complete a procedure GETMAX: PROC(VAL,ACT,RES); that has
exactly the same action from the caller's point-of-view as
FINDMAX of Exercise 19. GETMAX is to work by calling FINDMAX,
except that by keeping track of the kinds of calls GETMAX knows
when FINDMAX would fail (return with RES=0) so in these cases
GETMAX doesn't bother to call FINDMAX. It simulates FINDMAX's
action and returns directly. Do not change FINDMAX.

Section 2   The Uses of Procedures

Procedures provide two different capabilities:

1. The ability to write a section in terms of parameters so that it can be used for different variables at different times. This is effectively defining a new <u>operation</u> to be used in a program, like SORT(A,N) or SWAP(X,Y).

2. The ability to create an independent environment whose names are distinct from those of the rest of the program, and for which the total communication is clearly and completely specified. If a procedure is to be totally independent, it cannot make reference to any global variables.

2.1 <u>Subroutines</u>

The term "subroutine" is generally used to identify some sequence of statements that is needed in more than one place in a program. It is convenient to be able to write the common statements only once and use them as often and wherever necessary. If a subroutine is written in a general way, without commitment to particular variable names, its opportunity for use is clearly increased. This obvious use of procedures in PL/I was suggested by the examples of the preceding sections.

There is generally a sense of both <u>permanence</u> and <u>portability</u> in subroutines. That is, they are written so that they can be used in more than one program. There are various "libraries" of subroutines that are quite permanent and widely used. In effect, the built-in functions of PL/I -- SQRT, SIN, COS, MOD, etc. -- constitute such a library.

Subroutines can be considered a means of <u>extending</u> a programming language; of adding whatever operators or statements the user needs that the language doesn't happen to offer. In Part III we often used a statement at a higher level than PL/I, and then translated or expanded it into PL/I. By writing a subroutine to perform that task we effectively add that high-level statement to the language (at least temporarily). For example, in Section III.2.3 we developed a program to order the

elements of an array. If this were written as a procedure
with the array as argument then one could regard

        CALL SORT(A);

as part of the language. Moreover, the procedure could be saved
and reused in future programs whenever we had need of that
particular function. For all practical purposes we could now
think of "sort" as an operation available in our private
augmented-PL/I. In the development of future programs, once we
reached a point where the algorithm required "sort" we would not
have to refine that particular branch of the tree any further.

    Subroutines exploit both capabilities of procedures. The
first is obvious, but it is the second -- the independent
environment -- that allows a subroutine that contains no
references to global variables to be moved freely from one
program to another without any concern for whether the variables
in the subroutine happen to coincide with names in the host
program. This is possible because in SP/k, all variables must
be explicitly declared in each procedure.

2.2 Control Sections

    Procedures can be used simply to improve the clarity and
readability of programs. The techniques described in Part II,
which make small programs clear and understandable, don't always
work well when applied directly to large programs. For example,
if the units at the highest level are so long that it is
impossible to comprehend them as a single unit, then their role
and relationship to other units is less clear. The indentation
convention which makes vertical left-alignment significant in
understanding a program clearly works best if successive
statements with the same alignment appear on the same page. If
the successor to a particular unit is several pages away
vertical alignment is almost useless.

    Procedures can be used to alleviate all these problems by
reducing the apparent size of programs. Simply take some
convenient section of program, write it in some remote position
as an external procedure, and provide a CALL in its original
location. For example, suppose one has to perform some task on
each element of a 3-dimensional array:

```
          /* GRIMBLE THE ARRAY */
          DO I = 1 TO R BY 1;
              DO J = 1 TO S BY 1;
                  DO K = 1 TO T BY 1;
                      /* GRIMBLE AN ELEMENT */
                      END;
                  END;
              END;
```

This unit is clear as long as the expansion of the "grimble an element" task is not too large. If it is large, or if it involves many levels of nesting, it is worthwhile writing it as a procedure to be called by the unit shown above. These are not absolute bounds, but reasonable rules-of-thumb are:

1. No unit should be more than 50 lines (1 page) in length.
2. Nesting should not exceed 3 or at most 4 levels.

To maintain these limits, use procedures so that a call can replace some section of program.

Procedures should be routinely used in this way. In fact, any program of more than one or two pages should be entirely written in this manner. At the highest level the program should consist of little more than CALL statements. The main procedure, doing nothing but calling other procedures, serves as a <u>control</u> <u>section</u> of the program. It is short and shows clearly how the program is organized and the major steps in its action. A fine way to organize and present a large program is to have four sections:

1. A block of comments that fully and precisely describe the function of the program.
2. A block of comments serving as a "table of contents" for the following procedures.
3. A set of internal procedures, called by the control section.
4. A control section of not more than one page that calls various procedures to do the work.

Of course, some of the individual procedures may be so large that they would also benefit from the same treatment. Entry to such a procedure would encounter another control section, which would call other procedures. There is really no limit to how large a program can become, and still be understandable, if procedures are used to keep the apparent size down to where the techniques of Part II are effective.

2.3 <u>Sectional</u> <u>Independence</u>

A procedure containing no references to global variables is a usefully independent section of a program. Its communication with the rest of the program is <u>solely</u> <u>through</u> <u>its</u> <u>parameters</u>. When reading a program you can analyze each procedure separately, with complete confidence that no action (or mistake) elsewhere in the program will have the slightest effect on this procedure, except possibly in the way that it affects the values of arguments. The modularity sought in the discussion of "program units" in Part II is provided automatically by procedures.

When writing a program section, if you write it as an
internal procedure <u>and</u> declare all local variables in the
procedure you have less to worry about. You are entirely
concerned with <u>how</u> <u>to</u> <u>perform</u> <u>the</u> <u>required</u> action. You have no
concern that other sections of program will interfere with this
one, or that this section may have unexpected side effects
elsewhere. You need not remember what variable names have been
used elsewhere in the program; you can use whatever names are
most natural for this local use. For example, you can use I as
a subscript without wondering whether I is the index of some
outer loop, and hence must not be disturbed. <u>Warning</u>, because
of the PL/I rules for scope of names described in Section 1.8,
it is not always possible to detect that a programmer has failed
to declare a local variable if a global variable with the same
name has been declared in an outer block. Therefore, you should
always make sure that all local variables have been properly
declared.

This property is particularly useful when a program is to be
produced by a team of programmers. If each programmer (or
group) is assigned a separate procedure the communication
problems are minimized. Joint planning will concern only the
<u>function</u> of each procedure, and its <u>parameter</u> communication.
Given this "problem specification" the design and development of
the procedure can proceed as described in Part III, just as if
this were an independent problem. It should also be tested as
if it were an independent problem. The procedures should be
integrated into a final program only after there is great
confidence in their individual performance.

2.3.1 <u>Separation</u> <u>of</u> <u>Action</u> <u>and</u> <u>Control</u>

Recall the discussion in Section II.2 about the separation of
action and control. Schema (2a) was used as an example:

```
I = 0;
DO WHILE ( I < N );
   I = I+1;
   body
   END;
```

We wanted to state that this schema would repeat the body N
times regardless of what the body was. However, this statement
is true only if the body is restricted:

    1. it may not alter the values of I or N,
    2. and it may not execute a RETURN.

Suppose the body is written as a separate external procedure:

```
I = 0;
DO WHILE ( I < N );
    I = I+1;
    CALL BODY(...);
    END;
```

Now the body has no access to the variables I and N of the calling procedure (assuming that they are not given as arguments of the call and that any local variables named I and N (if any) are declared within BODY.) so it is not necessary to further restrict the body in this regard. The RETURN statement is now harmless in the body, since its execution will only accelerate return to calling procedure.

There is one other aspect of the question that was neglected in II.2 but should be mentioned here. For example, suppose the following were given as the body of the procedure:

```
DO WHILE ('1'B);
    END;
```

The procedure will never return from its first call, so obviously it will not be repeated N times. The guarantee of N repetitions only holds if the execution of the program is finite -- that is, if it will eventually terminate. For practical purposes, the guarantee only holds if the program will terminate in less than the time limit imposed. The DO WHILE loop shown here is obvious trouble, but unfortunately there are many less obvious ways to make an error in a program and have the same effect on execution. There might also be an error that terminates execution, which would also cause the procedure to fail to return.

Section 3   Recursive Procedures

A <u>recursive</u> <u>procedure</u> is one which calls itself -- a call of the procedure occurs within the body of the procedure itself, or in another procedure called by the original one. Recursion can be used quite extensively in programming, and in some cases can make difficult problems look easy. In fact, for some problems recursion is the natural way to describe the task.

3.1A_Simple_Example

The term <u>recursive</u> is derived from mathematics where some formulas are written using <u>recursive</u> <u>definition</u> - something is defined in terms of itself. For example, consider the function N! which for N > 0 is defined as

$$(3.1a)\qquad N! = N * (N-1) * (N-2) * \ldots * 2 * 1$$

This can also be defined recursively (in terms of itself) as

$$(3.1b)\qquad N! = \begin{cases} 1 & \text{if } N = 1 \\ N * (N-1)! & \text{if } N > 1 \end{cases}$$

We can write a recursive SP/k procedure to calculate N! for any positive integer N directly from this recursive definition:

```
          FACT: PROCEDURE(N,ANS);
             /* STORE N! IN ANS */
             DECLARE (N,ANS) FIXED;
             DECLARE (TEMP) FIXED;
             IF N = 1 THEN
                ANS = 1;
             ELSE
(3.1c)          DO;
                   CALL FACT(N-1,TEMP);
                   ANS = N*TEMP;
                   END:
          END /* FACT */;
```

PL/I requires keyword RECURSIVE to appear just before the semicolon in the heading of any recursive procedure. However in SP/k, all procedures are allowed to be recursive without any special declaration.

Consider the body of procedure FACT of (3.1c). If N is 1, the procedure stores 1 in ANS and returns, as required by definition (3.1b). If N > 1, then FACT is called a second time to store (N-1)! in TEMP. This value is then multiplied by N and the result is stored in ANS. This again satisfies definition (3.1b). Note that while discussing the call CALL FACT(N-1,TEMP); we don't worry about <u>how</u> FACT will work; we just assume that the procedure FACT will do its job -- will store (N-1)! in TEMP for us. That FACT also happens to be the procedure currently being executed should not disturb us; just think of it as two different procedures which just <u>look</u> the same.

This particular function N! is not a good example of a useful, efficient recursive procedure, since it can be written more easily and efficiently using definition (3.1a) as

```
FACT: PROCEDURE(N,ANS);
    /* STORE N! IN ANS */
    DECLARE (N,ANS) FIXED;
    DECLARE (I) FIXED;
    ANS = 1;
    DO I = 2 TO N BY 1;
        ANS = ANS*I;
        END;
    END /* FACT */;
```

However the recursive procedure for N! is short and simple enough to illustrate how recursion works and how we should deal with it, and we will use it extensively in the next section.

3.2 <u>Exploring Recursion</u>

Recursion may seem strange at first; it seems odd to be executing the same procedure two or more times at the same time. Let us motivate recursion as follows. Below we have written four procedures. (We have left out the declarations to save space). FACT1 will store in ANS the value N!, but only if N = 1. FACT2 produces N! if N≤2, by calling FACT1 to evaluate 1!. Similarly, FACT3 and FACT4 produce N! if N≤3 and N≤4, respectively, by calling on the other procedures. Thus we have written four different procedures, each of which calculates N! for a certain range of values of N.

These procedures are easy to understand, and obviously perform the required action. However, to be able to calculate 5! we must write a procedure FACT5, and for 6! a procedure FACT6, and so on. This is inconvenient.

Now note that all the procedures (except for the first) are similar, save for the <u>name</u> of the procedure being called. It would be useful to be able to have <u>one</u> procedure which we can call many times instead of many procedures once. Thus, we write the procedure FACT of (3.1c), with the same body as FACT2, FACT3 and FACT4 except for the name of the procedure being called. In effect, we can consider FACT to be as many procedures as we want. Each time it is called recursively, a new "copy" of the procedure is made and used for that call, and we can think of these different copies as having names FACT1, FACT2, FACT3, and so on.

```
FACT1: PROCEDURE(N,ANS);
   /* ANS = N! IF N = 1 */
   IF N = 1 THEN
      ANS = 1;
   ELSE
      Give error message;
   END /* FACT1 */;

FACT2: PROCEDURE(N,ANS);
   /* ANS = N! IF N ≤ 2 */
   IF N = 1 THEN
      ANS = 1;
   ELSE
      DO;
         CALL FACT1(N-1,TEMP);
         ANS = N*TEMP;
         END;
   END /* FACT2 */;

FACT3: PROCEDURE(N,ANS);
   /* ANS = N! IF N ≤ 3 */
   IF N = 1 THEN
      ANS = 1;
   ELSE
      DO;
         CALL FACT2(N-1,TEMP);
         ANS = N*TEMP;
         END;
   END /* FACT3 */;

FACT4: PROCEDURE(N,ANS);
   /* ANS = N! IF N ≤ 4 */
   IF N = 1 THEN
      ANS = 1;
   ELSE
      DO;
         CALL FACT3(N-1,TEMP);
         ANS = N*TEMP;
         END;
   END /* FACT4 */;
```

3.2.1 The Recursive Pattern

Most recursive definitions and recursive procedures have the
same pattern or flavor as does N!. For one or two values of the
argument, the result is defined nonrecursively, usually in a
quite simple manner. Thus, if N = 1, N! = 1. For all other
argument values, the result is defined recursively. This
recursive definition is arranged so that it is easy to see that
the recursion will terminate. For example for N!, if N > 1 we
have N! = N*(N-1)!. Here we see that the result for N! is
defined in terms of (N-1)! -- 5! is defined in terms of 4!
which is defined in terms of 3! and so on. Thus we must
eventually get to 1 and the process terminates.

As another example, we can define multiplication of two
positive, nonzero integers X and Y in terms of addition and
subtraction as follows:

$$X*Y = \begin{cases} X & \text{if } Y = 1 \\ X + X*(Y-1) & \text{if } Y > 1 \end{cases}$$

Y = 1 is the simple, nonrecursive case, while the second case is
recursive. The second argument Y decreases by one at each step
of the recursion, so that the process must terminate when Y = 1.

In general, any recursive procedure can be transformed into
one which is not recursive. The question then is why use
recursion? The answer is threefold:

1. A recursive procedure is often easier to understand and
prove correct.

2. Thinking recursively often leads to simpler algorithms,
even though they may finally end up in a nonrecursive form.

3. Recursive procedures tend to divide the problem into
smaller but similar ones which can be solved the same way,
and this often increases efficiency.

Once we understand the basic idea behind recursion, we find
that recursive procedures are much easier to understand than the
conventional iterative loops. Loops are hard because the way
they look is so different from the way they execute. The body
of the loop appears only once, but it may be executed any number
of times. This is also true of recursive procedures, but they
are easier to understand because of the way we read them. When
we see a call like CALL FACT(N-1,ANS); we can concentrate on
what FACT is doing, and leave until later how it does it. This
is much more difficult to do with iteration, and we have to
resort to invariant relations, as described in Section VII.2.

3.2.2 Executing Recursive Procedures by Hand

Executing recursive calls by hand is no more difficult than executing regular nested procedure calls. The only problem is that several boxes will exist for a procedure called recursively, one for each invocation which has not finished executing. To illustrate this, consider a call CALL FACT(3,X); in the main program, where the main program variables are as shown in Fig. 9a. We will now execute this call, assuming that FACT is an internal procedure, and show how the boxes are drawn at each point of execution. In order to keep track of which box for FACT to use at each point, we will put a superscript after the procedure name. Thus Fig. 9b shows the boxes just after the box for FACT is drawn for the main procedure call CALL FACT(3,X); but before the procedure body is executed. The superscript indicates the "level" of recursion.

The procedure body of FACT is now executed. Since $N \neq 1$, the call of FACT with arguments N-1 and TEMP is executed. Another box is drawn for this second call of FACT, labeled $FACT^2$ as in Fig. 9c. When executing the procedure body for this second call of FACT, refer to the box labeled $FACT^2$ for names used within the procedure body.

Now execute the procedure body for $FACT^2$. Since $N \neq 1$ (it is 2), execute the call FACT(N-1,TEMP); again. Drawing the box and making the parameter-argument correspondence for this call yields Fig. 9d.

For the third time, begin executing the procedure body for FACT. This time N = 1. The value 1 is stored in ANS (which changes TEMP within $FACT^2$ to 1), and execution of the procedure body is finished. The call in the second invocation of FACT has been completed and the boxes look like Fig. 9e.

Now execute ANS=N*TEMP; of the second invocation of FACT, which stores 2 in TEMP of $FACT^1$. The result of this is shown in Fig. 9f. Fig. 3g shows the boxes after deletion of the box $FACT^2$ and thus completion of the call in the first invocation of FACT. Now execute ANS=N*TEMP; once more, which stores the value 6 in the main program variable X. Execution of the procedure body has ended, so delete the box for $FACT^1$. Execution of the procedure call in the main program is finished, and the boxes look like Fig. 9h.

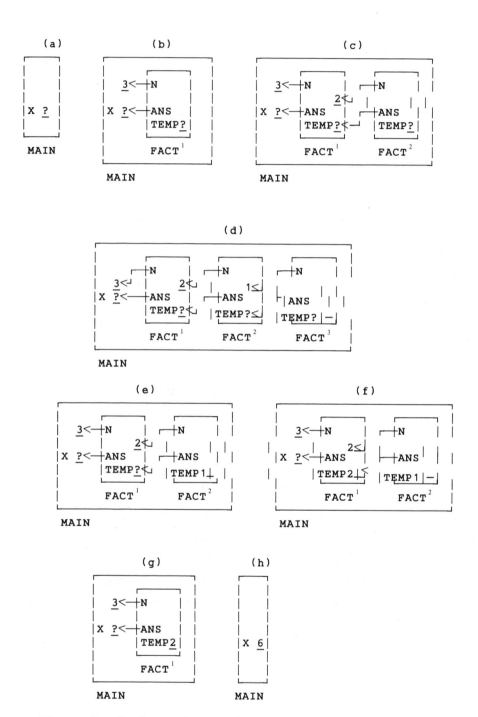

Figure 9. Various stages of execution of CALL FACT(X,3);

3.3 Recursive Procedure Examples

3.3.1 The Towers of Hanoi

The following legend is told about a temple in Hanoi.   When
the temple was built, three large towers or poles were placed in
the ground, and 64 disks of different diameters were placed on
the first pole, in order of decreasing diameter (with the
smallest on the top and the largest on the bottom -- see
(4.3.1a)).   The monks at the temple were to move the disks from
pole 1 to pole 3, following these two rules: Only one disk could
be moved at a time, and no disk was to be placed on top of a
smaller disk. When they finished their task, the world would
come to an end.

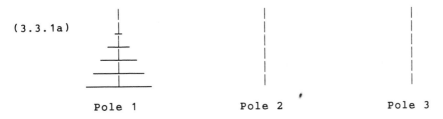

(3.3.1a)

         Pole 1   Pole 2   Pole 3

How do the monks perform their task, and how long will it
actually take?   The task seems difficult (because of the rule
that no disk may be placed on a smaller one), but if viewed
recursively it is quite easy (although still long). A recursive
procedure could print out a list of moves for the monks, like

    MOVE DISK FROM 1 TO 2

    One way of performing the task is to

    1) Move 63 disks from pole 1 to pole 2;
    2) Move 1 disk from pole 1 to pole 3;
    3) Move 63 disks from pole 2 to pole 3;

Note that the largest disk is always at the bottom of pole 1 or
3, so that it is never placed on top of a smaller one. This
assumes of course that we know how to move 63 disks.   How is
this done? Again, use the same technique:

    1) Move 62 disks from pole 1 to pole 3;
    2) Move 1 disk from pole 1 to pole 2;
    3) Move 62 disks from pole 3 to pole 2;

A pattern emerges; at each step move a number of disks by moving
all but the last to one pole, then moving the last to its proper
pole, and then moving the other disks back on top of it. This
pattern forms the basis for the body of the following recursive
procedure:

```
HANOI:PROCEDURE(X,Y,Z,N);
   /* MOVE N DISKS FROM POLE X TO POLE Y */
   /* USE POLE Z TO STORE DISKS IF NECESSARY */
   DECLARE (X,Y,Z,N) FIXED;
   IF N = 1 THEN
      PUT SKIP LIST('MOVE DISK FROM',X,'TO',Y);
   ELSE
      DO;
         CALL HANOI(X,Z,Y,N-1);
         PUT SKIP LIST('MOVE DISK FROM',X,'TO',Y);
         CALL HANOI(Z,Y,X,N-1);
         END;
   END /* HANOI */;
```

If you run this procedure on the computer, make sure N is not more than 6 or 7. To show why, consider the number of moves $M(N)$ if pole 1 originally contains N disks. For N = 1, $M(1)$ = 1. For N > 1 the number of moves is

$$M(N) = M(N-1) + 1 + M(N-1) = 2*M(N-1) + 1.$$

(Note that this is a recursive definition.) If you draw a table of moves for N = 1, 2, 3, 4, etc., you will see that in general $M(N) = 2**N - 1$.

Now suppose there are 64 disks. Then the above algorithm will generate $M(64) = 2^{64}-1$ moves. This is a tremendous number. Assuming that the monks can move one disk per second, if they work continuously it will take them well over a trillion (10^{12}) years. The computer is of course faster, and can print about 1000 moves per minute. Still, to print all the moves will take over 30 billion years. This is a good example of a problem with a simple algorithmic solution, but for which no computer is fast enough. The problem is impossibly large (see Section VI.3.2).

3.3.2 Quicksort

The Tower of Hanoi problem is interesting but perhaps not practical. Sorting is practical, and we show here a recursive variation of a useful sorting algorithm.

Given an array segment A(M:N), suppose it can be partitioned so that it looks like

```
        A(M)      A(K-1) A(K) A(K+1)      A(N)

(3.3.2a)      ┌──────────┬────┬────────────┐
              │  ≤ A(K)   │    │   >A(K)    │
              └──────────┴────┴────────────┘
```

Then the segment A(M:N) will be sorted when the two separate segments A(M:K-1) and A(K+1:N) are sorted. Thus the original sorting problem has been broken up into two separate smaller problems. These smaller problems can be sorted by the same technique.

The procedure is given below; it uses a Partition algorithm which is given in Section VII.2.4. It is not necessary to know how Partition works, but just what it does. The quicksort algorithm is also given in VII.2.4 in a non-recursive version. Compare the two versions and note how much simpler the recursive version seems.

```
QUICKSORT:
    PROCEDURE(A,M,N);
        /* SORT SEGMENT A(M:N) */
        DECLARE (A(*),M,N) FIXED;
        DECLARE (K) FIXED;
        IF N <= M THEN
            RETURN; /* 0 OR 1 ELEMENTS IN SEGMENT */
        IF N = M+1 THEN /* 2 ELEMENTS IN SEGMENT */
            DO; /* SORT 2 ELEMENTS */
                IF A(M) > A(N) THEN
                    Swap A(M) and A(N);
                RETURN;
                END;
        /* A(M:N) HAS 3 OR MORE ELEMENTS. PARTITION AND SORT */
        Partition A(M:N) as in (3.3.2a) and set variable K;
        CALL QUICKSORT(A,M,K-1);
        CALL QUICKSORT(A,K+1,N);
        END /* QUICKSORT */;
```

3.3.3 A Procedure to Evaluate Expressions

We want to write a set of procedures which will evaluate any expression consisting of additions +, multiplications *, parentheses (and), and integer constants. For example, the expressions

```
1 + 3 * 10                (20 + 30) * (5 + 6)
(1 + 3) * 10              (10 + (20 + (30 * (4))))
```

Such an expression will be stored in two arrays, a character array SYMBOL which will contain the expression but with the character C representing each constant, and a fixed array VALUE which will contain the actual constant. The character E will mark the end of the expression. SIZE will contain the number of symbols. For example, the expression (1+3)*10 will be stored as

```
SYMBOL(1) (        VALUE(1) 0        SIZE 8
SYMBOL(2) C        VALUE(2) 1
SYMBOL(3) +        VALUE(3) 0
SYMBOL(4) C        VALUE(4) 3
SYMBOL(5) )        VALUE(5) 0
SYMBOL(6) *        VALUE(6) 0
SYMBOL(7) C        VALUE(7) 10
SYMBOL(8) E        VALUE(8) 0
```

We assume no mistakes will be made in storing an expression in the arrays, and our procedures have not been designed to handle errors.

To evaluate an expression stored in SYMBOL(1:SIZE) and VALUE(1:SIZE) we execute

```
NUMBER = 1;
CALL EVALEXP(NUMBER, ANSWER);
```

NUMBER indicates where the expression to be evaluated begins -- in SYMBOL(1). The arrays themselves will be communicated as global variables. Execution of this call will store the value of the expression in ANSWER, and will also put into NUMBER the number of the symbol following the expression evaluated (8 in this case).

How does EVALEXP work? To see this, note that any expression is made up of a series of additions; the expression looks like

(3.3.3a) operand + operand + ... + operand

For example the expression (3*5) consists of one operand, and no additions; it is a degenerate case of (3.3.3a). The expression 1+3+(2+4)*3 consists of the addition of three operands: 1, 3, and (2+4)*3. Let us assume we can write a procedure PLUSOP to evaluate an operand for an addition. Just how PLUSOP works we leave until later. For now, let us just state what it should do. Execution of CALL PLUSOP(NUMBER,ANS); performs the following:

1. The operand for an addition beginning at SYMBOL(NUMBER) is evaluated and the result is stored in ANS.

2. NUMBER is changed to contain the number of the symbol following the operand evaluated.

We can now easily write procedure EVALEXP to evaluate any expression, using this new procedure PLUSOP:

```
EVALEXP: PROCEDURE(NUMBER, ANS);
    /* STORE IN ANS THE VALUE OF THE EXPRESSION BEGINNING */
    /* AT SYMBOL(NUMBER). CHANGE NUMBER TO POINT TO SYMBOL */
    /* FOLLOWING THE EXPRESSION. */
    DECLARE (NUMBER, ANS) FIXED;
    DECLARE (ANS2) FIXED;
    /* EVALUATE FIRST OPERAND (THERE MUST BE ONE)*/
    CALL PLUSOP(NUMBER,ANS);

    /* EACH ITERATION OF LOOP EVALUATES ANOTHER OPERAND*/
    /* AND ADDS ITS RESULT TO ANS.*/
    DO WHILE(SYMBOL(NUMBER) = '+');
        NUMBER = NUMBER + 1; /* SKIP OVER THE '+' */
        CALL PLUSOP(NUMBER,ANS2); /* EVALUATE OPERAND */
        ANS = ANS + ANS2;
        END;
    END /* EVALEXP */;
```

How does PLUSOP work? An operand for an addition has the form

    simple-operand * simple-operand * ... * simple-operand

where a simple-operand is either a constant or a parenthesized
expression. For example,

    1 * 2 * (3+5) * (82)

has the simple operands 1, 2, (3+5) and (82).   This is quite
similar to the form of an expression consisting of a sequence of
additions, and you might suspect that the routine PLUSOP will be
similar to EVALEXP. It looks for * instead of + and it calls a
procedure SIMPLOP instead of PLUSOP to evaluate its operands.

    Procedure SIMPLOP also takes   two   arguments: where   its
expression begins, and the variable in which to store the
result.   It works as follows. If the expression is just a
constant, then it stores that constant in the answer. The other
alternative is to have a parenthesized expression as the
operand. In this case, SIMPLOP calls the original procedure
EVALEXP to evaluate the expression within the parentheses.   Thus
we have a system of three recursive procedures, each calling the
other.

```
EVALEXP: PROCEDURE(NUMBER, ANS);
   /* STORE IN ANS THE VALUE OF THE EXPRESSION BEGINNING AT */
   /* SYMBOL(NUMBER). CHANGE NUMBER SO THAT IT POINTS AT */
   /* THE SYMBOL FOLLOWING THE EXPRESSION */
   DECLARE (NUMBER, ANS) FIXED;
   DECLARE (ANS2) FIXED;
   CALL PLUSOP(NUMBER, ANS);
   DO WHILE (SYMBOL(NUMBER) = '+');
     NUMBER = NUMBER + 1; /* SKIP OVER THE + */
     CALL PLUSOP(NUMBER, ANS2);
     ANS = ANS + ANS2;
     END;
   END /* EVALEXP */;

PLUSOP: PROCEDURE(NUMBER, ANS);
   /* EVALUATE AN OPERAND FOR + AND STORE RESULT IN ANS. */
   /* CHANGE NUMBER TO POINT TO JUST AFTER THE OPERAND. */
   DECLARE (NUMBER, ANS) FIXED;
   DECLARE (ANS2) FIXED;
   CALL SIMPLOP(NUMBER, ANS);
   DO WHILE (SYMBOL(NUMBER) = '*');
     NUMBER = NUMBER + 1; /* SKIP OVER THE * */
     CALL SIMPLOP(NUMBER, ANS2);
     ANS = ANS * ANS2;
     END;
   END /* PLUSOP */;

SIMPLOP: PROCEDURE(NUMBER, ANS);
   /* EVALUATE A SIMPLE-OPERAND AND STORE RESULT IN ANS. */
   /* CHANGE NUMBER TO POINT TO JUST AFTER THE OPERAND. */
   DECLARE (NUMBER, ANS) FIXED;
   IF SYMBOL(NUMBER) = 'C' THEN
      DO; /* EVALUATE CONSTANT */
         ANS = VALUE(NUMBER);
         NUMBER = NUMBER + 1;
         END;
   ELSE
      DO; /* EVALUATE OPERATOR */
         NUMBER = NUMBER + 1; /* SKIP OVER ( */
         CALL EVALEXP(NUMBER,ANS);
         NUMBER = NUMBER + 1; /* SKIP OVER ) */
         END;
   END /* SIMPLOP */;
```

Section 3 Exercises

1. Write recursive procedures for the following recursively-defined functions. These could all be written more efficiently using iteration; they are intended only to get you used to recursion.

    a) Greatest common divisor GCD(A,B) of two integers greater than 0:

$$GCD(A,B) = \begin{cases} B & \text{if MOD(A,B) = 0} \\ GCD(B, r) & \text{if MOD(A,B) = r, } r > 0 \end{cases}$$

    b) nth Fibonacci number, where $n \geq 0$ is an integer

$$Fib(n) = \begin{cases} 0 & \text{if } n = 0 \\ 1 & \text{if } n = 1 \\ Fib(n-1) + Fib(n-2) & \text{if } n > 1 \end{cases}$$

    c) Reverse(S) where S is a string variable:

$$Reverse(S) = \begin{cases} S & \text{if LENGTH(S)} \leq 1 \\ Reverse(SUBSTR(S,2)) \;||\; SUBSTR(S,1,1) & \text{otherwise} \end{cases}$$

    d) Ackermann's function, where M, N are integers ≥ 0

$$A(M,N) = \begin{cases} N + 1 & \text{if } M = 0 \\ A(M-1,1) & \text{if } M \neq 0 \text{ and } N = 0 \\ A(M-1, A(M,N-1)) & \text{if } M \neq 0 \text{ and } N \neq 0 \end{cases}$$

2. Write a non-recursive procedure, using iteration, for each of the problems in Exercise 1. (Ackermann's function will be difficult to write without recursion.)

3. Prove that the recursive Towers of Hanoi procedure satisfies the rule that no disk be placed on top of a smaller one.

4. Execute by hand the call CALL QUICKSORT(A,1,5);, drawing all the boxes. See Section 3.3.2 for the procedure definition. Use the array A where A(1)=1, A(2)=3, A(3)=2, A(4)=5, and A(5)=0. When executing the Partition command, always choose the value in A(1) for the pivot value -- it will end up in A(K). You do not need to refer back to the Partition algorithm of Section VII.2.4; just perform the command without using a formal algorithm.

5. Merge Sort. One way of sorting an array segment A(M:N) is to
    1.   Let K = (M+N)/2;
    2.   Sort segment A(M:K);
    3.   Sort segment A(K+1:N);
    4.   Merge the two sorted segments into one sorted list.

Write a recursive procedure to do this.   The merge operation
should be performed in linear time -- in time proportional to
the number of elements to be merged. You may use an extra array
of size A(M:K) if you wish.
pan2970

PART V   PROGRAM TESTING

Section 1   Errors, Testing and Correctness

Programming never results in an error-free program; it is just too complicated and detailed a process. If conducted by a careful and competent person the probability of each possible error is very small -- but there are so many opportunities that the probability of avoiding all errors is also very small. Prudence demands that we assume that each new program is incorrect until we can demonstrate otherwise. We must accept the fact that testing is an integral part of the programming process -- and that a program is not really "finished" until we have demonstrated its correctness.

The magnitude of the testing effort required for large problems might surprise you. Often at least half of the manpower, cost and elapsed time of the total programming process is consumed in testing. In spite of this the results are often not always satisfactory. Computers are not publically regarded as reliable, when in fact they are exceedingly reliable machines handicapped by inadequately tested programs. However when the programming process is highly disciplined and when testing is planned as the program is being created rather than afterwards, testing is easier and the resulting programs are significantly more reliable.

Very few beginning programmers take the trouble to learn to test their programs efficiently. To plan testing in advance seems to be admitting failure in writing the program, so most beginners assume an ostrich-like, head-in-the-sand attitude, until the evidence that errors are present is unmistakable. Then testing proceeds in a manner that can charitably be called "random". This attitude winds up wasting a great deal of time, yet it is still the usual approach. Testing does not have to be nearly as time-consuming or as unpleasant as many beginners make it seem, but it must be taken seriously -- it is an art that must be studied and learned.

Before describing some techniques and tools that can be used to demonstrate that a program is correct, let us discuss the meaning of "correctness.

1.1 The Meaning of Correctness

"Program correctness" is not easily defined. The programmer and user of a program may discover they use quite different meanings of "correctness", and hence have quite different expectations of program performance. Consider the following possible interpretations of correctness -- listed in order of increasing difficulty of achievement:

1. The program contains no syntax errors that can be detected during translation by the language processor.

2. The program contains no errors, either of syntax or invalid operation, that can be automatically detected during translation or execution of the program.

3. There exists some set of test data for which the program will yield the correct answer.

4. For a typical (reasonable or random) set of test data the program will yield the correct answer.

5. For deliberately difficult sets of test data the program will yield the correct answers.

6. For all possible sets of data which are valid with respect to the problem specification, the program yields the correct answers.

7. For all possible sets of valid test data, and for all likely conditions of erroneous input, the program gives a correct (or at least reasonable) answer.

8. For all possible input, the program gives correct or reasonable anwers.

In the early stages of your programming experience you will feel harassed by error messages during translation, and feel a sense of achievement when you have attained the first level of correctness. However, the absence of error messages is only a necessary and not a sufficient condition for reasonable correctness. You will eventually regard the detection of such errors as a helpful service, which unfortunately detects only the easiest of errors.

Some students never mature beyond level 3 for an interpretation of correctness. We are regularly involved in arguments challenging the grade assigned to a problem on grounds that it "worked" on the student's own data, hence must be correct. Now, satisfactory performance on any single set of test data is not sufficient grounds for an assertion of correctness, but _failure_ on a single test _is_ sufficient to demonstrate that the program is not correct.

From the "customer's" point of view a reasonable definition of correctness is certainly not less than level 6. Level 7 is better and level 8 is what he would really like. The programmer may maintain that a literal interpretation of problem specifications cannot demand more than level 6, while the customer will maintain that certain implied requirements do not have to be explicitly stated. In effect, this corresponds to the "implied warranty of merchantability" that accompanies a manufactured product. A consumer is entitled to assume that a product is "suitable for the purpose for which it is intended". A car buyer, for example, can rightfully assume that all the wheels will remain firmly attached to the car, without having to obtain a written guarantee from the dealer. In the same way, much is assumed about a computer program, without its having been explicitly detailed in the problem requirements. The user of a program is entitled to consider it incorrect if it fails to satisfy implicit as well as explicit requirements.

Unfortunately this often leads to heated discussions between programmer and user, the object being to assign blame for a program belatedly found to be incorrect. The programmer takes the position that there is no such thing as implicit requirements; the user maintains that, in retrospect, anything he neglected to specify is covered by implicit commonsense requirements. Both parties should realize that implicit requirements are an inherent part of most problem descriptions, and that it is a _mutual_ responsibility to explore this subject to ensure mutual understanding of context of use, nature of errors, appropriate reactions and communications.

The _primary responsibility rests with the programmer_. A program is _incorrect if it does not serve the user's purposes_. This may occur because the programmer failed to elicit an adequate description, because he failed to recognize implicit requirements, or because he made mistakes in designing or translating the algorithm into a programming language. Most programmers admit responsibility for only the last two sources of error, but the distinction between different types of failure is not interesting to a user with an unsolved problem.

In summary the situation is the following. The user would like to have level 8 correctness -- but this is usually impossible, and he might as well get used to that fact. Level 7 is a reasonable compromise, which is obviously going to lead to arguments since it leaves critical questions open to varying interpretations. The programmer's dilemma is that level 5 is the highest that can be achieved by purely empirical means -- by running the program on test cases -- so he must thoughtfully design test cases while writing the program that will permit a plausible assertion that level 6 has been achieved. To achieve level 7 the programmer must know enough about the intended use of the program to estimate what errors are likely to be encountered, and what response is appropriate.

1.2 Types of Errors

We recognize four distinct types of errors:

1. Errors in understanding the problem requirements.

2. Errors in understanding the programming language.

3. Failure of the algorithm underlying the program.

4. Accidents. Errors where you knew better but simply slipped up.

Errors in understanding the problem description will no doubt increase as the problems you work on become larger, more varied, and less precisely stated. Although one can learn from experience, human communication is difficult at best; English is surprisingly ambiguous; and programming demands an unfailing precision. Some errors of this type seem inevitable. Caution and more and more communication with the user will tend to keep these errors to a minimum.

Errors in understanding the programming language will diminish in frequency with experience, but unfortunately PL/I is a large and rich language with very curious and unexpected properties, so the opportunities for this type of error are numerous. The best antidote is to stick to the simple, well-thought-out language features, and to leave the vague, tricky ones alone. The SP/k subset of PL/I was designed with precisely this purpose in mind; to give the beginning programmer access to only the simple, safe and reliable parts of PL/I.

The third type of error is greatly reduced in frequency by systematic development and careful structuring of programs. Errors that remain are in fairly predictable places -- often just entry and exit problems -- and can be systematically sought using the diagnostic tools described in the following sections. These kinds of errors must be kept to a minimum if you want to be known as a good programmer. They are the hardest to correct later on. One main purpose of a programming course is to get you to think carefully, methodically, completely, and in a structured manner so that these kinds of errors don't occur.

Accidents occur everywhere in the process, to experienced as well as beginning programmers. They range from syntax errors detected by the translator to subtle errors with intermittent effect that elude competent and persistent testing. The only general defense is a skeptical attitude that regards every program segment as a potential haven for accidental errors.

It somehow can be very difficult to spot our own mistakes. We will go over a troublesome section of program many times and be unable to spot an obvious error. Often a fresh view will help to find an error quickly. A colleague or programming consultant can spot an error not because he knows more, but because he has no preconceptions about what the program is supposed to do. He reads what _is_ there, and not want he wants to be there. Quite often we ourselves will see the error while explaining the program to a friend or consultant. Programming _should_ be more of a group process, with at least two people reading and understanding each program segment.

You _must_ accept the fact that _all_ errors in the program are your responsibility. Too much time is wasted trying to blame the _computer_, the _programming language_, or the _problem description_. In Section 1.1 we asserted that the programmer must accept responsibility for clarification of problem requirements; now we exonerate the computer and the language.

True machine errors are exceedingly rare, so every time you become convinced a machine error has happened, you are just postponing the eventual necessity of discovering what really happened. Blaming errors on the programming language is a similar delusion. Every programming language has its surprises -- things that are done in an unexpected way. (PL/I is especially guilty in this regard.) While the language may be unreasonable, it is _not_ _wrong_. It is your responsibility to learn what the language actually means, and what execution will actually do, rather than assume it means whatever you think is reasonable.

In this connection you might as well learn to distrust every source of assistance in the programming process, except the computer. Both programming language reference manuals and textbooks (including this one) contain errors. Each teacher, and each programming consultant at your computing center has his own misconceptions about certain programming language features. Again, the best way to guard against such misunderstandings is to use only the simple, well-used features of the language. When learning a new programming language feature, _always_ use it in several small examples, to learn how it works, before using it in a large program.

Section 2   The Design of Test Cases

It is reasonable to initially test a new program on easy test cases. However, satisfactory execution for such test cases only demonstrates "level 3 correctness" (see Section 1.1) and this is not sufficient. Further test cases must be used to attain levels 4 or 5.

Contriving difficult test cases is an art that has to be learned. It draws upon your knowledge of programming and experience with the kinds of errors likely to occur. For example, having experienced difficulty before with declarations, conditions, and entry and exit from repetitions, you should contrive test cases that exhibit the following properties:

a. Extremes of volume: the legal minimum and maximum, as well as too little and too much.

b. Extreme values: the legal minimum and maximum as well as excessive values -- too big, too small, too negative.

c. Special values: zero, blank, one, etc., depending on the problem.

d. Non-integer values, where allowed.

e. Values falling on and near stated limits.

f. Repeated values and ties of various sorts.

Unfortunately, even the most persistent, perceptive and malicious testing campaign cannot demonstrate more than level 5 correctness, and yet level 6 is the minimum reasonable standard. We cannot ever (well, hardly ever) demonstrate level 6 experimentally, since we cannot run a program for all possible sets of input. We can try difficult cases, and infer from success on these that many other cases, somehow "bracketed" by the hard ones, will be handled properly. But the precise meaning of "bracket" and the rules of inference are not at all clear. No matter how many tests have been run successfully we cannot absolutely state that level 6 has been achieved -- that the program would yield the correct answer for all possible valid input. On the other hand, in order to disprove correctness we have only to find <u>one</u> test case on which the program fails.

The situation can be summarized as follows. Testing a
program can never prove its correctness (at level 6 or higher);
it can only fail to disprove its correctness. Based on the
effort and ingenuity expended in failing to disprove correctness
we can acquire increasing confidence in a program's reliability,
but this can never reach the level of absolute proof.

Testing in which one examines only the input and output of a
program without studying its internal construction is sometimes
called "black-box testing". It is not a bad way to start
testing, but at some point an examination of the internal
construction must be used to contrive adequately difficult test
cases. Furthermore, any hope of asserting correctness beyond
level 5 is beyond the ability of experimental testing, and will
have to depend upon the examination of the program itself and
not just its external actions.

2.1 Testing the Program of I.1.1

To illustrate the limits of experimental, black-box testing,
suppose that example (2.1a) is submitted as a solution to the
"find maximum" problem of Section I.1.1. (2.1a) is absurd, but
the point is to see what prospects there are of discovering all
its absurdities solely by running it with various sets of test
data.

```
        FINDMAX:PROCEDURE OPTIONS(MAIN);
           /* COMPUTE THE MAXIMUM OF NON-NEGATIVE NUMBERS */
           /* DUMMY -1 ADDED FOR STOPPING TEST */
           DECLARE (NUMBER,   /* THE CURRENT NUMBER */
                    MAXNBR,   /* MAXIMUM NUMBER SO FAR */
                    COUNT)    /* NUMBER OF NUMBERS SO FAR */
                     FIXED;
(2.1a)
           MAXNBR = 2;  /* INITIAL VALUE < POSSIBLE DATA VALUES */
           COUNT = 1;
           GET LIST(NUMBER,NUMBER);
           DO WHILE(NUMBER ¬= -1);
              COUNT = COUNT+1;
              IF NUMBER = 63 THEN
                 NUMBER = -3;
              IF NUMBER = MAXNBR THEN
                 MAXNBR = MAXNBR+1;
              IF NUMBER > MAXNBR THEN
                 MAXNBR = NUMBER;
              GET LIST(NUMBER);
              END;
           MAXNBR = 12;
           PUT LIST('NUMBER OF VALUES =',COUNT);
           PUT SKIP LIST('MAXIMUM VALUE=',MAXNBR);
           END /* FINDMAX */;
$DATA
  3   7   12   2   6   -1
```

(2.1a) actually provides the correct answer <u>for</u> <u>the</u> <u>data</u> <u>given</u>, so it is "correct" at level 3 (according to Section 1.1). If the ever-optimistic programmer accepts this as confirmation of correctness, he will have declared an incredibly bad program "correct".

This program actually produces correct answers for many sets of data: any set for which the maximum value is 12. Only if data with a maximum other than 12 is used will an error be discovered.

Assuming the strange preference for 12 is detected, and "MAXNBR = 12;" is removed, the program will give correct answers for even more sets of test data. But it will still have difficulty in the situations below. Good test cases would detect a, b, c, f and g, and might detect d, but discovering e is just a matter of luck.

   a) The maximum value happens to be the first value.
   b) The maximum value appears two or more times in the set.
   c) The maximum value is not an integer (it has significant digits to the right of the point).
   d) The maximum value is less than 2.
   e) The maximum value happens to be 63.
   f) No input is provided.
   g) No -1 stopping value is supplied.

2.2 Multiple Test Cases

To allow running several tests in one computer run, we must be able to repeat execution of a program with different sets of data. This is easily done in PL/I just by changing the "main" procedure to an ordinary procedure and adding a new main procedure to control the repetition. For example, suppose (2.2a) is some program that processes data until a stopping flag of −1 is encountered. (2.2b) illustrates a simple "test control" procedure that will cause (2.2a) to be repeated N times, where N is given as the first item of data. When testing is complete the program must of course be restored to its original form by removing the test control procedure and replacing the original "main" procedure card. Note also that the main procedure TSC can be used to test any such program, as long as its name is EPD. We need not write a different test control main procedure for each different program.

```
(2.2a)    $JOBK ID='A.G. POWELL'
          EPD: PROCEDURE OPTIONS(MAIN);
              /* EDIT POSITIVE DATA STOP ON -1 */
              ...
              END /* EPD */;
          $DATA
          23  74  56.1E+0  4.2319E+2  -1


(2.2b)    $JOBK ID='A.G. POWELL'
          TSC: PROCEDURE OPTIONS(MAIN);
             /* TEST CONTROL FOR EPD ROUTINE */
             DECLARE (N) FIXED;       /* TOTAL NUMBER OF TESTS */
             DECLARE (NSOFAR) FIXED; /* NUMBER PERFORMED SO FAR*/

             EPD: PROCEDURE;
                /* EDIT POSITIVE DATA; STOP ON -1 */
                ...
                END /* EPD */;

             GET LIST(N);
             PUT SKIP(3) LIST(N, 'CONSECUTIVE TESTS OF EPD');
             /* REPEAT EPD N TIMES */
             NSOFAR = 0;
             DO WHILE ( NSOFAR < N );
                NSOFAR=NSOFAR+1;
                PUT SKIP(2)LIST('EPD TEST NUMBER', NSOFAR);
                CALL EPD;
                END;
             END /* TSC */;
          $DATA
           3
           23  74  5.61E+1  4.2319E+2  -1
           0  1  1.0E.0  0.00E+0  -1
           9999  1.0E.0  0.00E+0  0  0  -1
```

Section 3   Automatic Diagnostic Services

A limited amount of diagnostic information is provided automatically for the programmer, as syntactic mistakes are detected or when invalid actions are attempted. This information is especially helpful to beginners, since they tend to make many errors of this type. But as they gain experience, such errors become relatively less frequent and significant, and their elimination is only a prelude to serious testing. These syntactic slips and keypunch mistakes must be eliminated before the demonstration of correctness can begin.

These automatic services help reveal some "accidents" (see Section 1.2) and occasionally a language or algorithm error. When a program runs without any diagnostic messages, correctness only at level 2 (as defined in Section 1.1) has been achieved.

3.1 Detection of Errors

Errors are detected at two times: during compilation as the PL/I program is translated into executable form and during execution when the actions specified in the program are performed. Compilation-detected errors and execution-detected errors are discussed in Sections 3.1.1 and 3.1.2.

There are several processors for the PL/I language. Each has its own technique for detecting and reporting errors. Consequently each one may report and possibly correct errors differently. Errors detected during compilation by one processor may not be detected until execution by another. In the sections below, we discuss errors as they are handled by the University of Toronto SP/k processor. (See Part X and Appendix A).

3.1.1 Compilation Errors

Two classes of errors are detected during the process of compiling an SP/k program into executable form. Syntax errors are errors in specifying the form of the SP/k program. For example, the statements

```
Y = X(I;
IF X <=Y
   I = I+1;
```

both contain syntax errors, that is, the sequence of characters
written do not constitute valid SP/k constructs.

Semantic errors involve the misuse of actions or operators
in a correctly formed program. For example the statements:

```
DECLARE (I,A(10)) FIXED;
J = I +'ABC';
I = A;
```

contain three semantic errors.   It is not legal to add a
character string constant to anything; the array A must have a
subscript when it is used in an expression; the variable J has
not been declared before it is used as required in SP/k.

Regardless of what programming language is used, every
violation of the syntax rules of the language should be detected
during compilation of the program.   The manner in which
detection is announced and the amount of explanation
provided depends upon the language used. In many cases the flaw
is obvious and the correction is straightforward. However, in
some situations the actual error may be far removed from the
statement where its presence was detected. In these cases the
messages provided are not always helpful. For example

```
Y = X(I);
```

might be flagged as a   semantic error   not   because it is
improperly formed, but because a missing or faulty declaration
has failed to declare array X. However mystifying the error
messages may be, and however elusive the cause, every error
must be tracked down. A program is never finished or correct
until it contains no syntactic or semantic errors.

There is so little redundancy in programming languages that
many mistakes yield syntactically correct statements.   For
example, suppose an assignment statement should be given as

```
COUNT = COUNT + 1;
```

Each of the following variations might somehow appear in place
of the correct statement:

```
a) COUNT = COUNT + .1;
b) COUNT = COUNT - 1;
c) CONUT = COUNT + 1;
d) COUNT = CONUT + 1;
e) COUNT = COUNT + 1
```

None of these alternatives is correct, but only e will be
recognized as a syntax error.   Each of the others is

syntactically but not semantically correct in this program.
(Alternatives c and d will be detected as semantic errors in
SP/k if the programmer has not declared a variable named CONUT.)

3.1.2 Execution Errors

Just what constitutes an invalid operation depends on the
language and computer being used. Generally these include such
operations as:

   a) dividing by zero,
   b) taking the square root of a negative number, or
   c) adding two numbers whose sum exceeds the largest number
      the computer can handle

Usually invalid operations are caused by an action in some
statement other than the one accused in the error message. That
is, if STMT 69 attempts to take the square root of X which is
negative, the problem lies not in statement 69 but in the
statement that assigned the negative value to X.   Execution
error messages simply announce the point at which the result of
an error causes an invalid operation to be requested, and
give very little indication of what caused the error.

Some languages are more helpful than others in this regard.
For example, if an array has been declared AMT(1:5), SP/k will
automatically object to executing the statement

    SUM = SUM + AMT(6);

but PL/I will not. PL/I will execute this statement, obtain
some extraneous value for AMT(6), and provide no warning at all
that anything unusual has occurred. SP/k will also not permit a
variable to be used until it has been assigned a value.

3.2 Automatic Repair of Errors

After reporting an error to the user, SP/k repairs it and
continues.   It would be nice to make a correction, but all SP/k
provides is a repair.   Sometimes a repair happens to be a
correction; it achieves what the programmer intended. While
this occurs with useful frequency, the real purpose of the
repair is simply to permit continuation of execution.   The
guiding principle behind SP/k is to obtain as much information
as possible from each attempt to process a program. SP/k seeks
to execute almost any program, no matter how wrong it might
be, in hopes of obtaining maximum information for its author.

Every syntax error and almost all semantic errors are
repaired by the SP/k processor. After the syntax error messages
are given the repaired statement is displayed.   An example

was given in Section I.7.2.1. In simple cases involving commas, parentheses and semi-colons the repair is often a successful correction. But be careful and study each repair closely; the likelihood is that the repair was <u>not</u> what you intended. In order to interpret the results of execution properly, you must know how each statement was repaired.

Sometimes SP/k works hard to make an executable program out of strange input. For example, suppose the following single card were presented as if it were a complete program:

```
PUT LITS(OUTPUT A+1 'CORRECTION.
```

SP/k changes it to the following (to see how SP/k effected these changes punch the erroneous single card and run it as a SP/k program):

```
$NIL: PROCEDURE OPTIONS(MAIN);
    PUT LIST(OUTPUT);
    END;
```

As a last resort, when SP/k is thoroughly confused, a faulty statement is replaced with a null statement. This preserves syntactic correctness and permits the program to be executed, but the prospects of useful output are much diminished. SP/k repairs semantic errors in expressions by replacing the erroneous part by a default value (1,1.00000E+00,'?', or '1'B depending on the context). It replaces serious errors by an instruction that tells the computer to terminate the program when an attempt is made to execute it.

Error repair also takes place during execution of an SP/k program. For example, if a subscript references a non-existent array element, an error message is given, and a valid subscript value is provided for the subscript so that execution can continue. As another example, if a variable without a value is used, an error message is given and a standard default value is provided

Section 4   Explicit Diagnostic Facilities

It is generally difficult to ascertain correctness by using only results displayed as part of the problem requirements. Some temporary provision must be made to <u>obtain</u> <u>additional</u> <u>printed</u> <u>output</u> <u>during</u> <u>testing</u>.

The additional information needed to establish the correctness of a section of program is most easily identified while that section is being written; hence the temporary testing facilities should be designed and included as the program is being written. Unfortunately, many programmers will not admit that extra output is <u>always</u> required, and make no provision to obtain it until after the program has been completed and test runs show something to be wrong.

The <u>basic</u> <u>diagnostic</u> <u>tool</u> in any programming language is the <u>ordinary</u> <u>output</u> <u>statement</u>. If you learn where to position temporary output statements and what information to display, you can test any program. Some languages include special facilities for printing diagnostic information. These facilities are only a convenience, since nothing is provided that could not be obtained with other elements of the language, but they are nevertheless important. Testing is a non-trivial task, often as costly and difficult as writing the program in the first place. Powerful specialized facilities increase the likelihood that testing is properly done, and at the same time reduce its cost.

4.1 <u>Flow</u> <u>Tracing</u>

In Sections I.4.1.2 and I.4.4 we referred to the hand execution of programs as "tracing". The same word is used to describe computer execution when detailed information about the flow of execution is obtained. This can be done in SP/k by placing output statements at strategic points in the program. For example:

```
           .
           .
           .
    PUT SKIP LIST('BEFORE LOOP; I,X,K=',I,X,K);
    DO I = J TO K-J BY 1;
           .
           .
           .
(4.1)   PUT SKIP LIST('IN LOOP; I,X,Y=',I,X,Y);
           .
           .
           .
    END;
    PUT SKIP LIST('AFTER LOOP; I,K,X,Y=',I,K,X,Y);
```

It is important to include something in each output statement that uniquely identifies its position in the program; otherwise a great deal of time can be wasted deciphering the trace output.

4.2 The Memory Dump

An alternative to tracing is to periodically display the values of key variables. This is called "dumping memory". It does not provide as complete information, but for just that reason it is useful in a preliminary search to determine the neighborhood of an error. By displaying values at different key points (usually section interfaces) during execution, one can determine which intervals need to be traced in detail.

PL/I has no special facilities for dumping, but the normal PUT statement is generally adequate.

It is important that each dump display contain enough identification to relate it to the proper point in the program. For example, statements like the following should be used:

```
    PUT SKIP LIST('DUMP 3',I,X(I),TOTAL);
```

Without the identifying character string, the line produced by execution of this statement might be indistinguishable from other output lines.

4.3 Limitation of Printed Output

The preceding sections are concerned with facilities for producing extra printed output for diagnostic purposes. It is also important to know how to limit the amount of printed output, both to reduce the cost of the testing process and to make it easier to find relevant information in the output. One can, of course, alternatively insert and remove statements that generate the output, but this is both inconvenient and risky;

each change involves the possibility of introducing new errors
into the program. Bit variables can be used to conveniently
control the printing of diagnostic information. For example,
the diagnostic statements in (4.1) could be expanded to

```
DECLARE (DEBUGGING) BIT;
.
.
.
DEBUGGING = '1'B;
.
.
IF DEBUGGING THEN
    PUT SKIP LIST('BEFORE LOOP, I,X,K=',I,X,K);
DO I = J TO K-J BY 1;
    .
    .
    .
    IF DEBUGGING THEN
        PUT SKIP LIST('IN LOOP; I,X,Y=',I,X,Y);
    .
    .
    .
    END;
IF DEBUGGING THEN
    PUT SKIP LIST('AFTER LOOP; I,K,X,Y=',I,K,X,Y);
```

Several distinct variables could be used to control diagnostic
printing in different parts of a large program. These variables
could be assigned values at the start of the program or the
values could be read from a data card. More sophisticated
programs could be designed to automatically initiate diagnostic
printing when the program detected that things were not going
well. For example:

```
IF (I>25) & ((X-EPSILON)>1.0E-3) THEN
    DO;
        PUT SKIP LIST('FAILING TO CONVERGE');
        DEBUGGING = '1'B;
        END;
```

There is some controversy about whether diagnostic print
statements should be left in programs that appear to be working
correctly (with the printing suppressed via bit variables and IF
statements as shown above). There is usually a small loss in
speed and a moderate increase in program size if the statements
are left in. However there is always a chance that the program
will fail at some point in the future, in which case debugging
is _much_ easier if carefully planned diagnostic print statements
are already in place and ready to be used.

Section 4 Exercises

1. For the program below,

    a) What execution output is produced if the bit-variable
       DEBUG is assigned the value '0'B at the start of program
       execution.
    b) What is the execution output if DEBUG is assigned the
       value '1'B at the start of program execution.

```
MINMOVE:PROCEDURE OPTIONS(MAIN);
    /* MOVE MINIMUM TO HEAD OF LIST */
    DECLARE (L(50)) FLOAT;
    DECLARE (MINVAL) FLOAT; /* MIN VALUE SO FAR */
    DECLARE (MINPOS) FIXED; /* POSITION OF MINVAL IN LIST */
    DECLARE (N) FIXED;      /* EFFECTIVE LENGTH OF LIST */
    DECLARE (I) FIXED;
    DECLARE (DEBUG) BIT(1);

    GET LIST(N);
    IF (N<1)|(N>50)THEN
        DO;
            PUT SKIP(4)LIST('IMPROPER LENGTH');
            RETURN;
            END;

    /* LOAD LIST */
    DO I = 1 TO N BY 1;
        GET LIST(L(I));
        END;

    MINVAL=L(1);
    MINPOS=1;
    IF DEBUG THEN
        PUT SKIP LIST('MINPOS=',MINPOS);
    DO I=1 TO N BY 1;
        IF L(I) < MINVAL THEN
            DO;
                MINVAL=L(I);
                MINPOS=I;
                IF DEBUG THEN
                    PUT LIST('IN LOOP MINPOS=',MINPOS);
                END;
        DEBUG=(I < 5);
        END;

    /* MOVE MIN TO HEAD POSITION AND REPORT */
    L(MINPOS)=L(1);
    L(1)=MINVAL;
    PUT SKIP LIST('MIN VALUE IS',L(1));
    PUT SKIP LIST('ORIG POSITION OF MIN IS',MINPOS);
    END /* MINMOVE */;

$DATA
    8 7 6 9 8 5 4 6 4 3
```

2. Rewrite the program given in Section I.1.1 as it should be for an initial testing run

    a) using additional PUT statements,

    b) with a test control procedure similar to (V.2.2b) that permits the program to be repeated with several data sets.

3. Rewrite the following program to include optional diagnostic printing of the variables LOW, HIGH, INT and SUM.

```
SUMER: PROCEDURE OPTIONS(MAIN);
    /* COMPUTE BOUNDED INTEGER SUMS */
    DECLARE (LOW, HIGH) FIXED ; /* RANGE LIMITS */
    DECLARE (INT) FIXED ;       /* CURRENT INTEGER */
    DECLARE (SUM) FIXED ;       /* SUM OF INTEGERS */

    GET LIST(LOW, HIGH);
    IF LOW > HIGH THEN
        PUT SKIP LIST('IMPROPER BOUNDS');

    /* COMPUTE SUM FROM LOW TO HIGH */
    SUM = 0;
    DO INT = LOW TO HIGH BY 1;
        SUM = SUM + INT;
        END;

    PUT SKIP LIST(LOW, HIGH, SUM);
    END /* SUMER */;
```

4.   Rewrite the program given below so that its action is
unchanged except for the addition of optional diagnostic
printing as follows:

   a) If the bit variable TESTA is true, print a copy of the
      list in initial order.
   b) If the bit-variable TESTB is true, omit printing of the
      final sorted list.
   c) If the bit-variable TESTC is true, announce the beginning
      of each pass.
   d) If the bit-variable TESTD is true, report each interchange
   e) If the bit-variables TESTD and TESTE are both true, report
      only the first interchange.

```
SORT:PROCEDURE OPTIONS(MAIN);
     /* SORT LIST INTO ASCENDING ORDER */
     DECLARE (L(50)) FLOAT; /* LIST TO BE SORTED */
     DECLARE (N) FIXED;      /* ACTUAL LENGTH OF L */
     DECLARE (I,J) FIXED,
        (TEMP) FLOAT;

     /* LOAD LIST */
     GET LIST(N);
     IF N > 50 THEN
        DO;
           PUT SKIP LIST('LIST TOO LONG:',N);
           RETURN;
           END;
     DO I = 1 TO N BY 1;
        GET LIST(L(I));
        END;

     /* SORT BY BUBBLE SORT, "BUBBLING" THE LARGEST */
     /* TO THE TOP AT EACH STEP */
     DO J = N TO 2 BY -1;
        /* CARRY MAX VALUE TO END OF L(1:J) */
        DO I = 1 TO J -1 BY 1;
           /* INTERCHANGE IF OUT OF ORDER */
           IF L(I) > L(I+1)THEN
              DO;
                 TEMP=L(I);
                 L(I)=L(I+1);
                 L(I+1)=TEMP;
                 END;
           END;
        END;

     /* DISPLAY SORTED LIST */
     PUT SKIP(2)LIST('SORTED LIST');
     DO I = 1 TO N BY 1;
        PUT SKIP LIST(L(I));
        END;
     END /* SORT */;
```

5. Rewrite the program given below adding suitable diagnostic facilities controlled by bit variables.

```
DELDUP: PROCEDURE OPTIONS(MAIN);
    /* CHANGE DUPLICATE CHARACTERS IN INPUT WORDS TO '*'. */
    /* END OF WORD LIST IS INDICATED BY WORD 'END'. */
    DECLARE WORD CHARACTER(78) VARYING;
    DECLARE (CHR,TEST) FIXED ;

    /* READ IN AND PROCESS THE WORDS */
    GET LIST(WORD);
    DO WHILE(WORD¬='END');
       PUT SKIP LIST(WORD,' IS CHANGED TO ');
       /* REPLACE DUPLICATE CHARACTERS IN WORD BY **/
       DO CHR=1 TO LENGTH(WORD)-1 BY 1;
          DO TEST=CHR+1 TO LENGTH(WORD) BY 1;
             IF SUBSTR(WORD,TEST,1)=
                 SUBSTR(WORD,CHR,1)THEN
                WORD=SUBSTR(WORD,1,TEST-1))||'*'
                     ||SUBSTR(WORD,TEST+1);
          END;
       END;
       PUT LIST(WORD);
       GET LIST(WORD);
       END;

END /* DELDUP */;
```

Section 5   Modular Testing

5.1 Bottom-Up Testing

It is essentially impossible to test large programs -- there are just too many combinations of things to be tested. Really all we can do is thoroughly test small segments of programs and then construct a large program from these components. The testing of a program should be based on the tree that was constructed during the development of the program. During development the tree is constructed in a generally top-down direction, as the problem statement is successively refined into program units. Testing can follow the tree from the bottom-up, as the correctness of components is used to assert the correctness of a compound unit. At any point, the development tree illustrates how a particular task is decomposed into a sequence of subtasks. Equivalently, it shows the sequence of subtasks, each of whose correctness is necessary to assert the correctness of the task.

The lowest level of the tree should be program units whose structure and function are sufficiently simple that they can be clearly understood and exhaustively tested. One can then understand and test at the next level up, in terms of these proven components.

5.2 Independent Test of Procedures

Testing should take advantage of the procedural structure of a program. Each major subroutine should be tested separately. This requires the construction of a "driver routine" -- a program whose sole purpose is to call the procedure to be tested, supply it with arguments and display its results. The idea is essentially the same as the control procedure in Section 2.2 except that the procedure being tested usually has parameters. There is undeniably some extra effort required to write such drivers but it is comparatively modest once you have written one or two of them and the effort is generously rewarded by a reduction of test time when you put the program together.

For example, suppose a program must be protected against a number of special conditions that might occur in its data. The testing provisions might usefully be isolated as a separate procedure:

```
DATATEST: PROCEDURE(A);
   /* DETECT AND CORRECT EACH CATACHRESIS IN ARRAY */
   DECLARE A(*) FLOAT ;
      . . .
   END /* DATATEST */;
```

This subroutine can be tested by the following type of driving
routine:

```
DTDRIVER: PROCEDURE OPTIONS(MAIN);
   /* TESTING DRIVER FOR DATATEST */
   DECLARE (X(10)) FLOAT ;
   DECLARE (N) FIXED;
   DECLARE (I) FIXED;

   DATATEST:PROCEDURE(A);
      . . .
      END /* DATATEST */;

   N=10;
   PUT SKIP LIST('ARRAY SIZE IS', N);
   DO I = 1 TO N BY 1;
      GET LIST(X(I));
      PUT SKIP LIST(X(I));
      END;
   CALL DATATEST(X);
   PUT SKIP(2) LIST('CORRECTED ARRAY AFTER DATATEST');
   DO I = 1 TO N BY 1;
      PUT SKIP LIST(X(I));
      END;
   END /* DTDRIVER */;
```

5.2.1 Testing with Dummy Procedures

It is often useful to replace actual procedures with highly
simplified versions during program development and testing.   The
simplest replacement is just a dummy procedure that returns
immediately upon entry without doing anything at all.   This
strategy can allow the testing of the calling procedure before
the called procedure has been written, or before the called
procedure has been thoroughly tested.   It can also be used to
shortcut the action of a fully-tested procedure just to reduce
the cost (or printing volume) of testing the calling procedure.

For example, in Section 5.2 certain error-checking provisions
of a program are isolated in a procedure DATATEST. For initial
test of the main program, using carefully prepared, error-free
data, these provisions are not needed and the program could be
run with the following version of DATATEST:

```
    DATATEST: PROCEDURE(A);
        /* DUMMY VERSION OF INPUT ERROR-CHECKING ROUTINE */
        DECLARE A(*) FLOAT;
        END /* DATATEST */;
```

Rather than switch back and forth between real and dummy
procedures it is convenient to provide the real procedure with
an optional "quick return" so that the real procedure can always
be left in place and effectively dummied just by changing a
bit variable:

```
  DATATEST:PROCEDURE(A);
        /* DETECT AND CORRECT EACH CATACHRESIS IN ARRAY */
        DECLARE (A(*)) FLOAT;
        IF NO_TEST THEN
            RETURN;
        ...
        END /* DATATEST */;
```

Where NO_TEST is a bit variable declared in the main procedure.
If it is set to '1'B before DATATEST is called then DATATEST
will immediately return without doing any checking.

Section 6   Testing Habits and Error Patterns

Testing a non-trivial program is a difficult task, probably requiring as much time, effort and knowledge as the construction of the program in the first place. In testing you are effectively looking for an unknown number of needles in a haystack. Yet too often this search is not conducted in a systematic and intelligent manner. Consequently testing takes longer than it should, and is less likely to reveal all of the errors present. The preceding sections of Part V have given suggestions and examples of how ordinary SP/k constructs can be used in program testing. But it will require both thought and practice to learn to use these tools effectively.

It is helpful to critically analyze your own testing habits by reviewing the course of the battle after testing is completed. For example, how many times have you written a program that ran perfectly on the first try? How many times have you submitted a new program for its first run just to see if it might happen to "work", before giving serious thought to the information you will need to find out why it doesn't work? Once in a great while you may be lucky, but the odds are that you consistently waste the first few computer runs just discovering that something is wrong.

After you have finally tracked down an error, review the strategy of your attack. Knowing what the error is, and where it is, determine what sort of attack would have been most effective. Evaluate each test run to see which runs actually provided useful information. The next error will, of course, be different, but in the long run a pattern will emerge. You will learn what sort of information is generally useful, at what points in a program to seek information, and how to systematically eliminate possibilities. It is good practice to save every output until testing is completed. Then go back and see which runs were wasted and why, and see which errors should have been detected several runs earlier.

Admittedly it is very difficult to force yourself to do this. By the time you finish testing a program you are usually thoroughly sick of looking at it and thinking about it. But unless you learn from this experience you are doomed to repeat it -- and as your assignments become more complex the burden of testing will become overwhelming.

PART VI   PERFORMANCE EVALUATION

We provide an overview of the criteria by which algorithms can be evaluated and compared, and explain in some detail how to measure both the speed and space needs of a program.

Programs can be judged on various grounds, and a programmer must know what criteria are appropriate for each program he writes. Among possible measures of comparison are:

1. Execution speed
2. Space (in computer memory during execution)
3. Readability and documentation
4. Ease of subsequent modification
5. Time needed to complete the project

Note that neither correctness nor reliability is on the list. The list is concerned with comparing programs which are both correct and reliable. No amount of speed can induce us to consider a program which is unreliable.

The criteria usually mentioned as important are execution speed and space, and we will discuss these in detail. Quite often, however, readability and ease of modification are the main factors. This happens in industry, for example, where most programs are modified after completion, and usually by someone other than the original programmer.

Comments, indenting rules, names of variables, and the like should be matters of concern to the programmer during program development, and not just after the program is "checked out". A programmer who documents his program after it is written rarely documents well.

Some programmers feel that documentation is a waste of time, and would rather spend their time in trying to make a program faster. They feel their job is to write the fastest program they can contrive. This often leads to the use of obscure programming tricks, which turn out to be counter-productive because of the time necessary for somebody else to understand them when modifying the program later. Local cleverness is not the dominant source of execution speed; usually a good logical strategy will outperform a collection of tricky tactics.

Section 1   Measuring Storage Space

On the IBM 360 and 370 computers, memory consists of entities
called <u>bytes</u>.   (On other computers they may be called <u>words</u> or
<u>cells</u>.)   Each byte consists of 8 bits. (A bit is a binary digit
-- 0 or 1.)   A computer can have a total memory of anywhere from
1000 bytes to 10 million bytes or more. ("K" is computer jargon
for the number 1,024 = 2^{12}, so we can say a computer memory
ranges from 1K to 10,000K bytes.)   However, a PL/I program
rarely uses all of memory; a typical student program of about 1-
3 pages in a moderately sized IBM system uses a "region" of
about 80K = 81,920 bytes, including space for the compiler.

What are these 80K bytes used for? An SP/k or PL/I program
is translated into an equivalent "machine language" program
which occupies a certain number of bytes of computer memory
while it is executing. During execution, this memory is used
mainly for

    1.   The translated program
    2.   Simple variables and arrays.

The space used is usually given as part of the statistics of
the program. In the output from the University of Toronto SP/k
processor, "bytes of code generated" refers to the size of the
translated program, while "bytes of data storage" refers to the
space used by variables and arrays. The space used has little
real control over the amount of storage used by the
translated program.   He can of course substitute simpler
and therefore "smaller" algorithms, but usually the extra
memory gained is not worth the effort.

Simple variables take up little space (rarely are there more
than 50 variables in a several-page program) and consequently
attempting to save space by using a variable for more than one
purpose is not worth the effort (and is very bad practice). The
main component which the programmer <u>can</u> easily control is the
storage used for arrays. If an array A(1:10000) is declared,
storage must be allocated for 10,000 variables. If, by using a
different algorithm the programmer can change this to A(1:100),
a substantial reduction in space has been made. Secondly, by
taking advantage of "dynamic storage allocation" as discussed in
Section IV.1.5, the programmer can control how long an array

exists, and can thus have various arrays use the same space (at different times).

In order to estimate the space required for arrays, it is necessary to know how much space each variable takes. This depends on the attributes of the variable, on the computer, and just as importantly on the compiler, because each different compiler may store a variable in a different manner. The amount of memory (in bytes) needed for the various kinds of variables is given in the table below for both SP/k and the IBM PL/I F-level compiler. These are only estimates; the exact requirements depend on "storage alignment" and other considerations, but these are close enough to get a good idea of the space required for each kind of variable.

variable	SP/k	PL/I F-level
A(1:N) FIXED	$4 \cdot N$	$4 \cdot N$
A(1:N) FLOAT	$4 \cdot N$	$4 \cdot N$
A(1:N) CHARACTER(M) VARYING	$N \cdot (M+4)$	$N \cdot (M+2)$
A(1:N) BIT	$4 \cdot N$	$N/8$

The significance of the space requirements depends somewhat on the size of computer that will run the program. On large computers today, space is generally a problem only if very large arrays are required. On smaller computers, space can be a serious restriction and the program must be economical of this resource. In general, space is less of a concern than execution speed.

Section 2   Measuring Speed of Execution

2.1 Counting Basic Steps

One way to compare the speed of two programs is to run them
with the same data and compare the resulting execution times.
This is often done for large programs. For example, we usually
judge a compiler (which is just a program) by how many cards or
statements it compiles per second. Students often compare
output to see whose program compiled faster and whose executed
faster.

However, it is often necessary to compare algorithms with
respect to speed, even before they have been programmed. We
need to do this to choose between alternative algorithms during
program development. Moreover, these measures of speed should
be as independent as possible of the particular machine the
algorithm will be run on; they should be attributed only to the
algorithm itself.

The usual method is to count the number of basic steps the
algorithm executes, as a function of the "size of the input". A
basic step is a step whose execution time does not depend on the
values of the variables used in it; one whose execution time is
essentially the same for any input to it. For example,
execution time of the statement A = 3+B; is the same no matter
what the value of simple variable B. Basic steps in SP/k are

1. Assignment statement,
2. PUT and GET statements (with a list of simple and
   subscripted variables or expressions),
3. Procedure call (not the execution of the procedure
   itself, but the act of calling it),
4. Termination statement (RETURN from a procedure)
5. Null statement,
6. The test in a WHILE loop or conditional statement.

In addition,

7. A "DO I = ..." loop is considered as the WHILE loop by
   which it is defined (see Section I.4.2.2).

As a first illustration, consider the following two loops:

```
(2.1a)    I = 1;                        For N >= 1, 4*N+2 basic
          DO WHILE(I<=N);               steps are executed (the test
              X = X+A(I);               I<=N N+1 times and the 3
              X = X+B(I);               statements in the body
              I = I+1;                  N times)
          END;
```

```
(2.1b)    I = 1;                        For N >= 1, 3*N+2 basic steps
          DO WHILE (I <= N);            are executed (the test I<=N,
              X = X + A(I) + B(I);      N+1 times; the 2 statements
              I = I+1;                  in the body N times)
          END;
```

Certainly, different basic steps take different times to execute, and by only counting basic steps we make some errors in estimating the execution time of programs. Segments (2.1a) and (2.1b) clearly perform the same task in essentially the same way, and yet we say that one uses 4*N+2 basic steps and the other 3*N+2. We would <u>like</u> to say that the two perform essentially the same, and will subsequently extend our terminology to that effect. But first let us look at more important differences that might occur in execution times.

Suppose we want to process an array A(1:N) in some manner. We have seven different algorithms to carry out that process. (2.1c) gives the number of basic steps executed in each as a function of N, the size of the array.

Algorithm	Number of basic steps executed
A1	SQRT(N)
A2	N+5
A3	2*N
A4	N^2
A5	N^2+N
A6	N^3
A7	2**N

(2.1c) labels rows A3.

We notice immediately that for "very small" N any of these algorithms can be used. If we assume each basic step takes roughly .0001 seconds to execute, for N=10 the fastest algorithm A1 takes .0003 seconds while the slowest takes .1024. Typically, when comparing the speeds of algorithms, we are not interested in execution times for small inputs, but only for large inputs. With small amounts of data almost any algorithm will do. As the amount or size of the data increases, we have to be more careful about which algorithm we use. Figure 1 illustrates this well.

Algorithm A1 is clearly the best (with respect to time), but any of the first three seem reasonable. For large values of N, A2 and A3 aren't too different (one is twice as fast as the other), and we might use other criteria besides time to choose between them. Algorithms A4 and A5 seem all right for "moderately sized" input, but as N increases past 1000 they

become useless. Algorithms A6 and A7 clearly cannot be used for
moderate values of N.

algorithm	N = 20	N = 50	N = 100	N = 1000
A1	.0004 sec	.0007 sec	.0010 sec	.0032 sec
A2	.0025 sec	.0055 sec	.0105 sec	.1005 sec
A3	.0040 sec	.0100 sec	.0200 sec	.2000 sec
A4	.0400 sec	.2500 sec	1.000 sec	100 sec
A5	.0420 sec	.2550 sec	1.010 sec	100.1 sec
A6	.8 sec	12.5 sec	100 sec	28 hrs
A7	105 sec	3570 yrs	$4*10^{18}$ yrs	----

Figure 1. Amount of Time Required as a Function of N

Consider A4 and A5. For large N they perform essentially the
same; the term N in N^2+N has little effect when N is large.
We next introduce terminology which puts A4 and A5 in the same
category.

2.2 The Order of Execution Time

Let f(n) and g(n) be functions. We say that

(2.2a)   f(n) is of order g(n), written O(g(n)), if there is a
          constant c > 0 such that, for all (except possibly a
          finite number of) positive values of n,

$$f(n) <= c*g(n).$$

Example 1. Let f(n) = n+5 and g(n)=n. Taking c=5, we see that
          n+5 = f(n) <= 5*g(n) = 5*n for n=1,2,3,... Hence n+5
          is O(n).

Example 2. Let f(n) = 2*n+5 and g(n) = n. Taking c = 7, we see
          that 2*n+5 <= 7*n   for n=1,2,3,... Hence 2*n+5 is
          O(n).

Example 3. Let f(n) = $(1/2)*n^2+n$ and g(n) = n^2. Taking c = 2
          we see that $(1/2)*n^2+n$ <= $2*n^2$, for n = 1,2,3,...
          Hence $(1/2)*n^2+n$ is $O(n^2)$.

If f(N) is the number of basic steps executed for a program with
"input size" N, and if g(N) satisfies the above definition, then
the following are equivalent:

    1. The algorithm runs in time proportional to g(N),
    2. The running time is order g(N),
    3. The running time is O(g(N)),
    4. It's an order g(N) algorithm,
    5. Execution takes time proportional to g(N).

We give below a table in increasing size of typical execution
time orders that seem to crop up in programming. (Other
orders occur, but not so often.) When we compare two programs

with respect to time which have different orders, all other
things being equal we choose the one with smaller order. Only
when comparing algorithms with the same order should we worry
about the constant involved. When comparing 4*N with $1/2*N^2$, we
choose the 4*N algorithm; when choosing between 4*N and 1/2*N we
choose the 1/2*N algorithm.

Order	term used
constant	fixed time (it contains only basic steps)
LOG2(N)	logarithmic algorithm (see Section 2.4)
SQRT(N)	
N	linear algorithm
N*LOG2(N)	
N*SQRT(N)	
N^2	quadratic (or N^2) algorithm
N^3	cubic (or N^3) algorithm
2**N	exponential algorithm
N!	factorial algorithm

Figure 2. Typical Execution Time Orders

2.3 Worst Case Versus Average Case Analysis

Consider the problem of finding a value X in an array B(1:N),
with N ≥ 1. We want to store in J an integer so that B(J) = X,
and if no such integer exists, we want to store 0 in J:

```
J = 0;
K = 1;
DO WHILE ((J = 0) & (K <= N));
   IF B(K) = X THEN
      J = K;
   ELSE
      K = K + 1;
   END;
```

If X is not in the array B(1:N), then the algorithm executes at
most 3*N+3 basic steps. If X is in the array, the algorithm
executes fewer basic steps. Thus in the worst case linear
search is an order N, or linear algorithm.

Sometimes we would rather know the average number of basic
steps executed if we ran the algorithm a very large number of
times with different data. This average is also called the
"expected" number, but the word "expected" is used in a special
statistical sense (meaning average) and not with the usual
English meaning. Consider linear search, assuming that X is in
the list. If the values of B(1:N) are assumed to be "randomly"
chosen, then X has an equal probability of appearing in any of
the elements B(I). On the average then, we may expect to look
halfway through the list before finding X, executing roughly
3*(N/2) basic steps, which is still linear.

If X may not be in the list, we can expect more than 3*(N/2) basic steps -- how many more depends on the probability that X doesn't appear. However, the algorithm is still linear on the average, since it is linear for the worst case. This is in fact why the algorithm is called "linear" search.

For linear search then, both a worst case and average case analysis show that the algorithm is linear in the size of the input. This is not always the case, and frequently the average speed is much better than the worst speed. Which analysis should we choose? This depends in part on how easy it is for us to compute. In general, average case analysis is much harder because it requires estimates of various probabilities, and involves more complex calculations. Worst case analysis is often quite easy; we need just identify the worst case data and count how many operations the algorithm executes with that data. It may however not be a realistic estimate, since the worst case may never arise with "real" input.

2.4 Analysis of Binary Search: Logarithms

We can perform a search for a value X more efficiently than linear search if the array B(1:N) is already _sorted_ into ascending or descending order. We do this ourselves whenever we look up a name in the telephone book. We don't begin at the beginning of the telephone book, but we turn roughly to where the name we want is, and decide by that entry which half of the book to continue looking in. Then we repeat the process with just this half of the telephone book.

We can write down this algorithm as follows, where at each iteration we actually look in the middle of the list where we expect to find the name:

```
    /* LOOK FOR X IN B(1:N), SET J TO ITS INDEX*/
    /* IF X IS NOT IN B(1:N), SET J TO 0.*/
    Let the list to be searched be B(1:N);
    J = 0;
    DO WHILE(X is not found & list to be searched is not empty);
       K = index of middle entry of list;
       IF B(K) = X THEN
          J = K;
(2.4a) ELSE
          IF B(K) < X THEN
             discard first half of list including B(K);
          ELSE
             discard second half of list including B(K);
       END;
```

To describe the list to be searched we use two variables FIRST and LAST. At any time during execution, the list still to be searched is B(FIRST:LAST). Thus the list is _not_ empty if

FIRST <= LAST. With this data refinement, (2.4a) is easily
translated into the following PL/I algorithm:


```
        J = 0;
        FIRST = 1;
        LAST = N;
        DO WHILE((J=0) & (FIRST <= LAST));
            K = (FIRST + LAST)/2; /* K = MIDDLE ENTRY */
(2.4b)  IF B(K) = X THEN
                J = K;
            ELSE
                IF B(K) < X THEN
                    FIRST = K + 1;
                ELSE
                    LAST = K - 1;
            END;
```

Let us perform a worst case analysis of (2.4b). Clearly the
worst case arises when the loop iterates as often as possible,
and this is the case when the value X is not in the list B(1:N).
In this case, $3+5*i+1$ basic steps are executed, where i is the
number of times the loop body is executed.

If N = 1, the loop body is executed once, because the whole
list B(1:1) is discarded if B(1) ¬= X. If N = 2, the first
execution of the loop body discards at least half the list,
leaving at most one element in it. Since we know that the loop
body executes only once if N = 1, we see that for N = 2 the loop
body is executed at most twice. Similarly, if $2<N\leq4$ the loop
body is executed at most 3 times, and if $4<N\leq8$ the loop body is
executed at most 4 times.

Table (2.4c) gives a list of possible values of N, all powers
of 2, and the corresponding number of loop iterations that can
occur. We see that if N is between $2**(n-1)$ and $2**n$ for an
integer n, then the loop iterates <u>at most</u> n+1 times. Hence the
number of basic steps executed is no more than $4+5*(n+1)$.

(2.4c)

N		number of iterations
1	$= 2^0$	1
2	$= 2^1$	2
4	$= 2^2$	3
8	$= 2^3$	4
16	$= 2^4$	5
32	$= 2^5$	6
64	$= 2^6$	7

If N = 2 raised to the power n, then n is called <u>the
logarithm to the base 2 of</u> N. It is written <u>LOG2(N)</u>. (LOG2 is
also a built$_{in}$ function in PL/I and is written this way.)
(2.4d) is a table of some values of N and corresponding
logarithms.

What is LOG2(9)? It lies somewhere between 3 and 4, as you
can see from table (2.4c). Exactly where it is doesn't really
matter from our point of view, and we will never ask you to
compute it. We just don't need to. What is important is to
note that the function LOG2(N) "grows much more slowly" than N
itself. When N = 1, LOG2(N) is quite close to it, but as N
grows to 1024, LOG2(N) only grows to 10. Thus an algorithm
which performs only LOG2(N) operations for input of size N is
far superior in speed to an equivalent linear algorithm.

(2.4d)

N	LOG2(N)	reason
1	0	$1 = 2^0$
2	1	$2 = 2^1$
4	2	$4 = 2^2$
8	3	$8 = 2^3$
16	4	$16 = 2^4$
256	8	$256 = 2^8$
1024	10	$1024 = 2^{10}$
32768	15	$32768 = 2^{15}$

The binary search algorithm runs in time proportional to
LOG2(N). This yields a tremendous saving over the linear
search. For example, if N = 32,768, linear search executes on
the average over 49,152 basic steps, while binary search
executes at most 84 steps! If a list is sorted, and if it
contains over 20 elements, say, then the crucial difference here
is that linear search is a linear algorithm while binary search
is logarithmic.

2.5 Analysis of Simple Program Segments

A Program Segment to Test Primeness

An integer greater than 1 is prime if it is exactly divisible
only by 1 and itself. The first few primes are 2, 3, 5, 7, 11,
13, 17, 19, 23, 29, 31. Segment (2.5a) tests whether a positive
integer > 2 is prime. Assuming the loop condition can be
implemented by a basic step (which it can), we see that the
algorithm performs at most 4+2*(N-2) basic steps to test the
primeness of N, and is thus linear.

```
      /* N CONTAINS AN INTEGER > 2.  STORE 1 IN ANS IF N IS A*/
      /* PRIME NUMBER, 0 OTHERWISE.  ALGORITHM TAKES AT MOST*/
      /* 4 +2*(N-2) STEPS, AND IS THUS LINEAR*/
      I = 2;
      DO WHILE ((I < N) & (I does not divide N evenly));
(2.5a)  I = I + 1;
      END;
      IF I = N THEN
        ANS = 1;
      ELSE
        ANS = 0;
```

We see two ways to improve this algorithm. First note that
the program tests whether 2, 4, 6, 8, ... all divide N evenly.
Obviously, if 2 does not divide N evenly, then no even number
will. This inefficiency is rectified in algorithm (2.5b).
Secondly, suppose a number J greater than SQRT(N) divides N
evenly. Then so does the number

$$N \: / \: J$$

which is <u>less</u> <u>than</u> SQRT(N). Hence it is not necessary to test
integers greater than SQRT(N) to see if they divide N evenly.
This change is made in (2.5c).

Which algorithm is better, (2.5b) or (2.5c)? (2.5b) cuts the
worst case execution time in half, but note that it is still
<u>linear</u>. Algorithm (2.5c) executes at most 4+2*(SQRT(N)-2) basic
<u>steps</u> and is thus an O(SQRT(N)) algorithm. Now if N>10,000 and
prime, (2.5b) executes over 10,000 basic steps, while (2.5c)
executes around 200.

```
          /* N contains an integer > 2.  Store 1 in ANS if N is a*/
          /* prime number, 0 otherwise.  Algorithm takes at most*/
          /* 5+2*(N/2 - 2) steps and is thus linear.*/
          IF 2 divides N evenly THEN
             ANS = 0;
          ELSE
             DO;
                I = 3;
                DO WHILE((I < N) & (I does not divide N evenly));
(2.5b)             I = I + 2;
                END;
                IF I = N THEN
                   ANS = 1;
                ELSE
                   ANS = 0;
             END;



          /* N contains an integer > 2.  Store 1 in ANS if N is a*/
          /* prime number, 0 otherwise.  Algorithm takes at most */
          /* 4+2*(SQRT(N)-2) steps and is thus O(SQRT(N)).*/
          I = 2;
          SQRTN = SQRT(N);
          DO WHILE((I <= SQRTN) & (I does not divide N evenly));
             I = I + 1;
(2.5c)    END;
          IF I divides N evenly THEN
             ANS = 0;
          ELSE
             ANS = 1;
```

<u>Generating</u> <u>a</u> <u>List</u> <u>of</u> <u>Unique</u> <u>Numbers</u>

Supppose the input consists of a list of N integers (N is already initialized), and we want to store these integers in an array B but with each unique integer appearing only once. Thus if N = 8 and the list is

      3   8   12   8   6   5   8   3

then upon termination of the algorithm B should contain

      3   8   12   6   5   -   -   -

where "-" indicates that the value in that position is immaterial. Let us also assume that a variable M should contain the number of unique integers in B upon termination. A simple program segment to do this is

```
          M = 0;        /* NO INTEGERS IN B YET */
          DO I = 1 TO N BY 1;
              GET LIST(INT);
(2.5d)        Search B(1:M) for INT and set J to 1 if found,
                  to 0 otherwise;
              IF J = 0 THEN
                  DO;
                      M = M + 1;
                      B(M) = INT;
                      END;
          END;
```

The operation Search B(1:M) will probably be done by linear search, since the array is not sorted. (Be careful in writing this search, however, since it must work when M = 0!) Thus each execution of "Search" takes time proportional to the current value of M. Execution of each of the other statements in the loop body takes essentially a constant time, so that for M sufficiently large, execution of the loop body alone is proportional to M.

The worst case arises when the search is as slow as possible at each iteration of the loop, and this occurs when the value being searched for is not in the list (i.e., when all N input numbers are different). For I=1 the search takes time proportional to 0; for I=2 it takes time proportional to 1, for I=3, 2 and so on. Thus the total search time is proportional to

$$0 + 1 + 2 + \ldots + (N-1) = N(N-1)/2 = N^2/2 - N/2$$

In the worst case, execution time is proportional to N^2.

Now suppose that there are only M different integers in the original list of N integers. We leave it to the reader to show that the worst case running time is O(N*M).

Printing Names in Alphabetical Order, Without Duplicates

Consider the following problem:

> The input is a list of roughly 5000 names of people. Some
> names, say about 30% of them, are duplicates. The program
> should   read   in these names and print them out   in
> alphabetical order, with each different name appearing only
> once. (This problem occurs frequently. For example the
> list might be a mailing list, a list of alumni and their
> addresses, a list of students and their courses, where each
> student's name appears once for each course, and so on.)

Recall that the last example (2.5d) was somewhat similar.
One solution to this problem consists of first making up the
list of unduplicated names as in (2.5d), then sorting the list,
and then printing it. The algorithm is:

            S1: Read in list and delete duplicates
                (algorithm (2.5d));
(2.5e)   S2: Sort the list;
            S3: Print the list;

This would probably be our first thought, since it is related to
a problem just studied. However, we know that S1 runs in time
proportional to M*N (if there are M unique names and N total
names), which is roughly .70N since about 30 percent of the
names are duplicates. Let us assume we can sort the list in
time proportional to N*LOG2(N).   This can be done by several
algorithms, for example heap sort of Section 2.7 and Quicksort
in Section VII.2.4. We show below the statements of (2.5e)
together with their execution time orders as functions of the
size of the input. Clearly the most time is spent in executing
S1, and we should look for a more efficient way of performing
it.

Statement	S1	S2	S3
Time	M*N	M*LOG2(M)	M

Suppose we leave all names in the list, including duplicates,
then sort using the N*LOG2(N) heap sort, and then print:

            Read names into list B;
(2.5f)   Sort B;
            Print B, but avoid printing duplicates.

Reading names into the list is now of order N, the number of
names; sorting is of order N*LOG2(N); and we should be able to
print B as stated in linear time (with respect to N), since all
duplicates of one name now appear together in the sorted list.
Hence, in this algorithm, the sorting dominates, and the whole
algorithm runs in time N*LOG2(N). This is much faster than
(2.5e).

A third possibility exists. Suppose after reading each new
name we immediately sort B:

```
M = 0;
DO I = 1 TO N BY 1;
    Read one name into NAME;
    Search sorted list B(1:M) for NAME;
    IF NAME not in list THEN
        Insert NAME into proper place in list B(1:M);
    END;
Print B;
```

This may seem like a good idea, but we leave it to the reader to
show that the total time spent inserting names into their proper
places will be of order M^2 and thus not very attractive. The
searching can be performed by binary search, but the insertion
will be too slow. This algorithm is called an insertion sort.

2.6 A More Complicated Example: KWIC Index

We will discuss the development of a program to produce a
"KWIC Index" as we did with other examples in Section III.2 but
now we can pay more attention to the choice of an efficient
algorithm.   It is also a good example of several points
discussed in III.3:

1. using notation to fit the problem,
2. the importance of analyzing all possibilities for a
   refinement, and
3. the importance of knowing which operations are to be
   performed on a data structure before deciding on its
   representation.

Without a top-down development, or at least a clear description
of the program at a high level, it would be difficult to even
see that there are so many choices to choose from.

2.6.1 The Problem and a First Refinement

(2.6.1a) KWIC Index. KWIC stands for "KeyWord In Context". Its
meaning is as follows: suppose we have a list of titles of
books, research articles, etc. For example,

               THE RENTED STOLE
               MYSTERY OF THE STOLEN RENT
               RENTED HOUSE MYSTERY
               STOLEN HOUSE
               RENT A MYSTERY RENT HOUSE

A KWIC index is a list of the titles arranged so that it is
easy to find out which of the titles contain each "key"
word. The KWIC index for the above list would be:

```
                         ┌──keyword column
                         │
              RENTED HOUSE MYSTERY
              STOLEN HOUSE
    RENT A MYSTERY RENT HOUSE
                    MYSTERY OF THE STOLEN RENT
         RENTED HOUSE MYSTERY
              RENT A MYSTERY RENT HOUSE
       RENT A MYSTERY RENT HOUSE
    MYSTERY OF THE STOLEN RENT
              RENT A MYSTERY RENT HOUSE
              THE RENTED STOLE
              RENTED HOUSE MYSTERY
         THE RENTED STOLE
              STOLEN HOUSE
       MYSTERY OF THE STOLEN RENT
```

In each title, words which are <u>not</u> articles, prepositions,
and the like are called <u>keywords</u>. In the index, each title
occurs once in the list for each keyword in the title, and
the titles are so aligned that the keywords all occur in
the same column. The titles are printed in alphabetical
order of the keywords. Note that if a keyword appears two
or more times in a title (e.g. RENT in "RENT A MYSTERY
RENT HOUSE"), the title appears two or more times under
that keyword in the final list.

Such a KWIC index is an invaluable aid to researchers in
finding books and articles. To find them, one just has to
search the list for relevant keywords and note down the
corresponding titles. A typical index may contain 1000 to 5000
different titles.

A program to produce a KWIC index is given the titles and the
list of "non-keywords" as input. The program must read the
titles and non-keywords, make up a list of possible keywords,
sort the list of keywords, and then print the titles according
to the list of keywords. Often, it will take several "runs" of
the program to get the index in shape. The list of non-keywords
may be changed from run to run to add more words than just
prepositions and articles. For example, the word "computer"
appears in many titles in computer science, and it may be
irrelevant to have a listing of 300 titles each with the keyword
"computer". Such cases may not be detected until after the list
is first printed.

The general outline (first refinement) for the KWIC index
program can be easily created from the above description. It
uses three "lists": TITLES is the list of titles, NONKEY the
list of non-keywords, and KEYWORDS the list of keywords.
Although they will probably be implemented in standard fashion
using arrays, we will not make that decision now, but just talk
in terms of lists. The first attempt at a program is:

```
                    S1: Read titles into list TITLES;
                    S2: Read non-keywords into list NONKEY;
(2.6.1b)            S3: Make up list KEYWORDS from the titles
                        and non-keywords;
                    S4: Sort the list KEYWORDS;
                    S5: Print the titles according to list KEYWORDS.
```

Refinements of statements S1 and S2 will depend on the input
format and we will not discuss them further. We are mainly
interested in statements S3, S4 and S5. Speed of execution will
be important since there can be so many titles (up to, say,
5000). First, note that a sort is involved. We will use an
N*LOG2(N) algorithm like heap sort (see Section 2.7) instead of
an N^2 algorithm like bubble sort. Hopefully we can refine S3
and S5 into algorithms no worse than N*LOG2(N).

In order to intelligently talk about speed, we must have some
estimate of the size of the lists. Suppose that

```
          1.  There are T titles.  T <= 5000.
(2.6.1c)  2.  On the average there are 5 keywords per title.
          3.  Each keyword appears about 5 different times.
              Thus there are roughly T different keywords.
          4.  There are a maximum of 10 words per title.
```

We don't know there are 5 keywords per title, or that there are
T different keywords, but these estimates are close enough in
order to make reasonable time estimates.

2.6.2 Analyzing and Refining Statement S3

In order to save space, let us first of all consider keeping
only the different keywords in KEYWORDS. No matter how many
times a keyword appears in titles, it will only appear once in
the list. Thus, for the sample input, the list KEYWORDS would
be

```
      HOUSE    MYSTERY    RENT    RENTED    STOLE    STOLEN
```

Statment S3 to make up the list of keywords must then perform as
follows:

```
          /* MAKE UP LIST OF KEYWORDS*/
          Set list of KEYWORDS to empty;
          For each word in each title
              DO;
                  IF that word is not in NOKEY THEN
                      DO;
(2.6.2a)                  Search KEYWORDS for the word;
                          IF the word isn't in KEYWORDS THEN
                              Add word to KEYWORDS;
                      END;
              END;
```

This looks similar to a problem discussed at the end of Section
2.5.   There, the problem was to read in a list of values and put
them in an array, but put each duplicated value in only once.
Here, we get the words from the titles, but that is the only
essential difference.   In Section 2.5, we saw that the approach
we just took led to an N^2 algorithm. Looking at (2.6.2a), we
see that a search of the keyword list is performed in time T.
This leads to a T^2 algorithm, as in the last section.

   If we want to have the algorithm run in time no worse than
$T \cdot LOG2(T)$, then we must revise it along the lines suggested by
the related problem of Section 2.5. We must first put all the
keywords in KEYWORDS, whether they are duplicates or not, then
sort, and then delete the duplicates:

                    S1: Read titles into list TITLES;
                    S2: Read non-keywords into list NONKEY;
(2.6.2b)   S3: Make up list KEYWORDS from the titles
                           and non-keywords;
                    S4: Sort the list KEYWORDS;
                    S4A:Delete duplicates from KEYWORDS;
                    S5: Print the titles according to list KEYWORDS.
S3 is now

       /* S3: MAKE UP LIST KEYWORDS FROM TITLES */
       Set list KEYWORDS to empty;
       For each word in each title
          DO;
              IF that word is not in NONKEY THEN
                 Put that word in list KEYWORDS;
              END;

We have lost the space advantage we were looking for in the
beginning of this section, but we have satisfied our speed
requirement. Indeed, statement S3 runs in time proportional to
the number of titles T, while the sort is still $T*LOG2(T)$.
Statement S4A can also obviously be done in time proportional to
the number of keywords, which is roughly 5*T. The only
statement to take care of now is statement S5.

2.6.3 Analyzing and Refining Statement S5 to Print the Titles

   Our first attempt at statement S5 is

   For each keyword in KEYWORDS
        DO;
(2.6.3a)   Search the titles and print those containing the
               keyword (if a keyword appears i times in
               a title, print the title i times);
            END;

Searching the titles will take time proportional to the number
of titles T.   Since this must be done T times (once for each

keyword), this is a T^2 algorithm, which is above our hoped-for upper bound of T*LOG2(T).

We have to process each keyword, so the only way of reducing the time in executing (2.6.3a) is to somehow get rid of the search through the titles each time. How can we do that? One possible way would be to keep with each keyword a list of the titles to be printed for that keyword, or better still, to keep a list of the positions of the titles in TITLES, to be printed.

Keeping such a list may be quite messy, but notice that if we don't delete duplicate keywords, then for each keyword in KEYWORDS we need only keep track of which title it appeared in and its character position in the title. For example, with the sample input, the keyword list could be represented by three arrays KEYWORDS, TITLENO, and CHARPOS, as follows:

KEYWORDS	TITLENO	CHARPOS		KEYWORDS	TITLENO	CHARPOS
(1) RENTED	1	5	(8) MYSTERY	3	14
(2) STOLE	1	12	(9) STOLEN	4	1
(3) MYSTERY	2	1	(10) HOUSE	4	8
(4) STOLEN	2	16	(11) RENT	5	1
(5) RENT	2	23	(12) MYSTERY	5	8
(6) RENTED	3	1	(13) RENT	5	16
(7) HOUSE	3	8	(14) HOUSE	5	21

Statement S5 will then look something like

```
DO I = 1 to number of keywords;
   N = TITLENO(I);
   POS = CHARPOS(I);
   Print the Nth title in TITLES with the POSth
      character in the keyword column;
   END;
```

This requires several changes in the higher level algorithm (2.6.2b). For example, we must delete S4A which deletes duplicate keywords. At this point we must back up to this algorithm, change it, and then proceed in top-down fashion to refine its statements once more. This we leave to the reader.

Now we can specify in detail the data structures that will be used:

1. The list of titles is kept in an array TITLES. TITLES(1) is the first title, TITLES(2) the second, and so on. There are T titles in the array.

2. The list of non-keywords is kept in an array NONKEY. NONKEY(1) is the first, NONKEY(2) the second, and so on.

3. The keywords are kept in three arrays KEYWORDS, TITLENO, and CHARPOS. The Ith keyword is in KEYWORD(I), and was added to the array because it was found in title

TITLENO(I), beginning at character position CHARPOS(I).
At any point, there are K keywords in the list.

In terms of these structures the algorithm is:
    S1: Read titles into TITLES;
    S2: Read non-keywords into NONKEY;
    S3: Make up keyword list in arrays KEYWORDS, TITLENO, and
        CHARPOS;
    S4: Sort array KEYWORDS. Whenever a swap of KEYWORDS(I)
        and KEYWORDS(J) (say) occurs, also swap TITLENO(I)
        and TITLENO(J), and CHARPOS(I) and CHARPOS(J);
    S5: Print the titles according to the keywords;

We have the following refinements of S3 and S5:

```
/* S3: MAKE UP LIST OF KEYWORDS, ASSUMING NONKEY IS*/
/* SORTED. IF  BINARY SEARCH IS USED TIME IS PROPORTIONAL*/
/* TO T*LOG2(NO. OF NON-KEYWORDS).  */
K = 0; /* KEYWORD LIST IS EMPTY */
DO I = 1 TO T BY 1;
   For each word in TITLES(I)
      DO;
         IF the word is not in NONKEY THEN
            DO;
               K = K + 1;
               KEYWORD(K) = the word;
               TITLENO(K) = I;
               CHARPOS(K) = position of keyword in title;
               END;
         END;
   END;


/* S5: PRINT TITLES. TIME PROPORTIONAL TO NUMBER OF */
/* KEYWORDS K. */
DO I = 1 TO K BY 1;
   Print out TITLES(TITLENO(I)), with character
      CHARPOS(I) appearing in the keyword column;
   END;
```

2.7 An Example: Heap Sort

Problem. Sort the array B(1:N) into ascending order.
(Assume B and N are already initialized.)

A number of sorting algorithms have already been given, but
all run in time proportional to N^2 in the worst case. The
algorithm developed here runs in time proportional to N*LOG2(N).
It requires a knowledge of "trees" and "heaps".

2.7.1 Binary Trees and Heaps

A binary tree is a collection of nodes (the underlined values
in the trees of (2.7.1a)) and branches (the lines connecting the
nodes), which satisfies certain properties. One node, called
the root node, has no branches coming down to it. Each other
node has one branch coming down into it from above. At most two
branches emanate downward from a node to other nodes.

Each node is labeled with an integer to its right. If i
labels a node, we use the notation NODE(i) to refer to the node
itself. In tree 1 of (2.7.1a) NODE(1)=8, NODE(2)=7, and
NODE(3)=5.

Any node is called the father of the nodes on branches
emanating downward from it. Similarly, they are called his
sons. Since each father can have at most two sons, we designate
them the left son and the right son. The position of a node is
important. A father can have only a left son, or only a right
son, or both. In tree 1 of (2.7.1a), node 1's sons are nodes 2
and 3, node 3's sons are 6 and 7. 7's father is 3.

A father's sons, his sons' sons, etc., are called his
descendants. Similarly, we talk of a node's ancestors -- his
father, father's father, etc. In tree 1 of (2.7.1a) node 2's
descendants are nodes 4, 5, 8, and 9; 9's ancestors are nodes 4,
2, and 1.

The root node is on level 1, his sons are on level 2, their
sons are on level 3, and so on.

We label the nodes in a very systematic manner. The root
node is node 1. If a node is labeled i, his sons are always
labeled 2i (the left son) and 2i+1 (the right son). Thus node
4's sons are nodes 8 and 9. Finally, we restrict our trees so
that if node i exists, then so do nodes 1, 2, ..., i-1. Thus
there are no "holes" in the tree. Tree 2 of (2.7.1a) does not
satisfy this restriction and we will not use this tree further.
This restriction is made so that later, when we attempt to map
the tree into PL/I arrays, we will have no trouble.

The following property will be useful: a binary tree is a
heap if for any node i,

NODE(each ancestor of i) $\geq$ NODE(i)

Tree 1 of (2.7.1a) is a heap, as you can see by inspection.
Tree 1 of (2.7.1b) is not, since NODE(4) < NODE(9).

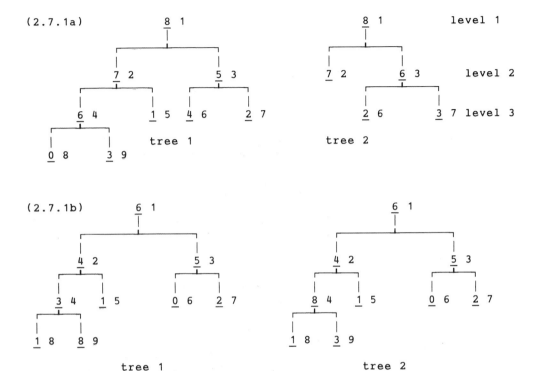

(2.7.1a)   tree 1

(2.7.1b)   tree 2

2.7.2 The Basic Heap Sort Algorithm

We now outline the basic algorithm for sorting B(1:N). First
of all, consider B to be a binary tree; the value in B(i) is
NODE(i) for any i. It is easy to calculate fathers and sons:

      father(B(i))   is   B(i/2)
      leftson(B(i))   is   B(2i)
      rightson(B(i))   is   B(2i+1)

We shall use terms like "father(i)" when referring to B because
we must think of it as a binary tree in order to understand the
algorithm. The sorting algorithm consists of two steps:

      S1: Make B(1:N) into a heap;
      S2: Sort the heap so that B(i) ≤ B(i+1) for i=1,...,n-1.

As we will see, each step can be done in time proportional to
N*LOG2(N) so that the whole algorithm runs in time proportional
to N*LOG2(N).

2.7.3 Making B(1:N) into a Heap

The algorithm is:

```
        DO I = 1 TO N BY 1;
(2.7.3a)    Make B(1:I) into a heap, assuming
              B(1:I-1) is already a heap;
        END;
```

Thus we make the tree into a heap one node at a time, in the
order the nodes are labeled. For example, consider tree 1 of
(2.7.1b).   The nodes 1 through 8 already form a heap. If we add
node 9 (value 8), we no longer have a heap since NODE(4) <
NODE(9). To make it into a heap we need only "bubble" the
offending value 8 up to its father, and to its father's father,
etc. until it has reached the root node or until it is finally
not greater than its father. Tree 2 of (2.7.1b) shows the first
step of this bubbling process, in which NODE(4) is exchanged
with NODE(9).

There is one important property necessary to follow the
subalgorithm given here. This is:

Suppose a tree would be a heap except for one node j where
NODE(ancestor of j) < NODE(j) for some ancestor. Then
NODE(father of j) < NODE(j). If we exchange the values of
NODE(father of j) and NODE(j) (as in the transformation of
tree 1 to tree 2 in (2.7.1b)), then the only offending
relations can be between NODE(father of j) and his
ancestors.

Work with examples, and then prove this for yourself.

With this property in mind, we can now give the following
algorithm for the English statement of (2.7.3a):

```
J = I;
DO WHILE (node J has a father);
    IF B(father of J) ≥ B(J) THEN
       stop;
    Swap B(father of J) and B(J);
    J = father of J;
    END;
```

Putting this together with (2.7.3a) and translating into SP/k
(except for the Swap) yields the following algorithm:

```
/* MAKE B(1:N) INTO A HEAP */
DO I = 1 TO N BY 1;
   /* MAKE B(1:I) INTO A HEAP ASSUMING B(1:I-1) */
   /* IS A HEAP */
   J = I;
   NOT_A_HEAP = '1'B;
   /* BUBBLE B(J) UP AS FAR AS IT WILL GO */
   DO WHILE((J>1) & NOT_A_HEAP); /* WHILE J HAS A FATHER */
      FATHER_OF_J = J/2.0E0;
      IF B(FATHER_OF_J) >= B(J) THEN
         NOT_A_HEAP = '0'B;
      ELSE
         DO;
            Swap B(FATHER_OF_J) and B(J);
            J = FATHER_OF_J;
            END;
      END;
   END;
```

Let us see why this is an N*LOG2(N) algorithm. Consider a value of I, and see how many times the body of the inner loop (the DO WHILE loop) is executed. Each iteration of the loop "bubbles" the offending value up one level in the tree. Hence the maximum number of times the body can be executed is the number of levels in the tree, minus one.

If the tree has 2 nodes the level is 2, if 4 nodes the level is 3, if 8 nodes the level is 4, and so on. The level is exactly FLOOR(LOG2(I))+1. Thus for a given value of I, the loop body is executed at most LOG2(I) times.

Hence the total number of times the inner loop body is executed is <u>at most</u>

   LOG2(1) + LOG2(2) + LOG2(3) + ... + LOG2(N)

and this is bounded above by N*LOG2(N). The total number of basic steps executed is bounded above by the sum of the following, and this sum is of the order N*LOG2(N):

   3*N   (basic steps in executing DO I = 1 TO N loop)
   2*N   (J=I; NOT_A_HEAP = '1'B, are executed N times)
   5*N*LOG2(N)   (steps executed in inner loop)

2.7.4 <u>Sorting the Heap</u>

The heap B satisfies the property B(father(i)) $\geq$ B(i). We want to change B so it satisfies the property B(i) $\leq$ B(i+1), since then the array will be sorted. Note that for any heap, the largest value is in the root node, and that if the heap is to look like a sorted array, that largest value must be put in the <u>last</u> node of the tree.

Algorithm (2.7.4a) has the following property which holds just before each execution of the loop body.

> B(1:I) is a heap. Every value in B(1:I) ≤ every value in B(I+1:N). The array segment B(I+1:N) is sorted in ascending order:

```
B(1)                              B(I) B(I+1)         B(N)
┌──────────────────────────────────┬──────────────────────┐
| These form a heap and are not     | These are sorted:    |
| greater than values in B(I+1:N)   | B(I+1)≤B(I+2),etc.   |
└──────────────────────────────────┴──────────────────────┘
```

Thus each execution of the loop body takes the largest number out of the heap B(1:I) and puts it in the correct position of the array.

```
          I = N;
(2.7.4a) DO WHILE (I > 1);
          Swap B(1) and B(I);
          I = I-1;
          Make B(1:I) into a heap;
          END;
```

The only thing left is to show how to make B(1:I) back into a heap. It is <u>not</u> a heap only because the new value in B(1) is too small (probably); this value just came from the previous last node of the heap. In order to make the tree back into a heap, then, we bubble this small value <u>down</u> as far as it can go, the opposite of what we did in the last section. However, the process is quite similar; we need only make sure we exchange it (if necessary) with its <u>larger</u> son.

```
    /* MAKE B(1:I) INTO A HEAP.  ONLY THE VALUE IN B(1) */
    /* DESTROYS THE HEAP RELATION */
    J = 1;
    NOT_A_HEAP = '1'B;
    DO WHILE((J has a son) & NOT_A_HEAP);
       K = left son of J;
       IF J has a right son THEN
          IF B(K) < B(right son of J)THEN
             K = right son of J;
       IF B(J) >= B(K) THEN
          NOT_A_HEAP = '0'B;
       ELSE
          DO;
             Swap B(J) and B(K);
             J = K;
             END;
       END;
```

Putting this all together with (2.7.4a) yields the following program; we leave it to you to show that it is also of the order N*LOG2(N).

```
/* SORT HEAP B(1:N). */
I = N;
DO WHILE (I > 1);
   Swap B(1) and B(I);
   I = I - 1;
   /* MAKE B(1:I) INTO A HEAP. ONLY THE VALUE B(1) MAY */
   /* DESTROY THE HEAP RELATION. */
   J = 1;
   K = 2*J;   /* K WILL BE J's LARGER SON */
   NOT_A_HEAP = '1'B;
   DO WHILE((K <= I) & NOT_A_HEAP);   /* WHILE J HAS A SON */
      IF K < I THEN
          IF B(K) < B(K+1) THEN
             K = K + 1;
      IF B(J) >= B(K) THEN
          NOT_A_HEAP = '0'B;   /* TERMINATES LOOP */
      ELSE
          DO;
              Swap B(J) and B(K);
              J = K;
              K = 2*J;
              END;
      END;
   END;
```

Section 2 Exercises

1. Show that the function

$$f(N) = c1 + c2 \cdot N$$

is order O(N), where c1 and c2 are constants. Any such function is said to be <u>linear</u> in N.

2. Show that the function

$$f(N) = c1 + c2 \cdot N + c3 \cdot N^2$$

is $O(N^2)$, where c1, c2 and c3 are any constants.   F(N) is a <u>quadratic</u> function.

3. Show that the function

$$f(N) = c1 + c2 \cdot N + c3 \cdot LOG2(N) + c4 \cdot N \cdot LOG2(N)$$

is O(N*LOG2(N)), where c1, c2, c3 and c4 are any constants.

4. Show that the function N + SQRT(N) is O(N). Show that it is <u>not</u> O(SQRT(N)).

5. Show that the function N+LOG2(N) is O(N) but <u>not</u> O(LOG2(N)).

6. Determine the order of execution time for each program segment of Exercise 2, Section I.5, in the worst case.

7. Consider the binary search algorithm of (2.4b). Suppose N = 16 and B = 1, 3, 5, 7, 9, 11, 13, 15, 17, 19, 21, 23, 25, 27, 29, 99.

    a) Execute algorithm (2.4b) by hand with X = 99.
    b) Execute algorithm (2.4b) by hand with X = 1.
    c) Execute algorithm (2.4b) by hand with X = 17.
    d) Execute algorithm (2.4b) by hand with X = 18.

8. Will binary search (2.4b) work correctly if, when discarding half the list, B(J) is <u>not</u> also discarded?

9. Binary search (2.4b) makes two array-element comparisons for each iteration of the loop, while the likelihood that the condition B(J) = X is true early during execution is quite low. Change the program to make only <u>one</u> comparison within the loop, say B(J) <= X. Then after the loop make a few comparisons to set J correctly.

10. The following algorithm, the <u>successive</u> <u>maxima</u> sorting algorithm, sorts array B(1:N) into ascending order. Find the order of the worst case execution time as a function of N.

```
/* SORT ARRAY B(1:N) */
DO J = N TO 2 BY -1;
   /* Swap values of B(1:J) to put largest in B(J) */
   DO I = 1 TO J-1 BY 1;
      IF B(I) > B(J) THEN
         Swap B(I) and B(J);
      END;
   END;
```

11. Below are two program segments to calculate the <u>mode</u> of an array A(1:N), where it is assumed that A is already sorted in ascending order. The mode is the most frequently occurring value; the mode of an empty array is arbitrarily taken as 0. Find an upper bound for the number of basic steps executed and the worst case order of execution time, for each. The second program may contain an execution error, due to the way PL/I and SP/k evaluate a condition like (J<N)&(A(J)=A(J+1)). Fix the error.

```
/* FIND THE MODE M OF SORTED ARRAY A(1:N), N>=1.   */
/* BEFORE AND AFTER EACH EXECUTION OF THE LOOP BODY, */
/* M IS THE MODE OF A(1:I), */
/* MCT = NUMBER OF TIMES M OCCURS IN A(1:I), */
/* LCT = NUMBER OF TIMES A(I) OCCURS IN A(1:I).  */
I = 1;
M = A(1);
MCT = 1;
LCT = 1;
DO WHILE(I<N);
   I = I + 1;
   IF A(I) ¬= A(I-1) THEN
      LCT = 1;
   ELSE
      DO;
         LCT = LCT + 1;
         IF LCT > MCT THEN
            DO;
               M = A(I);
               MCT = LCT;
               END;
         END;
   END;
```

```
/* CALCULATE THE MODE M OF SORTED ARRAY A(1:N).  */
/* BEFORE AND AFTER EACH EXECUTION OF THE MAIN LOOP BODY,*/
/* M = MODE(A(1:I)), */
/* MCT IS THE NUMBER OF TIMES M OCCURS IN A(1:I),*/
/* A(I) ¬= A(I+1)  (IF THEY BOTH EXIST).  */
I = 0;
M = 0;
MCT = 0;
DO WHILE (I < N);
   J = I + 1;
   DO WHILE ((J < N) & (A(J) = A(J+1)));
      J = J + 1;
      END;
   IF (J - I) > MCT THEN
      DO;
         M = A(J);
         MCT = J - I;
         END;
   I = J;
   END;
```

Section 3   Problems Impossible to Program

This section discusses three types of problems that are impossible to program -- no approach will yield an effective program. Sections 3.1 and 3.2 concern problems that are too vague or too large. Such problems occur frequently and the programmer must be wary of them. Section 3.3 introduces the existence of problems for which it can be proved that no effective program can be written.

3.1 Ill-Defined Problems

Many problems are just not understood well enough to program. We have suggested that in program development one use English commands and phrases, such as "solve", "find", "create", etc. This is useful, but it can lead to unwarranted optimism about the kinds of problems that can be programmed. Eventually, each of these commands must be refined or developed into the statements of a programming language. The process breaks down if, at any point in the development, one encounters a command that cannot be refined into program statements. For example, it is easy to write "solve", but it is sometimes difficult to figure out "how to solve". One can write "find" and not even be sure where to look.

It is often easy to disguise the inability to refine such a command. For example, in developing a program to select potential companions for an applicant to a computer dating service, one must at some point refine the meaning of "appropriate date" into program statements. No algorithm capable of doing this has yet been discovered. Nevertheless, scores of people have written programs to perform this task. Unfortunately, the use of a computer sometimes lends respectability or authenticity to an algorithm that would be laughable if performed by a human.

While it is often necessary to obtain approximate solutions to difficult or impossible problems, programming ethics demand that the approximation be clearly identified, and that the program not be used to obscure the dubiousness of the algorithm.

3.2 Impossibly-Large Problems

Most beginners are somewhat awed by the computer's speed. Programs that take hours to write are executed in seconds, and one begins to regard its speed as essentially infinite. Therefore, it is surprising and a bit disillusioning to discover problems that are clearly and precisely stated, easily programmed, but that require so much execution time that they are effectively impossible.

The following program makes the point. It does nothing, but takes at least hours to do so on the fastest computer. If a third level of loops were added to the nest it would become impossibly long for the fastest computers that exist.

```
FUTILE:PROCEDURE OPTIONS(MAIN);
   /* TWO LEVEL EMPTY DO NEST */
   DECLARE (I,J) FIXED;
   DO I = 1 TO 100000 BY 1;
      DO J = 1 TO 100000 BY 1;
         END;
      END;
   END /* FUTILE */;
```

As a more reasonable example, consider the following problem. Suppose a swimming coach has four swimmers to enter in a meet consisting of four events, and the rules specify that each swimmer may compete in only one event. The coach writes down his estimate of how many points each swimmer would earn in each event in a table of four rows (one for each swimmer) and four columns (one for each event). Now he wants to determine the assignment of swimmers to events to maximize the teams score.

We could try every possible assignment, add up the total score for each one, and select the assignment that gives the highest score. The structure of a program to do this is given below:

```
Initialize table of points;
Set max team score to zero;
For each possible assignment of swimmer 1 do
   For each possible assignment of swimmer 2 do
      For each possible assignment of swimmer 3 do
         For each possible assignment of swimmer 4 do
            If each event has exactly one swimmer assigned THEN
               DO;
                  Compute team score;
                  IF team score > max team score THEN
                     DO;
                        Save assignment of swimmers to events;
                        Set max team score to team score
                        END;
                  END;
```

The body of the innermost loop of this program will be executed $4^4=256$ times. For a similar program concerning ten swimmers and ten events (not an unreasonably large number) the innermost loop would be executed 10^{10} times. Since a computer will execute several thousand PL/I statements per second, and there are approximately 3×10^7 seconds in a year, this problem would take <u>at least months</u>, <u>and perhaps years</u> to execute (depending on the computer used). If that is not sufficiently discouraging, consider a problem with twelve swimmers and twelve events.

This algorithm involves "complete enumeration" -- it examines every possible solution in order to select the best. This brute force solution relies on the computer's speed, which is inadequate for the task. Fortunately, a more efficient algorithm is known that will easily obtain solutions for hundreds of swimmers and events. This so-called "assignment algorithm" is described in most operations research texts. (For example, see Section III.2 in Ford and Fulkerson, <u>Flows in Networks,</u> Princeton Press, 1962.) This particular problem can be programmed and solved on a computer, because a clever and efficient algorithm happens to be available. Unfortunately, there are many problems, as simple in form as this one, where no algorithm except complete enumeration is known, and in some cases it can be proved that no algorithm except complete enumeration exists.

In general, these problems have the characteristic that their computation time grows very rapidly with increases in size of the problem. If n is some key dimension of the problem, the computing time may depend upon n**n, 2**n, n! or some similar function of n. Such problems grow so rapidly with n that, while small problems (n = 3 or 4 or 5) can often be solved by hand, problems only two or three times as large (in terms of n) cannot be solved by the most powerful computers.

3.3 "Undecidable" Problems

For certain problems it can be proved that <u>no</u> effective program can be written. It is not just a matter of not having yet found an efficient algorithm, or not yet having computers that are fast enough -- it can be rigorously proved that no program is possible. One important branch of computer science is concerned with classifying problems according to degree of difficulty (rate at which execution time increases with increasing values of n) and, in particular, identifying such non-computable problems. In most cases rather sophisticated mathematical arguments are involved, but the following example will suggest the general nature of the problems and proofs.

Suppose one is asked to write a program TRUTHTEST that will be able to determine the truth or falsity of a certain restricted class of English statements. Assume that each such statement is identified by a comment that follows the statement. For example:

     ROSES ARE RED.   /* STATEMENT 23 */

After processing such a statement, TRUTHTEST would produce one of two possible outputs:

     STATEMENT 23 IS FALSE.   or   STATEMENT 23 IS TRUE.

   Suppose TRUTHTEST were presented with the following statement as data:

     STATEMENT 9 IS FALSE.   /* STATEMENT 9 */

If TRUTHTEST reports

     STATEMENT 9 IS FALSE.

it will be confirming the truth of the statement it is declaring to be false. This is a contradiction. If TRUTHTEST reports

     STATEMENT 9 IS TRUE.

it will be contradicting a statement that it claims is true. The only resolution of this paradox is to conclude that it is impossible to produce a program to do what TRUTHTEST is supposed to do.

   This difficulty does not lie in the definition of truth and falsity; this is not an example of an "ill-defined" problem, as discussed in Section 3.1. The following example should clarify the distinction. It is similar to the TRUTHTEST problem, but the task is more precisely defined. Nevertheless, it leads to the same type of paradox and conclusion of impossibility.

   Suppose we want a program to test other programs for the presence of an error called an "infinite iterative loop". If a program contains an infinite iterative loop (abbreviate this as "iil") it will never complete execution, and it would be useful to have a diagnostic program that would detect such errors before large amounts of computer time are wasted. Note that one cannot empirically test for such errors just by running the suspect program, because one could not distinguish between programs that would never terminate, and those that are just impossibly long (as in Section 3.2).

   The testing program TESTIIL loads a program P and data D into character arrays. TESTILL then determines whether P processing D contains an iil. If it does, the value 'NOHALT' is assigned to the variable RESULT; if it does not contain an iil the value 'HALT' is assigned. That is:

```
TESTIIL:PROCEDURE OPTIONS(MAIN);
   /* TEST FOR PRESENCE OF IIL */
   Declarations;
   Load program P and data D;
   IF P processing D contains an ill THEN
      RESULT = 'NOHALT';
   ELSE
      RESULT = 'HALT';
   PUT SKIP LIST(RESULT);
   END /* TESTIIL */;
```

For example, suppose P is

```
XLOOP: PROCEDURE OPTIONS(MAIN);
   DECLARE (X) FLOAT;
   GET LIST(X);
   DO WHILE(X = 3);
      END;
   END /* XLOOP */;
```

If D is 4, XLOOP processing D does not contain an iil, and TESTIIL should report HALT. If D is 3, then TESTIIL should detect an iil in XLOOP processing D and report NOHALT.

   If TESTIIL can be written, it would be trivial to write another program REPEAT that is very similar, but contains an extra WHILE loop. Furthermore, where TESTIIL will test any program P processing any data D, REPEAT considers only the special case where a program P processes a copy of itself. That is, data D is a copy of program P. (It is not unusual for one program to be read as data by another program. See Part X.)

```
REPEAT:PROCEDURE OPTIONS(MAIN);
   /* REPEAT IF ILL NOT PRESENT WHEN P PROCESSES P */
   Declarations from TESTIIL;
   Load program P;
   Copy program P to be used as data D;

   /* REPEAT TESTIIL UNTIL RESULT IS 'NOHALT' */
   RESULT = 'HALT';
   DO WHILE(RESULT = 'HALT');
      IF P processing D contains an ill THEN
         RESULT = 'NOHALT';
      ELSE
         RESULT = 'HALT';
      END;

   PUT SKIP LIST(RESULT);
   END /* REPEAT */;
$DATA
   Program P
```

Observe that REPEAT is designed so that

   a) REPEAT processing data P halts only if P processing data
      P does not halt, and
   b) REPEAT processing data P does not halt only if P
      processing data P does halt.

Since program P can be _any_ program, it can be the program
REPEAT. That is, write another copy of REPEAT after the $DATA
so that REPEAT processes itself. Now rewrite the observations
a) and b) with P = REPEAT:

   a) REPEAT processing data REPEAT halts only if REPEAT
      processing data REPEAT does not halt, and

   b) REPEAT processing data REPEAT does not halt only if
      REPEAT processing data REPEAT does halt.

Hence, assuming REPEAT halts leads to a contradiction, and
assuming it does not halt also leads to a contradiction. But
REPEAT _must_ either halt or not halt. The only flaw in the
argument is our initial assumption that a program TESTIIL could
be produced. Therefore TESTIIL cannot be written. No matter
what computer language is used, it is impossible to write a
program that will test an arbitrary program and set of data to
determine whether or not that program will halt.

   We should note that it is not impossible to write a program
that tests programs for some kinds of errors. For example one
could write a program that would test for missing semi-colons
(see Part X). Only certain types of errors, such as infinite
iterative loops, cannot always be detected.

   This is an example of a phenomenon called "undecidability".
The problem of determining whether program P processing data D
will ever halt is said to be "undecidable". This particular
problem was first proved undecidable by a British mathematician
Alan Turing in 1936 (ten years before the first modern
computer). The most readable contemporary exposition of the
idea is Chapter 8 of Minsky's Computation (Prentice-Hall, 1967).

PART VII   CONFIRMATION OF CORRECTNESS

Section 1   Proofs of Correctness

We have argued in Parts II and III that the systematic
development of a program, using only certain restricted
structures, will reduce the frequency and severity of errors --
but realistically we know that we cannot eliminate them
entirely.   In Part V we conceded this fallibility and presented
strategies and tools for testing programs -- for trying to
detect the existence of errors, and for locating and identifying
them.   But this process is not guaranteed either.   When our
testing reveals no further errors, it may be that no errors are
present -- but it could also mean only that our testing is not
sufficiently rigorous.   As noted in Part V, you can disprove the
correctness of a program -- by exhibiting an incorrect action --
but <u>failing</u> <u>to</u> <u>disprove</u> <u>correctness</u> is <u>not</u> the same thing as
<u>proving</u> <u>correctness</u>.

It would be nice to be able to prove the correctness of a
program, much as one proves a mathematical theorem, in a way
that does not depend importantly upon the skill of the
individual programmer. But the nature of a program and the
meaning of correctness of a program makes this exceedingly
difficult.

There are two aspects to a program. First of all, a program
is a <u>static object</u>. It exists on paper and we read it in this
form, usually from left-to-right and top-to-bottom. Secondly, a
program is <u>dynamic</u>, in that it is executed to produce a result.
The order of execution of statements is quite different from the
static order, and yet we attempt to understand the order of
events that take place during execution just from the static,
top-to-bottom description. This is complicated by the fact that
the order of events changes from execution to execution,
depending on the input data. Thus, when reading a program, we
are attempting to understand a multitude of <u>different</u> executions
of the program. From the static description, we would like to

understand   the   program   enough   to   <u>prove</u> that   <u>all</u> <u>possible</u>
executions are correct.

If we would be satisfied to prove properties about the static
version of a program things would not be so difficult, but about
all that one could prove about a static program is   that   it   is
syntactically correct.   The   proof of syntactic   correctness   is
sufficiently straightforward that it can be mechanized.   This is
considered   a standard part   of   the   task   of   translating   a
programming language and many translators do an adequate job   in
this   regard (see Part X).   However, as noted in Section   V.1.1,
a   reasonable meaning of correctness implies much more than   the
absence of syntactic errors.

The fundamental difficulty is that we   would   like   to   <u>prove</u>
properties   of   the   dynamic   aspect   of a program   <u>using</u>
<u>characteristics</u>   <u>of</u>   <u>its</u>   <u>static</u> version. The process is clearly
going to be aided if we make the static and dynamic aspects of a
program   as much alike as possible.   This   is   really what   the
concept   of   program   units in Section II.1 is all about.   For a
single statement the static and dynamic aspects   are   identical.
To   say   that   we   understand   what a written statement means   is
essentially   equivalent to saying that we   understand   what will
happen   when   it   is   executed.   If   we   can make a sequence of
statements behave as a single statement, then this   property   of
static-dynamic   identity   is preserved for a compound statement.
The compound statement will have component steps, but as long as
they   are   in strictly sequential   order   this   poses   no   great
difficulty.   For example, to say that the meaning (or execution)
of a compound statement S is

    1. perform S1,
    2. then perform S2,
    3. finally perform S3,

is not inherently different or more difficult than to   say   that
the meaning of an assignment statement is

    1. evaluate the expression on the right side,
    2. and assign its value to the variable on the left.

If one of the components Si of a compound statement is itself
compound this   does   not   change the situation. After   all,   the
evaluation   of the expression in   the   assignment statement   may
have   involved   the execution of a built-in function like SIN or
COS which is actually a substantial segment of program.   It   may
have   involved   a user-supplied   function procedure   (Section
IV.1.6)   and   there   is no limit   to the size   or complexity   of
program that   could be   included   in   that   procedure.   In
understanding the assignment statement we regard these functions
as   elemental tasks   --   performing   some   action   in a   clearly
specified order with respect to other tasks.   Each component   of
the compound statement is regarded in the same way.

In these terms we have some chance of making a convincing argument that a certain algorithm is correct for a particular problem. We may be able to argue that

    P1 then P2 then P3 is equivalent to P

and then that

    P21 then P22 is equivalent to P2.

Eventually, at some low level, we could show that program segment Si is equivalent to algorithm step Pi.

Alternative steps in the algorithm don't greatly complicate the argument:

    Pi1 then (either Pi2 or Pi3) then Pi4 ...

but repetition does complicate things. The following type of sequence is relatively hard to understand:

    P1 P2 P3 P2 P3 ... P2 P3 P4

It is hard to summarize this sequence with a statement that is true for any number of repetitions of the pair (P2,P3). This is the situation in which the static and dynamic aspects of a program differ most widely. There are two basic difficulties with repetition:

    1. We must be able to show that the loop will halt -- that is, that the condition that allows repetition will eventually terminate it.

    2. Provided the loop does halt, we must be able to show that the loop performs its intended function, no matter how many times the loop iterates.

We discuss this problem in the next section.

Section 2   Invariant Relations of a Loop

The dynamic execution of a loop is quite different from its static description, and we need some technique to connect the two. This will turn out to be a <u>relation</u> <u>about</u> <u>the</u> <u>values</u> <u>of</u> <u>the</u> <u>variables</u> <u>used</u> <u>in</u> <u>the</u> <u>loop</u> -- a statement about them which is either true or false. We illustrate first with an algorithm with which we are all familiar.

2.1 <u>An</u> <u>Example</u>: <u>Sorting</u>

Consider the successive-minima algorithm to sort an array A(1:N) where N≥0.

```
        I = 1;
        DO WHILE (I <= N);
(2.1a)      Swap values of A(I:N) to put smallest in A(I);
        I = I+1;
        END;
```

This algorithm halts with I = N+1, since I is increased by 1 each time the loop body is executed. Initially, the array A looks like the left diagram of (2.1b), while upon termination we want it to look like the right diagram of (2.1b). We want to be able to "prove" that it looks like the right diagram, but not just by mentally executing one or two cases.

```
            A(1)                 A(N)   A(1)                A(N)
           ┌─────────────────────┐     ┌────────────────────┐
(2.1b)     │ values may be unsorted │   │ values are sorted  │
           └─────────────────────┘     └────────────────────┘
```

We first draw a picture of array A that will turn out to describe <u>A</u> <u>at</u> <u>any</u> <u>point</u> <u>during</u> <u>execution</u>:

```
            A(1)        A(I-1) A(I)                          A(N)
           ┌───────────────────┬────────────────────────────┐
(2.1c)     │     sorted        │ each value in this partition │
           │                   │ ≥ each value in A(1:I₁)      │
           └───────────────────┴────────────────────────────┘
```

We now prove several points which lead to the conclusion that algorithm (2.1a) does indeed sort the array.

1. Picture (2.1c) describes the array just before execution of the loop -- after execution of I=1. (This is true because the array segment A(1:I-1) has no elements -- I-1=0. Thus all values are in A(I:N).)

2. Each iteration of the loop leaves the array as described by picture (2.1c) (but of course with I increased by 1). We show this below.

3. Because of point 2, (2.1c) describes the array after the last iteration, and after the loop has halted.

4. The loop halts with I=N+1 and picture (2.1c) describing the array. Since I=N+1 the segment A(I:N) contains no values. Thus the first partition A(1:I-1), which is A(1:N), contains all the values. Since this partition is always in sorted order, the array is sorted.

We have to show that each iteration of the loop leaves the array as described by picture (2.1c), that is, that number 2 above is true. Only execution of the loop body might change this picture, so let us consider one execution of the loop body with (2.1c) describing the array beforehand and with I≤N. Executing the first statement "Swap values" changes the picture to

A(1)   A(I_1)   A(I)   A(I+1)   A(N)
sorted	a value ≥ each value in A(1:I_1)	each value in this partition ≥ A(I)

This must be so since the smallest of A(I:N) is put into A(I). Note that now the segment A(1:I) is sorted. Thus executing the second statement I=I+1 of the body yields the picture

A(1)   A(I_1) A(I)   A(N)
sorted	each value in this partition ≥ A(I_1)

But if this picture holds after execution of the body, then so does picture (2.1c). Thus executing the body of the loop has not changed the picture.

This may seem like a lot of intricate detail to go through just to show the algorithm works. Why, it's obvious from just looking at the algorithm that it works! This may be true for this simple example, but we have illustrated a powerful technique which can and should be used with any loop. We discuss this in more general terms in the next section.

Note how picture (2.1c) connects the static description of the algorithm with the dynamic execution. (2.1c) is <u>always</u> <u>true</u>, no matter how many times the loop iterates, and we have shown this by considering only <u>one</u> execution of the loop body. In effect, picture (2.1c) is a picture of <u>what</u> <u>is</u> <u>not</u> <u>changing</u> during execution. Dynamic execution is hard to understand because the values of variables continually change, and the way they change depends on the input data. What the picture gives is an <u>invariant</u> <u>relation</u> about the variables -- a relation which is always true no matter what the input values are.

Picture (2.1c) can also be put into words as we show below. In this case the picture says it better:

(2.1d)   The array A(1:N) is partitioned into A(1:I-1) and A(I:N).   A(1:I-1) is sorted.   Each value in A(I:N) is not less than each value in A(1:I-1).

2.2 <u>The</u> <u>Invariant</u> <u>Relation</u> <u>Theorem</u>

We develop a simple but powerful theorem which can be useful in understanding any WHILE loop. First we must introduce some notation. Let P and Q be relations concerning the values of variables used in a sequence of statements S. We use the notation

$$|P| \quad S \quad |Q|$$

to mean: If P is true before execution of the sequence of statements S, then Q is true after execution of S.

For example, suppose I and N are FIXED variables and that

P	is the relation	$I < N$
S	is the statement	$I = I+1;$
Q	is the relation	$I \leq N$

Then $|P|$ S $|Q|$ is the statement

$$|I < N| \quad I = I + 1 \quad |I \leq N|$$

Note that $|I<N|$ I=I+1 $|I<N|$ is <u>not</u> true. This notation is important to the proper understanding of what follows. (It is suggested that you do Exercise 1 at this point, before proceeding.)

Now consider a loop

(2.2a)
```
      DO WHILE ( c );
         Body
      END;
```

where c is a condition and Body is a sequence of statements, and suppose

(2.2b) |P & c| Body |P|

where P is a relation about the variables used in the loop.
That is, execution of the Body with condition c true leaves
relation P true. Then, provided the loop halts, we know that

         |P| DO WHILE (c); Body END; |P & ¬c|

Why? During execution of the loop only execution of the Body
may change the relation P. But by (2.2b) execution of the Body
does not change the relation P. Thus P remains true after the
loops halts. Relation c must be false when the loop halts,
because that is the only way the loop may halt.

We have quite simply proved a very powerful theorem:

(2.2c) Invariant Relation Theorem

    Provided the loop halts, |P & c| Body |P| implies

            |P| DO WHILE (c); Body END; |P & ¬c|

P is called an invariant relation of the loop. It is a relation
concerning the variables of the program -- a statement about
them which is either true or false. It is invariant in that it
remains true after the loop halts if it is true before execution
of the loop begins.

    This theorem only applies if the loop halts because c becomes
false. It we terminate the loop by using a RETURN, we have
to use other means to check correctness. Such exits are of
course very useful at times, and we illustrate in later examples
how to handle them.

    Consider again the successive-minima algorithm of Section
2.1. We have:

    condition c: I ≤ N

    relation P: picture (2.1c) or equivalent form (2.1d)

    Body: Swap values of A(I:N) to put smallest in A(I);
                  I = I + 1;

    Upon halt: P & ¬c imply the array is sorted.

    It is sometimes difficult to find the right relation P.
There are an infinite number of invariant relations which
satisfy the hypothesis of the theorem. For example, the
relations

         array A(1:N) may be sorted
         I*0 = 0

are always true, but they are not useful in understanding any loop. We must look for the <u>one</u> relation P which, together with ¬c, implies the intended result.

Let us summarize by stating how the invariant relation helps us, how it connects the dynamic and static aspects of the loop. The loop has the form

```
DO WHILE ( c );
    Body
    END;
```

To understand the loop and prove it correct, we need to do the following four things (five if exits occur in the loop):

1. Find a relation P such that P & ¬c imply the intended result.
2. Prove that P is true just before execution of the loop.
3. Prove that |P & c| Body |P|.
4. Prove that the loop halts.
5. If the loop contains exits (i.e., RETURNS which terminate execution of the loop) the correctness of the results upon exit must be ascertained by other means.

We have to prove that execution of the body with c true leaves P true. We do <u>not</u> have to worry about how many times the loop will be iterated, and we do not have to worry about the dynamic execution of the loop; just about <u>one</u> dynamic execution of the <u>loop body</u>. This is very important.

Of course, the desired relation P is sometimes difficult to find. But often the programmer doesn't really understand his loop until he <u>does</u> find it. Without relation P he is still groping in the dark.

2.3 <u>Simple</u> <u>Examples</u> <u>of</u> <u>Invariant</u> <u>Relations</u>

We present here several program segments. Each is a simple loop together with initialization statements. With each, we also give the invariant relation which can be used to understand the loop. With each the reader should show, in the following order, that

1. The relation P is true before execution of the loop.

2. P and ¬c imply the desired result.

3. |P & c| Body |P|.

4. The loop halts.

This is enough to show that the loop is correct. From points 1 and 2 the reader will get the main idea behind the algorithm. From 3 and 4 he sees how the idea is carried out.

```
1.   /* STORE IN X THE MAXIMUM OF A(1:N). N >= 1 */
     /* THE INVARIANT RELATION OF THE LOOP IS: */
     /* X CONTAINS THE MAXIMUM VALUE OF A(1:I) */
     I = 1;
     X = A(1);
     DO WHILE(I ¬= N);
        I = I + 1;
        IF A(I) > X THEN
           X = A(I);
        END;

2.   /* SWAP VALUES OF A(I:N) TO PUT SMALLEST IN A(I).  */
     /* 1<=I<=N.  THE INVARIANT RELATION OF THE LOOP IS: */
     /* A(I:J) CONTAINS ITS ORIGINAL VALUES, BUT WITH */
     /* THE SMALLEST IN A(I) */
     J = I;
     DO WHILE(J ¬= N);
        J = J + 1;
        IF A(J) < A(I) THEN
           Swap A(J) and A(I);
        END;

3.   /* STORE IN SUM THE SUM OF VALUES IN A(1:N).  N >= 1 */
     /* THE INVARIANT RELATION OF THE LOOP IS:*/
     /* SUM CONTAINS THE SUM OF VALUES IN A(1:I). */
     I = 1;
     SUM = A(1);
     DO WHILE(I ¬= N);
        I = I + 1;
        SUM = SUM + A(I);
        END;

4.   /* SORT-BY-INSERTION.  SORT ARRAY A(1:N)*/
     /* THE INVARIANT RELATION OF THE LOOP IS: */
     /* THE ARRAY LOOKS LIKE          */

     /* A(1)          A(I)                      A(N)    */
     /*    ┌──────────┬──────────────────────────┐     */
     /* |  SORTED     | UNSORTED, NOT "LOOKED AT" |  */
     /*    └──────────┴──────────────────────────┘     */

     I = 2;
     DO WHILE(I <= N);
        Swap values of A(1:I) so that A(1:I) is sorted;
        I = I + 1;
        END;
```

5.   In SP/k, the following program will produce a runtime error
     message. Discover why and fix the program.

```
/* SWAP VALUES OF A(1:I) SO THAT A(1:I) IS SORTED,*/
/* ASSUMING THAT A(1:I-1) IS ALREADY SORTED.*/
/* THE INVARIANT RELATION FOR THIS LOOP IS:*/
/* A(1:J-1) IS SORTED & A(J:I) IS SORTED & */
/* IF 1 < J < I THEN A(J-1) <= A(J+1) */
J = I;
DO WHILE((J ¬= 1) & (A(J)<A(J-1)));
   Swap A(J) and A(J-1);
   J = J - 1;
   END;
```

6.   This is the binary search algorithm of Section VI.2.4. It
searches the array A(1:N) for a value X.   The invariant
relation theorem helps us in proving that if the loop
terminates normally, then X is not in the list. If X is in
the list, then the program stops when J is set to K.

```
/* BINARY SEARCH.  GIVEN A(1:N) AND X, STORE IN J A VALUE*/
/* SUCH THAT A(J) = X.  STORE 0 IN J IF X NOT IN LIST*/
/* THE INVARIANT RELATION OF THE LOOP IS:*/
/* IF X IS IN A(1:N), IT IS IN A(FIRST:LAST). */
FIRST = 1;
LAST = N;
J = 0;
DO WHILE((FIRST <= LAST) & (J = 0));
   K = (FIRST + LAST)/2.E0;
   IF A(K) = X THEN
      J = K;
   ELSE
      IF A(K) < X THEN
         FIRST = K + 1;
      ELSE
         LAST = K - 1;
   END;
```

2.4 More Complicated Examples

   The last section showed several algorithms with which the
reader was already familiar, in order to help gain facility with
invariant relations. Here we present new algorithms.   If the
reader has studied and understood the technique, these
algorithms will appear easy; otherwise they may be hard to
understand. Remember, it is not necessary to execute the
algorithm with a set of initial values in order to understand
it; indeed this sometimes tends to confuse the issue. It is
only necessary to go through the four points discussed at the
beginning of Section 2.3.

   Some of these algorithms contain nested loops. We have only
written the invariant relations where they indeed help. We have
also sometimes written a comment describing <u>what</u> the body of a
loop does, and written the statements to <u>perform</u> that function
underneath. When trying to understand the loops, read the

comment as the loop body. Later, you can read the statements to
make sure the statements do what the comment says.

```
1.   /* CALCULATE Z = A RAISED TO THE POWER B (A**B) */
     /* WHERE A AND B ARE INTEGERS > 0 */
     /* WITHOUT USING EXPONENTIATION*/
     /* THE OUTER LOOP HAS THE INVARIANT RELATION*/
     /*   Z*(X**Y) = A**B  and X>=0 and Y>=0 */
     Z = 1;
     X = A;
     Y = B;
     DO WHILE(Y ¬= 0);
        /* DECREASE Y, KEEPING INVARIANT RELATION TRUE */
        DO WHILE(MOD(Y,2) = 0);
           Y = Y/2.0E0;
           X = X*X;
           END;
        Y = Y - 1;
        Z = Z * X;
        END;
```

2. <u>Quicksort</u> This algorithm sorts an array A(1:N).   The
expected runtime is proportional to N*LOG2(N) although the worst
case is proportional to N^2.

   The algorithm uses a command "Partition A(L:U)..." which is
given as algorithm 3 below. To understand Quicksort itself, it
is <u>not</u> necessary to understand <u>how</u> Partition works, but only
<u>what</u> it does.

   Quicksort uses two additional arrays LOWER and UPPER and a
simple variable M. <u>Their</u> <u>definition</u> <u>is</u> <u>actually</u> <u>the</u> <u>invariant</u>
<u>relation</u> <u>of</u> <u>the</u> <u>loop</u>, which we now give:

   A(LOWER(1):UPPER(1)),   A(LOWER(2):UPPER(2)), ...,
   A(LOWER(M):UPPER(M)) are disjoint segments of the array A
   such that, if these M segments are sorted then the whole
   array is sorted.

Originally then, we have M=1, LOWER(1) = 1, UPPER(1) = N, and at
the end, when M=0 there are no segments in this list, and hence
the array must be sorted.

```
LOWER(1) = 1;
UPPER(1) = N;
M = 1;
DO WHILE(M ¬= 0);
    /* EITHER SORT SEGMENT A(LOWER(M):UPPER(M)) AND DELETE IT */
    /*    FROM LIST IF IT IS SMALL ENOUGH, */
    /* OR SPLIT IT INTO SMALLER SEGMENTS TO BE SORTED. */
    /*    IN THIS CASE REPLACE SEGMENT ON LIST BY THESE */
    /*    SMALLER ONES. */
    L = LOWER(M);
    U = UPPER(M);
    M = M-1;
    IF U = L+1 THEN /* A(L:U) HAS TWO ELEMENTS. SORT */
        DO;
            IF A(L) > A(U) THEN
                Swap A(L) and A(U);
            END;
    IF U > L+1 THEN
        DO;
            /* A(L:U) HAS MORE THAN TWO ELEMENTS */
            Partition A(L:U) into three segments
```

```
    A(L)   A(K-1)   A(K)   A(K+1)     A(U)
   ┌─────────────────┬─────┬────────────────────┐
   │    ≤ A(K)       │     │     > A(K)          │
   └─────────────────┴─────┴────────────────────┘
```

```
            and set K.

            /* A(L:U) WILL BE SORTED WHEN A(L:K-1)AND */
            /* A(K+1:U) ARE, ADD THEM TO LIST TO SORT; */
            /* PUTTING THE LARGER OF THE TWO SEGMENTS ON */
            /* LIST FIRST REDUCES STORAGE FOR LOWER, UPPER */
            IF U-K > K-L THEN
                DO;
                    M = M + 1;
                    LOWER(M) = K + 1;
                    UPPER(M) = U;
                    END;
            M = M + 1;
            LOWER(M) = L;
            UPPER(M) = K-1;
            IF U-K <= K-L THEN
                DO;
                    M = M + 1;
                    LOWER(M) = K + 1;
                    UPPER(M) = U;
                    END;
            END;
    END;
```

3. Partition algorithm. This algorithm is given an array segment A(L:U) as input. It rearranges the values of the array segment and stores an integer in variable K so that the array looks like

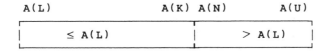

```
A(L)   A(K1)  A(K)  A(K+1)  A(U)
┌─────────────┬───┬───────────────┐
│   ≤ A(K)    │   │    > A(K)     │
└─────────────┴───┴───────────────┘
```

The value initially in A(L) will end up in A(K); this is used as
the "pivot" value. The main loop has the invariant relation:

```
A(L)         A(N)          A(K)          A(U)
┌────────────┬─────────────────┬───────────────┐
│   ≤ A(L)   │ unknown values  │    > A(L)     │
└────────────┴─────────────────┴───────────────┘
```

When the loop halts the array looks like

```
A(L)                     A(K) A(N)        A(U)
┌─────────────────────────────┬───────────────┐
│          ≤ A(L)             │     > A(L)    │
└─────────────────────────────┴───────────────┘
```

and we need only swap values of   A(L)   and   A(K)   to yield   the
desired result.

```
  N = L + 1;
  K = U;
  DO WHILE(N <= K);
     /* DECREASE K OR INCREASE N, KEEPING RELATION INVARIANT */
     IF A(N) <= A(L) THEN
        N = N + 1;
     ELSE
        DO;
           DO WHILE(A(K) > A(L));
              K = K - 1;
              END;
           IF N < K THEN
              DO;
                 Swap A(N) and A(K);
                 N = N + 1;
                 K = K - 1;
                 END;
           END;
     END;
  Swap A(L) and A(K);
```

2.5 Invariant Relations in Everyday Programming

Invariant relations should also be used in developing loops;
in getting ideas about how an algorithm should work. Often, the
use of an invariant relation can lead to a more efficient
algorithm.   Using an invariant relation gets us away from
thinking about how values change, which is hard to comprehend,
and instead gets us to think about how relations about values
remain the same, which is easier.

Suppose we have a problem which we feel will be solved by some sort of loop. We have some idea of how the loop will work, but the details are not clear. One good way of developing the loop is the following:

1. Write down a statement or picture of what the loop should accomplish; what we expect out of the loop.
2. Write down a statement or picture of what is known initially.
3. Tie the above two statements together with a more general statement which has the two as extreme cases. This should turn out to be the necessary invariant relation.
4. Now develop the initialization, the loop condition, and the body of the loop from the invariant relation.

Of course, it is really a trial and error process and these four steps will be repeated, in various orders, until the final loop emerges. But there is a major difference between this way of developing the loop and the typical way.

The typical loop is programmed by test cases. The programmer makes up some sample data and develops the program for it. He then makes up another set of sample data and modifies his algorithm to fit it. This process is repeated over and over until the programmer finally "feels" his program is correct. The chances are it is not, because he has developed it from a finite number of test cases.

The method outlined above has nothing to do with isolated test cases. It is more general because it works with relations about the variables, and not the values of the variables themselves. Thus, any set of data which satisfies the initial relations should be executed correctly.

We now give an example, due to E.W. Dijkstra, of developing a program this way.

Problem. Suppose we have an array $A(1:N)$, $N \geq 1$, which contains only the values 1, 2, and 3. Suppose we want the array sorted. Values of the array may be changed only by using the command "Swap $A(I)$ and $A(J)$".

We could of course use a general sort algorithm, but since the array values are so restricted we should be able to develop a more efficient algorithm. Initially the array looks like the diagram on the left below, while when the algorithm has finished, we want it to look like the right diagram. These two are the statements spoken of in the first two steps of the development process. In the diagram, "U" represents an unknown value.

```
A(1) A(N)              A(1)                        A(N)
┌─────────────┐        ┌───────┬───────┬───────┐
│    U's      │        │  1's  │  2's  │  3's  │
└─────────────┘        └───────┴───────┴───────┘
```

It seems logical to have a WHILE loop which at each iteration
puts one value into its correct partition, and a possible
candidate for the general picture is:

```
A(1)           A(N1)        A(N2)              A(U)      A(N)
┌──────────────┬─────────────┬─────────────┬──────────────────┐
│     1's      │     2's     │     3's     │       U's        │
└──────────────┴─────────────┴─────────────┴──────────────────┘
```

where N1 is the index of the first value that is not a 1,
      N2 is the index of the first value that is not a 1 or a 2,
      U is the index of the first unknown value.

This yields the simple algorithm

```
N1 = 1;
N2 = 1;
U = 1;
DO WHILE (U <= N);
    Determine partition for A(U) and put A(U) into it;
    END;
```

Moving A(U) into its partition may require two swaps. For
example, if A(U) is 1, we must first swap A(U) with A(N2) and
then swap A(N2) with A(N1). How can we reduce the number of
swaps to at most 1 at each iteration? Let us change the general
picture to the following, where the partition of unknowns now
appears between the 2's and 3's:

```
A(1)           A(N1)        A(FU)    A(LU)                A(N)
┌──────────────┬─────────────┬─────────────┬──────────────────┐
│     1's      │     2's     │     U's     │       3's        │
└──────────────┴─────────────┴─────────────┴──────────────────┘
```

where N1 is the index of the first non-1,
      FU is the index of the first unknown,
      LU is the index of the last unknown.

Using this relation we end up with the following algorithm

```
N1 = 1;
FU = 1;
LU = N;
DO WHILE(FU <= LU);
   /* DETERMINE PARTITION FOR A(FU) AND PUT IN PLACE */
   IF A(FU) = 1 THEN
      DO;
         Swap A(N1) and A(FU)
         FU = FU + 1;
         N1 = N1 + 1;
         END;
   ELSE
      IF A(FU) = 2 THEN
         FU = FU + 1;
      ELSE
         DO;
            Swap A(FU) and A(LU);
            LU = LU - 1;
            END;
   END;
```

This is a <u>linear</u> algorithm. The loop is iterated N times, and each iteration requires at most two comparisons and one interchange.

A subtle point should be noted about the definition of the variables. N1 was defined as the index of the first non-1, and was therefore initialized to 1. If we had defined N1 to be the index of the first 2, we would have had to initialize N1 to 0 since there are no 2's initially, just U's. The algorithm would have been more complicated. From the picture, we cannot tell whether N1 is the first 2 or the first non-1, and we must be careful to write down exactly what we mean.

Section 2 Exercises

1. Indicate whether the following statements are true or false.
   All variables are assumed to be FIXED.
   a) |I is even| I = I/2E0; |I is even|
   b) |I is negative| I = I*I; |I is non-negative|
   c) |Z = A**B & A and B are integers| B = B/2E0; A = A*A;
      |Z = A**B & A and B are integers|
   d) |true| DO WHILE (I is even); I = I/2E0; END; |I is odd|
   e) |I > 0| I = FLOOR(I/2E0); I = I-1; |I ≥ 0|
   f) |N > 0| SUM=1; DO I = 2 TO N BY 1; SUM=SUM*I; END;
      |SUM=N!|
   g) |N ≥ 0 & SUM = N!| N = N+1; SUM = SUM*N; |SUM = N!|

2. Consider the following program segment written to search
A(1:N) for a value X and set J accordingly. The only difference
between this segment and the binary search segment of Section
2.3 is in the statement which throws away half of the list.
Prove whether the program segment is correct or incorrect, and
if incorrect, indicate for what initial values it will not work.

```
FIRST = 1;
LAST = N;
J = 0;
DO WHILE((FIRST <= LAST) & (J = 0 ));
   K = (FIRST + LAST)/2.0E0;
   IF A(K) = X THEN
      J = K;
   ELSE
      IF A(J) < X THEN
         FIRST = K;
      ELSE
         LAST = K;
END;
```

3. For each of the following algorithms, write down what the
result of execution of each loop is, and then write down the
invariant relation which together with ¬c indicates that the
loop executes correctly.

```
a) /* REVERSE THE VALUES OF A(1:N).  N >= 1.  */
   LOWER = 1;
   UPPER = N;
   DO WHILE(LOWER < UPPER);
      Swap values of A(LOWER) and A(UPPER);
      LOWER = LOWER + 1;
      UPPER = UPPER - 1;
      END;
```

b) /* STORE 1 IN P IF I IS PRIME; 0 OTHERWISE. */
    P = 1;
    IF I <= 1 THEN
        P = 0;
    J = 2;
    DO WHILE((P=1) & (J*J<=I));
        IF MOD(I,J) = 0 THEN
            P = 0;
        ELSE
            J = J + 1;
        END;

4. A game is played by two players on a grid of points (of any size) as shown below. Player A first draws a horizontal or a vertical solid line between any two adjacent points. Then player B draws a dotted horizontal or vertical line. This process continues until there are no more lines to fill in. The game can thus be pictured as execution of the loop

    DO WHILE (there exists another move);
        Player A draws | or - ;
        Player B draws : or .. ;
        END;

The object of the game is for player A to draw a closed curve consisting of only solid lines, while B wins if he can prevent A from drawing a closed curve.
    Does there exist an algorithm for player B's move so that he can always win? If so, give it. This problem is most easily solved by considering an invariant relation of the loop which implies that A has not drawn his closed curve.

```
    .   .   .   .   .   .   .   .

    .   .   .   .   .   .   .   .

    .   .   .   .   .   .   .   .

    .   .   .   .   .   .   .   .
```

5. Write algorithms for the following problems. Each will be a simple loop, together with some initialization statements and the like. This loop should be developed from an invariant relation. That is, try to discover the relation first, then write the loop, not the other way around.

a) The GCD of two positive integers A and B, written GCD(A,B), is the greatest positive integer which divides them both evenly. Write a program to calculate the GCD of A and B. You may use the MOD function. The following facts about GCDs should help. First, GCD(A,B) = GCD(B,A). Second, if A = p·B where p is an integer greater than 0, then of course B is the GCD of A and B. Third, if

    A = p·B + r   where p ≥ 0 and 0 < r < B,

and p and r are integers, then GCD(A,B) = GCD(B,r). This follows easily by noting that any divisor of A and B must also divide r.

    Hint: Note that GCD(A,B) = GCD(B,r). Suppose we initialize variables X and Y to A and B respectively. Then GCD(X,Y) = GCD(A,B). Then making the assignments X=Y; Y=r; does not change this relation GCD(X,Y) = GCD(A,B).

b) A(1:K) and A(K+1:N) are each sorted in ascending order. Write an algorithm which sorts the whole array in linear time. (It will probably be a single loop.) You may use an extra array which has no more than K elements.

c) An array TEM(1:100) contains 100 temperatures. Print the number of temperatures above 100 and the number below 32.

PART VIII COMPUTER SOLUTION OF MATHEMATICAL PROBLEMS

by J. E. Dennis, Jr. and Jorge J. Moré

Many people study computer programming because they are interested in implementing algorithms to extract quantitative information from mathematical models in science and engineering. Our purpose in this part is to first discuss some of the difficulties that are encountered when implementing such algorithms, and then to study two representative mathematical problems in some detail.

We are faced with a problem in notation. The formulas in this part will generally be intended as mathematical rather than programming language statements. However, the computer text-editing system used to produce this book does not permit many of the usual mathematical notational conventions. In particular it does not permit subscripts, and permits only integer superscripts. Therefore, we have resorted to the usual programming convention for subscripts, and in order to increase the readability of our expressions, we restrict their generality, when possible, to use only integer superscripts. In all other cases we use mathematical symbols and conventions such as $\leq$ instead of $<=$. We indicate multiplication by proximity or $\cdot$ rather than $*$, and we use vertical lines $|\ |$ to indicate absolute value (rather than concatenation or "or", as in PL/I.) We will use the symbol $**$ to mean "raised to the power" as in PL/I (see Appendix B.6), e.g., $2**6=64$.

Section 1   Floating Point Numbers

Except for programming errors, the factors which usually account for unexpected results in numerical computations are as follows:

a) Most numbers cannot be represented <u>exactly</u> in the computer.

b) The results of the arithmetic operations performed by the computer are not, in general, <u>exact</u>.

c) Most mathematical problems require an <u>infinite</u> number of calculations.

In this section we will discuss how numbers are represented in the computer, and how this representation leads to a certain type of error called "roundoff error". We also discuss how roundoff error affects the different arithmetic operations.

1.1 <u>Representation</u> <u>of</u> <u>Floating</u> <u>Point</u> <u>Numbers</u>

We have already mentioned that some of the difficulties with executing numerical algorithms on the computer are due to the fact that most numbers cannot be represented <u>exactly</u> in the computer. Let us see what this means in terms of a specific example.

Consider a PL/I program which reads the number 69.4 from a data card, assigns the value to a variable which has been declared FLOAT and then prints the value of the variable. If you run the program you will find that the number printed out is 6.93999E+01, which is equivalent to 69.3999. On the other hand, if the number on the card is 69.5, then it is returned exactly, that is, as 6.95000E+01.

To understand these results, we need to know how 69.4 and 69.5 are stored in the computer, that is, the internal representation of a floating point number. PL/I as opposed to SP/k, allows the programmer to declare floating point numbers as being FLOAT DECIMAL or FLOAT BINARY depending on whether they prefer to think of the number in base 10 or base 2 (see Appendix B.5 for further details). The SP/k attribute FLOAT corresponds to the PL/I attributes FLOAT DECIMAL(6) or FLOAT BINARY(21). Since almost all versions of PL/I use the same internal representation for both FLOAT BINARY and FLOAT DECIMAL, variables, we will call their contents "floating point numbers". In this way the following discussion will apply to both cases.

A number can be written in terms of a <u>base</u> b, a <u>fraction</u> f, an <u>exponent</u> e, and a <u>sign</u>. If b=10 then this representation is just the number written as a decimal fraction times a power (the exponent) of 10. Most computers do not use base 10, but regardless of the base, any number can be written as a fraction f times a power of b. The fraction is also written in terms of powers of b, and this means that

$$f = d(1) \cdot b^{-1} + d(2) \cdot b^{-2} + \ldots, \text{ where } 0 \le d(i) \le b-1,$$

which in base b notation is abbreviated to

$$f = (0.d(1)d(2)\ldots)(\text{base } b).$$

The exercises at the end of this section will describe a method for finding the base b representation of a number.

A floating point number is also written in terms of a base and an exponent. In the IBM 360 and 370, b = 16. This means that 69.4 is $(0.4566\ldots)(\text{base } 16)$ because this number can be written as $f \cdot 16^2$ where

$$f = 4 \cdot 16^{-1} + 5 \cdot 16^{-2} + 6 \cdot 16^{-3} + 6 \cdot 16^{-4} + \ldots .$$

You can easily verify that 69.5 is just $(0.458) \cdot 16^2$ in base 16. By now you have probably guessed that 69.4 and 69.5 are treated differently by the computer because it can only hold finitely many digits of a fraction.

The representation of the fraction that the computer does save is called the <u>mantissa</u> and t, the number of digits in the mantissa, is the <u>precision</u> of the floating point number. Some computers, like the IBM 360 and 370, obtain the mantissa by truncating the fraction to t digits while for others the mantissa is obtained by rounding the fraction to the closest t digit number. For example, if b=16 and t=3 then the mantissa of 69.4 is 0.456 for truncation and 0.457 for rounding. In our discussion of floating point numbers we will assume that the mantissa is obtained by truncating the fraction to t digits, but regardless of the method used, the errors due to the finite precision of the computer are traditionally called <u>roundoff errors</u>. Since we are assuming that the mantissa is obtained by truncation, in our case a better name would have been "truncation errors", but this term is customarily used for another type of truncation error which is not associated with the finite precision of the machine.

PL/I on the IBM 360 allows t=6, called <u>single precision</u>, or t=14, called <u>double precision</u>. The default assumption is single

precision, so in order to use double precision, it is necessary
to declare attributes of DECIMAL FLOAT(16) or BINARY FLOAT(53).
Since double precision was not specified in the previous
example, 69.4 was represented internally in single precision as

$$(0.456666) \cdot 16^2 \text{ (base 16)}$$

and 69.5 was represented as

$$(0.458000) \cdot 16^2 \text{ (base 16)}.$$

On output the computer prints the base 10 representation of
these numbers.

Note that the internal representation of a floating point
number has a mantissa with a non-zero first digit. This
"normalized" form is always possible (unless the number is zero)
and clearly leads to maximum accuracy.

The t-digit floating point numbers can be thought of as a
finite subset of the real numbers. They are fairly densely
packed about zero, but become more widely separated further from
zero. The t-digit floating point representation T(x) of a real
number x is the member of this subset which is nearest to x
among all those members between x and 0. In particular, all
real numbers between two adjacent floating point numbers will
have the same floating point representation.

In the preceding paragraph we referred for the first time to
there being finitely many t-digit floating point numbers. This
is rather clear, for just as the computer must truncate the
fractional part of the number, so it can't allow more than
finitely many different exponents. The IBM 360 floating point
numbers are approximately between

$$5.4 \cdot 10^{-79} \text{ and } 7.2 \cdot 10^{75}$$

since the range of base 16 exponents is $-64 \leq e \leq 63$. When the
computer encounters a number not in this range it prints an
UNDERFLOW or OVERFLOW message. OVERFLOW is a common problem in
numerical computation, where it is often caused by dividing a
large floating point number by a small one. UNDERFLOW signals a
loss of accuracy since it warns that a number has been taken to
be zero because in its normalized form the exponent required is
too small. In general, when we see UNDERFLOW we <u>suspect</u> the
results of the computation, and when we see OVERFLOW we <u>discard</u>
them.

Unless the number of operations is rather large, the
increased cost of double precision isn't noticeable, so double
precision is generally advisable for small problems. In SP/k,
you do not have this choice since all floating point variables
are maintained in single precision form. This is not true in
PL/I.

You may wonder why PL/I specifies double precision variables
as FLOAT DECIMAL(16) or FLOAT BINARY(53) when the computer
represents them in either case with 14 base 16 digits. The
answer is that 16 decimal digits, 53 binary digits, and 14
hexadecimal (base 16) digits all give essentially the same
precision. We will explain why in the next section.

1.2 Roundoff Errors and Significant Decimal Digits

In the previous section we showed how a computer represents
any real number x in its floating point range by a floating
point number T(x) obtained from the leading t terms of the
number's expansion in powers of the base b. Clearly, this
approximation of x by T(x) sets a limit on the accuracy of any
subsequent calculations and we are thus led to ask what the
maximum possible accuracy is when we approximate x by T(x). To
answer this question we need a precise way to measure accuracy.

The generally accepted way to measure how accurately a number
y approximates another number x is in terms of significant
decimal digits. We would like to say that y has s significant
decimal digits as an approximation to x if when x and y are
represented as decimal numbers then the leading s digits agree
and the (s+1)st digits do not differ by more than five. This
definition suffices for x=10012, y=10034, or for x=10.012,
y=10.034, since it gives the same reasonable answer of three
significant decimal digits in either case. On the other hand,
in the previous section we stated that if x=69.4 then on the IBM
360 the single precision T(x) is 69.3999. This is clearly a
better approximation to x than 69.3 and yet in the above sense
they both have two significant decimal digits. All this is
meant to convince you that in order to give a precise and
reasonable definition of significant decimal digits we will have
to examine roundoff errors more carefully.

We begin by obtaining a bound on the magnitude of the error
committed by replacing T(x) by x. The quantity $|T(x)-x|$ is
called the absolute error of T(x) as an approximation to x,
while if $x \neq 0$ then $|T(x)-x|/|x|$ is the relative error.

Theorem: If $x \neq 0$ lies in the range of the base b floating point
        numbers of precision t, then

(1.2a) $|T(x)-x|/|x| < b^{**}(1-t)$.

We will prove (1.2a) for the case when t=6. This will
illustrate the general case, and you should prove (1.2a) in full
generality as an exercise. It is only necessary to give a proof
in the case that x>0 since the proof for a negative x differs
only in sign.

Now take any x>0 and represent it as a normalized base b
number. That is, set

    $x = (b^{**}e) \cdot [d(1) \cdot b^{-1} + \ldots + d(6) \cdot b^{-6} + \ldots]$

where $d(1) \neq 0$. Notice (since we will need it later) that $|x| > b**(e-1)$. Then since $t=6$,

$$T(x) = (b**e) \cdot [d(1) \cdot b^{-1} + \ldots + d(6) \cdot b^{-6}]$$

and thus,

$$T(x)-x = -(b**e) \cdot [d(7) \cdot b^{-7} + d(8) \cdot b^{-8} + \ldots].$$

Now make use of the fact that $0 \leq d(i) \leq b-1$ to replace $d(7)$, $d(8)$, etc., by $(b-1)$ and get

$$|T(x)-x| \leq (b**e)(b-1)[b^{-7} + b^{-8} + \ldots].$$

However,

$$b^{-7} + b^{-8} + \ldots = b^{-7}(1 + b^{-1} + b^{-2} + \ldots) = b^{-6}/(b-1)$$

since this is a geometric series. Therefore,

$$|T(x)-x| \leq (b**e)b^{-6} < b^{-5}|x|$$

where we have used the fact that $|x| > b**(e-1)$. Inequality (1.2a) now follows.

In general, if x and y are real numbers and y is an approximation to x, then $|y-x|$ is the _absolute error_ of y as an approximation to x while $|y-x|/|x|$ is the _relative error_ of y as an approximation to $x \neq 0$. Inequality (1.2a) indicates that if $y=T(x)$ then the absolute error is not a very good measure of the agreement between y and x if the magnitude of x is very large or very small. This is also true if y is any approximation to x. For example, if $y=10^{-6}$ and $x=10^{-5}$ then $|y-x| < 10^{-5}$ although y certainly isn't a good approximation to x. On the other hand, the relative error measures the number of fractional digits that x and y have in common. In fact, we will say that the _first s decimal digits_ of y are _significant_ as an _approximation to_ x, if $|y-x|/|x| \leq 5 \cdot 10**(-s)$. If you work out a few examples, you will see that this precise definition and the intuitive notion given at the beginning of this section essentially agree.

Now that we have these results we can determine the number of significant decimal digits in $T(x)$ as an approximation to x. We will only consider double precision in the IBM 360 with $b=16$ and $t=14$ although essentially the same results hold if $b=2$ and $t=53$. For any real number x in the range of floating point numbers, (1.2a) implies that the relative error of $T(x)$ as an approximation to x is bounded by 16^{-13} or about $2.2 \cdot 10^{-16}$. Therefore, $T(x)$ has 16 significant digits as an approximation to x so subsequent calculations which use $T(x)$ in place of x can only be expected to have at most 16 significant decimal digits. This explains why only 16 digits are printed as output by the computer, and why FLOAT DECIMAL(16) and FLOAT BINARY(53) give the same precision.

1.3 Errors in Floating Point Arithmetic

We have already discussed how roundoff errors arise as the result of converting a number x into its floating point representation. Roundoff errors also arise because the results of arithmetic operations performed on the computer are, in general, not exact. In order to illustrate these errors we will assume that we are working on a computer with base b=10 and precision t=4. You can observe similar errors on any computer, but this simple scheme makes it easier to really see what is happening.

First consider addition and suppose we want to add 163.9 and 24.36. On our computer they would be represented in normalized form as $(0.1639)10^3$ and $(0.2436)10^2$. However, since the computer can only perform additions by adding the mantissas of numbers with equal exponents, these numbers will be added in the form $(0.1639)10^3$ and $(0.02436)10^3$. In other words, the exponent of the number with the smaller exponent will be increased, and its mantissa will be shifted right by the same number of places. You can see that the result is $(0.1882)10^3$ which is the correct answer truncated to our working precision, t=4.

Although the example shows that the addition of two numbers has a small relative error associated with it, this is not the case when several numbers are added. For example, consider adding 0.556, 3.294, 24.36 and 163.9. Adding in decreasing order of magnitude the sum is 191.9. But if we add in the opposite order the sum is 192.1. Since the true sum is 192.11, the relative error for the sum in decreasing order is 21 times larger than in the reverse order.

If you have to add many numbers and you want high precision then you should try to add them in increasing order of magnitude. For most mathematical problems this is not convenient, so instead the sums are usually accumulated. This means that each intermediate sum is stored in double precision and then added to the next summand in double precision. The final result is then truncated to the working precision. If the sum in the previous example had been accumulated, then the final sum would have been 192.1 regardless of the order in which the sum was carried out.

Subtraction is similar to addition. However, note that if two almost equal numbers are being subtracted then there may be a loss of significance. For example, if x=136.5 and y=136.4 are approximations to 136.52 and 136.41, respectively, then both x and y have 4 significant digits. However, x-y=0.1 has one significant digit as an approximation to 0.11, the true difference.

It is not important to know precisely how the multiplication and division of two floating point numbers are carried out. It is important for you to know that these operations are carried out in such a way that the result equals the true answer truncated to the working precision. This means that the multiplication or division of two numbers gives rise to a small relative error. In fact, unlike addition and subtraction, it is even possible to prove that the relative error does not grow when several numbers are multiplied or divided. Unfortunately things aren't as good as they sound, since underflow and overflow occur much more frequently in this case and can be a source of error. For example, let x and y be floating point numbers and consider the calculation of $z = sqrt(x^2 + y^2)$. (Here and below, we intend "sqrt(arg)" to denote the nonnegative square root of arg.) If our machine with b=10 and t=4 restricts the exponent to $-9 \le e \le 9$, then you can verify that a straightforward calculation of z with $x = y = 10^{-6}$ gives z = 0 instead of $10^{-6} \cdot sqrt(2)$. This seems to be unavoidable in our computer, but in fact it isn't. We just have to be clever and see that the computation of z can also be carried out as follows:

Let $v = max\{|x|, |y|\}$

and $w = min\{|x|, |y|\}$.

Then, you can see that

$$z = v \cdot sqrt(1 + (w/v)^2),$$

and this time, for our example, we do obtain $z = 10^{-6} \cdot sqrt(2)$.

Now that we have talked about sums and products, we can discuss one of the most common numerical computations. From our discussion of the calculation of sums you can see that we should also be careful in the evaluation of inner products; that is, quantities of the form

$$(x(1) \cdot y(1)) + \ldots + (x(n) \cdot y(n)).$$

If high accuracy is desired, then inner products are usually accumulated. This means that each product $(x(i) \cdot y(i))$ is calculated in double precision and then this double precision number is added to the accumulated sum of the previous products. The final result is truncated to working precision.

As a final word of warning we mention that the accumulation of sums and inner products is <u>not</u> guaranteed to result in small relative errors unless cancellation does not occur. For example, consider

$$1.002 \cdot (1.003) + 0.9999 \cdot (-.9995) + 0.02000 \cdot (-0.2803).$$

Forming the products in double precision, i.e. with t=8, gives

$$(0.10050060)10^1 + (-0.9994005)10^0 + (-0.56060000)10^{-2}$$

which is zero in floating point addition with t=8. The true sum is easily seen to be $-0.5 \cdot 10^{-7}$.

Now that we have made you aware of roundoff errors, what can you do about them? Certainly it helps to work in extended precision, but still the best line of defense is to be aware of them so that you may be able to rearrange your calculations to lessen their effect.

Section 1 <u>Exercises</u>

1. The conversion of a decimal integer into base 2 notation is accomplished by a series of divisions by 2. The remainders, either 0 or 1, yield the digits of the fraction in reverse order, and the exponent is the number of divisions performed. For example, if the decimal integer is 69 we obtain

	quotient	remainder
69/2	34	1
34/2	17	0
17/2	8	1
8/2	4	0
4/2	2	0
2/2	1	0
1/2	0	1

The appearance of a zero quotient signals the end of the process. The result is that

$$69 = (.1000101) \cdot 2^7 \text{ (base 2)}.$$

To see that this algorithm works, note that if

$$69 = (.d(1) \ \ldots \ d(7)) \cdot 2^7,$$

then

$$69 = d(7) + d(6) \cdot 2 + d(5) \cdot 2^2 + \ldots + d(1) \cdot 2^6.$$

Therefore,

$$69/2 = 1/2 + 34 = d(7)/2 + d(6) + d(5) \cdot 2 + \ldots + d(1) \cdot 2^5,$$

so that d(7)=1 and

$$34 = d(5) \cdot 2 + d(4) \cdot 2^2 + \ldots + d(1) \cdot 2^5.$$

We can now divide 34 by 2 and proceed as before until we obtain a zero quotient.

   a) Write a program that will find the base 2 expansion of a decimal integer.

   b) Modify the program in a) so that it will find the expansion in any integral base b>1.

2. Write a program that will find the base 2 expansion of a decimal fraction. The algorithm for this program is very similar to the one described in Exercise 1, but now the number will be successively <u>multiplied</u> by 2.

3. Write a program that will perform the conversion between binary (base 2) and hexadecimal (base 16) numbers. An outline of the algorithm is as follows:

To go from hexadecimal to binary, replace each hexadecimal digit by its binary representation and (since $16=2^4$) multiply the exponent by 4. For example,

$(.458) \cdot 16^2$ (base 16) $= (.0100\ 0101\ 1000) \cdot 2^8$ (base 2).

To go from binary to hexadecimal, first increase the exponent and add leading zeroes to the fraction until the exponent is divisible by 4. Then replace each group of four binary digits by the corresponding hexadecimal digit and divide the exponent by 4. For example,

$(.10101) \cdot 2^{-6}$ (base 2) $= (.0010101) \cdot 2^{-4}$ (base 2)

$= (.2A) \cdot 16^{-1}$ (base 16).

We have used A ($=10$) for 1010, and similarly, B, C, D, E and F are used for the digits 11 through 15.

4. Let $x=1.0$ and $y=0.999$. Give the number of significant decimal digits, the absolute error and the relative error in y as an approximation to x. Repeat the exercise with the pairs $x \cdot 10^{-4}$, $y \cdot 10^{-4}$ and $x \cdot 10^4$, $y \cdot 10^4$.

5. a) Prove that $y=0$ never has any significant decimal digits as an approximation to any nonzero number x.

   b) Show that if $y \cdot x < 0$, then y has no significant decimal digits as an approximation to x.

6. Complete the proof of (1.2a) by showing that it holds for any precision t.

7. a) What is the <u>maximum</u> number of significant decimal of $T(x)$ as an approximation to x if you are working on a computer with $b=16$ and $t=6$? Assume $T(x) \neq x$.

   b) Since one hexadecimal digit can be represented by four binary digits it would seem that machines with $b=16$, $t=6$ and $b=2$, $t=24$ are equally accurate. Explain the fallacy in this argument.

8. a) Show that 0.2 has no significant decimal digits as an approximation to 0.1 but that 0.1 has one significant decimal digit as an approximation to 0.2.

b) Part a) shows that there is a lack of symmetry in the
definition of significant decimal digits; prove that it
can be removed by changing the definition to

$$|y-x| \leq 5(10**-s) \cdot \min\{|x|, |y|\}.$$

9. Write a program segment to read a given value of x and
compute the sum

$$1 + x/1! + x^2/2! + \ldots + x^{30}/30!$$

in ascending and descending orders. Compare the results for
x = ±10, ±5, ±0.1. Explain any differences.

10. Consider the following segment of a PL/I program:

```
A = 20.0E+0;
B = 0.1E+0;
C = A * B;
DO I = 1 TO C BY 1;
    PUT SKIP LIST(I);
    END;
```

What values of I will be printed? Check your answer by running
this program.

11. In real arithmetic (infinite precision), the two
expressions

$$99-70 \cdot sqrt(2) \quad \text{and} \quad 1/(99+70 \cdot sqrt(2))$$

are equal in value. Which expression is more accurate in finite
precision arithmetic? Why?

12. If $x(1),\ldots,x(n)$ are given numbers then $m=(x(1)+\ldots+x(n))/n$
is their mean or average and $v=((x(1)-m)^2+\ldots+(x(n)-m)^2)/n$ is
their variance. Show that in real arithmetic
$v=(x(1)^2+\ldots+x(n)^2)/n-m^2$. Which way of computing v is
preferable in finite precision arithmetic? Hint: Consider b=10,
t=3 and x(1)=\ldots=x(n)=0.905. Now compute v both ways for
$n=1,2,\ldots,5$.

Section 2   Library Functions (COS and SQRT)

Consider the statement Y = COS(X); where X is some floating point number, or the statement Y = SQRT(X); where X is now restricted to be nonnegative. When the computer executes these statements it will provide fast and accurate approximations to cos(x) and sqrt(x). How does it do this? Certainly, it does not have a table in which to look up the answer; this would require huge amounts of storage space and time. Instead for each value of x the computer generates an approximation to cos(x) or sqrt(x) by means of a few arithmetic operations.

2.1 Approximation by Polynomials

There are many methods for calculating a fast and accurate approximation to cos(x). Those readers with some knowledge of calculus are aware of a method based on Taylor's expansion of the cosine function. Since most people think that this is the way to calculate cos(x), we will first spend some time trying to convince you that this approach is not at all practical.

The approach that we have been referring to is based on the mathematical theorem that

(2.1a) $\cos(x) = 1 - x^2/2! + x^4/4! - x^6/6! + \ldots$

The right hand side of (2.1a) is called the "Taylor expansion" of the cosine function; the meaning of (2.1a) is that given any x and any accuracy factor ERROR, there is an integer n (which depends on x and ERROR) such that the sum of the first n terms on the right of (2.1a) is an approximation to cos(x) whose absolute error is less than ERROR. In other words, by adding enough terms we can get an approximation to cos(x) which is as accurate as desired.

There are many reasons why this approach is not reasonable. For one, how many terms do we need to take? In general, the larger |x| is, the more terms you need to take and this will slow down the computation. Even if you are willing to spend the time to compute enough terms in the right hand side of (2.1a), there is no guarantee that we will obtain an accurate answer. Equality in (2.1a) is a mathematical fact which depends on infinite precision; in finite precision (2.1a) is not true. For

example, if x=5.0 then with b=16 and t=6 the sum on the right of
(2.1a) equals 0.283655 but cos(5.0) = 0.283662... in infinite
precision.

It is fairly easy to see why we only obtain five significant
decimal digits: All the terms in the sum are restricted to
approximately seven decimal digits, but since the initial terms
like $5^4/4! = 26.04...$ are large, their initial two digits will
have to cancel in order to obtain an answer that is less than
one, and therefore only five decimal digits really contribute to
the accuracy of the sum. In addition, later terms will be small
and only their initial digits will contribute to the sum; after
the twelfth term they are negligible.

The cancellation that we have observed is due to the fact
that |x| is large and it will get worse if |x| is increased. If
|x| is small then (2.1a) is a reasonable way to compute cos(x).
Therefore, it is reasonable that practical methods for
evaluating cos(x) have an initial stage which allows you to
avoid the direct computation of cos(x) for large values of |x|.
The method that we will now describe shows that all the values
of cos(x) can be obtained from those of cos(x) and sin(x) for x
between 0 and (pi)/4 (where pi = 3.14159...).

First recall that the cosine is an even function, which means
that cos(-x) = cos(x), so we only need to consider nonnegative
x. Moreover, the cosine is a periodic function whose period is
p = 2pi. This means that cos(x + p·k) = cos(x) for any integer
k. To make use of this property first compute 4x/pi = q + f,
where q is an integer and f is the fractional part of 4x/pi.
Now express q as q = 8k + r where k and r are integers with
0≤r<8. Altogether, x = p·k + pi·(f+r)/4, so that periodicity
implies that

$$cos(x) = cos(pi·(f+r)/4).$$

Depending on the values of r we will have different results.
For example, if r = 0 then

$$cos(x) = cos(pi·f/4)$$

while if r = 1 then

$$cos(x) = cos(pi/2 - pi·(1-f)/4) = sin(pi·(1-f)/4).$$

Similar relationships hold for any 0≤r<8, so that
cos(pi·(f+r)/4) equals ±cos(pi·g/4) or ±sin(pi·g/4) where g = f
or g = 1-f.

The process just described is known as "range reduction".
Note that it consists of a clever use of the symmetries of the
cosine function; for other functions range reduction would take
a different form. If it is possible, range reduction is usually
beneficial, but the operations involved have to be carried out
with extreme care since they are very sensitive to errors.

Now that we have range reduction, the calculation of the cosine function will be complete if we can generate cos(x) and sin(x) for $0 \leq x \leq$ (pi)/4. For simplicity we only discuss the cosine function. In this case (2.1a) is reasonable since cancellation will not occur. In fact, if

(2.1b) $p(x) = 1 - x^2/2! + x^4/4! - x^6/6! + x^8/8!$,

then some thought will show that (2.1a) implies that

$$|p(x) - \cos(x)| < (pi/4)^{10}/10! = (2.5)10^{-8}$$

for $0 \leq x \leq$ (pi)/4.   Moreover,   since   in   this   range $\cos(x) \geq 1/\text{sqrt}(2)$, we also have

$$|(p(x) - \cos(x))/\cos(x)| < (3.5)10^{-8}.$$

This shows that p(x) always has eight significant decimal digits as an approximation to cos(x), so (2.1b) is adequate for single precision.

The function defined by (2.1b) is a polynomial of degree 8 in x, and degree 4 in x^2. Hence if we can find a polynomial of degree 3 in x^2 which approximates the cosine as well as (2.1b), then we should use this polynomial instead of (2.1b) since any work saving in a library function like the cosine is important because of the high frequency with which it will be used. It is indeed possible to find such a polynomial but the methods for doing this are beyond the scope of this book. The interested reader will find material on this topic in the references of Section 4.

2.1.1 Horner's Scheme

The point was made in Section 2.1 that any savings in the work required to execute a frequently performed task are generally worthwhile. Polynomial evaluation is certainly such a task if for no other reason than their frequent use in approximation.

Consider then the evaluation of a polynomial p of degree n

(2.1.1a) $p(x) = a(0) + a(1)x + a(2)x^2 + \ldots + a(n)(x**n)$.

If we evaluate (2.1.1a) in what would seem to be the obvious way -- evaluate a(i)(x**i) for i=0,1,...,n and add these terms together -- then this would involve n(n+1)/2 multiplications and n additions. To see this, note that the evaluation of a(i)(x**i) involves i multiplications and therefore the number of multiplications is

$$1 + 2 + \ldots + n = n(n+1)/2.$$

In analogy with the terminology introduced in Part VI, we say
that this is an n2 algorithm. Note however, that if we evaluate
(2.1.1a) from left to right, then each term needs only 2
multiplications and one addition. For example, if we have
evaluated

$$a(0) + a(1)x + a(2)x^2,$$

then we only need one multiplication to compute x^3 from x^2,
another multiplication for $a(3)x^3$, and an addition for

$$a(0) + a(1)x + a(2)x^2 + a(3)x^3.$$

In all, for (2.1.1a) we need 2n multiplications and n additions,
so this is an order n algorithm.

However, there is a still faster algorithm, known as Horner's
scheme. This method consists of a series of n nested
multiplications such that at each stage only one multiplication
and one addition occur. Thus Horner's scheme is also an order n
algorithm but requires only half as many multiplications as the
previous algorithm.

The idea of Horner's method is really simple. First note
that a first degree polynomial can be evaluated in one
multiplication and one addition. If we write a second degree
polynomial in the form

$$a(0) + a(1)x + a(2)x^2 = a(0) + (a(1) + a(2)x)x,$$

then it can be evaluated in two multiplications and two
additions. For a third degree polynomial, first write

$$a(0) + a(1)x + a(2)x^2 + a(3)x^3 = a(0) + (a(1) + a(2)x + a(3)x^2)x,$$

and then evaluate the polynomial in parentheses as above. The
idea of the algorithm should now be clear; a version of it is as
follows:

```
PX = A(N);
DO I = N-1 TO 0 BY -1;
    PX = X * PX + A(I);
    END;
```

Note that if the coefficients of the polynomials are decreasing
in magnitude, as in (2.1b), then for $|x| \leq 1$, the sum in Horner's
method will consist of an addition of terms of increasing
magnitude. Therefore, in cases like this we expect an accurate
evaluation of the polynomial.

2.2 Approximation by Iteration

The techniques discussed in Section 2.1 apply to the
evaluation of most functions, and in particular, to the
evaluation of sqrt(x). However, in this case we shall see that

although range reduction is possible, the final approximation of sqrt(x) is not obtained from a polynomial, but by a technique called "iteration".

First let us consider the form taken by range reduction.   If x is a floating point number in a base 16 computer then

        x = m(16**e)

where $1/16 \leq m < 1$ is the mantissa and e is the exponent. If e is even, say e=2c, then

        sqrt(x) = sqrt(m)·16**c,

while if e is odd, say e=2d-1, then

        sqrt(x) = (1/4)sqrt(m)·16**d.

By combining both cases we see that it is only necessary to evaluate sqrt(x) for $1/16 \leq x < 1$.

At this stage, in analogy with the previous section, it would seem reasonable to try to approximate the square-root function on the reduced range by a polynomial. However, this turns out not to be practical.

The method used depends on the fact that the number we are after, sqrt(m), is the positive solution of the equation $-m+x^2 = 0$. Consider then the graph of the function defined by $f(x) = -m+x^2$. If we have an approximation x(0) to sqrt(m) with x(0) > sqrt(m), then it is easy to obtain a better approximation x(1) with x(1) > sqrt(m). Just draw the tangent line to f at x(0) and take x(1) to be the intersection of this line with the x-axis. Finding x(1) is not difficult.   The   slope of the tangent line to f at x(0) is just the derivative f'(x(0)) so that the y-intercept equation of the tangent line is

        y = f'(x(0))(x-x(0)) + f(x(0)).

But f'(x(0)) = 2·x(0) and $f(x(0)) = -m + x(0)^2$ and thus

        $y = 2·x·x(0) - m - x(0)^2$.

Finally, since x(1) is the x-intercept of this line,

        $0 = 2·x(0)·x(1) - m - x(0)^2$

and rearranging terms,

        x(1) = (x(0) + m/x(0))/2.

There is no reason why this process cannot be repeated to obtain a still better approximation x(2) where

        x(2) = (x(1) + m/x(1))/2.

In general, if we have the kth approximation x(k), the (k+1)st
approximation x(k+1) is given by

(2.2a)   x(k+1) = (x(k) + m/x(k))/2.

   Geometrically, it is obvious that if x(0) > sqrt(m) then

        sqrt(m) < x(k+1) < x(k),

and that given any accuracy factor ERROR there will be an
approximation x(k) such that

        |x(k) - sqrt(m)| < ERROR.

Since sqrt(m) ≥ 1/4, we would also have

        |(x(k) - sqrt(m))/sqrt(m)| < 4·ERROR.

This would solve the problem of evaluating sqrt(m) if we could
answer   two   questions: 1) How do you choose   the   initial
approximation x(0)? 2) How do you decide which approximation to
take as sqrt(m)?

   These two questions are obviously related. We want an x(0)
which is close to sqrt(m) because this may mean that our fourth
approximation, say, will be the final one. On the other hand,
we do not want to spend too many operations in trying to find an
accurate x(0). In the following, these delicate matters will be
ignored and we will limit ourselves to presenting reasonable
solutions.

   An acceptable x(0) can be found as follows: First find the
straight line that best approximates (in the relative sense) the
square   root   function for 1/16 ≤ x ≤ 1; that is, determine
constants a and b such that

        max{|(sqrt(x) - (a+bx))/sqrt(x)| : 1/16≤x≤1 }

is minimal. Then set x(0) = a+bm. It turns out that a=2/9,
b=8/9, and that the resulting x(0) always has one significant
decimal digit as an approximation to sqrt(m).

   Deciding which approximation to accept as the final one is a
somewhat difficult question to answer theoretically. However, a
little experimentation will convince you that the third and
fourth approximations x(3) and x(4) will suffice for single and
double precision, respectively. The rule of thumb is that each
iteration roughly <u>doubles</u> the number of significant figures (and
recall that x(0) has one).

   To finish this section, we mention that the method used to
find the zero of the function f(x) = -m+x^2 is known as "Newton's
method". It can be used to find a zero of a general function f.

In fact, the same argument in terms of tangent lines and x-intercepts yields that Newton's method is given by

$$x(k+1) = x(k) - f(x(k))/f'(x(k)).$$

If $f(x) = -m+x^2$ then it is easy to verify that Newton's method reduces to (2.2a).

Section 2 <u>Exercises</u>

1. Show that sqrt(2) does not have a finite or repeating decimal representation. Do the same for cos(1) by using (2.1a).

2. Write an algorithm which accepts a positive integer q and finds integers k and r with $0 \leq r < 8$ and such that $q = 8k + r$.

3. Complete the discussion in the text by showing how $cos(pi \cdot (f+r)/4)$ can be expressed in terms of $cos(pi \cdot g/4)$ or $sin(pi \cdot g/4)$ where g=f or 1-f.

4. Verify the statements given in the text on the calculation of the right side of (2.1a). Evaluate it in three different ways: in ascending and descending order, and by Horner's method. In addition, evaluate the right side of (2.1a) for x=1.57 and explain why the result has a larger relative error than for x=5.0.

5. Let s(n,x) denote the sum of the first n terms on the right of (2.1a). Show that if $|x| \leq 2n$ then

$$|cos(x) - s(n,x)| \leq (x^{**}2n)/(2n)!$$

6. Write a procedure which, given an integer n and a float decimal x, will read in coefficients and evaluate the corresponding polynomial by Horner's method. Do not use any arrays.

7. a) Show that if $x(0) = 2/9 + (8/9)m$ then $x(1) > sqrt(m)$ for $1/16 \leq m < 1$.

   b) Verify that $|(x(0) - sqrt(m))/sqrt(m)| \leq 1/9$ for all $1/16 \leq m \leq 1$.

8. Verify, by experimentation, that the third iterate of (2.2a) suffices for single precision.

Section 3   Algorithms for Two Typical Problems

3.1 Simultaneous Linear Equations

The first of our typical problems is frequently encountered, not only for its own sake, but also as an intermediate step in the solution of other computational problems. It can be stated as follows: Given a vector (or one-dimensional array) b with n elements, and a matrix (or two-dimensional array) A with n rows and n columns, find a vector x of length n such that

(3.1a)
$$a(1,1) \cdot x(1) + \ldots + a(1,n) \cdot x(n) = b(1)$$
$$\ldots$$
$$a(i,1) \cdot x(1) + \ldots + a(i,n) \cdot x(n) = b(i)$$
$$\ldots$$
$$a(n,1) \cdot x(1) + \ldots + a(n,n) \cdot x(n) = b(n),$$

or show that there is no solution to this problem.

If n=2 then (3.1a) represents two straight lines, and the problem reduces to finding whether two lines intersect and the point of intersection. Similarly, for n=3, we have three planes and the problem is to find a point (if any) shared by these planes. In general, given a vector b, the system of equations (3.1a) can either have no solution, a unique solution, or an infinite number of solutions. In this section we will assume that (3.1a) has a unique solution.

The problem may seem trivial, but this is not so. For example, (3.1a) might have a solution vector of real numbers, but not a solution in floating point arithmetic. Moreover, you should realize that roundoff errors will probably change the matrix when it is read in, so that you will be solving a different system of linear equations. Clearly, all we can hope for is an approximate solution to (3.1a), but this problem is also not easy. For example, if

(3.1b)
$$0.66666 \cdot x(1) + 3.33334 \cdot x(2) = 4$$
$$1.99999 \cdot x(1) + 10.00001 \cdot x(2) = 12,$$

then you can verify that x = (1,1) solves this system exactly. Now consider the approximate solutions y=(1.1,0.9) and z=(6,0). Although y appears to be the better solution since it is closer to x, substituting y for x in (3.1b) gives

(3.733332, 11.199998)

instead of (4, 12), while the substitution of z for x in (3.1b) gives

(3.99996, 11.99994).

Thus, from this point of view z seems to be the better solution.

   Equations (3.1b) also illustrate another difficulty with linear systems. Suppose the right side of (3.1b) is changed to

(3.99996, 11.99994).

Then, as we have seen above, the <u>exact</u> solution is changed to (6,0).   Thus, a small relative change in the equations leads to a large relative change in the answer. Clearly, such a system is "ill-conditioned" and will cause problems. We will have more to say about (3.1b) in Section 3.1.3.

3.1.1 Gaussian Elimination

   Most of you have encountered linear systems before, and if so, you probably have solved   them by Gaussian elimination. Rather than give a formal   description we will   discuss this algorithm in connection with a system (3.1a) with n=3, but in such a way that the general algorithm is clear.

   Consider then

$$5 \cdot x(1) - 2 \cdot (2) + 3 \cdot x(3) = 10$$

$$(3.1.1a)\ 10 \cdot x(1) - 3 \cdot x(2) + 4 \cdot x(3) = 16$$

$$15 \cdot x(1) + 1 \cdot x(2) - 3 \cdot x(3) = 8.$$

   The first stage of Gaussian elimination consists of eliminating the unknown x(1) from the   second and   third equations. To do this, we multiply the first equation by 2, and subtract it from the second, then multiply by 3, and subtract it from the third to get

$$5 \cdot x(1) - 2 \cdot x(2) + 3 \cdot x(3) = 10$$

$$(3.1.1b)\qquad 1 \cdot x(2) - 2 \cdot x(3) = -4$$

$$7 \cdot x(2) - 12 \cdot x(3) = -22.$$

Thus, we have effectively reduced the problem to a smaller problem (in this case 2 by 2 but generally (n-1) by (n-1)) which doesn't involve x(1). If we can solve the smaller problem for x(2) and x(3) (generally x(2),...,x(n)) then x(1) could easily

be determining by substituting these values back into the first
equations.

   At this point, we can apply the same elimination strategy to
the smaller problem and eliminate x(2) from all except the first
equation of the problem.   In our example this results in

        5·x(1) - 2·x(2) + 3·x(3) = 10

(3.1.1c)   1·x(2) - 2·x(3) = -4

                2·x(3) = 6.

In the general case we would now have n-2 equations in n-2
unknowns and we would continue. In our example, n=3 and so we
have completed the forward elimination. From this you see that
for the general system (3.1a), the ith stage of the forward
elimination consists of eliminating x(i) from equations i+1
through n. This is done by forming the multipliers

        m(i,j) = a(i,j)/a(i,i)

for j = i+1,...,n, then multiplying the ith equation by m(i,j)
and subtracting it from the jth equation for j = i+1,...,n.

   Now that we have reduced our original 3 by 3 system to the
simple form of (3.1.1c) the solution can be obtained easily.
The third equation yields x(3) = 3. Substituting x(3) back into
the equation just above it yields x(2) = 2 and both of these
values substituted back into the next equation above, in this
case the first, results in x(1) = 1. This process is called
back substitution; in the general case it would be carried out
by the following PL/I program:

```
        DO I = N TO 1 BY -1;
           SUM = 0;
           DO J = I + 1 TO N BY 1;
              SUM = SUM + A(I,J)*X(J);
              END;
           X(I) = (B(I) - SUM)/A(I,I);
           END;
```

   Things don't always go so smoothly. If the coefficients of
the second equation in (3.1.1a) had been 10, -4 and 6 then the
second equation in (3.1.1c) would have been0=-4 and so no
solution would exist. A good program would not merely terminate
at this point but would return information to the user
concerning the nature of the failure.   Another hitch which
could occur does not imply the nonexistence of a solution.
Suppose A(2,2) had been -4 with all the other coefficients the
same as in (3.1.1a). Then the second equation in (3.1.1b) would
not involve x(2) and so it clearly couldn't be used to eliminate
x(2) from subsequent equations. The remedy to this difficulty
is simple; just interchange the second and third equations.

In general, this difficulty is caused by having $a(i,i)=0$ in the ith stage of the forward elimination, and thus, the multipliers can't be formed. The remedy is to interchange the ith row for any row j such that $a(j,i)\neq0$, although in practice j is chosen so that

$$|a(j,i)| \geq |a(k,i)|$$

for k = i,...,n. This modification which is made even when $a(i,i)\neq0$ is called <u>Gaussian</u> <u>elimination</u> <u>with</u> <u>partial</u> <u>pivoting</u>, and we will see in Section 3.1.3 that this is the method generally in use at present for solving (3.1a) except in those cases where A has some special property that makes special-purpose methods more suitable. Moreover, it can be shown that if (3.1a) has a unique solution then Gaussian elimination with partial pivoting will yield the answer provided all operations are performed in infinite precision arithmetic.

3.1.2 <u>Efficiency</u> -- <u>Gaussian</u> <u>Elimination</u> <u>vs.</u> <u>Cramer's</u> <u>Rule</u>

You have probably encountered <u>Cramer's</u> <u>rule</u> in your studies, and you may even have used it to solve systems of linear equations. If this is the case, you might want to know whether or not Gaussian elimination is more efficient than Cramer's rule in order to decide which algorithm to apply.

The standard way to measure efficiency in solving (3.1a) is in terms of the number of arithmetic operations necessary to obtain a solution. For linear equations, this is a reasonable measure since the only operations involved are arithmetic, but we shall see that the problem of Section 3.2 requires a different criterion.

Cramer's rule depends on the calculation of the determinants of certain matrices. The <u>determinant</u> of a matrix A with n rows and n columns is given by

(3.1.2a)   det A = $a(1,1)\cdot$det M(1,1) - $a(2,1)\cdot$det M(2,1)
              + a(3,1) det M(3,1) ... a(n,1) det M(n,1)

where M(i,1) is the (n-1) by (n-1) matrix obtained by deleting the ith row and first column of A. To calculate det M(i,1) we can apply this definition again and express det M(i,1) in terms of determinants of (n-2) by (n-2) matrices. By repeating this process, we eventually obtain det A expressed in terms of the determinants of 2 by 2 matrices, and since

$$\det \begin{bmatrix} a & b \\ c & d \end{bmatrix} = ad - bc,$$

this completes the calculation of det A.

However, the efficiency of this method for evaluating determinants is very poor. To see this let m(n) be the number of multiplications necessary to evaluate the determinant of an n by n matrix. Then (3.1.2a) implies that

$$m(n) = n \cdot m(n-1) + n,$$

and in particular, $m(n) > n \cdot m(n-1)$. But by the same reasoning $m(k) > k \cdot m(k-1)$ for any $3 \le k \le n$, and therefore,

$$m(n) > n \cdot (n-1) \cdot \ldots \cdot (3) \cdot m(2).$$

Since $m(2) = 2$, we finally have $m(n) > n!$.

This is an impossibly-large problem (as described in Section VI.3), even for small values of n. For example, on an IBM 360/65 a single precision multiplication takes approximately four microseconds ($4 \cdot 10^{-6}$ seconds). Since $15! = (1.3) \cdot 10^{12}$ this means that the calculation of the determinant of a 15 by 15 matrix by (3.1.2a) would take at least 2.6 years of computing time.

Now Cramer's rule states that if det A $\ne$ 0, then the solution to (3.1a) is given by

$$x(j) = \det A(b|j)/\det A,$$

where $A(b|j)$ is the n by n matrix obtained by replacing the jth column of A by b. Therefore, the above arguments would seem to imply that Cramer's rule is unreasonable. However, the correct conclusion is that if the determinants are calculated by (3.1.2a) then Cramer's rule is unreasonable. We shall later point out that it is possible to calculate determinants in about $n^3/3$ multiplications, but that even if the determinants are calculated in this manner Gaussian elimination with partial pivoting is more efficient.

To estimate the efficiency of Gaussian elimination, we will count the number of multiplications and divisions required by the forward elimination and the back substitution. It is important not to neglect the counting of additions and subtractions, since if this number is much larger, then it would determine the efficiency of the method. However, we shall let you verify that this is not the case in Gaussian elimination.

Since multiplications and divisions take almost the same amount of time to perform, we will count a division as a multiplication. Similarly, a subtraction is counted as an addition.

The ith stage of the forward elimination needs (n-i) divisions to form the multipliers. Moreover, to multiply the

ith equation by m(i,j) for j = i+1,...,n requires (n-i)(n-i-1)
multiplications. Altogether, the ith stage requires

   (n-i) + (n-i)(n-i-1) = (n-i)^2

multiplications, and the complete forward elimination needs

   (n-1)^2 + (n-2)^2 + ... + 1^2 = n(n-1)(2n-1)/6

multiplications.

   From the program segment we gave for back substitution, it is
easy to verify that this process uses

   n + (n-1) + ... + 1 = n(n+1)/2

multiplications. So we see that the most expensive part of
Gaussian elimination is the forward elimination, and this only
involves approximately n^3/3 multiplications. Since this is also
the most expensive in terms of additions, Gaussian elimination
is an n^3 algorithm. Moreover, Gaussian elimination with partial
pivoting is also an n^3 algorithm since there will be at most
n(n-1)/2 comparisons.

   It is interesting that Gaussian elimination with partial
pivoting is used to find the determinant of an n by n matrix in
approximately n^3 operations. In fact, the determinant of A is
not changed during the forward elimination except when two rows
are interchanged.   However, only the sign is changed, and this
happens only if the number of interchanges is <u>odd</u>. Since the
forward elimination will reduce A to an upper triangular matrix
-- a matrix such that a(i,j)=0 for i>j -- we only need to know
how to calculate the determinant of an upper triangular matrix.
But this is easy, since (3.1.2a) implies that the determinant of
an upper triangular matrix is the product of the elements on the
diagonal. In particular, the determinant of the matrix in
(3.1.1c) is 10, and therefore the determinant of the matrix in
(3.1.1a) is also 10. In summary, we have shown that the
determinant of an n by n matrix is an immediate by-product of
the forward elimination and therefore it can be calculated with
an n^3 algorithm. Since Cramer's rule requires the calculation
of n+1 distinct determinants, this makes Cramer's rule an n^4
algorithm.

3.1.3 <u>Ill-Conditioned</u> <u>Problems</u> <u>and</u> <u>Stable</u> <u>Algorithms</u>

   You have already seen an ill-conditioned problem; in
equations (3.1b) a small relative error in the righthand side
led to a large relative error in the solution. Geometrically,
it should be clear why this happens -- the lines represented by
(3.1b) are essentially parallel. Computationally, there is not
much that you can do with these problems except work in higher
precision. However, if the problem is very ill-conditioned then

even changing the data into the internal representation of the computer will drastically change the answer.

Let us now assume that our system of linear equations is not too ill-conditioned. Under this assumption, a method for solving (3.1a) is <u>stable</u> if it gives accurate results with respect to the working precision.

Without any pivoting, Gaussian elimination can't be considered stable since it can break down even in infinite precision arithmetic by having $a(i,i)=0$ at the ith stage of the forward elimination. Consider, for example, equations (3.1.1a) with $a(2,2)$ replaced by -4. However, if a zero causes problems in infinite precision, then maybe a small number will do the same in finite precision. Here is an example that will show that this is the case:

$$10-^4 \cdot x(1) - x(2) = -1$$
(3.1.3a)
$$x(1) + x(2) = 2$$

We assume that we are working on a computer with base $b=10$ and precision $t=4$. The result of the forward elimination is

$$10-^4 \cdot x(1) - x(2) = -1$$

$$10^4 \cdot x(2) = 10^4$$

so that $x(2) = 1$ and $x(1) = 0$. However, to four decimal places the correct solution is $x(1) = 0.9999$ and $x(2) = 1.0001$.

Note that (3.1.3a) is well-conditioned since the corresponding straight lines are far from parallel. Therefore, the conclusion is that without pivoting Gaussian elimination is not stable even for well-conditioned systems.

It is pretty clear what happened in (3.1.3a). We found ourselves having to add numbers whose magnitudes were so different that excessive roundoff errors resulted. An indication of this can be found in the magnitude change from 1 to 10^4 in the coefficient of $x(2)$ in the second equation. When Gaussian elimination is modified to be more stable, the changes are directed toward reducing the growth in the magnitude of the elements generated during the forward elimination. The partial pivoting strategy is one way to accomplish this. As mentioned in Section 3.1.1, this consists of interchanging rows at the ith stage of the forward elimination in such a way that

$$|a(i,i)| \geq |a(k,i)|$$

for $k = i+1,\ldots,n$. It follows that the multipliers $m(i,j)$ satisfy $|m(i,j)| \leq 1$, and therefore, at each stage of the forward elimination the elements can, at worst, double in size. In practice, however, this growth is usually not obtained, and

Gaussian elimination with partial pivoting is a stable algorithm.

Let us consider one last example:

$$10 \cdot x(1) - 10^5 \cdot x(2) = -10^5$$

(3.1.3b)

$$x(1) + x(2) = 2$$

Note that (3.1.3b) is well-conditioned, and that in fact, this example was obtained from (3.1.3a) by multiplying the first row by 10^5. Since in this case Gaussian elimination with partial pivoting does not interchange any rows, forward elimination gives

$$10 \cdot x(1) - 10^5 \cdot x(2) = -10^5$$

$$10^4 \cdot x(2) = 10^4$$

if the operations are carried out on a computer with b=10 and t=4. Therefore, x(2) = 1 and x(1) = 0 which is, of course, completely incorrect. What went wrong? The reason for the failure is that there is already a large difference in the magnitude of the elements of A. For this reason partial pivoting is usually implemented with a "scaling" or "equilibration" technique. Unfortunately this subject is not well understood, but at present scaling usually consists of dividing each row of (3.1a) by the absolute value of the element of maximum magnitude in that row. In (3.1.3b) this would amount to changing the system into (3.1.3a) which, as we have seen, can be adequately solved by Gaussian elimination with partial pivoting.

3.2 The Quadrature Problem

You are probably familiar with the problem of finding the area of a triangle or a circle. These are simple examples of the "quadrature problem", which is to find the area enclosed by a curve. This problem is not only geometrically interesting, but it is of great importance in science and engineering.

Instead of dealing with the completely general question, we will assume that we are given numbers a < b, and a procedure which accepts any x between a and b and returns a value f(x). This is a very important special case and if we think of f(x) as the height of a curve, then we want the area enclosed between the curve and the x-axis from a to b. For example, if someone gives us a=0, b=1 and f(x) = sqrt(1-x^2) then we are being asked to find the area of a quarter of a circle whose radius is one. Now, of course, you know the answer is pi/4 = 0.785398..., but suppose you had never seen the formula for a circle's area. How would you solve the problem then?

Those of you who have had calculus will probably recognize this problem as a special case of the more general problem of finding "the definite integral of a function". If this is the case, then you will realize, as you read this section, that the methods discussed here apply verbatim to this more general problem. Nevertheless, when the problem is treated from the point of view of finding an area, the methods for its solution become geometrically intuitive and therefore accessible to a wider audience.

Another remark is in order for the calculus student. A large percentage of the "indefinite integrals" which arise in practice can't be found in closed form. Furthermore, even when an antiderivative could be found it is often more accurate to ignore this and use a numerical quadrature method.

3.2.1 The Trapezoidal Rule

The simplest approach to solving our quadrature problem is to first subdivide the interval [a,b] into a series of smaller intervals in such a way that for each interval, say [c,d], the area of a trapezoid with a base of length d-c and sides of height f(c) and f(d), is a reasonable approximation to the area under the curve from c to d. Then the sum of the areas of these small trapezoids should be a good approximation to the area under the curve from a to b.

To illustrate this approach let us return to our example where a=0, b=1 and $f(x) = sqrt(1-x^2)$. As a first attempt we could divide [0,1] into two equal subintervals, calculate the areas of the corresponding trapezoids and take their sum as a tentative answer. Since the area of a trapezoid with base length of d-c and sides of height f(c) and f(d) is

T_AREA(c,d) = (d-c)(f(d)+f(c))/2

we would obtain 0.683 as our tentative answer. This is clearly not very good. To improve matters we could successively subdivide the interval into equal subintervals, calculate the corresponding area approximations and stop when two consecutive approximations agree to the desired accuracy. The result of this strategy is summarized in the table below:

Number of subintervals	Approximate areas
2	6.83012E-01
4	7.48927E-01
8	7.72454E-01
16	7.80813E-01
32	7.83775E-01
64	7.84824E-01
128	7.85195E-01
256	7.85326E-01
512	7.85372E-01
1024	7.85389E-01
2048	7.85394E-01
4096	7.85397E-01
8192	7.85397E-01

The results in this table were generated by the following method: The interval [a,b] was divided into n equal subintervals, each of length h = (b-a)/n. (In the above example n is a power of 2, but this is not important right now.) This introduces a set of partition points x(i), i=0,1,...,n where

(3.2.1a)   x(i) = a + h·i.

The area of the ith trapezoid is

$$(h/2)[f(x(i-1)) + f(x(i))],$$

and the sum of the areas of these trapezoids is

$$TR(n) = (h/2)\{[f(x(0)+f(x(1))] + \\ [f(x(1))+f(x(2))] + \\ ...+ [f(x(n-1))+f(x(n))]\}.$$

This formula can also be written as

(3.2.1b) TR(n) =
    h[(1/2)f(a) + f(x(1)) + ... + f(x(n-1)) + (1/2)f(b)],

and in this form the formula is known as the <u>trapezoidal</u> <u>rule</u>. The results in the previous table were then obtained by using (3.2.1b) and double precision on an IBM 360. However, only single precision answers were printed out. Finally, the computation was terminated when

$$|TR(n) - TR(2n)| < 10^{-6}$$

for some integer n.

There is a good reason why n was always doubled from one calculation to the next. Consider, for example, TR(512). Equation (3.2.1b) shows that to calculate TR(512) we have to call the height procedure 513 times. However, if you think about it, 257 of these values were already used in TR(256) and

so they will be repeat calls. Therefore you should be able to
compute TR(512) from TR(256) with only 256 additional procedure
calls. In fact, you should convince yourself that

(3.2.1c) TR(2n) = (1/2)TR(n) +
           h[f(x(1)) + f(x(3)) + ... + f(x(2n-1))]

where h = (b-a)/2n and x(i) is defined by (3.2.1a).

Although in our example we first computed TR(2), and then
used (3.2.1c) to compute the other values of TR(n), this is not
necessary. Usually n is initially chosen so that h = (b-a)/n is
relatively small; for example, choose n to be the smallest
integer such that n ≥ 10(b-a). Then TR(n) is computed from
(3.2.1b), and (3.2.1c) is used for the remaining values. Also
note that the computation of TR(2n) by (3.2.1c) represents a
real savings. Instead of 2n+1 procedure calls as (3.2.1b)
requires, only n calls are required. There is also a
corresponding decrease in the required number of arithmetic
operations.

3.2.2 Efficiency - Fixed vs. Adaptive Quadrature

How should we measure the efficiency of an integration
technique? Consider, for example, the following two methods for
finding the area under a curve. The first method chooses n such
that n ≥ 10(b-a) and then computes TR(n), TR(2n), TR(4n), ...,
by (3.2.1b) until

    |TR(m) - TR(2m)| < ERROR

for some integer m ≥ n where ERROR is a pre-specified accuracy.
The second method only differs in the fact that TR(n),
TR(2n),..., are computed by (3.2.1c).

In this case the second method is more efficient. The reason
is that clearly the main cost of finding an accurate
approximation to the desired area is measured by the number of
calls to the height procedure. Since this is true in general,
the efficiency measure for integration methods is usually taken
to be the number of calls to the height procedure necessary to
achieve some pre-specified accuracy.

We now would like to show that with this measure, the
trapezoidal rule is not very efficient when used to find the
area under certain curves. In fact, the example with a=0, b=1,
and $f(x) = sqrt(1-x^2)$ shows that the trapezoidal rule can use up
a tremendous number of procedure calls. To convince you that
this behavior is not typical, consider the problem a=0, b=1, and
f(x) = cos(x). In this case we have

n	TR(n)
20	8.41295E-01
40	8.41427E-01
80	8.41460E-01
160	8.41468E-01
320	8.41470E-01
640	8.41470E-01

The difference in behavior is due to the fact that for $f(x) = sqrt(1-x^2)$ the tangent line at x=1 is vertical. It is very difficult for a trapezoid to approximate the area of a curve near a point at which a vertical tangent line exists. In general, the trapezoidal rule is slow if the slope of the tangent line changes abruptly as the curve is traversed.

Another reason for the failure of the trapezoidal rule is that the points at which the height procedure is going to be evaluated are fixed in advance. These points are equally distributed throughout the interval [a,b] which means that the trapezoidal rule assumes that the curve behaves the same way throughout the interval, and this is not true for $sqrt(1-x^2)$.

Actually, it is not very difficult to modify the trapezoidal rule so that it adapts itself to the shape of the curve. The important modification that will be described below is called the adaptive trapezoidal rule while the trapezoidal rule as described in Section 3.2.1 is sometimes called the fixed trapezoidal rule.

The adaptive trapezoidal rule consists of a series of stages. In the first stage, subdivide the interval [a,b] into two equal subintervals by means of the midpoint m = (a+b)/2 and compare

    T1 = T_AREA(a,b)

with

    T2 = T_AREA(a,m) + T_AREA(m,b).

If T1 and T2 agree to the desired accuracy, then take T2 as the answer and stop. If they don't, then momentarily forget about the subinterval [m,b] and concentrate on [a,m]. The second stage is entirely analogous. The subinterval [a,m] is subdivided into two equal subintervals, and the corresponding T1 and T2 are computed. If T1 and T2 agree to the pre-specified accuracy then T2 is accepted as the area under the curve from a to m, and the above process is repeated on the interval [m,b]. If they don't agree, repeat the process on the left half of the interval [a,m].

Even from this vague description of the adaptive trapezoidal rule it should be clear that this scheme will concentrate the calls of the height procedure on the wiggly parts of the curve,

and therefore the adaptive trapezoidal rule should be more
efficient in the use of function values than its fixed
counterpart. However, it should also be clear that we will have
to keep track of the values produced by the calls to the height
procedure in order to avoid repeat calls. Since it may not be
clear how to save those values, we will now refine the
description of the adaptive trapezoidal rule, and in doing so we
will give a method for saving these values. You will probably
not be surprised to learn that this method is sometimes
implemented as a recursive procedure (see Section IV.3) although
we will not take this approach.

To fix ideas suppose that a=0, b=1, and let us concentrate on
the intervals being examined. For example, if T1 and T2 don't
agree to the desired accuracy, then during the first three
stages we successively generate

        [0,1/2]   [1/2,1]

        [0,1/4]   [1/4,1/2]   [1/2,1]

        [0,1/8]   [1/8,1/4]   [1/4,1/2]   [1/2,1].

Note that the leftmost interval is the one that is currently
being examined. At the fourth stage we would calculate

        T1 = T_AREA(0,1/8),

and

        T2 = T_AREA(0,1/16) + T_AREA(1/16,1/8).

If T1 and T2 agree to the desired accuracy, then T2 is accepted
as the area under the curve between 0 and 1/8. The process
would then start again, but now the list of intervals would be

        [1/8,1/4]   [1/4,1/2]   [1/2,1],

while if T1 and T2 had not agreed, then we would have had

        [0,1/16]   [1/16,1/8]   [1/8,1/4]   [1/4,1/2]   [1/2,1].

It is convenient to think of this list of intervals as being
a last-in first-out stack, with the rightmost interval at the
bottom, and the most recently generated intervals being inserted
at the top. To represent these stacks on the computer let
STK_A(J) be the left endpoint of the Jth interval on the stack,
and let STK_B(J) contain the right endpoint. For instance, in
our example, STK_A(1) = 1/2, STK_B(1) = 1, and at the end of the
third stage STK_A(4) = 0, STK_B(4) = 1/8.

The height of the stack is related to the length of the
smallest interval in the stack. In particular, if the length of
the smallest interval is 1/(2**k), then the length of the stack
does not exceed k+1. In the general case, the initial interval

is [a,b] so the lengths of the subintervals are each of the form
(b-a)/(2**k) for some integer k. Since this integer k indicates
the size of the interval it is called the <u>level</u> of the interval.
In our example, if on the fourth stage T1 and T2 do agree to the
desired accuracy, then on the stack we have

    level 1 intervals [1/2,1]

    level 2 intervals [1/4,1/2]

    level 3 intervals [1/8,1/4]

at the end of the fourth stage. If now, on the fifth stage, the
interval [1/8,1/4] is divided into halves and the corresponding
T1 and T2 don't agree then the level 3 interval [1/8,1/4] is
replaced by the two level 4 intervals [1/8,3/16] and [3/16,1/4].
In particular, note that if a level k interval is subdivided
then it is removed from the stack and replaced by two level k+1
intervals.

By now you should have a fair idea of how to implement the
adaptive trapezoidal rule. In particular you may have realized
that to keep track of the evaluations of the height procedure
you will need two more stacks: STK_FA(J) and STK_FB(J) will
contain, respectively, the height of the curve at the left and
right endpoints of the Jth interval in the stack. Moreover, you
will need another array to record the level of the jth interval
on the stack.

There is, however, one last but very important point that
must be made concerning the statement "T1 and T2 agree (or don't
agree) to the desired accuracy". The whole idea of the adaptive
trapezoidal rule is that, given a desired accuracy ERROR, the
adaptive trapezoidal rule will <u>automatically</u> provide an estimate
EST for AREA(a,b) -- the area under the curve from a to b --
such that

    |EST - AREA(a,b)| $<$ ERROR.

A technique for accomplishing this is based on the
observation that if EST1 and EST2 are the corresponding
estimates for AREA(a,m) and AREA(m,b) then we should require
that

    |EST1 - AREA(a,m)| $<$ ERROR/2,

and

    |EST2 - AREA(m,b)| $<$ ERROR/2.

In general, the acceptable error for a level k+1 interval should
be half of that acceptable for a level k interval. Thus, if we
are examining a level k interval [c,d] we should accept T2 as an
estimate for AREA(c,d) if

   $|T2 - AREA(c,d)| < ERROR/(2**k)$.

However, since we don't know $AREA(c,d)$ we try to satisfy this
requirement by asking that

(3.2.2a) $|T2 - T1| < ERROR/(2**k)$.

Therefore, in our example, we should accept T2 as an
approximation to $AREA(0,1/8)$ if

   $|T2 - T1| < ERROR/2^3$

since [0,1/8] is a level 3 interval.

   Interestingly enough, in practice criterion (3.2.2a) is very
stringent. In other words, the absolute error of your final
estimate for $AREA(a,b)$ will be much smaller than ERROR.
Therefore, instead of (3.2.2a) you could use

   $|T2 - T1| < ERROR/(g**k)$

where 1<g<2. Our limited experiments indicate that g=1.4 is a
good value, but you should determine your own favorite choice of
g. In some implementations, agreement is required between
three, rather than two, successive levels.

   Finally, as an example of the power of the adaptive
trapezoidal rule, we mention that for a=0, b=1, and
$f(x) = sqrt(1-x^2)$ this algorithm (with g=1.4 and $ERROR=10^{-6}$)
obtained a value of 7.85396E-01 in just 437 calls of the height
procedure as opposed to 8192 calls for the fixed rule. For a=0,
b=1, and $f(x) = cos(x)$, it obtained 8.41469E-01 in 255 procedure
calls versus 640 for the fixed rule.

3.2.3 Simpson's Rule

   We have already noted that the trapezoidal rule is
inefficient if at some point the area under the curve cannot be
conveniently approximated by trapezoids. One way to deal with
this defect is to localize the problem and concentrate the calls
of the height procedure at points near the trouble spot; this
philosophy leads to the adaptive trapezoidal rule. On the other
hand, you may believe that the defect is due to the simplicity
of the trapezoid, and that if the area under the curve were
approximated by a more sophisticated shape, then the resulting
rule would be more efficient. Let us consider this approach.

   First note that an alternate way of looking at the
trapezoidal rule on each subinterval is to say that we are
approximating the curve by a straight line, and taking the area
under this line as an approximation to the area under the curve.
From this point of view it is easy to extend the trapezoidal

rule by approximating the curve on each subinterval with a
parabola instead of a line.

To apply this idea consider a curve f defined on an interval
[a,b].   Now subdivide [a,b] into 2n equal subintervals by means
of the partition points

    x(i) = a + h·i   i=0,1,...,2n

where h = (b-a)/(2n). The area under the parabola that goes
through the points (x(j),f(x(j))) for j=2i-2,2i-1,2i is then

    (h/3)[f(x(2i-2)) + 4f(x(2i-1)) + f(2i)],

and the sum of all these areas is

    S(2n) = (h/3)[f(a) + 4f(x(1)) + 2f(x(2)) + 4f(x(3))
          + ... + 2f(x(2n-2)) + 4f(x(2n-1)) + f(b)].

This   last   formula   is known as Simpson's rule, and the
geometrical arguments given above indicate that it will be more
efficient than the trapezoidal rule.   This often turns out to be
the case.   Also note that the two rules are closely related.   In
fact, given TR(2n) and TR(n) it is easy to calculate S(2n) by
means of

(3.2.3a)   S(2n) = (4TR(2n) - TR(n))/3.

Simpson's rule can also be used in the adaptive form.   In
this case we proceed as before subdividing intervals in halves,
but now we make use of the formula

(3.2.3b)   P_AREA(a,m,b) = (b-a)[f(a)+4f(m)+f(b)]/6

where m is the midpoint of a and b. In fact, the first stage
would consist of estimating the area under the curve from a to b
by calculating

    T1 = P_AREA(a,m,b),

and

    T2 = P_AREA(a,p,m) + P_AREA(m,q,b),

where p and q are the midpoints of the intervals [a,m] and
[m,b], respectively. Of course, we can implement this adaptive
Simpson's rule by using stacks as in the adaptive trapezoidal
rule, but now we need another stack, say STK_FM. Then STK_FM(J)
would contain f(m) where m is the midpoint of the Jth interval
in the stack.

Section 3 <u>Exercises</u>

1. For Gaussian elimination:

    a) Find the number of additions and comparisons done during
    the forward elimination.

    b) Verify that the number of multiplications in the back
    substitution is $n(n+1)/2$.

    c) Find the number of additions in the back substitution.

2. Show that (3.1.2a) implies that the determinant of an upper
triangular matrix is the product of the elements on the
diagonal.

3. a) Find the solution to (3.1a) where

$$A = \begin{bmatrix} 1 & 2 & 2 \\ -1 & -3 & 2 \\ 2 & 0 & 6 \end{bmatrix}$$

    and b = (0, 4, 8) by Gaussian elimination with partial
    pivoting.

    b) What is the determinant of A?

4. Write and test a procedure that will solve (3.1a) by Gaussian
elimination with partial pivoting. This procedure should have
at least the following parameters:

    N, the order of the system
    A, the coefficient matrix
    B, the righthand side
    X, the solution vector.

There should be appropriate messages in case of failure.

5. Write and test a procedure that will execute the adaptive
trapezoidal rule. This procedure should have at least the
following parameters:

    A, the left endpoint of the interval
    B, the right endpoint of the interval
    EST, the final estimate for the area
    ERROR, the desired absolute error in EST
    MAX_LEVEL, the maximum number of levels allowed
    CALLS, the total number of calls of the height procedure
    MAX_CALLS, the maximum number of calls allowed.

The procedure should either run successfully, or terminate when
MAX_CALLS or MAX_LEVEL is exceeded. In either case appropriate
messages should be printed. Note that A, B, ERROR, MAX_LEVEL,

and MAX_CALLS have to be set by the user, but that the other
parameters will be set by the procedure. You may also want to
have other parameters; for example, the name of the height
procedure, or MIN_LEVEL so that you will be assured that the
height procedure will be called a sufficient number of times.

6. Write a procedure as in exercise 5 for the adaptive Simpson's
rule and compare it with the adaptive trapezoidal rule.

7. The following applies to the procedures defined in exercises
   5 and 6:

   a) Replace the use of STK_A and STK_B by the use of one
   stack for the length of the intervals and a variable which
   contains the left endpoint of the interval on top of the
   stack.

   b) Investigate the effect of calling these procedures with
   arguments A > B.

   c) Modify these procedures so that they will test for
   relative errors instead of absolute errors.

8.   a) Verify equation (3.2.3a).

     b) Show that if f is a parabola then formula (3.2.3b) gives
        the area under this parabola from a to b.

Section 4   Suggestions for Further Reading

We hope to have whetted your appetite for numerical analysis and to this end we have compiled a very brief list of references in this section.

The books by Shampine and Allen, and Conte and de Boor are two of the better introductory books on numerical analysis; they should be intelligible to anyone who has had calculus.

If you want to find out more about the effects of finite precision arithmetic on mathematical computation, the standard reference is the book by Wilkinson. Fike's book is an excellent introduction to the topic of computer evaluation of mathematical functions. Linear equations are treated by Forsythe and Moler in a very readable manner. Moreover, this book contains several excellent programs for solving systems of linear equations.

Numerical integration, the more exact description of the topic of Section 3.2, is surveyed by Davis and Rabinowitz. The last chapter is of special interest since it deals with automatic integration and contains several programs.

Finally, the book edited by Rice contains several good articles on the interaction between mathematics and computer programming.

Conte, S. and C. de Boor, _Elementary Numerical Analysis, An Algorithmic Approach_, 2nd edition, McGraw-Hill, 1972

Davis, P. and P. Rabinowitz, _Numerical Integration_, Blaisdell, 1967

Fike, C., _Computer Evaluation of Mathematical Functions_, Prentice-Hall, 1968

Forsythe, G. and C. Moler, _Computer Solution of Linear Algebraic Systems_, Prentice-Hall, 1967

Rice, J. (editor), _Mathematical Software_, Academic Press, 1971

Shampine, L. and R. Allen, _Numerical Computing: An Introduction_, W. B. Saunders, 1973.

PART IX   FILE PROCESSING APPLICATIONS

Three-quarters of the world's computers are engaged in processing the information generated by modern economic society. This usage began in the late 1950's and has grown very rapidly. By now it is difficult to imagine how business, government, banking, insurance, or even large universities could manage their activity without computing systems.

From a technical point of view, these computer applications are distinctive for what they do, and not just from the origin of the problem. The principal difference lies in the quantity and form of the information that is to be processed. There are also significant differences in the manner in which programs are developed, and the manner in which they are used.

Those involved in mathematical applications of computers often have a rather supercilious attitude toward business-oriented computing. This attitude reflects considerable innocence as to what is involved. The mathematics are elementary to be sure, but the problems of handling huge volumes of information and protecting it from the clumsiness and cupidity of people are exceedingly difficult. Typically the programs for file processing are dominated by concern for exceptions. Processing the 99% of activity that is legitimate and accurate may be relatively straightforward; detecting and handling the other 1% often requires great care and ingenuity.

The problems considered in the earlier sections of the book have all shared a significant characteristic -- they have been self-contained with respect to the computer. That is, all of the data necessary for execution has accompanied the program, and the complete results have been delivered on printed output during execution. Now we consider problems that involve collections of information called "files", that are more-or-less permanently stored in the memory of a computer. Programs will draw upon information in a file that is already resident in the computer system when the program arrives. Similarly, the results of execution are in part reflected in changes in the contents of the file, and only partly displayed on printed output.

Section 1   Files

Files are collections of information. We are concerned with
collections that have the following properties:

a) They are in "machine readable" form -- that is, they can
   be stored and processed by a computer.

b) They are highly structured (like a dictionary, rather
   than a novel).

c) They are highly repetitive in structure (a relatively
   small pattern is repeated many times).

d) They are sufficiently large to preclude storage in the
   main memory of current computers.

e) They have a relatively long life.

Generally, a file represents some set of <u>entities</u> in the real
world -- people, vehicles, courses, buildings, etc. -- and
contains whatever information about these entities is relevant
for some well-defined purpose. At any instant in time, the
particular information in a file is said to constitute a
"generation" of that file, and represents an instantaneous
status report for the entities described.   A sequence of
generations represents a <u>history</u> for these entities.

1.1 <u>Structure of a File</u>

A file will normally contain the <u>same</u> <u>kind</u> of information
about each of the entities that it represents. The specific
values will be different for each entity, but the format and
interpretation of the information will be the same for each.
The information pertaining to one entity is called a "record",
so a file consists of a set of records, one for each entity that
it represents. Each unit of information in a record is called a
"field". A field is analogous to a variable in that it is a
location in memory; it has a name and a value.

For example, a file might contain biographical information
about the current students at a university. There would be one
record for each student. Each record would have fields

representing the student's name, his campus address, telephone
number, college, year, faculty adviser, etc. Each record would
have a similar set of fields, with of course, different values.
For example:

Field-names:	Values: Record 1	Record 2	Record 3
NAME	JIM CORDY	D. BARNARD	M. FOX
ADDRESS	416 DORM 5	201 ELM AVE	256 HUDSON ST.
TELEPHONE	128 1110	256 9030	370 1652
COLLEGE	ENGINEERING	ENGINEERING	AGRICULTURE
CLASS	FRESHMAN	SENIOR	SOPHOMORE
ADVISER	WORTMAN	HOLT	HUME

Fields are somewhat analogous to arrays in that they have
multiple values. That is, each field has a value in each
record. Some values may of course be blank or zero. A program
must have a way of referring to one particular value
(corresponding to a subscripted variable) and this is discussed
in Section 2.1.1.

1.2 Events and Transactions

A file is intended to describe the status of a set of
entities for a particular purpose. When an event occurs that
changes the status of an entity represented by the file, the
corresponding file information must be changed or the file no
longer gives an accurate description of status. The information
generated by such an event is called a "transaction", and the
process of accepting a transaction and changing the file
contents accordingly is called "updating" the file.

For example, in the student biographical file of Section 1.1,
a relevant event would be the change of a student's telephone
number. The corresponding transaction would have to specify
which student (to designate a particular record), which field is
to be altered, and the new value to be stored.

Another significant event would be the entry of a new
student. The transaction would include values for many
different fields, and updating would involve the creation of a
new record and its addition to the file.

1.3 Storage Systems

Up to this point it has not been necessary to consider how
information is stored in a computer. A variable could just be
considered a location in memory, and the assignment and
retrieval of its value is straightforward and automatic. We

have only needed a relatively small amount of storage for program and data and this could be accommodated in "main memory" or "primary memory" of the computer. But the sizes of many files preclude their storage in main memory, so that alternative physical devices, and more complex programming are involved.

Files are generally relatively large collections of information. For example, a student biographical record might consist of 1000 characters, so a file for 15,000 students would involve 15 million characters of information. If the student record included academic, financial and medical information it could easily require 10,000 characters, so the file would be 150 million characters.

In general, files range in size from 10^5 to 10^{12} characters, with 10^6 to 10^9 being the most common range. These quantities are sufficiently large that, at least with current computers, the entire file cannot be stored in main memory at one time. Current main memories can contain anywhere from 10^4 to 10^7 characters, and most computer systems have less than 10^6 characters of main memory. (To put these numbers in perspective, this book contains about 10^6 characters.)

This means that for file processing, a multi-level memory system must be used. The main memory is relatively small, fast and expensive, and it is supplemented by a "secondary memory" that is relatively large, slow and cheap.

1.3.1 Storage Devices

In all current (so-called "third generation") computing systems, memory is implemented by using various electro-magnetic devices. These are magnetic elements with the following characteristics:

a) They have two stable magnetic states that can be recognized electronically.

b) They are capable of being changed electronically, from one of these states to the other.

c) They will remain in whichever state has been established, after the changing force is removed.

These characteristics provide the necessary abilities to read, write and remember.

It is also desirable for the magnetic element to be physically small, durable and cheap, and for it to be capable of being read and written very rapidly with very low power.

The magnetic device used for main memory in most third generation computers is the magnetic core. This is a tiny ring

of ferrous material. These cores are arranged in a square grid,
and are threaded with wires to read and write. Magnetic cores
are relatively fast (read or write in 10^{-6} seconds). (Much
smaller and faster devices are now being developed, so by the
late 1970's cores will probably be regarded with some historical
amusement as large, slow and crude devices.) They are also
relatively costly (roughly $1 per character for large System 360
memories from IBM). The largest core memories in use today have
a capacity of 16 million characters. However, capacities
between 50,000 and 2 million are much more common.

The alternative magnetic element is simply a tiny section of
a continuous magnetic surface. The material must be locally
magnetizable -- adjacent sections must be capable of being read
and written independently. Reading or writing a particular
section is accomplished by physically moving it past a
stationary coil, called a "read/write head".

The magnetic surface may be supported and transported in
several different ways. One method is as a surface coating on a
thin plastic tape. The standard computer tape is one-half inch
wide and one-half mile long. Each character is recorded in a
section across the width of the tape, with (typically) 1600
characters in each inch of length. There are gaps (between
records) in which no information is recorded, but a full tape
reel can contain about 30 million characters of information.

Alternatively, the magnetic surface can be supported on a
rigid disc, rotating on a central spindle, somewhat like a
phonograph record. Information is recorded in 200 concentric
(not spiral) rings called "tracks" on the surface, and each
character can be read or written as rotation of the disc brings
it under a stationary read/write head. Several discs are
usually stacked vertically on a common spindle, with a
read/write head for each disc. Such a "disc pack" (IBM 2316,
for example) can store about 28 million characters.

Just like their counterparts for music recording, computer
tapes and discs are removable. They can be dismounted from the
computer, and stored in what is called an "off-line library".
They can later be remounted on the computer system and the
information they contain further processed. Since the tapes and
disc packs themselves are not prohibitively expensive (about $15
and $400, respectively) libraries with several hundred disc
packs and several thousand reels of tapes are not uncommon.

With such libraries, the amount of information that can be
stored in a form accessible to a computer is almost unlimited.
However, at least at present, the computer requires the
assistance of a human operator to select reels and packs from
the library and mount them on the reading devices.

The significant distinction between tapes and discs as
secondary memory devices lies in the physical distance between a
required section of information and the read/write head that

will transmit it to main memory. On a disc, the information is at most a full revolution away from the read/write head. The delay until the required information reaches the read/write position (called "latency" delay) is at most a few hundredths of a second. On a magnetic tape the information could be at the opposite end of the reel -- one-half mile of tape away -- and the delay would be measured in minutes while the tape is wound from one reel to another. Consequently, tape storage can only be efficiently used for information that will be required in a predictable order. Fortunately, many files are processed in this way (see Section 2.1.1) and tapes are widely used. On discs, all information is more-or-less equally accessible (except for variations in latency time) and information can be accessed in unpredictable or random order without great loss in efficiency.

1.3.2 Two-Level Memories

In most computer systems today, the main memory is supplemented by a secondary memory of magnetic tapes and/or magnetic discs. The secondary memory can also be considered to have two levels -- the tapes and discs currently mounted "on-line" (on the reading devices), and those on racks in the "off-line" library. The different levels of memory differ in capacity, speed of access, and mode of use. The computer can read and write in main memory in microseconds (millionths of a second), in secondary memory (which involves physical movement of a tape or disc) in milliseconds (thousandths of a second), and in the off-line library (requiring human assistance) only in minutes.

Main memory is used in very small increments -- corresponding to individual variables. Secondary memory is used in terms of blocks of information (representing one or several records), and the off-line library is used in terms of entire files. That is, at any given moment, only a few files have been selected from the library and are mounted on the reading units of the computer. One (or at most several) records have been selected from these files and copied into main memory for processing. The computer cannot really process information in secondary storage; it can only transfer it in blocks in and out of main memory. The computer cannot process information in the off-line library at all, it can only print out messages to the operator and wait until the tape or disc-pack containing the required file has been mounted on a reading device.

Section 2   File Processing Programs

Once information has been moved into main memory, the program
proceeds as we have described in earlier sections, but in file
processing the programmer has certain additional tasks, as noted
in Section 2.1. Section 2.2 describes the languages that are
used for this type of programming. Sections 2.3 and 2.4
describe differences in the ways that problem specifications are
developed and documented for file processing.

2.1 Functional Requirements

The programs that have been considered up to this point have
been concerned only with the main storage of the computer. Both
the program itself, and all the variables and arrays with
which it dealt, were easily stored in main memory. The
card reader and the printer have been the only other components
of the computing system that were of concern. Now we
consider programs that must also communicate with magnetic tape
and disk storage units, and control the transfer of information
back and forth between main and secondary storage.

2.1.1 Control of Secondary Storage

In earlier sections the PL/I GET and PUT statements have been
regarded as means of communicating with the card reader and the
printer. In fact, the GET and PUT statements can be used to
access files as well by explicitly specifying the name of a file
in the statement (see Appendix B.3). SP/k uses an alternative
set of PL/I statements that are more appropriate for doing file
input and output. We describe these statements below.

A file must be declared before it can be used in a program.
(SP/k makes an exception to this rule for the standard card
reader input file SYSIN and the standard printer output file
SYSPRINT.) In SP/k a file declaration has the form:

    DECLARE (file-name) RECORD FILE;

This declaration specifies that file-name will be used as the identification of a file on secondary storage in the statements described below.

The OPEN statement requests the operating system to prepare a file on secondary storage for processing by the program. Two forms are permitted in SP/k:

```
OPEN FILE (file-name) INPUT;
OPEN FILE (file-name) OUTPUT;
```

The keyword INPUT specifies that the file specified by file_name will be read; the keyword OUTPUT specifies that the file will be written. Details of the processing performed by the OPEN statement depends on the file and on the operating system and are beyond the scope of this book. A file must be opened before it is used.

Once a file has been opened for input, one record at a time may be read from the file using the statement:

```
READ FILE (file-name) INTO (structure-name);
```

where structure name identifies a particular kind of PL/I variable called a "structure" (see Section 2.1.2). In SP/k, all structures read from (or written to) a particular file must have the same form.

To write information into a file, it must first be opened for output (a file cannot be opened for both input and output at the same time). Then the file can be written using the statement:

```
WRITE FILE (file-name) FROM (structure-name);
```

where again, structure-name must specify a PL/I structure variable.

For example, a program processing student records of the form described in Section 1.1 could declare a structure variable called STUDENT to hold the information about one student and then read information about successive students, one at a time, from secondary storage using the statement:

```
READ FILE (INPUT_FILE) INTO (STUDENT);
```

The program could create an updated file of student records by writing this same structure out onto a new secondary file, as in:

```
WRITE FILE (OUTPUT_FILE) FROM (STUDENT);
```

A program signals to the operating system that it is finished processing a file by executing the statement:

```
CLOSE FILE (file-name);
```

The operating system performs whatever actions are necessary to
terminate operations on the file. The CLOSE statement is often
used in changing the use of a file from input to output or vice-
versa. A typical sequence of events in a file processing
program might be to open a file for output, write some
information into the file, close the file, open the file for
input and then read and process the information that has been
stored on the file.

    This much of the process is fairly obvious and
straightforward; other parts are not. The management of files
in   secondary storage   is not nearly as automatic as the
management of variables· in main memory. The programmer must
explicitly control both the location and structure of the file
in secondary storage. For example, when using the IBM OS/360
operating system the actual assignment of a file to a particular
physical location in secondary storage is specified by a "DD
statement" in a language called the "Job Control Language"
(usually abbreviated "JCL").   DD statements specifying   the
location of all relevant files will accompany the PL/I program.
In the program the name to be used for a file is specified by a
declaration. For example:

    DECLARE (INPUT_FILE) RECORD FILE;

This relates the file-name in the program to the name specified
in a DD statement, while the attributes in the declaration
specify the manner in which the file is organized. These
matters are quite complex and exacting, but must be learned
if one is going to process files.

    The other complex aspect of this matter is knowing <u>which</u>
values of NAME,   ADDRESS, and COLLEGE the READ statement
refers to. Recall from Section 1.1 that there is a set of
values for these variables in each record in the file. The
programmer must indicate <u>which</u> <u>record</u> in the file is the source
or target of his READ or WRITE statement.

    This same concept has been present in the reading of data
cards, but we have not discussed it as such. For example, in
the program segment

    DO WHILE(X ¬= 0);
        GET LIST(X);
        ...
        END;

the data cards contain many different X's, or more precisely,
contain many values that will provide a sequence of different
values for the variable X as they are read into main memory.
There is no ambiguity in the GET statement, since it means read
the <u>next</u> value from the data stream and assign it to
variable X. Neither is there ambiguity in other statements that
reference X -- they refer to the variable (or location) in main

memory, and hence to the last value that was assigned to that
location. The data stream is an example of a "sequential" file,
in which there is a natural ordering among the values. READ
or WRITE with respect to a sequential file always imply the
next value.

Alternatively, files may be "direct" or "random" (instead of
sequential) for situations where one would like to be able to
select particular records, without having to process all records
in their natural order. With such files the next record is not
implied by any ordering, and phrases must be specified in the
READ or WRITE statement to indicate what record is desired.
Such files can be processed in PL/I, but only sequential files
are available in SP/k.

A file processing program proceeds by moving a copy of one
record at a time from secondary storage into main memory. The
fields of the record provide the values for corresponding
variables. The program operates upon these variables in main
memory just as the programs described in earlier sections of the
book. When a statement references a variable, it is referring
to the value in main memory and not to one of the many
corresponding fields in secondary storage. Hence the statement
implicitly refers to whichever record was last copied from
secondary to main memory. A small file processing program is
presented in Appendix A.2.8.

2.1.2 Data Aggregates

The variables representing the fields of a record are
logically related to each other, and often subjected to similar
processing. For example, one will read all of the fields into
main memory, move them from one set of variables to another in
main memory, and eventually copy them all back to the file in
secondary storage. It is very convenient to be able to specify
this logical relationship between variables, and then use it to
simplify programming.

In PL/I this is done by declaring a "structure". By
prefixing "level numbers" to consecutive identifiers in a
declaration one can show the logical relationship between
variables and assign identifiers to groups of variables. For
example, one might declare the variables representing the fields
of a student biographical record as follows:

```
DECLARE 1 STUDENT,
          2 NAME CHARACTER(30) VARYING,
          2 CAMPUS_RESIDENCE,
               3 ADDRESS CHARACTER(30) VARYING,
               3 TELEPHONE CHARACTER(7) VARYING,
               3 DINING_HALL_CODE CHARACTER(3) VARYING,
          2 HOME,
               3 PARENT_GUARDIAN CHARACTER(25) VARYING,
               3 ADDRESS CHARACTER(30) VARYING,
               3 TELEPHONE CHARACTER(10) VARYING,
          2 REGISTRATION,
               3 COLLEGE CHARACTER(12) VARYING,
               3 CLASS CHARACTER(2) VARYING,
               3 GRADE_AVG FLOAT,
               3 ADVISER CHARACTER(20) VARYING;
```

The identifiers that are followed by type attributes are
variables, and are used in the usual way. The identifiers that
have no type attributes, and are immediately followed by
identifiers with a higher level number, are called "structure
names". They are simply convenient names for the set of
variables that follow them. For example, CAMPUS_RESIDENCE
refers to the group of three variables ADDRESS, TELEPHONE and
DINING_HALL_CODE that follow it. In some contexts in PL/I
(assignment, input, output) one can use a structure name instead
of writing each of the variables that it represents.
CAMPUS_RESIDENCE is a "minor structure" because it is a part of
a larger structure; STUDENT is a "major structure" since it is
not part of a larger structure. (A major structure always has a
level number of 1.) Having defined this structure one could
read a record from a file just by writing

```
     READ FILE(STUDENTS) INTO (STUDENT);
```

This would cause information to be read from the file and
assigned to the variables in the structure in the order NAME,
CAMPUS_RESIDENCE.ADDRESS,   CAMPUS_RESIDENCE.TELEPHONE,
CAMPUS_RESIDENCE.DINING_HALL_CODE,   HOME.PARENT_GUARDIAN,
HOME.ADDRESS, etc. Structure names can be used in an analogous
way in output and assignment statements.

Note that, unlike an array, all variables in a structure do
not have to have the same type attributes. Note also that the
same identifier can be repeated in a structure. ADDRESS and
TELEPHONE are variables in the minor structure CAMPUS_ADDRESS,
and the same two identifiers are used in the minor structure
HOME. When one needs to refer to one of these variables it is
necessary to "qualify" the name to indicate which one. In PL/I
one would write either CAMPUS_RESIDENCE.ADDRESS or HOME.ADDRESS.

Such structures, or data aggregates, do not really add any
new capability to a programming language, since equivalent
statements could be written in terms of the individual variable
names. However, since it is not uncommon for records to have
several hundred fields there is a substantial convenience in

writing programs in a language that provides the ability to handle groups of variables as a single element.

In SP/k, some restrictions are placed on the use of structures and files. A special form of the PL/I declaration statement

DECLARE 1 variable LIKE identifier;

is used to allow the definition of a structure (or array of structures) with the same template (variable names and attributes) as some previously declared structure. The identifier must be a major (level 1) structure variable. The newly-declared structure variable only inherits the template of identifier, not its dimensionality. If the new structure variable is to represent an array, its dimensions must be explicitly given. The structure referred to by LIKE must not itself have been declared using LIKE.

In SP/k, (unlike PL/I) structures cannot contain other structures and are thus of only one level. Thus the only valid level numbers are 1 and 2. A variable in a structure is always referred to by the name of its containing structure, followed by a period, followed by the variable's name. If either the structure or the variable is an array, parenthesized subscripts must immediately follow the appropriate name. The structure declaration:

```
DECLARE 1 X,
        2 A (10) FIXED,
        2 B CHARACTER (20) VARYING,
        2 C BIT,
        1 Y LIKE X;
```

creates two structures named X and Y containing variables X.A, X.B, X.C and Y.A, Y.B, Y.C respectively.

Some versions of PL/I do not permit structures containing CHARACTER VARYING variables to be read from or written to files, but this is permitted in SP/k.

2.1.3 Format Control

File processing problems are typically very demanding with respect to the format of printed output. Often this is written on special printed forms, rather than plain paper, and the output format must be precisely specified so that each value is placed in the correct box, or is properly aligned with respect to pre-printed titles. Part of the output is used directly as business documents -- checks, bills, purchase orders, invoices, etc. The program must follow the conventions that have been established for such documents.

In general, the output of a file processing program is distributed to large numbers of different users, none of whom can be assumed to know anything at all about the problem, the file or the program. Each output document must be self-contained -- that is, completely self-explanatory.

One particularly fussy requirement occurs in the traditional display of dollar totals. The display format varies, depending upon the value being displayed. For example:

Value:	Display form:
00012345.67	$ 12,345.67
00000045.67	$ 45.67
09812345.67	$ 9,812,345.67
00000000.00	.00
00000000.01	$ .01
-00012345.67	$ 12,345.67 CR

While you could write a subroutine to achieve this format using only the PL/I facilities described in the earlier sections, it would not be a trivial routine. Fortunately, this is not necessary, since PL/I has an automatic editing facility to achieve this format. See the description of the P format item in Appendix A.2.

A language to be used for file processing programs must permit the flexible control over format that is demanded by these considerations. Moreover, since programmers in this area seem to spend an inordinate fraction of programming time on format control, the convenience of the language in this respect has major bearing on the productivity of programmers using it.

2.2 Languages for File Processing

Programming languages vary significantly in their provisions for the tasks described in Section 2.1. Some languages (such as APL, BASIC or LISP) simply do not permit the programmer much control over secondary storage, so their use for file processing is very limited. In other languages (such as FORTRAN or ALGOL) these tasks are possible, but not convenient. (For example, neither FORTRAN nor ALGOL has any provision for data aggregates, as described in Section 2.1.2.) However, some languages have been specifically designed for file processing.

2.2.1 General-Purpose Languages

Without question the standard general-purpose language for file processing is COBOL. In view of the early success of FORTRAN for mathematically-oriented problems, a group of computer users with file processing problems organized to define a language of comparable convenience and power, oriented to their problems. This CODASYL Committee produced a definition of COBOL in 1960. The United States Government was heavily represented in this effort, and the computer manufacturers were encouraged to make COBOL available on their machines by means of strong indications that sales to the Government would be dependent on COBOL capability.

COBOL is comparable to PL/I, and you could probably read a COBOL program and have a general idea of what it accomplishes based on your experience in PL/I. The similarities between the two languages are more important than the differences (although one would not get this impression from listening to a militant advocate of either). The syntax and keywords are different, but the same functions are performed -- declaration, assignment, sequence control, input and output.

A COBOL program is divided into four "divisions". The first two, called "identification" and "environment", correspond to blocks of PL/I comments describing the purpose of the program and its operating requirements. Declarations are collected in the "data division", and the "procedure division" corresponds to the main procedure in PL/I.

Some COBOL statements are quite similar to their PL/I counterparts (IF and GO TO, for example); others look different but perform a familiar task:

    PERFORM TAXLOOP VARYING I FROM 1 BY 1 UNTIL N

Comparable assignment statements in PL/I and COBOL are:

    A = B + C;   ADD B AND C TO A

    D = E * F;   MULTIPLY E AND F GIVING D

    G = H * (U + V);   COMPUTE G FROM H * (U + V)

    A = B;   MOVE B TO A

The most significant difference between the two languages (and the greatest weakness in COBOL) is the area of program structure. The procedure division can be subdivided into "sections" and "paragraphs" but the facilities provided to invoke paragraphs, pass arguments to them, and isolate them from other program actions, are very limited.

An example of a COBOL program paragraph is the following (from an IBM 360 COBOL manual -- C28-6516):

    PROCESS-SORTED-RECORDS SECTION.
     PARAGRAPH-3. RETURN SORT-FILE-1 AT END GO TO PARAGRAPH-4.
     IF FIELD-FF = FIELD-EE WRITE FILE-3-RECORD FROM
     SORT-RECORD GO TO PARAGRAPH-3 ELSE
     MOVE FIELD-EE TO FIELD-EEE MOVE FIELD-FF TO FIELD-FFF

```
MOVE FIELD-AA TO FIELD-AAA MOVE FIELD-BB TO FIELD-BBB
MOVE SPACES TO FILLER-A, FILLER-B WRITE FILE-2-RECORD.
GO TO PARAGRAPH-3.
PARAGRAPH-4.  EXIT.
```

The academic world tends to regard COBOL as verbose, clumsy and inelegant, and tries to ignore it, although there are probably more COBOL programs and programmers in the world than there are for FORTRAN, ALGOL and PL/I combined. For the most part, only schools with an immediate vocational objective provide instruction in COBOL.

PL/I is the second most important general-purpose language for file processing. It was designed in the early sixties by a committee of IBM language specialists and users of IBM computers. Their objective was to provide a single language that would be useful for both mathematical computing and file processing, and would possess the structure and elegance that were present in ALGOL. Unfortunately, the design committee was under severe time constraints and the result was not as attractive as it might have been. Nevertheless, IBM embraced the new language and announced the demise of both FORTRAN and COBOL. That obituary turned out to be premature, to say the least. Even if PL/I is a better language than either FORTRAN or COBOL many users felt that it was not enough better to be worth the effort to retrain programmers and convert program libraries. This reluctance was encouraged by the fact that IBM neglected to provide an efficient translator for PL/I (see Section X.2) until 1971.

It now seems unlikely that PL/I will ever succeed in replacing either FORTRAN or COBOL. Instead of unifying a computing world that was divided in two by a language barrier, PL/I has created a three-language situation in the United States. (In the rest of the world ALGOL is also important.) But it is equally unlikely that either FORTRAN or COBOL, at least in their present form, will continue in major use indefinitely. Both of these languages were pioneering efforts, and it would indeed be surprising if experience and research does not eventually lead to their retirement. Successor languages (whatever they may be called) are likely to offer many of the features now present in PL/I.

You should realize that you have been introduced to only a fraction of the full PL/I language -- perhaps one-quarter. (See Appendix B.) The features that have been omitted here have been, for the most part, those associated with file processing.

2.2.2 Specialized File Maintenance and Retrieval Systems

Beginning in the late sixties there has been a rapid development of a new type of programming language for file processing applications. Languages of this type have come to be

known as "data base management systems" or "file maintenance and
retrieval systems". These languages do not have the general
capability of COBOL or PL/I, but are intended to serve the more
common tasks of routine file processing -- processing
transactions to update a file, and extracting information from a
file to produce reports, lists and analyses. For these limited
purposes the specialized languages are substantially easier to
use than either COBOL or PL/I.

One of the least flexible of these languages is called RPG.
Since it is distributed by IBM it is also the most widely used.
(In fact, it is believed to be the most widely used of all
programming languages.) An RPG programmer is guided by a
variety of specially-printed programming forms. He fills in
designated spaces to specify the structure of the file, the
format of transactions on punched cards, and the desired format
of printed output. An experienced RPG user can write such
"programs" in a fraction of the time that would be required to
write a PL/I program to perform the same task. MARK IV is
another language of substantially greater power and flexibility,
but similar to RPG in its dependence on a multitude of special
forms.

Not all of these languages depend on special programming
forms, and some have achieved a reasonably readable syntax. For
example, in a language called ASAP, a retrieval program for the
student biographical file described in Section 2.1.2 might
appear as:

```
FOR ALL STUDENTS WITH COLLEGE = 'ENGINEERING' AND
        GRADE_AVG > 3.0,
    PRINT A LIST OF:
        NAME, ADDRESS, FACULTY_ADVISOR, GRADE_AVG,
    ORDERED BY GRADE_AVG.
```

In the same language a program to update the file would be:

```
FOR ALL STUDENTS SELECTED BY KEY IN FEBRUARY_DATA,
    FORMATTED BY BIOGRAPHICAL_CARD_FORMAT,
    UPDATE THE RECORD.
```

The equivalent PL/I or COBOL program would be several pages
long, would take much longer to write and test, and would be
much less easily understood by the person who requested the
program.

This development has been very rapid, and is still somewhat
chaotic. The CODASYL Committee has recently become interested
in the subject, and may well have the same standardizing
influence on file maintenance systems that it exerted on behalf
of COBOL a decade earlier. At present these file maintenance
languages are somewhat restricted in capability, but their power
will probably increase as they are further developed. They
would seem to demonstrate that languages considerably more

natural and convenient to use than PL/I or COBOL can be developed.

2.3 Defensive Programming

A programmer in this area must be a confirmed and practicing pessimist. A framed copy of Murphy's Law --

"ANYTHING THAT CAN GO WRONG, WILL"

should hang on his wall, and his programs should reflect his belief that this maxim accurately describes the world in which he works. The quality of his programs can largely be measured by their ability to maintain composure in the face of exceedingly difficult circumstances. Four aspects of this difficulty are cited in the following sections.

2.3.1 Operating Environment

Contrast the life cycle of a typical "student program" and a typical production file processing program. The student program has the following characteristics:

a) It is developed from a concise, precise, unambiguous statement of a problem, that is provided by someone who knows what he wants and whose requirements do not change during the life of the program.

b) One person is responsible for developing an algorithm, and writing and testing the program. When the program is finished the same person is responsible for "using" it -- setting control values, supplying data, and interpreting results.

c) The program is independent of other programs and data.

d) The worst that can happen as a result of a program error is the waste of a computer run (or a low grade).

e) After very brief use (often a single run of the finished program) the program is discarded.

On the other hand, the file processing program has the following characteristics:

a) It is developed from a vague statement of requirements from someone who isn't sure precisely what he needs, who has no idea what a computer is capable of doing, and who sometimes hopes that the computer will be incapable of handling the job. Moreover, the requirements, such as they

are, will change periodically as the program is being
developed and used.

b) Many people are involved. The problem may be refined by
one person (a "systems analyst"), programmed by a second,
tested by a third, documented by a fourth, and used by many
others. The program may be written by several people
working independently, and will surely be modified by
several people during its lifetime. Few of these people
have much appreciation of the total problem, and few have a
deep commitment to making the program work.

c) The program is related to a file whose content (and even
form) changes; it shares this file with many other
programs, all of which are changing and most of which
contain errors.

d) The worst that can happen as a result of a program error
is that a valuable, perhaps irreplaceable file will be
damaged or destroyed, and that erroneous information will
be distributed and acted upon.

e) The program (with modifications) may be run regularly
for many years.

The difference might be compared to learning to drive an
automobile on a large, empty parking lot, and driving an
ambulance in Manhattan during rush hour.

The dominant characteristics that dictate how programs must
be written are the necessity for communication (many people are
involved), and the certainty of change. The harsh realities of
the file processing environment demand a fanatical attention to
systematic program development, consistent style, adequate
documentation, and exhaustive testing. Casual and intuitive
procedures, that may suffice in the hospitable environment in
which a student learns to program, are just not adequate for
real programs.

2.3.2 File Protection

In this type of application the programmer must adopt the
view that file protection is as important as file processing.
In the first place, a file is an object of considerable value;
in the second place, it is under more or less continuous
assault. These assaults may be accidental -- the results of
errors -- or deliberate unauthorized attempts to extract or
alter information, or even to destroy the file. The effect is
the same; to cause the file to fail to represent the required
status information. Protection is a very complex issue. In
order to suggest what is involved it is useful to divide the
problems into issues of integrity, accuracy and security.

The maintenance of file integrity means physically safeguarding the device on which the file resides against catastrophic damage. Files are susceptible to damage by some of man's ancient hazards such as floods (computing centers are often ground floor or below), fire (and the malfunction of fire extinguishing systems) and riots (computing centers have become popular symbolic targets). It is also possible for either the computer or the human operator to malfunction in such a way as to damage the storage device and render all or part of a file unreadable. A file can be misused in an unfortunate number of ways. For example, the wrong generation of a file can be used, a file can be processed by the wrong program or with the wrong input transactions, or a device already containing a file can be considered empty and reused for another file.

Accuracy in this context refers to the validity of the information in the file. (This is not related to the concept of accuracy discussed in Part VIII.) This requires screening out erroneous transaction input that is trying to introduce inaccurate information.

Security is a more modern risk, and one that promises to become increasingly important. This is the task of restricting access to the information in the file to those individuals who have a legitimate and authorized right to it. As computer files accumulate increasing amounts of confidential and valuable information there are increasing incentives to indulge one's curiosity by browsing, or to augment one's resources by felonious alterations. Although there are some difficult ethical and legal problems in defining what access is legitimate and who is to authorize whose access to what, there is also the technical issue of how to _enforce_ whatever restrictions are agreed upon. Basically, it means that a file cannot regard every program as having the same privileges.

The details of solutions to these problems are well beyond the scope of this book, but they are major problems in file processing and we feel that the neophyte programmer should be made aware of them. Some of these matters involve physical protection (locks, fireproof vaults, etc.) and are not the direct concern of the programmer, but in general, these problems have a major effect on the way file processing programs should be designed. For example, a program must write detailed identification information into the beginning of each file that it creates, and it must _check_ the identification of each file that it processes and _absolutely_ _refuse_ _to_ _proceed_ if it is not correct. In this way, the program can offset the error of an operator who brings the wrong file, or the wrong generation of the right file, from the tape/disc library to mount on the reading device.

The basic protection mechanism is simple and traditional -- _make_ _and_ _retain_ _extra_ _copies_. Often in updating a file, one creates a complete new generation, incorporating the new transaction data, and not actually changing the previous

generation. The "father" generation of the file is used to
create the "son" generation, and both are retained in the
library. In fact, most installations use a "grandfather-father-
son" library system in which at least three generations of each
file are retained. In this way, if the current generation of a
file is destroyed, or found to be faulty because of a program
error or improper data, one can recover by recreating the new
generation from backup generations. Of course, for such
practices to offer a high degree of protection it is necessary
to go to the bother of storing some portion of the backup
library off site so that the same disaster cannot destroy all
generations of the file.

One could conceivably become so obsessed with these risks as
to over-protect the file. If the protection mechanisms make it
too difficult or costly for a legitimate, authorized individual
to use the file, the value of the entire system is reduced.
Similarly, if the file is so carefully protected against input
transactions that legitimate, accurate update information is
rejected or delayed, the information in the file will become
obsolete and its utility diminished. While one should keep this
risk in mind, over-protection is not a widespread problem in
file processing.

2.3.3 Error Treatment

One of the corollaries of Murphy's Law states that every
conceivable error will eventually be made, and unfortunately,
many inconceivable errors will also be made. One must
understand that a "computer file processing system" actually
involves a great number of frail and fallible human beings.
They write programs, supply data and operate the computer, and
are susceptible to errors in every act. The point is not to
bewail the characteristics of the human race, but only to remind
the programmer of these universal and inevitable
characteristics, and demand that he write programs in such a way
that they are useful in the real world, and do not require
unrealistic assumptions about the world.

A properly designed file processing program is dominated by
tests, checks, exceptions and error conditions. Most of these
provisions concern very rare events -- the probability of one
particular error occurring on one particular transaction is very
small, but the probability that that error will never occur on
any transaction for the life of the system is also small. These
frequent, usually unnecessary tests, exact a penalty in computer
time, but in general a faster program with reduced protection is
not an economical design in the long run.

For example, suppose you are writing a subroutine, and are
told that the key argument will always be nonnegative. In
scientific computing you might be able to believe such a promise
and program on the assumption that the argument will never be

negative.   In file processing you interpret the statement to
mean that the argument is _supposed_ to be nonnegative, but both
you and whoever made the promise know that the program will
receive bad data, and will someday be modified in some
unpredictable way by someone who is unaware of that promise.
Therefore, prudence demands that your subroutine start with
something like the following:

```
IF ARG < 0 THEN
    CALL ERROR3(ARG);
```

   Detection of errors is only part of the problem. What action
should the program take upon detection? In general, automatic
correction is a risky business and is rarely used for this type
of problem.   The   usual strategy is to call for human
intervention and assistance.   However, the program should
provide a maximum amount of information to facilitate the
correction.   For example, the message

```
ERROR ENCOUNTERED -- BAD DATA.
```

is not much help, but

```
FIELD CONTENT ERROR:
    ON DATA CARD 1208 THE AMOUNT FIELD IMPROPERLY
    CONTAINS A NON-NUMERIC CHARACTER.
```

would greatly simplify locating and correcting the faulty card.

   Some errors must be immediately and irretrievably _fatal_.
That is, the program must stop and refuse to proceed no matter
how it is coaxed.   Such a case would occur when improper file
identification is discovered.   However, there are many errors
that cannot practically be treated in this way. For example, it
is not unusual for 1% of data cards to be in some way faulty, so
that in a large file update there could easily be several
hundred data errors.   To stop on each such error, demand that it
be corrected, and then restart the run is just not practical.
The errors should be detected, rejected, and listed in such a
way that the corrections can all be made at once. If the number
and severity of such errors is high enough, it _may_ be necessary
to repeat the run, but more often the run is accepted and
corrections are made in the next update.

2.3.4 System Evolution

   The life of a file is generally measured in months or years;
hence it follows that programs to process that file are also
relatively long-lived. However, the detailed specification of
just what processing has to be done will change fairly often.
This means that unless the program can be modified from time to
time to meet these changing requirements it will become obsolete
and useless, and have to be replaced. Hence, in designing and

writing a file processing program one should assume that the program will be subjected to frequent and serious modifications throughout its life.

Typically, the modifications of a program are made by someone other than the original author (although it hardly matters, since by the time of modification even the author will have forgotten most of the necessary detail). This puts a great premium on clarity and consistency in programming, and adequacy of documentation. Both contribute importantly to a reduction in the time required for the subsequent programmer to understand the program and the manner in which it should be modified, and also increase the chances of effecting a modification without causing unfortunate side-effects. A bit of obscure cleverness, perpetrated in the name of "efficiency", is not likely to make this future programmer tell everyone what an ingenious programmer you are.

2.4 Systems Analysis

The task of precisely defining the problem in file processing applications is sufficiently difficult and time-consuming that it is often viewed as a separate task, to be performed by someone other than the programmer. One who analyzes problem requirements and plans the overall strategy of the computer solution is called a "systems analyst". When the overall programming task is divided in this way the translation to a programming language is often called "coding" (rather than programming).

A systems analyst can be considered to be responsible for the initial levels of the program development (see Part II), and the coder for the final levels. The exact division of labor will vary with the problem, and depend upon the capability of the individuals concerned. Obviously, a systems analyst must know how to program, since the initial levels of the development will define the structure of the program. Usually these analysts have been successful programmers, and have been promoted to this position of greater responsibility. In addition to their design role, they frequently act in a supervisory role with respect to several coders.

The other side of the analyst's responsibility is the interface with the user. In this he needs impossible amounts of tact, patience and judgement. He must discover precisely what has to be done by talking with people who see only a tiny corner of the whole picture, who have no idea what the power and limitations of the computer imply, and who may well feel threatened by the whole process. He must decide to what extent to just mechanize the task as it has been done previously, and to what extent to use the opportunity to alter the basic process. It is very much an art, and the difference in results between a good systems analyst and a mediocre one is spectacular.

Part IX <u>References</u>

<u>ASAP</u> <u>System</u> <u>Reference</u> <u>Manual</u>, Compuvisor Inc., Ithaca, N. Y.

Awad/DPMA, <u>Automatic</u> <u>Data</u> <u>Processing</u> <u>Principles</u> <u>and</u> <u>Procedures</u>, <u>2nd</u> <u>Edition</u>, Prentice-Hall, 1970

Brightman, R. W., and J. R. Clark, <u>RPG</u> <u>Programming</u>, MacMillan, 1970

CODASYL Systems Committee, <u>Survey</u> <u>of</u> <u>Generalized</u> <u>Data</u> Base <u>Management</u> <u>Systems</u>, May 1969 (available from ACM)

CODASYL Systems Committee, <u>Feature</u> <u>Analysis</u> <u>of</u> <u>Generalized</u> <u>Data</u> <u>Base</u> <u>Management</u> <u>Systems</u>, May 1971 (available from ACM)

CODASYL Systems Committee, <u>Data</u> <u>Base</u> <u>Task</u> <u>Group</u> <u>Report</u>, April 1971 (available from ACM)

Conway, R.W. and D. Gries, <u>An</u> <u>Introduction</u> <u>to</u> <u>Programming</u>, Winthrop, 1975

Conway, R. W., W. L. Maxwell and H. L. Morgan, "On the Implementation of Security Measures in Information Systems", <u>Communications</u> <u>of</u> <u>the</u> <u>ACM</u>, April 1972

Kernighan, B.W., and P.J. Plauger, <u>The</u> <u>Elements</u> <u>of</u> <u>Programming</u> <u>Style</u>, McGraw-Hill, 1974

<u>MARK</u> <u>IV</u> <u>Reference</u> <u>Manual</u>, Informatics Inc., Sherman Oaks, Calif.

Martin, J., and A. Norman, <u>The</u> <u>Computerized</u> <u>Society</u>, Prentice-Hall, 1970

McCracken, D. D., <u>A</u> <u>Guide</u> <u>to</u> <u>COBOL</u> <u>Programming</u>, Wiley, 1963

Olle, T. W., 'MIS: Data Bases', <u>Datamation</u>,, November 15, 1970

Pollack, S. V. and T. D. Sterling, <u>A</u> <u>Guide</u> <u>to</u> <u>PL/I</u>, Holt Rinehart and Winston, 1969

<u>USA</u> <u>Standard</u> <u>COBOL</u>, <u>X3.23-1968</u>, <u>ANSI</u>, 1968

PART X   PROGRAMMING LANGUAGES
AND TRANSLATORS

Section 1   Translation of Programs

Almost as soon as one understands a programming language, one begins to wish that the designers of that language had done various things a little differently. By now, you may have some ideas as to how you would "improve" upon PL/I. Let us consider how one might go about actually implementing such ideas.

1.1 Translation from PL/X to PL/I

Suppose we wanted to program in a hypothetical language called PL/X which differs from PL/I in only three respects:

1) Declarations begin with the keyword CREATE followed by one or more blanks instead of DECLARE,

2) Printed output is produced by a statement with the form

        PRINT_ONE_LINE(list of variables);

3) The keyword FINISH_PL/X is placed at the end of a program (on a separate card, starting in column 1), immediately preceding the $DATA card.

For example, (4.1.1a) of Part I, written in PL/X, would look like the following:

```
      ADDER: PROCEDURE OPTIONS(MAIN);
         /* ADDING PROGRAM */
         CREATE (X,Y,Z) FLOAT;
         /* X,Y ARE NUMBERS TO BE ADDED */
(1.1a)   /* Z IS THE RESULT */
         GET LIST(X,Y);
         Z = X+Y;
         PRINT_ONE_LINE(Z);
         END /* ADDER */;
      FINISH_PL/X
      $DATA
      15E+0 10.0E+0
```

We would like to be able to write programs in PL/X and have them executed on a computer, but unfortunately there is no computer that "understands" PL/X. However there are computers that understand PL/I, so if a PL/X program could be "translated" into an equivalent PL/I program, then the PL/I program could be executed to produce the desired results. Moreover, the PL/X programmer might not be told that his program required translation into PL/I, and he might be led to believe that a computer understood PL/X and could execute his program directly.

We have deliberately designed PL/X so that the translation would be simple so that the general idea of such a translation will not be obscured by details. An algorithm to perform this translation is:

```
Read a PL/X source card into CARD
DO WHILE (CARD does not begin with 'FINISH_PL/X');
    Within CARD change 'CREATE' to 'DECLARE'
        and 'PRINT_ONE_LINE' to 'PUT SKIP LIST '
    Write out CARD as a PL/I source line
    Read next PL/X source card into CARD
    END;
```

A PL/I program to perform this translation is given below. The PL/X program of (1.1a) is shown as data for this translation program. This translator will actually work -- it will take any PL/X program as input, and print out an equivalent PL/I program that could be punched on cards and executed on a computer.

This translator will transform the character sequences "CREATE " and "PRINT_ONE_LINE" wherever they occur. This means that they not only cannot be used as identifiers; they must not be used in a comment or a literal, or as part of an identifier. That is, 'NOW CREATE TABLE', and /* RECREATE INDEX */ would be changed by this simple translator. A slightly more complicated translator would make these additional restrictions unnecessary.

```
X_TO_I: PROCEDURE OPTIONS(MAIN);
    /* PL/X TO PL/I TRANSLATOR */
    /* READS ANY ARBITRARY PL/X PROGRAM --- */
    /* PRODUCES AN EQUIVALENT PL/I PROGRAM */
    DECLARE (CARD) CHARACTER(80) VARYING,  /* SOURCE LINE */
        (COL) FIXED;   /* CARD COLUMN */

    GET SKIP EDIT(CARD) (A(80));
    DO WHILE(SUBSTR(CARD,1,11) ¬= 'FINISH_PL/X');
        /* CHANGE 'CREATE ' TO 'DECLARE' AND 'PRINT_ONE_LINE' */
        /* TO 'PUT SKIP LIST ' */
        /* BEFORE EACH EXECUTION OF BODY 'COL' POINTS */
        /* TO POSITION TO LEFT OF NEXT SCAN POSITION */
        COL = 0;
        DO WHILE(COL < 73);   /* 73 = 80-LENGTH('CREATE ') */
            COL=COL+1;
            IF SUBSTR(CARD,COL,6) = 'CREATE ' THEN
                DO;
                    CARD=SUBSTR(CARD,1,COL-1) ||'DECLARE'||
                        SUBSTR(CARD,COL+6);
                    COL = COL+5;
                    END;
            IF COL < 66 THEN   /* 66 = 80-LENGTH('PRINT_ONE_LINE')*/
                IF SUBSTR(CARD,COL,14)='PRINT_ONE_LINE' THEN
                    DO;
                        CARD=SUBSTR(CARD,1,COL-1)||
                            'PUT SKIP LIST ' || SUBSTR(CARD,COL+14);
                        COL = COL+14;
                        END;
            END;
        PUT SKIP LIST(CARD);            /* PRINT REVISED CARD */
        GET SKIP EDIT(CARD) (A(80)); /* READ NEXT CARD */
        END;
    END /* X_TO_I */;
$DATA
    ADDER: PROCEDURE OPTIONS(MAIN);
        /* ADDING PROGRAM */
        CREATE (X,Y,Z) FLOAT;
        /* X,Y ARE NUMBERS TO BE ADDED */
        /* Z IS THE RESULT */
        GET LIST(X,Y);
        Z = X + Y;
        PRINT_ONE_LINE(Z);
        END /* ADDER */;
    FINISH_PL/X
```

The output from this program, if executed with the data shown, would be:

```
ADDER: PROCEDURE OPTIONS(MAIN);
    /* ADDING PROGRAM */
    DECLARE(X,Y,Z) FLOAT;
    /* X,Y ARE NUMBERS TO BE ADDED */
    /* Z IS THE RESULT */
    GET LIST(X,Y);
    Z = X + Y;
    PUT SKIP LIST (Z);
    END /* ADDER */;
```

1.2 Programs as Data

The computing process can be viewed in a general way as shown in the following diagram:

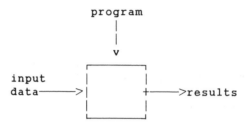

A program is loaded into a computer. Execution of this program causes input data to be read and manipulated to produce results. Initially, we considered input data and results that were entirely numeric. Then, in Section I.9, the concept of a variable was extended to permit values that included non-numeric characters. We alluded to the existence of "text processing" programs, and described the initial development of a text editor in Sections III.2.5 and III.3.2.

Now we are suggesting that there are certain text processing programs that read strings which are statements of a programming language, and manipulate these strings to produce as output equivalent elements of some other programming language. That is, one program called a "translating program" or "translator", reads another program, called a "source program", as input data, and transforms this to produce a third program, called an "object program", as output. This object program can, in turn, be loaded into a computer to process input data to produce results. Schematically, this can be shown as:

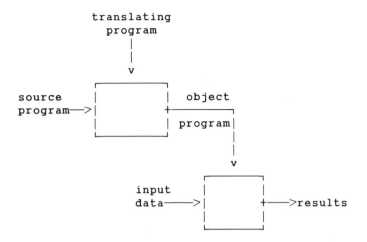

In Section 1.1 we devised a "source language" PL/X, that was
very similar to the "object language" PL/I, so that the
translator could be short and simple. It should be obvious that
we could devise many different source languages, some of which
could differ very markedly in form and function from PL/I. For
example, in Section IX.2.2.2 examples are given in a source
language that bears strong resemblance to English. The only
limitation on the design of a source language is the ability to
produce a translator that will transform programs in the source
language into some object language that is "understood" by a
computer.

Such translators are non-trivial, and their development
represents one major branch of the field of computer science.
The subject has received considerable attention, and the
problems and techniques of translation are quite generally and
widely understood. A great variety of source languages are
available to programmers today, because many different
translators have been produced.

It should not come as a complete surprise that PL/I and SP/k
are also source languages. They are not "understood" by a
computer, any more than PL/X is; they require translation into
an object language before they can be executed on a computer.
This is true not only of PL/I, but also of all the programming
languages that are in general use today -- FORTRAN, BASIC,
COBOL, APL, etc. None of these is the natural language of any
computer. They have all been designed to be more-or-less
convenient for human programmers, and programs written in any of
them must be translated before they can be executed.

It should also be apparent that this translation could take
place in several stages. For example, in Section 1.1, a PL/X
program was translated into an equivalent PL/I program, but this
PL/I program, in turn, must be further translated before it can
be executed.

However many translation stages may be required, eventually
the program must be transformed into a "real" computer program
-- one that can be executed directly by some computer. This
real program must be written in the "machine language" for
whatever computer is to be used for execution. Each different
type of computer has a unique machine language, into which every
program to be executed on that computer must be translated. For
example, programs to be executed on IBM 360 computers may be
written in PL/I, FORTRAN, COBOL, APL or several score of other
source languages -- but every one of these programs must be
translated into the same 360 machine language before it can
actually be executed.

The same source language can be used on different types of
computers. For example, FORTRAN can be used on many different
computers, since translators have been written to translate
FORTRAN programs into equivalent machine language programs for
these various computers.

1.3 Translation to Machine Language

A machine language is no more difficult to learn or
understand than PL/I, but is unquestionably more difficult to
use. For a given problem, it takes several times as long to
write a program in machine language as it does in PL/I. Largely
for this reason, very few programs are written directly in
machine language today. (This was not always the case. In the
first decade of computing, before "high-level" languages and
translators for them became available in the late 1950's, all
programs were written in machine language.)

A machine language program consists of a sequence of
instructions. Each instruction specifies the execution of one
of a repertoire of elemental operations that are "built into"
the computer. This specification is called the "operation code"
portion of the instruction. Most instructions also specify an
operand to be combined with the result of previous operations.
For example, an instruction may specify that "the value of X is
to be added to the results of previous computation". The
operands, or variables, are not specified by identifiers as in
PL/I, but are specified by their physical location in the memory
of the computer. Each memory location has a unique identifying
number called an "address"; the address of the operand is
specified in the instruction.

As a brief example, let us describe the machine language
instructions produced by translation of a PL/I assignment
statement. Suppose variables have been created and assigned
locations in memory as follows (as a result of the translation
of a PL/I declaration):

        X _ [float] in location with address 2132
        Y _ [float] in location with address 2134
        Z _ [float] in location with address 2204
        W _ [float] in location with address 2311

The PL/I assignment statement

        X = Y + Z - W;

could be translated into a sequence of machine language
instructions much like the following. In each instruction the
first two characters are the operation code, and the last four
are the operand address:

        682134
        662204
        622311
        602132

Their execution would proceed as follows:

  682134 Clear the result of previous computation from the
         "arithmetic unit" of the computer, and copy the value from
         the memory location whose address is 2134 into the
         arithmetic unit.

  662204 Add the value from memory location 2204 to the value
         already in the arithmetic unit.

  622311 Subtract the value in memory location 2311 from the
         value already in the arithmetic unit.

  602132 Store a copy of the value that is in the arithmetic
         unit into memory location 2132.

    The number of machine instructions produced by the
translation of different PL/I statements varies greatly. The
number for an assignment statement depends upon the complexity
of the expression on the right side of the statement. Some
statements may be translated into a single machine instruction;
a complex PUT EDIT statement may require over one hundred
machine instructions.

    Translation from a source language like PL/I into machine
language is obviously more complicated and difficult to perform
than the translation from PL/X into PL/I illustrated in Section
1.1. However, the general idea remains the same -- a source
program is read as data, and a machine language object program
is produced as output. It would be quite feasible to translate
PL/X directly into machine language, rather than use PL/I as an
intermediate stage. A program to perform this PL/X-to-machine-
language translation could be written in PL/I.

Section 2   Types of Translators

2.1 Measures of Performance

Many different machine language programs will perform the same computing task. These programs might differ in size, efficiency, or in the manner in which they react to errors in the input data. Beyond such functional differences, programs differ just because there are many different ways of performing each of the elemental subtasks that comprise a program, just as there are many ways of conveying the same idea in English.

Since there are different machine language object programs to perform a given task, all translators do not necessarily produce the same object program from the same source program. A translator must first of all be correct -- it must produce an object program that is logically equivalent to the source program -- but after correctness there are several possible secondary criteria against which a translator could be judged. A translator could be designed:

1) to produce an efficient object program;

2) to translate as efficiently as possible;

3) to provide as much assistance as possible to the author of the source program in eliminating errors;

4) to be as simple as possible, in order to minimize the cost, effort and time required to produce the translator.

Hence for a given pair of source and object languages there can be a number of different translators with significantly different characteristics. For example, there are at least a dozen significant translators from PL/I to IBM 360 machine language. Older source languages (such as FORTRAN) have accumulated an even greater number of translators.

As far as the PL/I programmer is concerned, any of these PL/I translators will permit him to execute his program on a computer, but the choice of translator may nevertheless be very important since different translators will provide him with vastly different degrees of assistance in finding and correcting his errors, and present him with considerably different bills for the computer time required to translate his program, and to execute the resulting object program.

2.2 Compilers and Interpreters

Two principal strategies are used in the construction of translators. In the first of these the entire source program is translated into an object program before any execution of the object program takes place. Translation and execution are distinctly different phases, and once translation has been completed, neither the source program nor the translator need be present while the object program is being executed. A translator that employs this strategy is called a "compiler".

The second strategy interleaves translation and execution. As soon as a statement of the source program is translated, the resulting segment of object program is executed immediately. After it has been executed, the segment of object program is discarded, and the next statement of the source program is translated and executed. When execution of a source statement must be repeated (for example, statements in the body of a WHILE loop), it must be re-translated from source form for each execution. The object program exists only in segments, and never as a complete program at any point in time. Obviously, both the source program and the translator must be present throughout the process. A translator that employs this strategy is called an "interpreter". Most interpreters perform a preliminary translation of the entire source program into an internal form, but this form is more similar to the source language than machine language. "Statements" from this internal program are translated and executed, as described above.

The strategies described above are idealized, or extreme. All real translators employ both strategies to varying degrees and in different contexts. Although every translator is a mixture of the two, each is generally classified as either a compiler or an interpreter depending upon which of the idealized models it most closely resembles.

Considering translators for PL/I, the IBM PL/I-F translator, Cornell's PL/C translator, and IBM's "PL/I Optimizer" are all compilers. PL/I-F is a general-purpose compiler, PL/C is a compiler intended to reduce translation time and maximize diagnostic assistance, and the Optimizer is a compiler designed to produce an efficient object program at the expense of increased translation time. The SP/k translator developed at the University of Toronto is also a compiler. There are also a number of interpreters for PL/I, including IBM's "PL/I Checkout Compiler" (called a compiler for reasons known only to IBM).

Interpreters are generally easier to construct than compilers, and provide more effective control over the execution of the object program. Unfortunately, some interpreters also require considerably more computer time, due to the repeated translation of iterated source statements. It is not uncommon to have an interpreter require twenty times as much computer time as a compiler, to execute the same source program.

Section 3   The SP/k Compiler

SP/k is a <u>subset</u> of the full PL/I language. The PL/I statements included in SP/k were selected to make it easy for students to learn to program in PL/I. Because SP/k is a subset, programs written in SP/k can be compiled and executed using several different PL/I compilers including the IBM PL/I compilers and the Cornell PL/C compiler. However, these compilers do not restrict the programmer to the SP/k subset. It is also possible to write a compiler that processes exactly the SP/k subset and nothing else. This section describes such a compiler that was developed at the University of Toronto.

Programs under development (especially those written by students) have several well-known properties. These programs:

   a) contain errors,
   b) require frequent re-translation, and
   c) require relatively little execution.

Consequently, the Toronto SP/k compiler was designed to provide a substantial amount of diagnostic information and to perform translation as rapidly as possible. To make the SP/k language available to a wide audience (high schools through universities), the SP/k compiler was designed so that it could be used on both very small and very large computers.

3.1 <u>Design of the SP/k Compiler</u>

The design goals for the Toronto SP/k compiler called for a compiler that:

   a) was highly diagnostic,
   b) performed translation rapidly,
   c) did not need to produce efficient object programs, and
   d) was adaptable to run on several computers.

This set of goals dictated a particular choice among the possible strategies described in Section 2. One of the key decisions was not to try and produce object programs in the machine language of any existing computer. Instead, an "SP/k machine" was designed that had a machine language especially well suited to the execution of SP/k programs. The SP/k compiler translates SP/k programs into the machine language of this SP/k machine. A program called a <u>simulator</u> was written to execute programs in the SP/k machine language by simulating the

effect of each SP/k machine instruction. This strategy meant
that the SP/k compiler could be very small and simple and that
it was relatively easy to produce versions of the compiler to
run on different computers.

3.2 SP/k Compiler Structure

The SP/k compiler was designed using the top-down program
development techniques described in Part III.   At the highest
level, the compiler can be described by:

1. compile and execute an SP/k program

The next refinement of the compiler leads to the steps:

1a. Read, analyze, and list, an SP/k source program
1b. Generate an equivalent SP/k machine language program
1c. Execute the SP/k machine language program

These steps correspond to the three major phases of the SP/k
compiler. The first phase is called the scanner-parser-lister.
It performs the functions indicated by the following refinement:

1a1. Read an SP/k source program and separate it into basic
     language elements called tokens (scanner)
1a2. Analyze the structure of the program and produce
     information for the second phase (parser)
1a3. paragraph and list the SP/k source program (lister)

The second phase of the compiler is called the semantic
analyzer. It accepts a condensed form of the source program
from the first phase, performs some processing on it and then
produces an object program in the machine language of the SP/k
machine. This phase can be described by the refinement:

1b1. process declarations and allocate storage
1b2. process internal procedures
1b3. process statements and generate machine code

Note that these three refinements correspond to the three
major entities that occur in the body of an SP/k program (see
Appendix A.4). Also note that this refinement describes a
recursive algorithm because step 1b2 will require the processing
of declarations, (possibly) internal procedures, and statements.
Further refinement of the semantic analyzer phase leads to steps
for processing each type of declaration and statement in the
SP/k subset. For example, the next level of refinement for 1b3
can be described using the "case statement" (see Appendix B.10).

```
FOR each statement in the program DO

    CASE depending on statement type OF

        assignment: 1b3a. process assignment statement
        if:         1b3b. process if statement
        do while:   1b3c. process do while loop
        iterative:  1b3d. process iterative do loop
        put:        1b3e. process put statement
        get:        1b3f. process get statement
        call:       1b3g. process call statement
        return:     1b3h. process return statement

    END;
```

The final phase of the SP/k compiler is the simulator that executes a program in SP/k machine language by simulating each machine language instruction. The first level of refinement for this phase is:

```
1c1. initialize SP/k machine
1c2. execute machine language program
1c3. print execution summary
```

The next level of refinement for 1c2 leads to

```
DO WHILE (instruction ≠ halt);

    CASE depending on instruction type OF

        load/store:    1c2a. execute load/store instruction
        arithmetic:    1c2b. execute arithmetic instruction
        allocation:    1c2c. execute allocation instruction
        input/output:  1c2d. execute input/output instruction
        control:       1c2e. execute control instruction
        misc:          1c2f. execute miscellaneous instruction

    END;

    fetch next instruction

END;
```

Further refinement leads to code to simulate each SP/k machine instruction.

3.3 Error Detection and Repair

Part of the processing performed by all three phases involves the detection and attempted correction of errors. We will describe the compiler's general strategy for error detection and correction here; specific examples are given in Appendix A.5. The first phase detects errors in the syntax of SP/k programs

(recall Section V.3). While analysing the structure of a
program it detects any sequence of tokens (basic language
elements) that cannot possibly form a valid SP/k program. The
strategy used for the repair of syntax errors is to delete
and/or insert the tokens necessary to produce a valid SP/k
program. The exact algorithm used to make the repairs is beyond
the scope of this book. Often this repair strategy results in
correcting the program to what the programmer had intended, but
this is not always so.

The second phase detects semantic errors in programs, that
is, errors that are not readily apparent from just the structure
of the program. For example, use of a variable in an expression
is valid in SP/k if and only if that same variable has appeared
in a declare statement. When the second phase processes
declarations (step 1b1) it builds a symbol table that contains
information about each variable that has been declared. When
statements are processed in step 1b3, the symbol table is used
to verify that each variable is being used correctly. The error
repair strategy used by the second phase is very similar to that
used by the first. It deletes and adds information as necessary
to transform an incorrect program into a legal one. For example
misuse of a variable in any expression will usually result in
replacing the reference to the variable by a standard default
value (1, 1.0E+0, '?', or '1'B depending on the type of value
required).

The third phase, the SP/k machine simulator, detects and
attempts to repair errors that depend on the dynamics of program
execution. For example, each value used as an array subscript
is checked to make sure that it lies within the range of valid
subscripts for the array on question; each use of a variable is
checked to make sure that the variable has previously been
assigned a value. The simulator attempts to repair errors
involving misuse of variable by replacing the value of the
variable by one of the standard default values described above.

3.4 An SP/k Translation Example

In this section we present an example to illustrate the
various stages in the translation of an SP/k program from source
to executable form. Consider the source program:

```
T:PROCEDURE OPTIONS(MAIN);
DECLARE(I) FIXED;
   I = 12300;
   PUT SKIP LIST(I+43);
END /* T */;
```

This program is read by the scanner in the first phase of the
compiler (step 1a1) and divided up into a sequence of language
tokens as shown in Figure 1a. The parser (step 1a2) reads this
sequence of tokens and produces the stream of information in

Figure 1b for the second phase. The lister sub-phase (step 1a3)
uses the information produced by the parser and the scanner to
paragraph and list the program as shown below:

```
    T:PROCEDURE OPTIONS(MAIN);
        DECLARE (I) FIXED;
        I = 12300;
        PUT SKIP LIST(I+43);
        END /* T */;
```

The lower-case words in Figure 1b describe the essential
structure of the source program to the semantic analysis phase.
This phase processes the information to produce the SP/k machine
language program in Figure 1c. The simulator phase then
executes the machine language program.

a) scanner output	b) parser output	c) semantic analyzer output
T	identifier,T	ENTER
:	main-program	LINE 1
PROCEDURE	new-line	ALLOCATE_FIXED I
OPTIONS	indent	LINE 2
(	declare	LOCATE_FIXED I
MAIN	identifier,I	LITERAL_FIXED 12300
)	fixed-scalar	ASSIGN
;	end-declare	LINE 3
DECLARE	new-line	PUT_SKIP
(	identifier,I	LOAD_FIXED I
I	expression	LITERAL_FIXED 43
)	fixed-constant,12300	ADD_FIXED
FIXED	end-expression	PUT_FIXED
;	assign	LINE 4
I	new-line	HALT
=	put-skip	
12300	put-list	
;	expression	
PUT	identifier,I	
SKIP	fixed-constant,43	
LIST	add	
(	end-expression	
I	put-expression	
+	end-put	
43	end-program	
)		
;		
END		
/* T */		
;		

Figure 1. Steps in the Translation of a Source Program

Part X <u>References</u>

Aho, A. V., and J. D. Ullman, <u>The Theory of Parsing,
    Translation, and Compiling</u>, Prentice-Hall, 1972

Conway, R. W., and T. R. Wilcox, "Design and Implementation of a
    Diagnostic Compiler for PL/I", <u>Communications of the ACM</u>
    March, 1973

Gries, D.,   <u>Compiler Construction for Digital Computers</u>,
    Wiley, 1971

Holt, R.C. and D.B. Wortman, "Structured Subsets of the PL/I
    Language", Technical Report CSRG-55, Computer Systems
    Research Group, University of Toronto, October 1973

IBM, <u>A Programmer's Introduction to the IBM System/360
    Architecture, Instructions, and Assembler Language</u>,
    Publication C20-1646, International Business Machines
    Corporation.

McKeeman, W.M., J.J. Horning, and D.B. Wortman, <u>A Compiler
    Generator</u>, Prentice-Hall, 1970

Sammet, J. E., <u>Programming Languages: History and Fundamentals</u>,
    Prentice-Hall, 1969

APPENDIX A   Specifications for SP/k

SP/k is a sequence of subsets of the PL/1 language that has been developed for the purpose of teaching computer programming. SP/k was developed at the Computer Systems Research Group, University of Toronto. This appendix is an adaptation of a technical report by Richard C. Holt and David B. Wortman.

Since SP/k is a compatible subset of PL/1, SP/k programs can be run under a variety of compilers, including the University of Toronto's SP/k compiler and Cornell University's PL/C compiler. Details about running SP/k programs under the SP/k compiler are given in Section A.1.4.

Appendix A.1 <u>Preliminary</u> <u>Definitions</u>

In the interest of making PL/1 more suitable for pedagogic purposes, SP/k restricts or eliminates many PL/1 features. In SP/k every variable must be declared. Declarations are not allowed to specify number bases (binary versus decimal) or precisions; this avoids problems arising from the precision rules of full PL/1. Implicit conversions are not allowed among numeric, logical and character types, thereby eliminating conversion anomalies.

Features implied by the following keywords are not in SP/k: BINARY, COMPLEX, INITIAL, EXTERNAL, POINTER, GOTO, ON and BEGIN. The following PL/1 features are eliminated: fixed-length character strings, label variables, operations on entire arrays or structures, pseudo variables, data directed input-output, static allocation, controlled allocation, based allocation, multitasking, and compile-time processing.

Instead of giving a complete list of the omitted PL/1 features, we will specify SP/k by giving a list of included features. Language features introduced by subsets SP/1 to SP/8 are summarized in the following table.

Subset   Features Introduced

SP/1   Characters: letters, digits and special characters
           Constants: fixed, float and character string
           Expressions: +, -, *, /, fixed to float conversion
           Simple output: put list
           Mathematical built-in functions: mod, sin, cos, atan,
                 log, exp, sqrt.

SP/2   Identifiers and variables
           Declarations: fixed and float
           Assignment statements (with float to fixed conversion)
           Simple input: get list

SP/3   Comparisons: <, >, =, <=, >=, ¬=
           Logical expressions: &, |, and ¬
           Selection: if-then-else and compound statement
           Repetition: while loop and indexed loop
           Paragraphing
           Logical constants: '0'B (false) and '1'B (true)
           Logical variables: the bit attribute

SP/4   Character string expressions: concatenation
            Character string variables (varying length only)
            Character string comparison and blank padding
            Character string built-in functions: length and substr

SP/5   Arrays (including multiple dimensions)

SP/6   Procedures: subroutines and functions
            Calling and returning
            Arguments and parameters
            Side effects and dummy arguments
            Arrays and character strings as arguments

SP/7   Detailed control of input and output: get and put edit

SP/8   PL/1 structures (one level only)
            Files: open and close
            Record oriented input and output: read and write

   The following sections give detailed specifications for each
subset. In describing the subsets, we will use this notation:

            [item] means the item is optional
            |item| means the item can appear zero or more times

When presenting the syntax of language constructs, items written
in upper case letters, for example,

       PROCEDURE

denote keywords; these items must appear in SP/k jobs exactly as
presented. Items written in lower case letters, for example,

       statement

denote one of a class of constructs; each such item is defined
below as it is introduced.

Appendix A.2 SP/k Subsets

In this section we present a detailed description of the
eight SP/k subsets of PL/I.

A.2.1 SP/1: Expressions and Output

We now begin the specification of the first subset.

A character is a letter or a digit or a special character.

A letter is one of the following:

A B C D E F G H I J K L M N O P Q R S T U V W X Y Z $ # @

A digit is one of the following:

0 1 2 3 4 5 6 7 8 9

A special character is one of the following:

+ - * / ( ) = < > . : ; ? % & | ¬
ᵇ (blank)
' (apostrophe or single quote)
_ (break character or underscore)

A fixed constant is one or more digits (without embedded
blanks), for example:

4 19 243 92153

A float constant consists of a mantissa followed by an exponent
(without embedded blanks). The mantissa must be one or more
digits with an optional decimal point. The exponent must be the
letter E, followed by an optional plus or minus sign followed by
one or more digits. The following are examples of float
constants.

5.16E+00 50E0 .9418E24 1.E-2

Note that a fixed constant may not contain a decimal point.
Note also that a float constant need not contain a decimal
point, but must contain an exponent.

There is a maximum allowed number of digits in a fixed
constant. There is a maximum allowed number of digits in the
mantissa of a float constant and a maximum allowed magnitude of
exponent. (These maximum values will vary from implementation
to implementation; see Appendix A.5.)

A literal (or character string constant) is a single quote (an
apostrophe), followed by zero or more occurrences of non-single-
quote characters or twice repeated single quotes, followed by a
single quote. The following are examples of literals:

        'FRED'   'X=24'   'MR. O''REILLY'

There is an implementation-determined maximum length of
character strings (see Appendix A.5).

Each constant must appear entirely on one card, i.e.,
constants must not cross card boundaries.

In SP/1, an expression is one of the following:

        fixed constant
        float constant
        literal
        +expression
        -expression
        expression + expression
        expression - expression
        expression * expression
        expression / expression
        (expression)
        built-in function

Float and fixed values may be combined in expressions. When
a fixed value is combined with a float value, the result is a
float value.

Evaluation of expressions proceeds from left to right, with
the exceptions that multiplications and divisions have higher
precedence than (i.e., are evaluated before) additions and
subtractions and that parenthesized sub-expressions are
evaluated before being used in arithmetic operations. Unary
operations (+ and -) are evaluated before binary operations.
Division (/) can be used only when one or both of the operands
are float values. Division of a fixed value by a fixed value is
not allowed. The following are examples of legal expressions.

        -4+20   2*8.5E+00   (4.0E+01-12.0E+01)/-2

The values of these three expressions are, respectively, 16,
17.0E+00, and 4.0E+01.

Character strings cannot be used in arithmetic operations.
In SP/k there are no implicit conversions from numeric values to
character string values or vice versa.

An SP/1 built-in function call is one of the following:

```
MOD( expression , expression )
SIN( expression )
COS( expression )
ATAN( expression )
LOG( expression )
EXP( expression )
SQRT( expression )
```

The MOD function accepts two fixed expressions as arguments and produces a fixed result. The SIN, COS, ATAN, LOG, EXP, and SQRT mathematical functions accept a single fixed or float expression as an argument and produce a float result. Appendix A.4 gives a more detailed description of SP/k built-in functions.

An SP/1 <u>statement</u> is one of the following:

```
PUT [SKIP] LIST(expression |,expression| );
PUT PAGE LIST(expression |,expression| );
```

An SP/1 <u>program</u> is: T:PROCEDURE OPTIONS(MAIN);
                                |statement|
                                END;

Remember that the notation |statement| means zero or more statements. The following is an example of an SP/1 program:

```
T:PROCEDURE OPTIONS(MAIN);
    PUT SKIP LIST(2, 'PLUS', 3, 'MAKES', 2+3);
    END;
```

The output from this example is: 2   PLUS   3   MAKES   5

Output produced by the PUT LIST statement is placed in successive "fields" across the print line. All fields have the same width. A new print line is started when all fields on a line have been used, or when SKIP (or PAGE) is used in the PUT LIST statement. (See Appendix A.5 for the number of and size of these fields.)

When a literal is printed by a PUT LIST statement, its enclosing single quotes are removed. In addition, twice repeated single quotes in a literal are printed as one single quote. A long string may use several print fields. If the printed string exactly fills all the columns of a field, then the next field is skipped.

There may be slight differences in the handling of certain aspects of the SP/1 subset by different compilers. These differences include the following:

1. Length of character strings. Most compilers allow character strings to be at least 127 characters long.

2. Number of digits in fixed values. Most compilers allow at
    least 5 digits.

3. Number of digits in the mantissa of a float value. Most
    compilers allow at least 6 mantissa digits.

4. Magnitude of float values. Most compilers allow the
    magnitude of float numbers to be at least 1.00000E+36.

5. Use of columns of punch cards for programs. Some compilers
    allow only columns 2 through 72 of a punch card to be used
    for the program. All 80 columns of a punch card can be
    used for data.

(See Appendix A.5 for more details on the above points.)

A.2.2 SP/2: Variables, Input and Assignment

We now begin the specifications of the second subset, SP/2.

An identifier is a letter followed by zero or more letters,
digits, or break characters (underscores). An identifier cannot
contain embedded blanks. Most compilers allow identifiers to be
at least 31 characters long. Some compilers limit the
identifier which names a program to 7 characters.

An SP/2 program is: identifier:PROCEDURE OPTIONS(MAIN);
                             |declaration|
                             |statement|
                             END;

A declaration is: DECLARE(variable |,variable|)attribute
                           |,(variable |,variable|)attribute|;

An attribute is one of the following:
                        FIXED
                        FLOAT

A statement is one of the following:
                        PUT [SKIP] LIST(expression |,expression|);
                        PUT PAGE LIST(expression |,expression|);
                        variable = expression;
                        GET [SKIP] LIST(variable |,variable|);

In SP/2, each variable is simply an identifier. (There are
no arrays in SP/2.)

In SP/k all variables must be declared.

In SP/2 an expression may be a variable.

Float values may be assigned to fixed variables. Any non-integer part of such a float value is truncated before the assignment without a warning message. Fixed values may be assigned to float variables with automatic conversion.

The items in the data (the input stream) read by GET LIST statements must be separated by at least one blank. When a GET LIST statement is executed, one data item is read for each variable in the statement.

Each item in the input stream must be a literal, a float constant, a fixed constant or a non-integer fixed constant. A non-integer fixed constant is one or more digits with a decimal point. The following are examples of non-integer fixed constants:

            3.14159   243.12

Non-integer fixed constants can not appear in programs, but can appear in data.

Any numeric constant (float, fixed or non-integer fixed) can be read (and will be automatically converted if necessary) into a float variable. Similarly, any numeric constant can be read (and will be automatically truncated if necessary) into a fixed variable. There are no automatic conversions from character string values to numeric values or vice versa.

A keyword is any of the special identifiers, e.g., PROCEDURE, GET, and LIST, that are part of the SP/k syntax. A variable can not be given the same name as a keyword.

Any number of blanks (or card boundaries) can appear between symbols, e.g., between constants, keywords, identifiers, operators +, -, *, / and the parentheses (and). When constants, keywords or identifiers are adjacent, for example, the adjacent keywords PUT and LIST, they must be separated by at least one blank.

A comment consists of the characters /* followed by any characters except the combination */ followed by the characters */. A blank cannot appear between the / and * or between the * and /. Comments can appear wherever blanks can appear. A comment must not cross a card boundary. Hence, any comment which would cross a card boundary should be closed by */ at the end of one card and continued by /* on the next card. In general, it is good practice for comments to appear on separate lines or at the ends of lines. Some compilers do not allow the initial /* of a comment to start in card column 1. Comments cannot appear in the data.

A.2.3 SP/3: Logical Expressions, Selection and Repetition

A condition is one of the following:

```
'0'B
'1'B
logical variable
¬condition
condition & condition
condition | condition
comparison
( condition )
```

A condition is called a logical expression. The constant '0'B means "false" and '1'B means "true".

A comparison is one of the following:

```
expression < expression
expression > expression
expression = expression
expression <= expression
expression >= expression
expression ¬= expression
```

An attribute is one of the following:

```
FIXED
FLOAT
BIT
```

Variables declared to have the BIT attribute are called logical variables. Logical variables can be operands in the logical operations of and (&), or (|) and not (¬). Float and fixed values cannot be operands of logical operations.

(Some compilers, namely, PL/C and PL/1 F, do not allow logical variables to be declared as simply BIT. For these compilers, the attribute BIT(1) must be used instead.)

The and operator (&) has higher precedence than the or operator (|). Logical variables can be compared, assigned, read, and printed. Logical variables can be compared only for equality or inequality.

There is no implicit conversion between numeric values (fixed and float) and logical values. Logical values cannot participate in arithmetic operations.

An SP/3 <u>statement</u> is one of the following:

```
PUT [SKIP] LIST(expression |,expression| );

PUT PAGE LIST(expression |,expression| );

variable = expression;

GET [SKIP] LIST(variable |,variable| );

IF condition THEN
   statement
[ELSE
   statement]

DO WHILE(condition);
   |statement|
   END;

DO identifier = expression TO expression [BY expression];
   |statement|
   END;

DO;
   |statement|
   END;
```

In the indexed loop (second DO loop above), the index variable (identifier) must have been declared to be a fixed variable. Each expression is evaluated once at the beginning of the execution of the loop. If the BY clause is omitted, a step size of 1 is assumed.

When the third expression (step size) is positive, the indexed loop is equivalent to the following:

```
start = first expression;
limit = second expression;
step  = third expression (or 1 if no by clause);
identifier = start;
DO WHILE(identifier <= limit);
   |statement|
   identifier = identifier + step;
   END;
```

If the third expression is negative, the comparison in the above DO WHILE group becomes >=.

The following is an example of an SP/3 program.

```
SP3:PROCEDURE OPTIONS(MAIN);
   /* PROGRAM TO SUM N INTEGERS FROM INPUT */
   DECLARE(N,X,TOTAL)FIXED;
   TOTAL=0;
   GET LIST(N);
   DO WHILE(N>0);
      GET LIST(X);
      TOTAL=TOTAL+X;
      N=N-1;
      END;
   PUT LIST('TOTAL IS',TOTAL);
   END /* SP3 */;
```

Paragraphing rules are standard conventions for indenting program lines. Some compilers provide automatic paragraphing of programs. If this feature is available, it should be used.

A set of paragraphing rules can be inferred from the method used to present SP/k constructs. For example, the DO WHILE loop was presented in the following form:

```
DO WHILE(condition);
   |statement|
   END;
```

This form means that the statements enclosed in a DO WHILE loop should be indented beyond the level of the opening "DO WHILE" line. The construct "END;" which marks the physical end of the loop should be indented to the same level as the enclosed statements.

Comments should be indented to the same level as their corresponding program lines. The continuation(s) of a long program line should be indented beyond the line's original indentation. If the level of indentation becomes too deep, it may be necessary to abandon indentation rules temporarily, maintaining a vertical positioning of lines.

A.2.4 SP/4: Character Strings

An attribute is one of the following:

```
FIXED
FLOAT
CHARACTER(maximum length) VARYING
BIT
```

Variables declared to have the attribute CHARACTER(maximum length)VARYING are called character string variables. In the declaration of character string variables, maximum length must be a fixed constant. The concatenation operator (||) can be used to join two strings together. Both of its operands must be character strings.

Two built-in functions, SUBSTR and LENGTH, operate on character string values. The SUBSTR built-in function can accept two or three arguments. (SUBSTR cannot be used as a PL/1 pseudo variable.) See Appendix A.5 for a detailed description of SUBSTR.

The LENGTH built-in function has one argument, which must be a character string value. Character strings can be compared, assigned, read and printed. When character strings of different lengths are compared, the shorter string is automatically extended (on the right) with blanks to the length of the longer string.

In general, a character string variable assumes the length of the string which is assigned to it (or read into it via a get list statement). However, if the maximum length of the variable being assigned to is less than the length of the string being assigned, then before assignment the assigned value is automatically truncated (on the right) to this maximum length.

There is no implicit conversion between character string values and numeric or logical values.

A.2.5 SP/5: Arrays

The form of declaration remains as it was:

        DECLARE(variable |,variable|)attribute
          |,(variable |,variable|)attribute|;

However, the form of variable is now allowed to specify array bounds. In a declaration, a variable is now:

          identifier [(range |,range|)]

A range is one of the following:

        fixed constant
        [-] fixed constant : [-] fixed constant

The first form of range assumes the lower bound is 1, and specifies the upper bound. The second form specifies both the lower and upper bounds.

In an expression, or in a GET LIST statement, a variable has the form:

        identifier [(expression |,expression|)]

Each array index expression must have a numeric value. A float value used as an array index will be truncated to a fixed value.

Array elements may be compared, assigned, read, and printed on an element by element basis, in the same way as simple variables with similar attributes.

A.2.6 SP/6: Procedures

In SP/6 the form of program is extended to allow the definition of (internal) procedures.

A SP/6 program is: identifier:PROCEDURE OPTIONS(MAIN);
                           |declaration|
                           |definition|
                           |statement|
                     END;

A definition is: identifier:PROCEDURE [(identifier |,identifier|)]
                           [RETURNS(attribute)] ;
                           |declaration|
                           |definition|
                           |statement|
                     END;

Two new statements are added:

          CALL procedure name [(expression |,expression|)];
          RETURN [(expression)];

All parameters to a procedure must be declared. Parameters are passed to procedures "by reference"; this means that when a procedure assigns a value to a parameter, the corresponding argument in the call to the procedure actually receives the value. If an array is a parameter, then the ranges for each array index must be specified by an asterisk (*) in the procedure. If a character string is a parameter, then the maximum length of the character string must be specified by an asterisk (*) in the procedure.

A subroutine is a procedure which does not have the RETURNS clause in its definition. A subroutine can be invoked only by the CALL statement. A subroutine is terminated: (a) by executing a RETURN statement without the RETURN expression, or (b) after the physically last statement of the subroutine body is executed.

A function is a procedure which has the RETURNS clause in its definition. A function can be invoked only by using its name (with arguments if required) in an expression. Return from a function must be via a RETURN statement having an expression

whose attribute matches the attribute given in the RETURNS
clause. (It is legal to have a fixed value as the RETURN
expression in a float function and vice versa; automatic
conversion of returned values will take place for these cases.)

A.2.7 SP/7: Edit Input and Output

Statements giving explicit control of the format of input and
output data are introduced.

A statement is one of the following:

a. PUT SKIP [(lines to skip)];
b. PUT [SKIP[(lines to skip)]] LIST (expression
      |,expression|);
c. PUT PAGE LIST (expression |,expression|);
d. PUT [SKIP[(lines to skip)]] EDIT (expression
      |,expression|)(format item |,format item|);
e. PUT PAGE EDIT (expression |,expression|)
      (format item |,format item|);
f. PUT PAGE;
g. variable = expression;
h. GET SKIP [(cards to skip)];
i. GET [SKIP[(cards to skip)]] LIST (variable
      |,variable|);
j. GET [SKIP[(cards to skip)]] EDIT (variable
      |,variable|)(format item |,format item|);
k. IF condition THEN
      statement
   [ELSE
      statement]
l. DO WHILE (condition);
      |statement|
      END;
m. DO identifier=expression TO expression [BY expression];
      |statement|
      END;
n. DO;
      |statement|
      END;
o. CALL procedure name [(expression |,expression|)];
p. RETURN [(expression)];

PUT EDIT statements (forms d and e above) allow the
specification of a particular number of columns to be printed.
When successive items are printed via a PUT EDIT statement, each
item is printed immediately next to the preceding item. This is
in contrast to PUT LIST statements, which cause items to be
printed in equal fields across the page. GET EDIT statements
(form j above) are analogous and allow the specification of

particular card columns to be read. This means that EDIT data
items need not be separated by blanks.

It is possible to use both LIST directed input-output and
EDIT directed input-output in the same program. To avoid
confusion, LIST and EDIT directed input-output should not be
mixed in printing a particular line, or in reading a particular
card. Those who insist upon mixing the two for printing a
single line should understand the following details. LIST
output always proceeds to the next standard output field, while
EDIT output always starts at the current position. LIST output
actually prints a blank after each item; hence, when an EDIT
item follows a LIST item on a print line, the two will be
separated by a blank. Those who insist upon mixing LIST and
EDIT directed input when reading a single card should understand
the following details. Each LIST data item must be followed
immediately by a blank. If the next read is via a GET EDIT
statement, the current position is taken to be that just beyond
this blank. Following the reading of a data item via GET EDIT,
scanning for a LIST data item begins just beyond the EDIT item.

In the PUT SKIP forms (a, b, and d above), lines to skip can
be any numeric expression; if the value is float, it is
truncated to fixed. If the lines to skip clause is omitted from
the SKIP clause, then the remainder of the current line is left
blank and output continues on the next line.

If the value of lines to skip, call it x, is positive, then
the printer will return to column 1 while performing x line
ejects. Putting this another way, the remaining columns (if any)
of the current line will be left unchanged, and x-1 blank lines
will then be printed. If x is zero (or negative), the effect is
a return to column 1 of the current line (with no line eject).
Note: omitting the lines to skip clause, causes the default x=1
to be used.

In the GET SKIP forms (h, i, and j above), if the cards to
skip clause is omitted from the SKIP clause, the remainder of
the current card is ignored, and input continues from the next
card.

In the GET SKIP forms, cards to skip can be an expression. If
it is a float value, it is truncated to a fixed value. This
fixed value, call it x, must be at least 1. The next x cards
(where the remainder of the current card counts as one card)
will be ignored. Note: SKIP(1) is equivalent to SKIP with the
cards to skip clause omitted.

If a SKIP clause is specified and the current card or line is
positioned after the last valid data column, then one card or
line is counted as having been skipped by moving to the next
card or line even though there were no available data columns to
be skipped.

A *format* *item* is one of the following:

```
X(width)                              (to skip columns)
COLUMN(position)                      (to skip columns)
F(width [,fractional digits] )        (for numeric values)
E(width, fractional digits)           (for numeric values)
A[(width)]                            (for character strings)
B(width)                              (for logical values)
P picture specification               (to print dollars)
```

The X and COLUMN format items are used only for control of the format (skipping columns). The other format items, F, E, A, B, and P, are data transferring items. In the EDIT forms (d, e, and j above) there must be the same number of data transferring format items as there are data items to be transferred. The last format item of a list must be a data transferring item and can not be X or COLUMN.

The terms *position*, *width*, or *fractional* *digits* must be arithmetic expressions; usually these are fixed constants. If the value is float, it is truncated to a fixed value.

The format item X(width) causes *width* columns to be skipped on input, or *width* blanks to be printed on output. If *width* is negative it is treated as zero. (Note: punch cards have 80 columns. Lines have 120 columns on many printers; however, other printers may provide, for example, 72, 80 or 132 columns.)

The COLUMN format item causes skipping of columns until the column numbered *position* is reached. If *position* is zero or negative, or if *position* is greater than the size of the card or line, it is replaced by one. If the current card or line is already positioned after column *position*, a skip to the next card or line is performed, followed by skipping columns until the column numbered *position* is reached.

The F and E format items are used to read and write either FIXED and FLOAT variables.

For F and E format items on output, fractions are rounded and not truncated when insufficient space is allocated for the fractional digits. The values printed under control of F and E format items are right-justified and padded on the left with blanks.

On input, the F format item causes the next *width* columns to be read as a fixed number. If *fractional* *digits* is given in the format item, it must be at least one and it specifies the insertion of a decimal point the given number of places from the right of the number, producing a non-integer fixed constant; the effect is that if the decimal point is omitted from the data, scaling occurs. If *fractional* *digits* is omitted, the data is assumed to be an integer fixed constant. If a decimal point appears in the input data, then the actual value of the data is

used, ignoring the specified <u>fractional digits</u>. The number
being read may be preceded or followed by blanks. A completely
blank field is read as zero. (Note: when a non-integer fixed
constant is read into a FIXED variable, the value is truncated
to an integer.) On output, if <u>fractional digits</u> is not
specified, an integer is printed with no decimal point, but if
it is specified, a non-integer fixed constant is printed with
the designated precision of fraction. In no case does the F
format item cause scaling on output; note that integers always
have a zero-valued fraction.

The E format item on input causes the reading of a field of
size <u>width</u> containing a float constant. If a decimal point is
present in the float constant, the specification of <u>fractional</u>
<u>digits</u> is ignored. Otherwise, a decimal point is inserted
<u>fractional</u> <u>digits</u> from the right of the mantissa (the effect is
that if the decimal point is omitted in the data, scaling
occurs). If the field is completely blank, this is an error.
The exponent can be omitted from values read under control of
the E format item. On output, the number is printed as a float
constant. (Note: the <u>fractional digits</u> field must be specified
in the E format item.)

When using an E format item on output, the float value is
printed in the form mD.|f|Esdd where m is a possible leading
minus sign, D is a non-zero digit (unless the float value is
zero), |f| is the string of fractional digits, s is a plus or
minus sign, and dd is the exponent magnitude. The field width
must be at least large enough to print the float value. In
particular, the number of columns specified by <u>width</u> should be
at least seven plus <u>fractional digits</u>.

The A format item is used for the transfer of character data.
The specified number of characters are transferred. On input,
quotes are not required around the data item. On output, if the
field is wider than the data item, the item is left-justified
and padded with blanks on the right; if the field is not as wide
as the data item, the item is truncated on the right. On output
<u>width</u> can be omitted and then the current length of the data
item is used. (The <u>width</u> field must be specified for input.)

The B format item is used for transfer of logical (declared
BIT) data items. On input, the value can be preceded or followed
by blanks. On output, the value is printed left-justified and
padded on the right with blanks. Logical data values are 0 or 1
(not '0'B or '1'B as they are within a program and for LIST
input-output).

For format items F, E, A, and B, <u>width</u> must be greater than
zero.

The P format item is used for writing numbers, usually as
dollar values. Numbers cannot be read using the P format item.
Only FIXED values can be written using this format item. Each P
format item consists of the letter P followed by a sequence of

picture <u>elements</u> in quotes. For example, P'$ZZ,ZZ9.99DB' is a P
format item whose sequence of picture elements is $ZZ,ZZ9.99DB.
The following picture elements can be used.

<u>element</u>   <u>use</u>

.   period insertion
,   comma insertion
$ floating dollar sign
Z   digit position, suppress zero
9   digit position
CR   negative indicator
DB   negative indicator

These elements must appear in a picture specification in this
order. First, zero or more dollar signs with optional   periods
and commas.   Next, zero or more Zs with optional periods and
commas. Next, one or more 9s with optional periods and commas.
Finally, an optional CR or DB; this is printed for negative
numbers.

The period is printed where specified if a digit is to be
printed to its immediate left, otherwise a blank is printed.

(Note: since FIXED variables must have integer values in
SP/k, dollar values should be represented internally as cents.
When printing such a value, the decimal point for dollars can be
inserted using a period in a picture specification.)

Similarly, a comma is printed where specified if a digit is
to be printed to its immediate left, otherwise a blank is
printed.

The dollar sign indicates that a digit may be printed, unless
the digit is a leading zero in which case blank is printed,
except for the rightmost of a series of such dollar sign
positions, and here a dollar sign is printed. The dollar sign
will also "float" across commas and periods that are embedded in
a series of dollar signs.

The Z signifies printing of a digit unless it would be a
leading zero, in which case a blank is printed.

The nine signifies that a digit (0 to 9) is to be printed.

The credit symbol (CR) or debit symbol (DB) is printed only
if the number is negative. If a negative number is to be
printed, then DB or CR must be present.

The following is an example of the use of a picture format
item:

    PUT EDIT(21612)(P'$ZZ,ZZ9.99DB');

This statement will print $ʬʬʬ216.12ʬʬ (the symbol ʬ represents a blank). Now consider this statement:

    PUT EDIT(PROFIT)(P'$$,$$9.99DB');

This table gives the output for selected values of PROFIT:

PROFIT	output
259271	$2,592.71
39100	$391.00
2516	$25.16
5	$0.05
-481	$4.81DB

A.2.8 SP/8: Structures and Files

The form of declaration is extended to allow definition of structures and files.

A declaration is one of the following:

a. DECLARE (variable |,variable|)attribute
    |,(variable |,variable|)attribute|;
b. DECLARE 1 variable,
            2 variable attribute
            |,2 variable attribute|;
c. DECLARE 1 variable LIKE identifier;

Form b allows the definition of structures: an aggregate of several fields or data items. The fields can have different attributes, and can be arrays. Arrays of structures are defined by including ranges in the variable following the integer 1 in the declaration. Structures cannot contain other structures as fields and thus have only two levels.

Form c allows the definition of a structure or array of structures with the same template (field names and attributes) as another structure. The identifier must be a structure identifier. The newly-declared structure variable only inherits the template of identifier, not its dimensionality. If the structure variable is to represent an array, the ranges must be explicitly given. The structure referred to by LIKE must not itself have been declared using LIKE.

A field of a structure is always referred to by the name of its containing structure, followed by a period, followed by the field name. If either the structure or the field is an array, parenthesized subscripts must immediately follow the appropriate name(s).

The following is an example of a declaration of a structure:

```
DECLARE 1 OBSERVATION(100),
          2 TIME FIXED,
          2 SIZE FIXED;
```

Execution of the following statement assigns 12 to the TIME field of the 23rd element of the structure array:

```
OBSERVATION(23).TIME=12;
```

Structures can be read into, written from, assigned, and passed as parameters. No other operations can be performed on structures. One structure can be assigned to another only if one is LIKE the other or both are LIKE the same structure. Similarly, if a structure is passed as a parameter, the formal parameter that it corresponds to must be LIKE it, or they must both be LIKE the same structure.

Fields of structures can be used in LIST or EDIT input and output statements, but whole structures cannot be transferred by these statements.

An <u>attribute</u> is one of the following:

```
FIXED
FLOAT
CHARACTER (maximum length) VARYING
BIT
RECORD FILE
```

A variable with the attribute RECORD FILE allows access to a collection of records external to the main memory of the computer. A field of a structure cannot have the attribute RECORD FILE. This collection is called a <u>dataset</u> or <u>file</u>. Arrays of files are not allowed, and files cannot be assigned, compared, or passed as parameters. Each record corresponds to a structure. The data set consists of records with the same template. Some compilers restrict the name of a file to be at most seven characters long. One record at a time can be transferred from the dataset to a structure or from a structure to the dataset by using READ and WRITE statements, respectively.

The following statements are introduced:

```
a. OPEN  FILE(file name) INPUT;
b. OPEN  FILE(file name) OUTPUT;
c. CLOSE FILE(file name);
d. READ  FILE(file name) INTO(structure name);
e. WRITE FILE(file name) FROM(structure name);
```

The parenthesized file name following the keyword FILE in forms a to e must be an identifier that was declared with the attribute RECORD FILE.

Files allow sequential access to datasets. The OPEN statement
establishes a communication path between the file variable and
an external dataset. When an OPEN statement is executed, the
file is positioned at the first record of the dataset. An OPEN
must be the first operation performed on any file.

A file opened for INPUT can only have READ or CLOSE performed
on it. A file opened for OUTPUT can only have WRITE or CLOSE
performed on it.

The CLOSE statement dissolves the communication path between
the file variable and the associated external dataset. A file
can be closed and reopened in a program, and the mode (INPUT or
OUTPUT) is independent of previous usage of the file. Within a
given program, all structures transferred to and from a
particular file must be LIKE each other, or LIKE the same
structure.

The following SP/8 program reads a dataset into an array of
structures, sorts these structures into ascending order by TIME
and writes the sorted array to a new file.

```
1    SORT:PROCEDURE OPTIONS(MAIN);
2       DECLARE (NUMBER_OF_RECORDS) FIXED,
3          (I,J) FIXED;
4       DECLARE (INFILE,OUTFILE) RECORD FILE;
5       DECLARE 1 OBSERVATION(100),
6                2 TIME FIXED,
7                2 SIZE FIXED;
8       DECLARE 1 WORK_RECORD LIKE OBSERVATION;

9       /* READ IN THE UNSORTED STRUCTURES */
10      GET LIST(NUMBER_OF_RECORDS);
11      OPEN FILE(INFILE) INPUT;
12      DO I=1 TO NUMBER_OF_RECORDS;
13         READ FILE (INFILE) INTO (OBSERVATION(I));
14         END;
15      CLOSE FILE(INFILE);

16      /* SORT THE VECTOR OF STRUCTURES */
17      DO I=1 TO NUMBER_OF_RECORDS-1;
18         DO J=1 TO NUMBER_OF_RECORDS-I;
19            IF OBSERVATION(J).TIME>OBSERVATION(J+1).TIME THEN
20               DO;
21                  WORK_RECORD=OBSERVATION(J);
22                  OBSERVATION(J)=OBSERVATION(J+1);
23                  OBSERVATION(J+1)=WORK_RECORD;
24                  END;
25            END;
26         END;
```

```
27        /* WRITE OUT THE SORTED VECTOR */
28        OPEN FILE(OUTFILE)OUTPUT;
29        DO I=1 TO NUMBER_OF_RECORDS;
30            WRITE FILE(OUTFILE)FROM(OBSERVATION(I));
31            END;
32        CLOSE FILE(OUTFILE);

33        END;
```

Some PL/1 compilers such as PL/C do not support LIKE in declarations. To run under such a compiler, line 8 of the example program could be changed to:

```
DECLARE 1 WORK_RECORD,
          2 TIME FIXED,
          2 SIZE FIXED;
```

Some compilers such as PL/C do not allow READ and WRITE to transfer elements of an array of structures. To run under such a compiler, line 13 could be changed to:

```
READ FILE(INFILE) INTO(WORK_RECORD);
OBSERVATION(I)=WORK_RECORD;
```

Line 30 could be changed in a similar way.

Appendix A.3 Statement Syntax of SP/6

A job is: $JOBK
                     program
                    $DATA
                     [data]

A program is: identifier:PROCEDURE OPTIONS(MAIN);
                       |declaration|
                       |definition|
                       |statement|
                       END;

A declaration is: DECLARE(variable |,variable|)attribute
                       |,(variable |,variable|)attribute|;

An attribute is one of the following:
                    FIXED
                    FLOAT
                    CHARACTER(maximum length)VARYING
                    BIT

A definition is: identifier:PROCEDURE[(identifier |,identifier|)]
                       [RETURNS(attribute)];
                       |declaration|
                       |definition|
                       |statement|
                       END;

Notation: [item] means the item is optional.
          |item| means the item is repeated zero or more times.

A <u>statement</u> is one of the following:

```
            PUT [SKIP] LIST(expression |,expression| );
            PUT PAGE LIST(expression |,expression| );
            GET [SKIP] LIST(variable |,variable| );
            variable = expression;
            IF condition THEN
               statement
            [ELSE
               statement]
            DO WHILE(condition);
               |statement|
               END;
            DO identifier = expression TO expression
               [BY expression];
               |statement|
               END;
            DO;
               |statement|
               END;
            CALL procedure name [(expression |,expression|)]
            RETURN [(expression)];
```

Appendix A.4 Built-in Functions in SP/k

a.   An arithmetic built-in function.

     MOD(i,j):remainder of i divided by j; i and j must be
              fixed values and j must not be equal to zero.
              The result is fixed.

b.   Mathematical built-in functions.

     For these functions, the arguments may be float or fixed.
     The result is float.

     SIN(x) - sine of x radians.
     COS(X) - cosine of x radians.
     ATAN(x) - arctangent of x in radians.
     LOG(x) - natural logarithm of x.
     EXP(x) - e to the x power.
     SQRT(x) - square root of x.

c.   String built-in functions.

     LENGTH(s) - number of characters (currently) in string s.
     SUBSTR(s,i[,j]) - substring of s from i-th to last
              character [or from i-th character for a length of
              j characters].

   In SUBSTR, s must be a character string value; i [and j] must
be fixed or float; the result is a character string. The values
of i and j are truncated to fixed values. The substring selected
by i [and j] must be contained entirely within s.   This means
$i \geq 1$; $j \geq 0$; $0 \leq i+j-1 \leq \text{length}(s)$.   Otherwise there is an
error. Some compilers, such as PL/C, require that i must be at
most equal to the length of s. Other compilers, such as SP/k,
allow i to be one more than the length of s when j is zero or j
is omitted.

Appendix A.5 <u>The</u> <u>Toronto</u> SP/k <u>Compiler</u>

A compiler has been developed at the University of Toronto to support the SP/k language. Generally, an SP/k program that runs without errors under the SP/k compiler will run with the same results under other PL/1 compilers such as PL/C or the IBM PL/1 compilers.

As of summer 1976 there exist versions of the SP/k compiler that run on IBM 360/370 computers, Univac 90/30 computers, and Digital Equipment Corp., PDP-11 computers. Persons interested in obtaining an SP/k compiler should contact;

> SP/k Distribution Manager,
> 216 Sandford Fleming Building,
> Computer Systems Research Group,
> University of Toronto,
> Toronto, Ontario, Canada.

As of August 1976, these compilers support subsets SP/1 to SP/7. SP/8 is not yet implemented.

A.5.1 <u>SP/k</u> <u>JOB</u> <u>CARD</u> <u>PARAMETERS</u>

The first card of an SP/k job is called the job card, for example

    $JOBK ID='JAN STURGIS'

In some computer installations, the characters $JOB are not used, and are replaced by other characters. The ID parameter as shown in this example job card causes the name JAN STURGIS to be printed in a header box preceding the printing of the SP/k program. The three characters ID= are optional, so the above job card is equivalent to

    $JOBK 'JAN STURGIS'

Other parameters can be given on the job card, as we show in this example:

    $JOBK ID='BERT PATKAU',STMTS=10000,LINES=300

The parameter STMTS=10000 specifies that the job is to be
allowed to execute 10000 statements before being terminated for
excess running time. The parameter LINES=300 specifies that the
job is to be allowed to print, via PUT statements, 300 lines
before being terminated for excess lines. STMTS can be
abbreviated as S and LINES can be abbreviated as L. Individual
computer centers may have different job card parameters.

A.5.2 Handling Errors in SP/k Programs

When an error is found in an SP/k program, the SP/k compiler
generally makes an attempt to repair the error. The programmer
is warned that these repairs are not to be taken as intelligent
advice for producing a correct program, but instead as a method
of allowing processing to continue. This strategy of automatic
error repair is intended to minimize programmer frustration and
the number of required computer runs.

We will now show how a number of common errors are handled.
Since compilers are always being modified, the treatment of
these errors by a particular version of the SP/k compiler may
differ slightly from what we present.

Here is the listing of a simple SP/k program in which the
PROCEDURE OPTIONS(MAIN) line has been forgotten.

```
    1
      ?
****     SYNTAX ERROR IN PREVIOUS LINE.   LINE IS REPLACED BY:
    1 $NIL:PROCEDURE OPTIONS(MAIN);

    2     PUT LIST('HELLO');
    3     END;
```

As you can see, the missing line is supplied by the compiler and
the program is given the name $NIL. The program is executed and
prints HELLO.

If the programmer forgets a semicolon, the compiler is often
able to insert it, as is shown in the following listing:

```
    2     PUT LIST('HELLO')
                          ?
****     SYNTAX ERROR IN PREVIOUS LINE.   LINE REPLACED BY:
    2     PUT LIST('HELLO');
```

If the programmer forgets the right-hand quote mark of a
literal, the compiler inserts a quote mark, although probably
not in the desired place. In the following example, the quote
mark between the O of HELLO and the right parenthesis has been
omitted. The compiler inserts a quote mark after the semicolon.
As a result, the line requires a new right parenthesis and
semicolon because the original right parenthesis and semicolon

were absorbed into the literal. Note that the right quote mark
was not present on the card, but was inserted by the compiler.

```
    2      PUT LIST('HELLO); '
```

```
 ****      STRING IS ENDED WITH QUOTE(')
```

```
 ****      SYNTAX ERROR IN PREVIOUS LINE.  LINE IS REPLACED BY:
    2      PUT LIST('HELLO); ');
```

When this is executed, it will print HELLO); instead of HELLO.

    In the next example, a forgotten right parenthesis is
inserted by the compiler.

```
    2      PUT LIST('HELLO';
                            ?
 ****      SYNTAX ERROR IN PREVIOUS LINE.  LINE IS REPLACED BY:
    2      PUT LIST('HELLO');
```

In the next example, the keyword PROCEDURE has been misspelled.

```
    1 SAMPLE:PROCDEURE OPTIONS(MAIN);
                  ?
 ****      SYNTAX ERROR IN PREVIOUS LINE.  LINE IS REPLACED BY:
    1 SAMPLE:PROCEDURE OPTIONS(MAIN);
```

The following SP/k program does not make sense because it tries
to use the value of the variable named INCHES, but INCHES is
never given a value. This error is detected during execution of
the program. To allow the program to continue execution, INCHES
is given the value 1.

```
    1 SP2:PROCEDURE OPTIONS(MAIN);
    2      DECLARE(CENTIMETERS,INCHES)FLOAT;
    3      CENTIMETERS=2.54E0*INCHES;
    4      PUT LIST('LENGTH IS',CENTIMETERS);
    5      END /* SP2 */;
 ****ERROR IN LINE 3: FLOAT VARIABLE HAS NO VALUE; 1.0E+00 USED
 LENGTH IS        2.54000E+00
```

The next program attempts to read data items into two variables:
WIDTH and HEIGHT. The data as provided by the programmer
contains only one data item, so the program is stopped because
it attempts to read beyond the end of the data.

```
    1 SP2:PROCEDURE OPTIONS(MAIN);
    2      DECLARE(WIDTH,HEIGHT)FLOAT;
    3      GET LIST(WIDTH,HEIGHT);
    4      PUT LIST('AREA IS',WIDTH*HEIGHT);
    5      END /* SP2 */;
 ****ERROR IN LINE 3: NO MORE INPUT DATA
```

    The next program has WEIGHT misspelled as WIEGHT in line 4.
The compiler assumes (wrongly) that WEIGHT and WIEGHT are

different variables; fortunately, it warns us about its wrong
assumption. Note that the value of WEIGHT remains 7.5E0.

```
1 SP2:PROCEDURE OPTIONS(MAIN);
2    DECLARE(WEIGHT)FLOAT;
3    WEIGHT=7.5E0;
4    WIEGHT=2.2E0*WEIGHT;
5    PUT LIST('WEIGHT IS',WEIGHT);
6    END /* SP2 */;
****ERROR IN LINE 4: UNDECLARED VARIABLE ASSUMED FIXED
WEIGHT IS      7.50000E+00
```

In the next program, the values of NUMBER were not read
inside the loop. As the program now stands, there is an
infinite loop because NUMBER is not changed inside the loop.

```
1 SP3:PROCEDURE OPTIONS(MAIN);
2    DECLARE(NUMBER,SUM)FIXED;
3    SUM=0;
4    NUMBER=0;
5    DO WHILE(NUMBER¬=-99999);
6       SUM=SUM+NUMBER;
7       END;
8    PUT LIST('SUM IS',SUM);
9    END /* SP3 */;
****ERROR IN LINE 6: EXECUTION LIMIT EXCEEDED
```

The next program tries to find the last name of Bill
McKeeman, but since the name McKeeman contains 8 and not 9
letters, the substring does not lie within the string.

```
1 SP4:PROCEDURE OPTIONS(MAIN);
2    DECLARE(NAME,LAST_NAME) CHARACTER(20) VARYING;
3    NAME='BILL MCKEEMAN';
4    LAST_NAME=SUBSTR(NAME,6,9);
5    PUT LIST('LAST NAME IS',LAST_NAME);
6    END /* SP4 */;
****ERROR IN LINE 4: SPECIFIED SUBSTRING NOT WITHIN STRING
LAST NAME IS   ?
```

In the next program array NAME contains elements NAME(1:4).
The program is supposed to read four names followed by the dummy
name ZZZ. When the program runs, there is an error because an
attempt is made to read ZZZ into the non-existant element
NAME(5). The error can be corrected by increasing the declared
upper bound of NAME to 5.

```
 1 SP5:PROCEDURE OPTIONS(MAIN);
 2   DECLARE(NAME(4))CHARACTER(20)VARYING;
 3   DECLARE(I)FIXED;
 4   I=1;
 5   GET LIST(NAME(I));
 6   DO WHILE(NAME(I)¬='ZZZ');
 7      PUT LIST(NAME(I));
 8      I=I+1;
 9      GET LIST(NAME(I));
10      END;
11   END; /* SP5 */;
****ERROR IN LINE 9: SUBSCRIPT OUT OF RANGE;  LOWER BOUND USED
```

A.5.3 Characteristics of the SP/k Compiler

The various compilers for PL/1 differ in their treatment of certain constructs of the PL/1 language. Generally, conservative use of these constructs results in programs that work well under most of the compilers. In this section we list limits of the SP/k compiler and those language aspects that it may handle in its own particular way.

Error Recovery. A large number of errors in programs will be automatically "repaired".

Card boundaries. Identifiers, keywords, constants and comments may not cross card boundaries in a program. Constants read by GET LIST may not cross card boundaries. If a constant uses the last columns of one card and another constant uses the first columns of the next card, the two constants are read separately.

Use of card columns for programs. When a program is prepared using punch cards, all 80 columns are used.

Two character operators. This compiler does not in general enforce the convention that blanks may not be embedded in two character operators such as >=. (In fact, it allows blanks in >=, <= and ¬= but not in ||.)

Length of identifiers. Identifiers can be at most 31 characters long.

Width of print fields. For printers with 120 or 132 columns, there are 5 fields per print line with 24 columns per field. For printers with 72 or 80 columns, there are 5 fields per line with 14 columns per field.

Form of printed numbers. Each fixed or float value printed by a PUT LIST statement is right-justified in the first 12

columns of the next print field. Float values are printed in
the form mD.dddddEsdd where m is an optional minus sign, D is a
non-zero digit, each d is a digit, and s is a plus or minus
sign. (Exception: D is zero when the float value is zero.)

Range of fixed values. Fixed values have a maximum magnitude
of 999999999.

Non-integer fixed constants. Non-integer fixed constants,
e.g., 214.8, are flagged as errors in programs and are
automatically converted to float. Non-integer fixed constants
are accepted (without error messages) in data.

Range of float values. Float values have a maximum magnitude
of 1.00000E+36.

Precision of float arithmetic. Float arithmetic is accurate
to approximately 6 significant figures.

Length of character strings. Character strings can be at
most 127 characters long.

Definition before use. The definition of a procedure must
appear before its invocation. (Calling a following procedure
which has the same name and parameter attributes as a global
procedure will result in a call to the global procedure instead
of a call to the following procedure; no error message will be
issued.)

Checks for recursion. Any procedure (except the main
procedure) can be called recursively; the RECURSIVE attribute is
neither required nor permitted.

Conversion of arguments. Conversion of fixed scalar
arguments to float scalar formal parameters (and vice versa) is
automatic and creates a dummy argument.

Dummy arguments. Arguments preceded by a unary plus or
enclosed in parentheses will have a dummy argument created.
Assignment of a value to a parameter having a dummy argument
does not change the value of the actual argument.

Division of fixed values. Division of fixed values, for
example 7/3, results in an error message, and the truncated
value of the quotient is used.

Collating sequence. The version of the SP/k compiler that
runs on the IBM 360/370 has IBM standard (EBCDIC) order of
characters for comparisons:

b-.<(+|&!$*);¬-/,%_>?:#@'="ABCDEFGHIJKLMNOPQRSTUVWXYZ0123456789

The version of the SP/k compiler that runs on the DEC PDP-11 has
the international standard (ASCII) order of characters for
comparisons:

ƀ|#$%ε'()*+,-./0123456789:;<=>?@ABCDEFGHIJKLMNOPQRSTUVWXYZ_¬

Since the characters | and ¬ are not standard ASCII characters,
they are printed as the exclamation point and the caret.

Reserved words. The following SP/k keywords must not be
used as names of variables or procedures. In addition, no
identifier should begin with the characters $JOB.

BIT	ELSE	INPUT	PAGE	THEN
BY	END	INTO	PROCEDURE	TO
CALL	FILE	LIKE	PUT	VARYING
CHARACTER	FIXED	LIST	READ	WHILE
CLOSE	FLOAT	MAIN	RECORD	WRITE
DECLARE	FROM	OPEN	RETURN	$DATA
DO	GET	OPTIONS	RETURNS	$JOB
EDIT	IF	OUTPUT	SKIP	

A.5.4 Acknowledgements

The design of SP/k has been the result of work with many
people. Valuable suggestions have been provided by T. Hull, J.
Horning, C. Phillips, D. Corneil, K. Sevcik and many others.
The SP/k compiler implementation team consisted of R.C. Holt,
D.B. Wortman, D. Barnard , J. Cordy, M. Fox, and K. Fysh and was
assisted by B. Clark, F. Ham, and B. Patkau.

SP/k and PL/I BIBLIOGRAPHY

1. Holt, R. C., "Teaching the Fatal Disease (or) Introductory Computer Programming Using PL/1", Assoc. for Computing Machinery SIGPLAN Notices, 8, 5 (May 1973) 8-23.

2. Conway, R. and Gries, D., "An Introduction to Programming: A Structured Approach Using PL/1 and PL/C-7", Winthrop Publishers, Cambridge, Mass., 1976 (2nd edition).

3. Conway, R.W. and Wilcox, T.R., "Design and Implementation of a Diagnostic Compiler for PL/1", Communications of the ACM, March 1973.

4. IBM System 360 PL/1 Reference Manual, Form C28-8201.

5. IBM PL/1 Language Specifications, Form C28-6571.

6. Pollack, S.V. and Sterling, T.D., A Guide to PL/1, Holt Rinehart Winston, 1969.

7. IBM: OS PL/1 Checkout and Optimizing Compilers. Language Reference Manual, Form SC33-0009-2.

8. ECMA.TC10/ANSI.X3J1 (European Computer Manufacturers Association and American National Standards Institute), "PL/1 Basis/1-11", February 1974.

9. Wortman, D.B., "Student PL - A PL/1 Dialect Designed for Teaching", Proceedings of Canadian Computer Conference, Montreal, June 1972.

10. Holt, R. C. and Wortman, D. B., "Structured Subsets of the PL/1 Language", Technical Report CSRG-55, Computer Systems Research Group, University of Toronto, October 1973.

11. Hume, J.N.P. and Holt, R.C., Structured Programming using PL/1 and SP/k, Reston Publishers, September 1975.

12. Conway, R.; Gries, D. and Wortman, D.B., An Introduction to Structured Programming using PL/1 and SP/k, Winthrop Publishers, 1976.

13. Barnard, D. T., "Automatic Generation of Error-Repairing and Paragraphing Parsers", Technical Reeport CSRG-52, Computer Systems Research Group, University of Toronto, April 1975.

15. Cordy, J. R., A Diagramatic Approach to Programming Language Semantics, Technical Report CSRG-67, Computer Systems Research Group, University of Toronto, March 1976.

APPENDIX B   Summary of PL/I

This appendix attempts to give a concise, readable definition of the important parts of PL/I. It is included in this book as an aid to to the programmer who has learned SP/k and wants to explore full PL/I. As you will learn from reading this Appendix, full PL/I is a very large and intricate language that will take considerable effort to learn. The SP/k subset of PL/I was designed to allow an easy introduction to programming in PL/I while omitting most of its complexities. SP/k includes only those PL/I statements described in Appendix A.

Describing the full PL/I language is difficult, since the original IBM System 360 PL/I (F) Language Manual, File No. GC28-8201, (herein referred to as IBMFM) is 455 pages long. Naturally we cannot describe all of PL/I carefully, completely, and with examples. We have concentrated on those features which we feel are most useful in programming. Others are listed and perhaps explained, but in less detail. Occasionally we omit a form of a statement or attribute because it is not needed; its usefulness is low, relative to the space needed to describe it.

The reader must have some knowledge of programming. This part of the book is intended as reference material, rather than an introduction. It was, however, designed with the beginner in mind. For example, for procedure definitions we show a simple form, and then later the complete form. The beginner will need to read only Appendices B.1 and B.2, B.3 on statements (just the few statements he needs to know), the simple form of the declaration given in Appendix B.4, and Appendix B.6 on variables, scope of names and the like.

Appendix B.1 <u>Conventions</u>

We use a different terminology than is typically used for PL/I. IBMFM calls END, BEGIN, and other such entities "statements". We feel this is misleading and makes the language description longer and more difficult to read. An algorithm is a sequence of statements (or commands) which, when executed, produce a desired result. A <u>program</u> in PL/I, which represents an algorithm, should consist of a sequence of executable statements, with comments, headings, and declarations to describe the entities the statements work on.

Thus we reserve the term "statement" for an entity which is to be executed, usually in sequence. We should be able to describe how to execute a particular kind of statement out of context; that is, knowing only the attributes of variables that it manipulates, but not knowing what statement precedes or follows it.

In describing the syntax of statements and declarations we use the following notation:

1. Square brackets [and] surround an option -- something that may be omitted if desired. For example, if the construct form is

    identifier [(exp)];

then it may be used in either of the forms

    identifier;   or   identifier(exp);

Similarly, identifier [(exp [, exp])] ; permits the possibilities

    identifier;   identifier(exp);   and identifier(exp,exp);

2. Braces | and | enclose a term that may occur 0, 1, 2, 3 or more times. For example, the form

    CALL entry-name [(argument |, argument|)] ;

means that the statement can look like

```
          CALL entry-name ;
or        CALL entry-name(argument);
or        CALL entry-name(argument, argument);
or        CALL entry-name(argument, argument, argument);
etc.
```

3. Words in capital letters are PL/I keywords (e.g. BEGIN and END). They should not be used for any other purpose. See Appendix B.2.

4. Terms in small letters denote general classes of elements in the language. The less-used ones will be described where they appear. The more important ones, together with their meanings, are given below:

array-ref   A reference to an array or a cross section of an array (e.g. C or C(*,2)).

attribute   A property or characteristic of a name which helps determine how the name is to be used. Examples are FIXED, BINARY, and RECURSIVE. Attributes are listed and described in Appendix B.5.

constant   Constants are described in Appendix B.2.

declaration PL/I declarations are described in Appendix B.4.

entry-name An identifier used to define an entry point in a procedure. See "Procedure definition" in Appendix B.4.

exp   Any PL/I expression.

file-name   An identifier used to name an input-output file.

label   An identifier used to label a statement.

ON-unit   A substatement of an ON statement. See the ON statement in Appendix B.3.

procedure definition   A procedure; it is described in Appendix B.4.

statement   Any one of the PL/I executable statements described in Appendix B.3. The BEGIN block, Compound statement, IF statement, Iterative statement (loop) and ON statement are "complex" statements, since they contain other statements as part of them. All others are called "simple" statements.

<u>structure-ref</u>   A reference to a structure or part of a
structure.

<u>variable-name</u>   The name of a variable. For a simple
variable this is just the identifier used to name it.
For a subscripted variable this is the identifier
followed by a (, followed by the constant subscripts
separated by commas, followed by a).   For example,
A(1) and B(2,3), but <u>not</u> A(I) and B(2,K).

   A variable name can also be a qualified name
yielding part of a structure (e.g. X.Y.P).

<u>variable-ref</u>

1.A reference to a simple or subscripted variable.

2.   A reference to an array.

3. A so-called "pseudo-variable", which is sometimes
used to reference <u>part</u> of a value of a variable, or
the whole value but in an unconventional way.   These
are: SUBSTR, COMPLEX, IMAG, REAL, and UNSPEC.

4.   A cross section of an array (e.g. C(*,2)).

5. A qualified name, which refers to part of a
structure (e.g. X.Y   B(I).Z).

Appendix B.2 <u>Preliminary</u> <u>Definitions</u>

A <u>program</u> in PL/I has the following form:

  entry-name : PROCEDURE OPTIONS(MAIN);
             |declaration|
             |procedure definition|
             |statement|
             END entry-name ; -

The two entry-names must be the same. The declarations (see Appendix B.4) describe the variables used in the program. The statements are the algorithmic part of the program; they are executed, generally in the order they appear, to produce results. The procedure definitions define other subprograms that the statements can invoke to perform specific subtasks.

The statements of the program refer to and manipulate simple variables, arrays, labels of statements, and so forth. Statements are described in Appendix B.3.

A <u>job</u> submitted to the computer consists of a program, together with data to be read by the program and any necessary control cards. For SP/k jobs, see Appendices A.3 and A.5.

<u>Identifiers</u> <u>and</u> <u>Keywords</u>

An identifier is a single alphabetic character (A through Z, $, #, and @) possibly followed by 1 to 30 alphanumeric characters and/or break characters. The alphanumeric characters are the alphabetic characters and the digits 0 through 9. The break character is the underline character "_".

Examples: B FILE3 $21 @ PRICE_PER_DOZEN

A keyword is an identifier that, when used in the proper context, has a specific meaning. In PL/I keywords are not reserved and can be used as names of variables, etc. (although it is not wise to do so). In SP/k however, the keywords are reserved and may not be used as identifiers. The SP/k keywords are listed in Appendix A.5.2.

<u>Use</u> <u>of</u> <u>Blanks</u>

Except for the following cases, blanks may appear <u>anywhere</u> and have no particular meaning.

1. They may <u>not</u> appear between adjacent characters of an identifier, keyword, constant, or composite symbol (one made up of two characters, like /* and **).

2. One or more blanks <u>must</u> separate adjacent identifiers, keywords, and/or constants.

3. Within a character string constant, a blank is treated as any other character. Thus 'A BC' is the string consisting of an A followed by a blank followed by a B followed by a C.

Comments

A comment has the form

/*   any sequence of characters   */

where the sequence of characters may <u>not</u> include "*/". A comment has no effect on execution of the program, and is used only to make the program more understandable. A comment is permitted wherever a blank is permitted (except in a character string) and is logically equivalent to a blank.

In SP/k, a comment must fit on one card -- it may not extend to two or more cards..

Constants

In PL/I the following kinds of constants can be used:

1. A decimal fixed point constant. Examples are: 831   003 .0016 391.416

2. A decimal floating point constant. Examples are: 18E-2 4E+30 .001E6

3. An imaginary decimal number. This is a decimal fixed or floating point number followed directly by "I". Examples are: 18E-2I   003I

4. True, or false, which in PL/I must be written as '1'B and '0'B respectively. (They are <u>bit</u> <u>strings</u>.)

5. A <u>literal</u>, which is a quote ' followed by a sequence of characters, followed by a quote '. Examples are 'SIN TABLE' 'ABCD*$.' and '' (the null string). The characters within the quotes can be any punchable characters, including a blank. A quote to be placed in a string constant must be punched twice. Thus, 'A''B' is the string constant whose three characters are A, ', and B, in that order.

One can specify that a string is to be repeated several times. For example, (3)'AB' is shorthand for the string constant 'ABABAB'. (3) is called the "string repetition factor". String repetition cannot be used in SP/k.

6. A binary fixed point constant, which is like a decimal fixed point constant except that only the digits 0 and 1 may be used, and that the character B must directly follow the number. Examples are: 1011100B .0010B, and 1.10B, whose decimal values are 92, 0.125 and 1.5.

7. A binary floating point constant, which is a binary fixed point number, followed by E, followed by an optionally signed decimal integer exponent, followed by B. The exponent specifies a power of 2. Examples are: 1011E-31B 1.10E2B (which is equivalent to .110E3B)

8. An imaginary binary number. This is a binary fixed or floating point number followed directly by I. Examples are: 0.1BI 100001000E+200BI

9. A bit string constant. This is a sequence of 0's and 1's enclosed in quotes and followed by B. A repetition factor may be used as for character string constants. In SP/k the only allowable bit string constants are '0'B and '1'B; repetition factors are not allowed. Examples are: '1'B '0'B '00000'B ''B.

10. A label constant. Labels may be assigned to label variables as values.

462

Appendix B.3 Executable Statements

We present here the commands, or executable statements of PL/I, in alphabetical order. Each statement described in this Appendix can be optionally preceded by a series of labels, which serve to name that statement:

⏐label :⏐ statement

The new student will be interested only in

1. "Assignment to scalars"
2. "Compound statement"
3. "IF statement"
4. "Iterative statements (loops)"
5. "PUT LIST" and "GET LIST"

Declarations are discussed in Appendix B.4.

When looking at the explanation of these statements, make sure you understand the notation and definitions discussed in Appendices B.1 and B.2. You will find material in these discussions which you do not need; this must happen if we are to explain the full language here. You must therefore read with a discerning eye, and skip what is not necessary for you to learn. For example, when reading about GET LIST, you will find that there are three forms of the GET statement. Since you are only interested in GET LIST, don't even look at the form and discussion of the others. Next, the first paragraph of the discussion of GET has to do with the "input" part of the statement. After reading half the paragraph you will note that leaving out "input" means that the data following the $DATA card will be used as input. This is all you need to know, so there is no reason for you to read the rest of that paragraph.

Several PL/I statements are not described here, because they are not in SP/k, or because they are beyond the scope of this book. These are:

1. Statements used to give control over storage allocation to the programmer. These are: ALLOCATE and FREE.

2. Statements dealing with "parallel processing" or "multi-tasking": DELAY, UNLOCK, and WAIT.

3. Some statements used for "record" input-output. In addition, normal input-output on files other than the

standard ones is not explained in full detail. The record
I/O statements are: DELETE, LOCATE, and REWRITE.

4. The DISPLAY statement, which is used to communicate
with the computer operator.

5. The FORMAT statement.

See IBMFM for complete details on these, and other details we
have left out because of space restrictions.

<u>Assignment statement</u>   There are three forms of the assignment
    statement.   These   are   discussed   separately   under
    "Assignment to scalars" (the conventional one), "Assignment
    to arrays", and "Assignment to structures".

<u>Assignment to arrays</u>

    Form: array-ref ¦, array-ref¦ = exp [, BY NAME] ;

        where exp is a scalar expression or an array
        expression. The arrays referenced and any array
        operands of the expression must have the same number
        of dimensions and identical bounds.

    Execution: This is <u>not</u> executed as a conventional
        assignment statement. The expression is <u>not</u> first
        evaluated and then assigned to the arrays referenced.
        Instead, the assignment statement is executed as if it
        were a number of nested loops (the number depending on
        the number of dimensions of the arrays) which
        evaluates an expression and assigns to one array
        element at a time, in row-major order. For example,
        suppose A(1:20,1:40) is an array. The statement A
        = A / A(1,1); is executed as if it were

                DO I = 1 TO 20 BY 1;
                   DO J = 1 TO 40 BY 1;
                      A(I,J) = A(I,J)/A(1,1);
                      END;
                   END;

        This execution first changes A(1,1) to 1, and then
        leaves the rest of the array elements unchanged since
        A(1,1)=1.   As another example, A = 5*A(1,1); is
        executed as if it were

                DO I = 1 TO 20 BY 1;
                   DO J = 1 TO 40 BY 1;
                      A(I,J) = 5*A(1,1);
                      END;
                   END;

The statement inside the generated loops will be a
scalar or structure assignment statement; in the
latter case it will be further expanded as described
under "Assignment to structures". If the original
array assignment has BY NAME appended to it, then so
will the generated statement inside the loops (this is
used for assignment to structures).

Assignment to scalar variables

Form: variable-ref |, variable-ref| = exp ;

The variable-refs must reference scalar variables;
evaluation of the expression must yield a scalar
value.

Execution: the statement is executed as follows:

1. The variables referenced are determined in
left to right order. This means evaluating
subscripts, etc.

2. The expression is evaluated.

3. The value of the expression is assigned to the
variables determined in step 1, in left to right
order. The value is converted, if necessary,
to the characteristics of each variable
according to the rules given in Appendix B.6.

If the variable-ref is a fixed length string, the
string exp is truncated on the right if too long or
padded on the right (with blanks for character strings
and zeros for bit strings) if too short. If the
variable-ref is a VARYING string and the value of the
expression is longer than the maximum length allowed,
the value is truncated to this maximum length and
assigned. Otherwise the length of the variable-ref
is changed to the length of the value.

SP/k Restriction: No implied conversion between string,
bit, and arithmetic data is performed. Thus if I
is fixed, I='23'; is invalid.

Assignment to structures

Form 1: structure-ref |, structure-ref| = exp ;

All structure-refs must have the same number k (say)
of immediately contained items. The exp must yield a
scalar or a structure value. All structure operands
of the expression must have exactly k immediately
contained items.

Execution: this is not a conventional assignment statement. The expression is <u>not</u> evaluated and then assigned. Instead, the statement is executed as if it were k simpler assignment statements. The ith one is derived from the original assignment statement by replacing each structure operand and reference by its ith contained item. For example, suppose we have

```
1 ONE                     1 TWO
   2 PART1                    2 PART3
      3 RED                      3 RED
      3 WHITE                    3 WHITE
   2 PART2                    2 PART4
```

The assignment statement ONE=TWO+2; is executed like the two assignments below. Note that the first is still a structure assignment statement, while the second is a scalar assignment.

```
ONE.PART1 = TWO.PART3 + 2;
ONE.PART2 = TWO.PART4 + 2;
```

Form 2: structure-ref ¦, structure-ref¦ = exp, BY NAME;

The exp must be a structure expression.

Execution: Execution is equivalent to execution of the assignment statements generated by the following rule: Each immediate item of the leftmost structure-ref is examined in turn, as follows:

> If each structure-ref and each structure operand has an immediately contained item with the same identifier as the item being examined, an assignment statement is generated. It is derived by replacing each structure operand and reference with its immediately contained item that has that identifier. If the generated statement is a structure or array of structures, then BY NAME is appended.

For example suppose we have the structures

```
1 ONE                     1 TWO
   2 PART1                    2 PART1
      3 RED(30)                  3 RED(30)
      3 BLUE                     3 WHITE
   2 PART2                      3 BLUE
```

The assignment statement ONE = TWO + 2 * ONE, BY NAME; is evaluated as if it were

```
ONE.PART1 = TWO.PART1 + 2 * ONE.PART1, BY NAME;
```

which in turn is evaluated as if it were the two
statements below. Note that the first statement below
is an array assignment statement.


```
ONE.PART1.RED = TWO.PART1.RED + 2 * ONE.PART1.RED;
ONE.PART1.BLUE= TWO.PART1.BLUE+ 2 * ONE.PART1.BLUE;
```

BEGIN block

Form: |label:|
      BEGIN
          |declaration|
          |procedure definition|
          |statement|
          END [label];

The label following the END (if it appears) must be
the same as one of the labels preceding the BEGIN. Be
careful; the PL/I rules state that if a label follows
the END, any ENDs missing from within the block will
be automatically inserted, without warning, just
before the block END. Therefore, omit no ENDs.

PL/I also allows the declarations, statements, and
procedure definitions to be intermixed, but it is a
good practice to keep them separated.

Execution: The variables declared and the procedures
    defined may be referenced by their names only while
    executing the block. For more on scope rules, see
    Appendix B.6.1. The BEGIN block is executed as
    follows:

        1.Variables are created and initialized
        according to the declarations.

        2.The statements in the block are executed in
        order.

        3.The variables created in step 1 are destroyed.

    See also the GO TO and RETURN statements.

CALL statement

Form: CALL entry-name [(argument |, argument|)] ;

Each argument can be a variable, constant, expression,
file-name, label, label variable, entry-name or
mathematical built-in function. The number of

arguments must be the same as the number of parameters specified at the definition of the entry-name.

SP/k Restriction: Scalars may not be used as arguments for array or structure parameters.

Execution:

> 1.A correspondence is set up between parameters and arguments, as described in Appendix B.6.5.

> 2. The variables of the procedure determined by the entry-name are created.

> 3.The sequence of statements of the procedure, beginning at the entry point defined by entry-name, is executed, until the last one has been executed or until a RETURN is executed. When a parameter is referenced, it refers to the corresponding argument. The parameter is <u>not</u> a variable and never contains a value of its own.

> 4.The variables created in step 2 are destroyed.

See also the GO TO statement.

CLOSE statement

Form: CLOSE FILE(file-name)⎨,FILE(file-name)⎬ ;

Execution: Execution causes the files designated to be closed; the file-name is disassociated from the data set with which it was associated upon opening. The file can be reopened. A CLOSE need not be executed for each file, since all files are automatically closed upon termination of the program. Closing an unopened file has no effect. For more information, see IBMFM.

Compound statement

Form: ⎨label :⎬
     DO;
        ⎨statement⎬
     END [label];

The label following the END (if it appears) must be the same as one of the labels preceding the DO. Be careful; the PL/I rules state that if a label follows the END, any ENDs missing from within the compound statement will automatically be inserted, without warning, just before the compound statement END. Therefore omit no ENDs.

Execution: The statements are executed, in order. See also
the GO TO and RETURN statements.

DECLARE, This is not a statement, but a declaration or
specification. See Appendix B.4.

Conditional statement   See "IF statement".

DO   See "Compound statement" and "Iterative statement".

ENTRY   ENTRY is not a statement. See "Procedure definition"
(Appendix B.4) for the use of the ENTRY definition in
specifying multiple entry points. See the ENTRY attribute
(Appendix B.5) for the use of an ENTRY attribute.

GET statement

Form1:GETLIST(variable-ref|,variable-ref|)   [input]
                        [SKIP[(exp)]] [COPY] ;

Form2:GETEDIT(variable-ref|,variable-ref|)format   [input]
                        [SKIP[(exp)]] [COPY] ;

Form3:GET DATA   [input] [SKIP[(exp)]] [COPY] ;

Execution of all of these has to do with reading in or
skipping data. "input" is usually left out, which
means that the data are read from the standard input
file SYSIN (that is, the data are taken from the cards
following the $DATA card.) If "input" has the form
"FILE(file-name)" then the data are taken from that
file. If "input" has the form "STRING(variable-ref)"
then the variable-ref must be to a string variable.
In this case, the data are taken from this string,
beginning with the first character. This is useful in
changing data previously read from character to
arithmetic form.

The presence of COPY causes the data to be written
onto the standard print file, as read. This is useful
for debugging purposes. COPY may only be present if
"input" is not STRING.

SKIP is equivalent to SKIP(1). SKIP may not be
used when the "input" is STRING.

The order of the various options "input", SKIP and
COPY is immaterial; they may also be placed just after
the keyword GET and before LIST, EDIT, or DATA.

Execution:
1.If SKIP(exp) is present, the exp is evaluated and
converted to yield an integer w. If w < 1, w is set
to 1. w records (usually cards) are then skipped on

the input file. (If in the middle of a record, the
rest of the record is skipped; this counts as 1 skip).

2. The data are read into the variables specified,
depending on the Form used, as described below. The
difference lies in the format of the input data being
read.

Form 1: GET LIST(variable-ref |, variable-ref|)

    Constants are read and assigned to the
variables in the list, in left to right order.
Any necessary conversion occurs exactly as in an
assignment statement.

    The input must consist of constants separated
by a comma and/or one or more blanks. Each
constant is a signed or unsigned number (e.g.
-32), a character string (e.g. 'AB C'), a bit
string (e.g. '1'B), or a complex constant (e.g.
32-21I).

    If the variable-ref is an array or structure,
constants are read and assigned to each element
of the array or structure, in order. For arrays,
this is done in row-major order. For example,
for an array A(1:2,1:2), the assignment proceeds
in the order A(1,1), A(1,2), A(2,1), A(2,2).

Form 2: GET EDIT (variable-ref |, variable-ref|)
                       format

    The data are read and stored into the
variables using the format. See Appendix B.9 on
formats. The variables are assigned in the same
order described for GET LIST.

Form 3: GET DATA

    The input must have the form

      variable-name = constant |,variable-name =
                    constant ;

One or more blanks may be used in place of, or
together with, the comma. In effect, the input
looks like a sequence of assignment statements.
The variable-names may be names of simple or
subscripted variables. A qualified name must be
fully qualified. The constants have the form
described in GET LIST. The constants are
assigned to the variables, which of course must
be referenceable at the point where the GET DATA
statement appears.

For example, if the data contains

A(1)=3 B= 21 C(1,3)='AB' ;

then 3 is assigned to A(1), 21 to B and the string 'AB' to C(1,3).

GO TO statement

Form: GO TO label ;   or   GO TO variable-reference ;

"GOTO" may be used in place of "GO TO".

Execution: Statements are usually executed in the order in which they occur. This normal sequencing can be changed by executing a GO TO. Control is transferred to the statement labeled "label", or to the label which is the current value of the variable-reference. Execution cannot cause a transfer into an inactive block (one not currently being executed), or into a loop from outside the loop.

Execution causes the termination of any BEGIN block, procedure, IF statement, or compound statement whose scope does not include the target of the jump. This termination occurs just as if the block or procedure were exited normally, in the sense that all variables created at the beginning of the procedure or block are destroyed.

END   See "BEGIN block", "Compound statement", "Iterative statement", and "Procedure definition".

IF statement   Form: IF exp THEN
                     statement[1]
                   [ELSE
                     statement[2]]

The exp must yield a scalar value. IF statements can be nested. If so, an ELSE belongs with the closest possible preceding THEN. For example,

IF exp^1 THEN
   IF exp^2 THEN
      s^1
   ELSE
      s^2

is equivalent to

IF exp^1 THEN
   IF exp^2 THEN
      s^1

```
        ELSE
            S²
      ELSE
        ;
```

SP/k Restriction: The exp must yield true or false ('0'B or '1'B).

Execution:
1. The expression is evaluated to yield a value. This value is usually "true" ('1'B) or "false" ('0'B); if not, it is converted to a bit string (in SP/k it <u>must</u> be a logical value, no conversion is performed).

2. If the result of step 1 is true ('1'B or a bit string which contains at least one bit which is '1'B) then statement^1 is executed; otherwise statement^2 is executed if it is present.

<u>Iterative</u> <u>statement</u> <u>(loop)</u>

Form 1: |label:|
```
        DO WHILE (exp);
            |statement|
        END [label];
```

The label following the END (if it appears) must be the same as one of the labels preceding the DO. Be careful; the PL/I rules state that if a label follows the END, any ENDs missing from within the loop will automatically be inserted, without warning, just before the loop END. Therefore omit no ENDs.

Execution: This is exactly equivalent to execution of

```
        L1: IF exp THEN
                DO;
                    |statement|
                    GO TO L1;
                END;
```


Form 2: |label:| DO variable-ref = exp^1 TO exp^2 [BY exp^3]
```
                        [WHILE(exp⁴)] ;
                    |statement|
                    END [label];
```

The remarks about the label following the END for Form 1 apply here also. If "BY exp^3" is missing, "BY 1" is implied. "TO exp^2 BY exp^3" may also be written as "BY exp^3 TO exp^2".

Execution: Let V1, V2, and V3 be variables with the type attributes of exp^1, exp^2, and exp^3 respectively, which are not used elsewhere in the program. Execution is exactly equivalent to executing the sequence:

Determine variable-ref -- say it is to variable VAR;

```
        V1 = exp¹;
        V2 = exp²;
        V3 = exp³;
        VAR = V1;
    LOOP:
        IF(V3 >= 0) & (VAR>V2) THEN
            GO TO NEXT;
        IF (V3<0) & (VAR<V2) THEN
            GO TO NEXT;
    WHILETEST:
        IF ¬(exp⁴) THEN
            GO TO NEXT;
        |statement|
        VAR = VAR + V3;
        GO TO LOOP;
    NEXT:;
```

where if "WHILE (exp^4)" is missing, statement WHILETEST is deleted.

Form 3: |label :| DO variable-ref = spec |, spec| ;
                     |statement|
                     END [label];

The remarks given for Form 1 about the label following the END apply here also. Each spec (specification) has the following form (see Form 2):

exp^1 TO exp^2 [BY exp^3] [WHILE exp^4]

Execution: This is exactly equivalent to executing the following sequence of loops, where variable-ref and |statement| are as above, and the superscript on the specs denote the order of the specifications above:

```
        DO variable-ref = spec¹ |statement| END;
        DO variable-ref = spec² |statement| END;
        DO variable-ref = spec³ |statement| END;
                        . . .
```


Null statement   Form: ;

Execution: Execution of the null statement does nothing.

ON statement

Form 1: ON condition [SNAP] SYSTEM ;
Form 2: ON condition [SNAP] ON-unit

The possible conditions are given in Appendix B.7.
The ON-unit may be any unlabeled statement except a
compound, iterative, IF, RETURN, or another ON
statement. It may be an unlabeled BEGIN block.

Execution: Execution of an ON statement indicates how an
interrupt for the specified condition is to be
handled. If Form 1 is used, or if no ON statement has
been executed for a certain condition, the standard
system action is taken. This is usually to print an
error message and stop.

If Form 2 is used, the condition's occurrence
causes the ON-unit to be executed. After it has
finished executing, control usually returns to the
point where the interrupt occurred. (This varies
according to the condition; see IBMFM for complete
details.)

In effect, the ON-unit is a procedure, which is
called into action not by an explicit call, but by the
raising of some condition.

The presence of SNAP causes a list of all blocks
and procedures active at the time the interrupt occurs
to be printed, just before executing the ON-unit or
the standard system action.

Note that execution of an ON statement does not
cause the ON-unit to be executed; it causes the ON-
unit to be associated with the condition. After
execution of the ON-statement, the ON-unit is said to
be "pending". That is, the ON-unit is awaiting the
occurrence of the condition. If SYSTEM was specified,
then the "standard system action" for that condition
is pending. (When the program begins execution, the
standard system action is pending for each condition.)

We use the term "ON-action" to mean either a
programmer-defined ON-unit or the standard system
action. Only one ON-action can be pending for any
condition at one time. However, each active block or
procedure in the program can have a different pending
ON-action for each condition. When a block or
procedure begins execution, the pending actions are
what they were just before execution began. When that
block or procedure is finished, the ON-actions revert
to what they were before entry. If the exit is by way
of a GO TO, the ON-actions are those of the block
containing the statement jumped to.

Execution of an ON statement within a block or procedure changes the ON-action only for that block or procedure. Executing a second ON-statement within the block or procedure completely cancels the previously pending ON-action. It is possible to recover the ON-action of a surrounding or calling block using the REVERT statement.

See Appendix B.7 and IBMFM for more details on the ON-statement and conditions.

OPEN statement   Form: OPEN FILE(file-name) |options|
                         |, FILE(file-name) |options|| ;

Some possible options are: SEQUENTIAL STREAM RECORD INPUT OUTPUT TITLE(exp) PRINT LINESIZE(exp) and PAGESIZE(exp). All exps must yield scalar values. These options need not be present; they augment the attributes specified in the file declaration.

Execution: Each file is opened by associating the file-name with the data set. The option INPUT or OUTPUT is used to indicate whether the file will be read or written.

Usually, the first eight characters of the file-name are used as the operating system's name for the data set. If the file-name is a parameter, the identifier of the argument and not the parameter, is used. If the option TITLE(exp) is used, the name for the data set is assumed to be the first eight characters of the string expression.

The LINESIZE option can be used only with a STREAM OUTPUT file. The value of the expression is used as the length of each line of the file. If no LINESIZE is given for a PRINT file, 120 is used.

PAGESIZE (exp) is used to indicate the number of lines on one page. The default is 60. PAGESIZE can only be used for PRINT files.

This is a sketchy description. See IBMFM for complete details.

PROCEDURE, PROC This is not a statement. See "Procedure definition" in Appendix B.4.

PUT statement

Form 1: PUT   [output] position ;

Form 2: PUT LIST(exp |, exp|)   [output] [position] ;

Form 3: PUT EDIT(exp |, exp|) format [output] [position] ;

Form 4: PUT DATA (variable-ref |, variable-ref|)
                                       [output] [position] ;

The order of the options "output" and "position" is
immaterial; they may also be placed directly after
PUT.

Execution: Execution of all these have to do with writing
data on an output file or into a variable. In the
normal case, "output" is missing and the standard
output file SYSPRINT is used. If "output" has the
form "FILE(file-name)" the data are written out on
that file. If "output" has the form "STRING(variable-
ref)" then the data are not written out on a file, but
are assigned to the string variable referenced,
beginning with its first character. In the latter
case the position option may not be present.

The forms for "position" are

        PAGE [LINE(exp)]   (only for PRINT files)
        SKIP [(exp)]
        LINE(exp)   (only for PRINT files)

where the exps must yield integers. SKIP is
equivalent to SKIP(1).

Execution proceeds as follows:

1. If PAGE is present, the current output page is
ended and a new one is begun.

2. If LINE(exp) is present, exp is evaluated and
converted to an integer w. If $w \leq 0$, it is changed to
1. Blank lines are written out so that line w of the
current page is the <u>next</u> one to be formed and written
out.

3. If SKIP(exp) is present exp is evaluated and
converted to an integer w. w lines are then skipped.
For non-PRINT files, w must be greater than 0. For
PRINT files (like the standard one) $w \leq 0$ has the
effect of writing at the beginning of the current line
again.

4. If Form 1 is used no transfer of data takes place.

5. The data are written out, depending on the form used. The form to use depends on the format of the output desired, as explained below:

Form 2: PUT LIST(exp |, exp|)

For PRINT files (like the standard output file SYSPRINT) the values of the expressions are written out, 24 columns each, in a standard format. Each line has five fields and each field contains one value. If an exp is missing (but not the corresponding comma) a blank field is written. If a string value covers exactly 24 characters, the next field will be left blank. If a string value contains more than 24 characters, it uses as many fields as necessary.

Form 3: PUT EDIT(exp |, exp|) format

The values are written out according to the format. See Appendix B.9 for details.

Form 4: PUT DATA(variable-ref |, variable-ref|)

Each reference may be to a scalar value, an array, or a structure variable. For PRINT files (like the standard output file SYSPRINT), the values are written out in the form

variable-name = constant

with a blank between each. The last one is followed by a semicolon. Arrays are written in row-major order.

READ statement

Form: READ FILE(file-name) INTO (structure-name);

Execution: This statement causes information to be read from the file specified by file name into the level-1 structure designated by structure-name. The SP/k restrictions on the read statement are described in Appendix A.2.8.

PL/I includes several other forms of the read statement that are beyond the scope of this book. See IBMFM.

RETURN statement   Form: RETURN [(exp)] ;

> Execution: RETURN; is to be used only within a procedure
> invoked by a CALL statement. Execution causes
> immediate termination of the procedure and the
> procedure call.

> RETURN(exp); is to be used only within a procedure called
> as a function. Execution causes immediate termination
> of the function; the value of the expression is
> returned as the value of the function. (It is of
> course first converted to the attributes
> specified by the RETURNS option of the procedure
> definition. See Appendix B.4.)

REVERT statement   Form: REVERT condition;

> Execution: This statement is used in connection with the ON
> statement. Execution causes cancellation of the
> pending ON-action for the condition. The pending ON-
> action of the last block executed becomes pending
> again. See the ON statement.

SIGNAL statement   Form: SIGNAL condition;

> Execution: This statement simulates the interrupt specified
> by the condition. If the condition is enabled, the
> current ON-action for that condition is executed.

STOP statement   Form: STOP;

> Execution: Execution of the program is terminated.

WRITE statement

> Form: WRITE FILE(file-name) FROM (structure-name);

> Execution: The inverse of the read statement described
> above. See Appendix A.2.8 for SP/k restrictions and
> IBMFM for other options that are beyond the scope of
> this book.

Appendix B.4 <u>Definitions</u> <u>and</u> <u>Declarations</u>

Definitions and declarations are used to define attributes of

1) variables, arrays, structures, and files
2) procedures and entry points to procedures
3) parameters of procedures

Except for the entry point definition, declarations and definitions may be placed anywhere within a block or procedure; they are <u>not</u> executable statements but just descriptions of things. However, it is suggested that these definitions and declarations be placed as described under "BEGIN block" (Appendix B.3) and "Procedure definition" (Appendix B.4), so that they may be easily found by the reader.

<u>Declaration</u> (simple)

Form: DECLARE (name |, name|) |attribute| ;

1. If there is only one name, the parentheses are not needed. Thus the following two are equivalent:

DECLARE (A) FIXED DECIMAL;
DECLARE A FIXED DECIMAL;

2. Each name has the form "identifier", in which case it is a simple variable name, a file-name, a label or an entry-name; or the form

identifier($exp^1:exp^2$ |, $exp^1:exp^2$|)

in which case it is an array named "identifier" of subscripted variables. It has as many dimensions as there are pairs "$exp^1:exp^2$". The exps are evaluated and converted to integers at the time the array is created. For each dimension, exp^1 must not be greater than exp^2. The subscript range is exp^1, exp^1+1, ..., exp^2.

In a bound pair "$exp^1:exp^2$", "exp^1" can be omitted if exp^1 is the constant 1. Thus, A(50,20) is equivalent to A(1:50,1:20).

3. The typical attributes that will be used, together
with their meanings in PL/I, are:

FIXED DECIMAL   The variable can contain integers
    in decimal notation from -99999 to +99999.

FIXED BINARY   The variable can contain integers
    in binary notation from -32767 to +32767
    (in decimal).

FLOAT DECIMAL   The variable can contain a
    floating point number of the form

$$\pm.ddddddE\pm dd$$

where the d's are digits 0-9. The exponent
dd has the range -78 to +75 (approximately).

FLOAT BINARY   The variable can contain a binary
    floating   point   number
    $\pm.bbbbbbbbbbbbbbbbbbbbbbE\pm dd$ where each b is
    a bit 0 or 1, and the d's are digits. The
    exponent   represents   a power   of   2.
    Binary floating point numbers range from
    2^{-260} to 2^{252} (approximately).

CHARACTER(x)   where x is an integer between 1
    and 32767. The variable can contain a string
    of x characters.

CHARACTER(X) VARYING   where   x is an integer
    between 1 and 32767.   The variable can
    contain a string of 0 to x characters. Upon
    creation of the variable, it is initialized
    to contain 0 characters (the null string).
    The number of characters in the variable at
    any point depends on the last assignment to
    it.

BIT(x) where x is an integer between 1 and 32767.
    The value of the variable is a string of x
    bits.

BIT(x) VARYING As in CHARACTER(x) VARYING, except
    that the value is a string of x bits
    instead of a string of characters.

4. Two (or more) declarations may be written as one
by replacing the semicolon of the first and the
DECLARE of the second by a single comma. For example,

DECLARE (A,B) CHARACTER(10), C FIXED BINARY;

is equivalent to

```
DECLARE (A,B) CHARACTER(10);
DECLARE C FIXED BINARY;
```

5. PL/I allows implicit declaration of variables, but
it is advisable to explicitly declare every name used
in the program. It is also advisable to specify all
the data attributes for each variable; the defaults
are too ad hoc to remember. See the beginning of
Appendix B.5 for a list of default attributes.

6. See "Procedure definition" and "BEGIN block" for a
discussion of where declarations go and what effect
they have.

7. Possible attributes are listed in Appendix B.5.

<u>Declaration</u>   (of structures)A <u>structure</u> is a hierarchical
collection of names. The names at the bottom of the
hierarchy are names of simple variables or arrays. The
name at the top is called the <u>structure</u> name. Space does
not permit a full, lucid explanation of structures, and we
restrict ourselves to discussing an example. Consider the
declaration

```
DECLARE 1 STUDENT,
          2 NAME CHARACTER(20),
          2 ADDRESS,
              3 STREET CHARACTER(20),
              3 CITY CHARACTER(20),
              3 ZIP_CODE FIXED DECIMAL,
          2 TRANSCRIPT,
              3 NO_OF_COURSES FIXED DECIMAL,
              3 COURSE_NAME(50) CHARACTER(10),
              3 GRADE(50) CHARACTER(1);
```

The name of the structure is STUDENT. It can be used to
refer to the whole structure. STUDENT.NAME refers to the
part of the structure containing his name -- a
CHARACTER(20) variable.   STUDENT.NAME   is   called   a
<u>qualified</u> <u>name</u> -- it consists of the sequence of names
in the hierarchy, beginning with the structure name,
which ends up at that variable name. The qualified name
STUDENT.ADDRESS refers to a <u>minor</u> <u>structure</u> of the whole
structure.   To reference the various parts of the address,
use   STUDENT.ADDRESS.STREET,   STUDENT.ADDRESS.CITY,   and
STUDENT.ADDRESS.ZIP_CODE.

Note that two parts of the TRANSCRIPT structure are
arrays of character variables. The (qualified) name of one
of these arrays is STUDENT.TRANSCRIPT.COURSE_NAME. To
refer,   say,   to   the   Ith   element,   use
STUDENT.TRANSCRIPT.COURSE_NAME(I).

To declare an <u>array</u> <u>of</u> <u>100</u> <u>structures</u> , each capable
of holding the record of one student, change the first line
of the declaration to

    DECLARE 1 STUDENT(1:100),

We could then refer, say, to the Ith grade of the Jth
student using

    STUDENT(J).TRANSCRIPT.GRADE(I).

Structures are useful in collecting several items of
information together under one name. For example, to pass
the student record to a procedure we need only give the
argument STUDENT; it is not necessary to pass each of the
individual parts as arguments.

It is not always necessary to use the complete qualified
name to reference part of a structure. Only enough of it
must be present to make the reference unambiguous (in
SP/k, the complete qualified name must be used). For
example, if there is no identifier GRADE being used, except
in this structure, then one can used the name GRADE instead
of the qualified name STUDENT.TRANSCRIPT.GRADE. Generally,
one should include the name of the structure; for example,
write STUDENT.GRADE, OR STUDENT.CITY.

The only difference in structure declarations and normal
declarations is in the use of <u>level</u> <u>numbers</u> just preceding
the name of a part of the structure. The structure name
must have level 1; all its immediate subparts should have
level 2, <u>their</u> immediate subparts should have level 3, and
so on. The immediate subparts are generally referred to as
immediate <u>items</u>.

PL/I gets its idea for structures from COBOL. More
recent languages, for example PASCAL and ALGOL 68, have a
much more useful, flexible way of declaring structures.

Procedure definition (simple)

    Form: entry-name: PROCEDURE [(parameter |, parameter|)] ;
                      |parameter declaration|
                      |declaration|
                      |statement|
                      END entry-name ;

1. The entry-name is used to call the procedure. The
entry name after END must be the same as the one
preceding PROCEDURE. Be careful; the PL/I rules state
that any ENDs omitted from within the procedure
definition will automatically be inserted, without

warning, just before the procedure END.   Therefore, omit no ENDs.

2.   This simple form of the procedure definition does not apply to the main program definition. See Appendix B.2 or the general procedure definition which follows.

3.   Each parameter is an identifier.

4.   The parameter declarations describe the attributes of the arguments corresponding to the parameters when the procedure is called.   All parameters should be specified here. The parameters are <u>not</u> variables and never receive a value of their own.

   Parameter declarations look exactly like normal declarations, except that

      a) The length of a string or bounds for an array may be specified by using *.   Thus CHARACTER(*) would be the attribute used for a character string, while A(*,*) would   describe   a two-dimensional array.   In SP/k one <u>must</u> use * in these positions for parameters.

      b) Since a parameter is not a variable, it may not have storage attributes STATIC, AUTOMATIC, or BASED.   PL/I   allows a parameter to have the attribute CONTROLLED, but this attribute is not included in SP/k.

5.   The declarations describe variables which are internal to this procedure, or EXTERNAL variables that the procedure may use.   The non-STATIC variables (the usual ones) are created when the procedure is called, and are destroyed when its execution ends.

6.   When the procedure is invoked, the statements are executed, in order, until either a RETURN; is executed or until the last statement has been executed. See also the GO TO statement. Upon termination, all variables created at the beginning of the procedure execution (see point 5 above) are destroyed.

Procedure definition (general)

```
Form: entry-name: |entry-name :|
         PROCEDURE [ (parameter |, parameter| )]
            [OPTIONS(MAIN)] [RECURSIVE]
            [RETURNS ( |attribute| )];
               |parameter declaration|
               |declaration|
               |procedure definition|
               |statement|
            END [entry-name] ;
```

All the points discussed under "Procedure definition (simple)" apply here. In addition,

1. OPTIONS(MAIN) is used to designate the main procedure which the system should call to begin execution.

2. RECURSIVE must be specified if the procedure is to be invoked recursively -- if it may be called while it is still executing. In SP/k the RECURSIVE attribute is neither required nor permitted.

3. The RETURNS phrase is not used if the procedure is to be invoked using the CALL statement. It is used only if the procedure is a <u>function</u>. The attributes in the RETURNS phrase specify the attributes of the value that will be returned as the value of the function. Only type attributes for arithmetic and string quantities are allowed; a function cannot return an array, structure, file-name, label or entry point.

4. The procedure definitions define procedures which can only be called from within this procedure.

5. If the entry-name appears after the END, it must be the same as one of the entry-names preceding the PROCEDURE phrase.

Appendix B.5 Attributes

We list here a brief summary of the more important attributes of variables. Each scalar variable has a set of attributes which help describe it. These are called type, scope and storage attributes. In addition, an _initial_ attribute can be given. These classes of attributes are described below:

1. _Type_ attributes. These indicate what kind of value the variable can contain.

    a)For arithmetic variables, these attributes fall into the following classes:

        1.A _base_ attribute, DECIMAL or BINARY. One should always be given.

        2.A _scale_ attribute, FIXED or FLOAT. One should always be given.

        3.A _mode_ attribute, REAL or COMPLEX. The default is REAL. Almost all variables are REAL so there is no need to give this attribute explicitly.

        4.A _precision_ _attribute._ In general, this is not needed.

    b)For character variables, the attribute is CHARACTER, and perhaps VARYING.

    c)For bit strings, the attribute is BIT and perhaps VARYING.

    d) For labels, the attribute is LABEL.

2. _Scope_ attributes. These are INTERNAL and EXTERNAL. They help indicate in what part of the program the variable can be referenced by its name.

3. _Storage class_ attributes. These are AUTOMATIC and STATIC. They help indicate when and where the variable is to be created and destroyed.

4. _INITIAL_ attribute. This specifies what the initial value of the variable is. This can be used only if the initial value is to be a constant.

PL/I provides defaults, in case a variable is not declared or in case only a partial list of attributes is given. For variables, the scope definition default is INTERNAL, while the storage class attribute default is AUTOMATIC. These are the usual cases and there is no need to give these attributes explicitly.

The default for the other attributes defining a variable are rather ad hoc (they are historically grounded in FORTRAN), and should not be used, except for REAL. Default attributes for base, mode and type depend upon the identifier name. For identifiers beginning with any letter I through N, the default attributes are REAL FIXED BINARY (15,0). For identifiers beginning with any other character, the default attributes are REAL FLOAT DECIMAL (6). If BINARY or DECIMAL and/or REAL or COMPLEX are specified, FLOAT is assumed unless FIXED has been specified. If FIXED or FLOAT and/or REAL or COMPLEX are specified, DECIMAL is assumed unless BINARY has been specified.

Got it? Now forget it and give the attributes explicitly.

Several attributes are not described here, either because they are beyond the scope of the book, or because they are not that useful for the space the explanation takes. They are:

1. "Parallel processing" or "multi-tasking" attributes. They are EVENT, EXCLUSIVE, and TASK.

2. File-name attributes. These are BACKWARDS, BUFFERED, DIRECT, KEYED, SEQUENTIAL, STREAM, ENVIRONMENT and UNBUFFERED.

3. Attributes concerning programmer-control of storage and "pointer" variables. These are ALIGNED, BASED, CONTROLLED, DEFINED, OFFSET, PACKED, POINTER, POSITION, UNALIGNED, and UPDATE.

4. Attributes used to help the compiler "optimize" the program. These are IRREDUCIBLE and REDUCIBLE.

5. The PICTURE attribute, which is used to define special internal formats of data and to specify editing of data.

The following description of attributes is based on the version of PL/I defined by the IBM F-level compiler. See IBMFM. If no form is given for an attribute, then the form is just the symbol itself. For example, the AUTOMATIC attribute is written "AUTOMATIC". Abbreviations for attributes are given in parentheses.

AUTOMATIC (AUTO) and STATIC attribute   Two other storage class attributes, CONTROLLED and BASED, are not described here.

1. AUTOMATIC means that the variable is created when the block in which it is declared is entered, and destroyed when execution

of the block is finished.   This   is   the   conventional   default
attribute,   and   it   need   <u>not</u>   be   given   for   any   variable.   An
EXTERNAL   variable   may <u>not</u> be   AUTOMATIC.   In SP/k, all variables
have the AUTOMATIC attribute.

2.   STATIC specifies that the variable is to be created when the
<u>program</u>   begins   execution, and is to be destroyed only when the
program terminates.   The bounds of any STATIC array   or   string
variable must be given as integer constants, since the variables
are   to   be   created before program   execution begins. A   STATIC
variable can only be referenced within the block in which it   is
declared, but remains a variable and retains its value after the
block execution is finished.

    Note that STATIC   affects   only   the   <u>storage</u>   <u>class</u>   of   the
variable,   and   not   the <u>scope</u> of its name (which is INTERNAL or
EXTERNAL).   For example, there can be several   STATIC variables
named X, each internal to a different block.

<u>BINARY (BIN)</u> and <u>DECIMAL</u> <u>(DEC)</u> attributes   Arithmetic   values
    may   be   stored   in   the   computer   in decimal   or   binary
    representation.   The number of bits   (digits)   of   accuracy
    depends on the attributes of the variable as follows:

> FIXED BINARY   15 bits   plus   sign.   The   range   in
>   decimal is -32767 to +32767.
> FLOAT BINARY   21 bits   plus sign for the   mantissa.
>   The range is   approximately $2-^{260}$ to
> 2^{252}.
> FIXED DECIMAL   5 digits plus sign (-99999 to +99999)
> FLOAT DECIMAL   6 digits plus sign for the   mantissa.
>   The range is approximately 10^{-78} to
> 10^{75}.

    See also the "Precision attribute".

<u>BIT</u> and <u>CHARACTER</u> <u>(CHAR)</u> <u>attribute</u>

> Form 1: BIT(length) [VARYING]
> Form 2: CHARACTER(length) [VARYING]

>   "length" must be an expression   which   when   evaluated
>   can be converted to an integer.

> Use: The value of a variable   with   this   attribute   is   a
>   string of "length" bits   for   Form   1,   or "length"
>   characters for Form 2.   If VARYING is present, the
>   string consists of 0 to "length" characters, depending
>   on the   last   assignment to it.   Upon creation of the
>   variable, its length is set   to   0   --   the   variable
>   contains   the null string.

>   For   parameters,   in   SP/k   use   "*"   instead   of
>   "length",   since   the   length   depends   on   the
>   corresponding argument.

<u>BUILTIN</u> <u>attribute</u>   Any reference to a name with this attribute
is a reference to the built-in function or pseudo-variable
with the same name. The name can have no other attributes.
A parameter may not have this attribute. This is used to
reference a built-in function in a block contained in
another block in which the name has a different meaning.

<u>CHARACTER</u> <u>(CHAR)</u> <u>attribute</u>See "BIT attribute".

<u>COMPLEX</u> <u>(CPLX)</u> <u>attribute</u>See "REAL attribute".

<u>DECIMAL</u> <u>(DEC)</u> <u>attribute</u>See "BINARY attribute".

<u>Dimensioning</u> <u>of</u> <u>Arrays</u>See "Declaration" in Appendix B.4.

<u>ENTRY</u> <u>attribute</u>

    Form: ENTRY [(|attribute| |, |attribute| |)] ;

        A name associated with the ENTRY attribute is an entry
point of a procedure. The first set of attributes
describes the first parameter of the entry point, the
second set of attributes the second parameter, and so
on. If a parameter is an array a special attribute
(*) for a one-dimensional array, (*,*) for a two-
dimensional array, etc. must be used as the <u>first</u>
attribute in the set.

  Use: There are three reasons for using this attribute:

        1. In PL/I an external procedure can be compiled
separately. In this case, when a program contains a
call on that procedure, it cannot know what its
parameters are. The ENTRY attribute serves to
indicate the attributes of the parameters. For
example,

DECLARE P ENTRY(FIXED DECIMAL, (*,*) FLOAT DECIMAL);

indicates that procedure P has two parameters, a fixed
decimal variable, and a float decimal two-dimensional
array. The procedure P does not have to appear in
this program, but may be compiled at a later time.

        2. An argument may be the name of a procedure. In
this case the declaration for the corresponding
parameter must describe the procedure and <u>its</u>
parameters using the ENTRY attribute.

        3. In PL/I (<u>but</u> <u>not</u> <u>in</u> <u>SP/k</u>), argument attributes
must match parameter attributes <u>exactly</u> unless an
explicit ENTRY attribute is given for the entry point.
If we want to call a procedure P(X) where the
parameter X is fixed binary, with CALL P(2);, then we
must write

```
PROGRAM: PROCEDURE OPTIONS(MAIN);
   DECLARE P ENTRY(FIXED BINARY);
          ...      CALL P(2);
          ...
P: PROCEDURE(X);
   DECLARE X FIXED BINARY;
          ...
   END P;
END PROGRAM;
```

In SP/k, the ENTRY attribute is neither required nor allowed.

EXTERNAL (EXT) and INTERNAL (INT) attributes   These are called
scope attributes. They specify in which part of a program a
name may be referred to. INTERNAL means that the name can
only be referenced within the block in which it is
declared (and of course within contained blocks).   It is
not necessary to give the INTERNAL attribute; it is the
conventional, default scope attribute.

   EXTERNAL specifies that the variable can be referred to
within any block containing an external declaration for it.
For example, if two external procedures and the main
program all contain identical EXTERNAL declarations for the
same   variable   I, then each can reference that same
variable.   There are not three variables I, but just one
variable I which they can all reference.   An EXTERNAL
variable must be STATIC; its name can contain no more than
seven characters.

FILE attributeThis indicates that the identifier is a file-
name.

FIXED and FLOAT attributesFIXED specifies that the value of
the variable is to be kept in fixed point form. Typically,
this means the value is an integer, but see the "Precision
attribute" for more information.

   FLOAT specifies that the value is to be kept in floating
point. The number of digits (bits) of accuracy remains the
same no matter what the value, but the value need not be in
any certain range. See the "Precision attribute" and the
"BINARY attribute".

FLOAT attribute   See "FIXED attribute".

GENERIC attribute   This attribute allows different procedures
to have the same name; which one is called will depend on
the attributes of the arguments.

INITIAL (INIT) attribute Form: INITIAL (item |, item|)

   Each item in the list can be a signed or unsigned
constant (see Appendix B.2 for constants).   The

INITIAL attribute can be associated only with a variable or array. Only one constant can be specified for a simple variable; the multiple items are used for arrays.

Use: The constants are assigned as initial values to the corresponding variables at the time the variables are created. Thus, all three variables A, B and C in the following declaration are initialized to 3:

DECLARE (A,B,C) FIXED DECIMAL INITIAL(3);

For arrays, the constant values are assigned to the subscripted variables of the array in row-major order. Consider for example the declaration

DECLARE (A(1:2), D(1:2,1:2)) INITIAL(1,3,5,7);

Upon creation, the variables will be

```
A(1)    1        A(2) 3
D(1,1) 1     D(1,2) 3     D(2,1) 5     D(2,2) 7
```

If not enough constants are supplied, the left-over array elements are not initialized. If there are too many constants, then the left-over constants are ignored.

One can supply an asterisk * instead of a constant for an item. This means that the corresponding array element will not be initialized. For example,

DECLARE E(1:3) FIXED DECIMAL INIT (3,*,2);

creates   E(1) 3   E(2) ???   E(3) 2

Iteration specification: To abbreviate a sequence of identical items an "iteration factor" may be used. For example, the item (4) 3 is equivalent to 3, 3, 3, 3.

The iteration factor is any expression that can be evaluated and converted to an integer. (For STATIC variables it must be an unsigned integer.) There are two forms for this:

1.   (iteration-factor) item (this is equivalent to "iteration-factor" items.)

2.   (iteration-factor) (item |, item|) (this is equivalent to the list of items repeated "iteration-factor" times.)

An iteration factor less than or equal to zero causes the item(s) to be skipped. For example, the following two are equivalent:

```
INIT( (2)*, (3)(*,3,6), 0(*), (3)8)
INIT(*,*, *,3,6,*,3,6,*,3,6, 8,8,8)
```

The item (2)'AB' is equivalent to 'ABAB', because (2) implies string repetition and is not an iteration-factor. With a string constant, to get an iteration-factor the string repetition must be there also. Thus (2)(1)'AB' specifies two elements and is equivalent to 'AB', 'AB'.

LABEL constants: A label constant assigned an initial value must be known within the block where the declaration occurs.

INPUT and OUTPUT attributes These are attributes of a file-name (see "FILE attribute"). INPUT specifies that the file is to be read; OUTPUT that it is to be written.

INTERNAL (INT) attribute See "EXTERNAL attribute".

LABEL attribute A variable or array with this attribute can contain only a label constant. It may not contain an entry-name of a procedure.

Length of String Variables See "BIT attribute".

LIKE attributeThis attribute allows a structure to be declared to have exactly the same template (data items and types) as some other structure. The principle use of the LIKE attribute is in allowing the definition of a complex structure to be written once and then used to declare several compatible variables. Also see Appendix A.2.8.

OUTPUT attribute See "INPUT attribute".

Precision attribute for arithmetic variables

Form: (number-of-digits [, scale-factor])

1. The number-of-digits is an unsigned decimal integer; the scale-factor is an optionally-signed decimal integer.

2. The precision attribute must immediately follow a FIXED, FLOAT, DECIMAL, BINARY, REAL or COMPLEX attribute.

Meaning: The number-of-digits specifies the minimum number of decimal digits (or bits for binary) to be maintained for the value of the variable. The maximum allowable number is 15 for DECIMAL FIXED, 31 for BINARY FIXED, 16 for DECIMAL FLOAT, and 53 for BINARY FLOAT.

The scale factor may be specified only if the variable is FIXED; it must be in the range -128 to +127. It specifies the assumed position of the binary or decimal point -- that is, the number of fractional bits or digits. If omitted, 0 is assumed and the value is an integer.

Typically the precision attribute is omitted. The default in this case is

```
(5,0)   for FIXED DECIMAL     (15,0) for FIXED BINARY
(6)     for FLOAT DECIMAL     (21)   for FLOAT BINARY
```

Examples: We give below some sample attributes and indicate to the right the corresponding format of a value with those attributes. In the examples, d stands for a digit, and b for a bit.

```
FIXED DECIMAL(5,0)      ddddd
FIXED DECIMAL(5,2)      ddd.dd
FIXED DECIMAL(5,7)      .00ddddd
FIXED DECIMAL(5,-2)     ddddd00.
FIXED BINARY(6,7)       .0bbbbbb
FLOAT DECIMAL(8)        .dddddddd*10**dd
FLOAT DECIMAL(6)        .dddddd*10**dd
FLOAT BINARY(10)        .bbbbbbbbbb*2**dd
```

PRINT attribute   The data file associated with a file-name with the attribute PRINT will eventually be printed. Each line (record) is written out with an extra character at its beginning, which is used by the printer to determine when to skip to a new page, to a new line.

REAL and COMPLEX (CPLX) attributes   REAL specifies that the value of the variable is a real number. REAL is the default attribute and need not be explicitly stated if FIXED, FLOAT, DECIMAL, or BINARY are used. COMPLEX specifies that the value is a complex number, consisting of real and imaginary parts.

RECORDattribute   This attribute is used to specify the characteristics of a file on secondary storage. See IBMFM for details.

RETURNS attribute   This is used in connection with the ENTRY attribute to help describe an entry-name. It indicates that the entry-name is called as a function, and describes the attributes of the value returned as the result of the function. The form of the RETURNS attribute is exactly the same as the form of the RETURNS phrase in a procedure definition (see Appendix B.4).

<u>STATIC</u> <u>attribute</u>   See "AUTOMATIC attribute".

<u>VARYING</u> <u>(VAR)</u> <u>attribute</u>   See "BIT attribute".

Appendix B.6 Variables, Values and Expressions

We consider how variables are referenced and changed. The kinds of values that can be assigned to variables have already been listed in Appendix B.4 under "Declaration (simple)", and in Appendix B.5 in the discussion of the Precision attribute. Constants for the different kinds of values have been described in Appendix B.2.

Appendix B.6.1 Scope and Recognition of Names

Assume for the moment that all identifiers are explicitly declared or defined. Note that the presence of a label preceding a statement, or an entry-name preceding PROCEDURE or ENTRY, constitutes its definition. "Block" means either a BEGIN block or a procedure definition.

The use of an identifier in a program always refers to a declared or defined identifier; it represents some entity -- a variable, array, entry point in a procedure, etc. That part of the program where an entity may be referred to by its identifier is called the scope of that entity. The scope has nothing to do with the question of when that entity is created or destroyed; it only indicates where it may be referred to by its name. The scope of an entity depends on where it is declared or defined relative to the blocks of the program.

The scope of an entity named with an identifier is the block in which its declaration or definition appears, including any contained blocks, except those blocks (and blocks contained in them) where another declaration or definition of that same identifier occurs.

For example, consider the program below, where the lines to the right show the scope of the corresponding identifiers. The identifiers X, W and B are each declared twice; we use superscripts to distinguish them.

PL/I allows the use of identifiers without having to declare them. For such undeclared identifiers, PL/I inserts a declaration with default attributes which are determined from the way in which the identifier is used. For an explanation of "contextual" and "implicit" declarations see IBMFM.

$$A \quad X^1 \quad Y \quad M \quad W^1 \quad X^2 \quad W^2 \quad B^1 \quad B^2$$

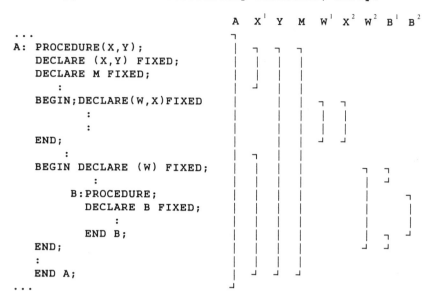

```
...
A: PROCEDURE(X,Y);
     DECLARE (X,Y) FIXED;
     DECLARE M FIXED;
        :
     BEGIN;DECLARE(W,X)FIXED
        :
        :
     END;
        :
     BEGIN DECLARE (W) FIXED;
        :
        B:PROCEDURE;
          DECLARE B FIXED;
             :
          END B;
     END;
     :
     END A;
...
```

Appendix B.6.2 <u>Referencing Variables, Arrays and Structures</u>

In Appendix B.1 we discussed variables, arrays and structure references briefly. We elaborate a bit more here. We illustrate assuming the declarations

```
DECLARE (A, B(1:20,1:20)) FIXED DECIMAL,
         C CHARACTER(20),
         D CHARACTER(20) VARYING;
DECLARE 1 PERSON,
         2 NAME CHARACTER(20),
         2 ADDRESS,
             3 STREET CHARACTER(20),
             3 CITY CHARACTER(20),
             3 ZIPCODE CHARACTER(5);
DECLARE 1 UNIVERSITY,
         2 NAME CHARACTER(20),
         2 ADDRESS(5),
             3 CITY CHARACTER(20),
             3 ZIPCODE CHARACTER(5);
```

Within the scope of a declaration, one references variables, arrays and structures declared in that declaration as follows:

1. To reference a simple variable use its name (e.g. A , C).

2. To reference an array, use its name (e.g. B).

3. To reference a subscripted variable, use the form

        array-name (exp |, exp|)

The number of exps must equal the number of dimensions of the array. To find out which element of the array is referenced, evaluate the subscripts and convert to integers, from left to right. For example, if I has the value 1 and J the value 2, then A(I,J+1) refers to the subscripted variable A(1,3).

4. To reference a cross section of an array, use a form like that of a subscripted variable, but use an asterisk * for a subscript for which a whole "row" is wanted. For example, B(*,1) is the one-dimensional array consisting of B(1,1), B(2,1), ..., B(20,1). B(7,*) is the array consisting of B(7,1), B(7,2), ..., B(7,20). B(*,*) represents the whole array. A cross section is an array with as many dimensions as there are asterisks in the cross section reference.

The following program segment stores in array T(1:20,1:20) the transpose of the array B:

```
        DO I = 1 TO 20;
            T(I,*) = B(*,I);
        END;
```

5. To reference a structure, use its name (e.g. PERSON).

6. To reference a part of a structure use a qualified name. This is the sequence of identifiers, starting from the name of the structure and leading down to the name of the structure part desired, separated by periods. For example, to refer to the value STREET of the substructure ADDRESS of the structure PERSON, use

        PERSON.ADDRESS.STREET

Note that the declaration for UNIVERSITY allows for 5 different addresses; UNIVERSITY.ADDRESS is a qualified name which refers to an array. UNIVERSITY.ADDRESS(1).CITY refers to the city for the first address.

It is not necessary to fully qualify such a reference; only enough names must be given to make the reference unambiguous. Thus STREET, PERSON.STREET, or ADDRESS.STREET would be equivalent to PERSON.ADDRESS.STREET. ADDRESS, however, is ambiguous since it could refer to either PERSON.ADDRESS OR UNIVERSITY.ADDRESS.

7. Pseudo-variables. A pseudo-variable is a phrase which allows one to reference a subpart of a variable, or two variables which are thought of as being one. For example, the SUBSTR pseudo-variable allows one to use part of a string as a variable, just as we use A(3) to reference part of an array.

Most of the pseudo-variables allow arrays as arguments, in which case the pseudo-variable refers to an array of values.

Pseudo-variables may not be nested. Thus UNSPEC(REAL(A)) = '00'B is invalid.

The pseudo-variables COMPLETION, ONCHAR, ONSOURCE, PRIORITY, STATUS and STRING are beyond the scope of this book. The other pseudo-variables are:

1. COMPLEX(a,b) -- In an assignment statement like COMPLEX(A,B) = 1+2I; the real part "1" is assigned to the variable A, while the imaginary part "2" is assigned to variable B. If either A or B is an array, they both must be arrays with identical bounds.

2. IMAG(c) -- This refers to the imaginary part of the complex variable c. If c is an array, IMAG(c) refers to the array of imaginary parts of c.

3. REAL(c) -- This refers to the real part of the complex variable c. If c is an array, REAL(c) refers to the array of real parts of c.

4. SUBSTR(string, i [, j]) -- This refers to the subpart of the character string or bit string "string", beginning with character (bit) i and ending with character (bit) i+j-1. No other characters (bits) of the string are changed by an assignment to SUBSTR. The pseudo-variable is always non-VARYING. Thus, execution of SUBSTR(C,1,1) = ''; does not delete the first character from C, but just sets it to a blank. If j is missing it is assumed to be i+LENGTH(string)-1.

    If one argument is an array, they all must be, with identical bounds.

5. UNSPEC(s) -- s can be a string or arithmetic variable or array. The value being assigned to it is evaluated, converted to a bit string (if possible), and assigned to s <u>without</u> <u>further</u> <u>conversion</u> to the attributes of s.

8. To reference a function, use the same format as the call of a procedure, except that the keyword CALL and the semicolon are omitted.

Appendix B.6.3 <u>Expressions</u>

An expression is something which, when evaluated, yields a value. The expression "2" yields the value 2; if A is a variable with current value 3, then the expression "A" yields the value 3 while the expression "A+2" yields the value 5.

An expression can be a single constant, a reference to a variable, or a combination of "operators" and "operands", with perhaps parentheses to indicate the order in which the operators should be evaluated.

Operands of Expressions

These may be

1. Constants.

2. References to variables, as described in Appendix B.6.2.

3. References to built-in functions, as described in Appendix B.8.

4. References to user-defined functions (procedures with RETURNS attributes).

Operators

PL/I allows the following operators:

        + - * / ** < ¬< <= =
        > ¬> >= ¬= | & and ||

Their descriptions appear below:

1. Arithmetic operators -- These operators have only arithmetic operands. Unless otherwise specified, if the operands of an operator have the same arithmetic attributes, so does the result. Thus addition of two fixed decimal numbers yields a fixed decimal number. The result of an operation in which the two operands do not have the same attributes is discussed in Appendix B.6.4. Remember that a constant like 3 or -2.45 is fixed decimal.

    a) + x   -- The result is the value of x.

    b) - x   -- The result is the negative of the value of x.

    c) x + y --This is conventional addition: 1+5 is 6.

    d)x - y --This is conventional subtraction: 2-5 is -3.

    e)x * y --This is conventional multiplication: 2*5 is 10.

f) x / y -- This is conventional division. Be very careful if both operands are fixed point. In this case the result is also fixed point but is not rounded to an integer. Because of the PL/I precision rules, 25+1/3 is 5.333333 and not 25.333333.

g) x ** y -- This is conventional exponentiation. That is, x is multiplied by itself y times. If y is not an unsigned integer constant, then x is converted to floating point and floating point exponentiation is performed. Some special cases are:

    1. If x=0 and y>0 the result is 0.
    2. If x=0 and y≤0 an error results.
    3. If x≠0 and y=0 the result is 1.
    4. If x<0 and y is not fixed (an integer) an error results.
    5. If x=0 and y is complex with real part >0 and imaginary part =0, the result is 0.
    6. If x=0 and y is complex but does not fit (5), an error results.

h) x < y,   x ¬< y,   x <= y,   x = y
   x ¬> y,   x >= y,   x > y,   x ¬= y

These are the arithmetic comparison operators. They yield the value "true" ('1'B) or "false" ('0'B), depending on whether the relation is true or not. "¬=" stands for not equal, "<=" for less than or equal, etc. For example,

```
1  < 2 yields true     1 ¬< 2 yields false
1 <= 2 yields true     1  = 2 yields false
1  > 2 yields false    1 ¬> 2 yields true
1 >= 2 yields false    1 ¬= 2 yields true
```

2. Character string operators

a) x || y   -- The result of this concatenation is a character string consisting of the characters of x followed by those of y. For example,

```
'ABC' || 'DXY' yields 'ABCDXY'
'ABC' || ''    yields 'ABC'
'AB ' || 'DXY' yields 'AB DXY'
```

b) x < y,   x ¬< y,   x <= y,   x = y
   x ¬> y,   x >= y,   x > y,   x ¬= y

These are the character string comparison operators. They have the same form as the arithmetic comparison operators. A comparison is evaluated as follows: first, the shorter of the two operands is extended with blanks until the two have the same length. Then a left-to-right character by character comparison is performed until the result is determined. The result is '1'B if the relation is true; '0'B otherwise. The collating sequence given at the end of Section I.9.2.2 is used to make the comparison. Examples are:

```
'A' <= 'A'       yields true
'A' <= 'AB'      yields true
'AB'<= 'A'       yields false
'A' = 'A '       yields true
```

3. <u>Bit</u> <u>string</u> <u>operators</u>   -- These always take bit strings as operands, and always yield a bit string result.

   a) ¬ x --The result is a bit string the same as x but with every bit reversed. ¬ '10011'B yields '01100'B.

   b) x | y   -- If one operand is shorter than the other, the shorter is extended on the right with zeros until they are the same length. Then a bit-by-bit operation is performed to yield a bit-string with the same length. For each bit, the result is 1 if either operand has a 1 in that position, and is 0 otherwise. For example,

```
'1010'B | '1100'B yields '1110'B
'1'B    | '1101'B yields '1101'B
```

   c) x & y   -- The shorter operand is extended with zeros until both operands have the same length. Then a bit-by-bit operation is performed to yield a value with that length. For each bit, the result is 1 only if both operands have a 1 in that position. For example,

```
'1010'B & '1100'B yields '1000'B
'1'B    & '1101'B yields '1000'B
```

   d) x || y   -- The result is a string of bits consisting of those in x followed by those in y.

   e) x < y,   x ¬< y,   x <= y,   x = y
      x ¬> y,   x >= y,   x > y,   x ¬= y

   These bit comparison operators yield '1'B if the relation is true, and '0'B otherwise. The shorter operand is first extended with zeros until both operands have the same length. Then a left-to-right bit-by-bit comparison is made of the two operands until the result is determined. See also the arithmetic and character string comparison operators.

Expressions and the Priority of Operators

Expressions follow conventional mathematical notation, where parentheses may be used to indicate the order of evaluation of the operators. For example,

      - A + B * C + D * (E + F)   is evaluated as follows:

      1.   Evaluate -A
      2.   Evaluate B*C
      3.   Evaluate -A + B*C (using the results of steps 1 and 2)
      4.   Evaluate E+F
      5.   Evaluate D*(E+F) (using the result of step 4)
      6.   Evaluate -A+B*C + D*(E+F) (using the results of
                                            steps 3 and 5)

Operations are performed using the following table of priorities of operators:

```
prefix +  prefix -   ¬   **     (highest)
*  /                            |
infix +  infix -                |
||                              |
<  ¬<  <=  =  ¬=  >=  >  ¬>      |
&                               V
|                            (lowest)
```

If two or more operators on the same level appear next to each other, the operations are performed in left-to-right order. The exception to this rule is the top line. If two or more operators from the top line of the table appear next to each other, the operations are performed in right-to-left order. For example,

      A * -B is evaluated as A * (-B)
      A + B + C is evaluated as (A + B) + C
      A ** -B is evaluated as A ** (-B)
      A ** B ** C is evaluated as A ** (B ** C)

Array and Structure Expressions

PL/I allows array expressions which yield arrays of values, and structure expressions which yields structures of values. An array expression is evaluated element by element. Thus if A(1:3) is (3 8 2) and B(1:3) is (2 1 2), then A*B is the array (6 8 4). This is not conventional array multiplication.

Any operator described for conventional expressions can also be used for arrays, but be careful. An array operation implies that same operation being applied to the individual elements of the array (or array operands), to yield an array of the same size. Read "Assignment to arrays" and "Assignment to structures" in Appendix B.3 before using array expressions.

In an array expression all array operands must have identical bounds. In a structure expression, each structure operand must have the same structure.

Appendix B.6.4 Data Conversion

Quite often, values have to be converted from one form to another -- FIXED DECIMAL to FLOAT DECIMAL, bit string to character string, etc. These conversions occur when evaluating an expression, when assigning a value to a variable, and in similar situations. In PL/I, evaluation of operations and conversion of values is a difficult problem, mainly because of the way precision attributes are defined and used. The typical programmer will not use these precision attributes; instead he will rely on the default attributes given by PL/I.

We describe only a simplified version of the data conversion rules and assume that the precision attributes are not explicitly used. Those people who want to understand why 25+1/3 = 5.33333 are encouraged to read IBMFM.

Remember that constants like 3.14 are actually fixed decimal values. To be sure of results, when using a constant as an operand of a division, write it with an exponent: 3.14E0.

Conversion During Arithmetic Operations

During evaluation of an operation like x*y, if the arithmetic attributes of the operands differ, some conversion must be performed before the operation can take place. The rules for the order of this conversion are:

1. If one operand is binary and the other decimal, the decimal operand is converted to binary.

2. If one operand is fixed and the other floating point, the fixed point operand is converted to floating point form. The one exception to this rule is with exponentiation. If in x**y, x is FLOAT and y FIXED, no conversion is necessary; the result is still FLOAT. If in x**y, both operands are FIXED, then x is converted to floating point form unless y is an unsigned integer constant.

3.   If one operand is REAL and the other COMPLEX, the REAL
operand is converted to COMPLEX.   The one exception is
exponentiation. If in x**y, y is a fixed point integer, no
conversion is necessary.

Results of Conversion

Bit string to character string   -- Each bit 1 becomes the
        character 1; each bit 0 becomes the character 0. The
        length of the result is the length of the original
        value.

Character string to bit string   -- The character string
        should contain only the characters 1 and 0; any other
        causes an error message to be printed (the CONVERSION
        condition is raised). Each character 1 becomes the
        bit 1; each character 0 becomes the bit 0.

Mode conversion   -- Conversion from complex to real is
        done by deleting the imaginary part of the complex
        number.   When converting from real to complex, a zero
        imaginary part is added to the real value.

Base conversion   -- Converting from DECIMAL FLOAT to
        BINARY FLOAT, or vice versa, causes no changes in the
        number, since both are internally stored in the same
        representation.   Conversion from DECIMAL FIXED   to
        BINARY FIXED can cause the number to be truncated, so
        significant digits may be lost.   This is because
        DECIMAL FIXED has the range -99999 to +99999, while
        BINARY FIXED has the range   -32767 to 32767.   For
        example, the fixed decimal number 32769 will be
        converted to 1000000000000001B and then truncated to
        1B.   Conversion from BINARY FIXED to DECIMAL FIXED
        causes no problems.

Scale conversion   -- Conversion from FIXED to FLOAT may
        cause problems because the FLOAT representation allows
        fewer digits (or bits) than the FIXED representation.
        Conversions from FLOAT to FIXED may cause the   least
        signicant digits (bits) to be discarded. Truncation,
        not rounding, is performed.

Appendix B.6.5 Parameter-Argument Correspondence

Suppose we have a call CALL P(A1); of a procedure defined as

    P: PROCEDURE(P1);
        DECLARE P1 ...;
            :
        END P;

The parameter-argument correspondence is set up before the actual execution of the procedure statements. Once this link between parameter and argument is made, it is not changed for the duration of the procedure execution.

The way the correspondence between P1 and A1 is set up depends on the attributes of both P1 and A1. In general, P1 must be attached (by an arrow) to a line containing the value of the argument. The declaration of P1 does not indicate that P1 is a variable; it just indicates what the attributes of the corresponding argument must be. In the above example, an assignment to P1 changes A1 immediately.

We have generally indicated parameter-argument correspondence by an arrow from the parameter to the argument:

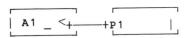

We now describe the way in which the parameter-argument linkage is done when a procedure is called, depending on the attributes of the parameter.

Scalar parameter   The parameter represents a variable that is neither an array nor a structure. The argument must be an expression (a constant, scalar variable, or more general expression). The linkage is drawn as follows: if the argument is a simple or subscripted variable whose data attributes match those of the parameter exactly, then the arrow is drawn from the parameter to the argument:

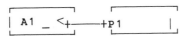

Note that the arrow is drawn before the procedure statements are executed. If the argument is a subscripted variable, the subscripts are evaluated just once, before execution of the procedure statements, in order to determine which variable is being passed to the procedure.

If the argument is anything else (a constant, an expression which is not a variable, a variable in parentheses, like (I), a variable with different attributes from the parameter), the following happens:

1. A new variable, say TEMP, is automatically created; its attributes are those of the parameter.

2. The argument is evaluated and assigned to
TEMP. Normal conversion rules for an assignment
statement apply.

3. An arrow is drawn from the parameter to TEMP:

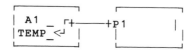

TEMP is called a "dummy argument".

If the parameter is a fixed length string and the
argument a VARYING string, a dummy argument is created
with a length equal to the <u>maximum</u> length of the
argument.

If the parameter has the attribute LABEL, then the
argument must be a label or a label variable.

<u>Array</u> <u>parameter</u>   If the parameter is an array, the
argument must be an array expression or a scalar
expression. A scalar expression will be automatically
converted to an array of the appropriate size in which
every element has the value of the expression. The
array operands of the array expression must have the
same number of dimensions as the parameter.

If the argument is an array or a cross section of
an array with the same attributes as the parameter,
then an arrow is drawn from the parameter to the
argument:

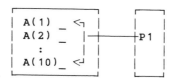

In <u>any</u> <u>other</u> <u>case</u>, an array TEMP (say) with attributes
of the parameter and dimension of the argument is
created, the argument is assigned to the array TEMP
and an arrow is drawn from the parameter to TEMP. Any
conversion is performed as in an assignment statement.
TEMP is called a "dummy array argument".

Structure parameter   If the parameter is a structure, then the argument must be a structure expression or a scalar expression. The correspondence is similar to the correspondence for array parameters.

Entry-name parameter   If the parameter is an entry-name, the argument must be the name of a procedure (or function).   It can be the name of a mathematical built-in function, like SIN.   The number and attributes of parameters declared for the parameter and the argument must be the same.

File-name parameter   The argument must also be a file-name. The attributes of the parameter are ignored.

Appendix B.7 <u>Conditions</u> <u>and</u> <u>Prefixes</u>

During execution of a program an exceptional condition such as OVERFLOW (a floating point number becoming too large) or ZERODIVIDE (division by zero) can cause an <u>interrupt</u> to occur. Execution of the program is temporarily halted, a certain statement is executed, and then the program terminates or execution resumes, depending on the condition and what the programmer wants. Generally, a standard system action is performed when the interrupt occurs. However, the programmer himself can indicate what should take place, using the ON statement. We will call the statement to be performed when the condition occurs the "ON-action" for that condition.

The typical programmer will usually use only the CHECK and ENDFILE conditions.

Appendix B.7.1 <u>Prefixes</u> <u>and</u> <u>Their</u> <u>Use</u>

For each possible condition that can occur, the programmer can indicate whether or not the ON-action should be executed if the condition occurs. The programmer does this by placing a "condition prefix" before the statement in which the condition may occur. If the ON-action should be executed, it is said to be "enabled"; of not, it is "disabled". For example, suppose we do not want an ON-action to execute if division by zero takes place in a statement A=B/C;. Then we should write

    (NOZERODIVIDE) : A = B / C;

If division by zero does occur, the programmer won't know about it, and some undefined value will be stored in A.

The complete form of a statement is

    |prefix :| |label :| statement

A prefix has the form

    (cond |, cond|)

where each "cond" is a condition as specified in Appendix B.7.2. A "cond" may also be a condition with the letters NO immediately preceding it (no intervening blanks). A prefix attached to a statement signifies that each condition is to be enabled (if just the condition is used) or disabled (if NO precedes the condition). The statement can be any simple statement, BEGIN block, IF statement, or loop. A procedure definition may also be prefixed, which means the condition applies to the execution of the whole procedure. There are some restrictions on which conditions may be used as prefixes; these will be explained under the particular conditions.

One may of course enable a condition for a block, and disable it for part of that block. For example,

```
(ZERODIVIDE): BEGIN; ...
              (NOZERODIVIDE): A=B/C;
                ...
              END;
```

A prefix applies to the statement to which it is attached, but <u>not</u> to any procedure called by that statement. The scope of a prefix is statically defined, like the scope of an identfier in a declaration. Prefixes attached to IF, ON, compound, and iterative statements are treated differently:

1. A prefix attached to an IF applies only to the evaluation of the expression following the IF, and not to the statements following THEN or ELSE.

2. A prefix attached to an ON statement does not apply to the ON-unit.

3. A prefix attached to a compound statement has no effect.

4. A prefix attached to an iterative statement does not apply to the substatements of the loop.

B.7.2 Conditions

Unless otherwise noted, the following three points hold for an interrupt:

1. The standard system action when an interrupt occurs is to print a message and raise the ERROR condition.

2. In PL/I, the result of the operation causing the interrupt is undefined.

3. Upon normal termination of a ON-unit, control returns to the point <u>following</u> the operation which caused the interupt.

The conditions are listed below. Permissible abbreviations are shown in parentheses. Unless otherwise noted, the form of the condition used in a prefix or as a condition is the keyword itself. For example, the form of the ERROR condition is "ERROR".

The following conditions are not discussed here; see IBMFM for details: AREA, KEY, PENDING, RECORD and TRANSMIT.

CHECK   Form: CHECK(name |, name|)

where each name is the name of a simple variable, array (but <u>not</u> a subscripted variable), a structure, an entry-name, or a label. A name cannot be a parameter in PL/I,

This particular prefix may <u>only</u> be attached to a BEGIN block or a procedure definition. The names appearing in the CHECK prefix refer to names known <u>within</u> that block or procedure.

The CHECK condition is raised in the following cases:

1. If a name is a variable, array or structure, the condition is raised whenever it is assigned a value, or whenever <u>part</u> of it is assigned a value, or after a return from a user-defined procedure which had that name as an argument which was <u>not</u> a dummy argument.

2. If a name is a label, the condition is raised just before execution of the statement with that label.

3. If a name is an entry-name, the condition is raised when the entry-name is invoked.

Raising CHECK has no effect on the statement being executed; it is used primarily to obtain output to help debug a program. The standard system action is to print out the name on SYSPRINT together with its value if it has one. If an ON-unit is given, upon its termination, execution continues at the point where the interrupt occurred.

CHECK is <u>not</u> raised if

1. An assignment occurs because of an INITIAL attribute.

2. An assignment is made through a parameter. (But CHECK will be raised upon return from the corresponding procedure if the argument is not a dummy argument.)

CONDITION   Form: CONDITION (identifier)

    The identifier is given by the programmer. No
declaration or definition can be given for it; its
appearance with a CONDITION in an ON, SIGNAL, or REVERT
statement constitutes its declaration. It is given the
attribute EXTERNAL.

    CONDITION is raised by execution of a SIGNAL statement
that specifies the appropriate identifier. It cannot be
disabled.

CONVERSION (CONV) NOCONVERSION (NOCONV)   This occurs whenever
    an illegal conversion is attempted on a character string
    value. (For example, when a character other than 0 or 1
    occurs in a string being converted to a bit string.) Upon
    termination of an ON-unit, control returns to the beginning
    of the statement and the conversion is retried.

ENDFILE   Form: ENDFILE(file-name)

    This occurs when an attempt is made to read when no more
data exists on the file. Another attempt to read from the
same file will cause another interrupt. Upon normal
termination of an ON-unit, the statement that caused the
interrupt is immediately terminated. This condition cannot
be disabled.

ENDPAGE   Form: ENDPAGE(file-name)

where the file referred to is a PRINT file.

    This occurs when an attempt is made to start a new line
beyond the last line specified for the current page. The
last line is the limit given when the file was opened, or
the default of 60. When ENDPAGE is raised, the current
line number is 1 greater than that specified. ENDPAGE is
raised only once per page, and it is possible to continue
writing on the same page by specifying a null ON-unit. An
ON-unit can start a new page by executing PUT PAGE for that
file.

    The standard system action is to start a new page. Upon
normal termination of the ON-unit, control returns to the
point of the interrupt and the operation is performed
again. If it is raised while data is being written, the
data is written on the current line after the ON-unit is
executed. If ENDPAGE results from LINE or SKIP this action
is ignored.

    ENDPAGE may not be disabled.

ERROR   This is raised in the following cases:

1. As a result of the standard system action for an interrupt which is "print a message and raise the ERROR condition.

2. As a result of an error during execution for which there is no ON condition.

3. As a result of execution of SIGNAL ERROR;

The standard system action is to raise the FINISH condition. ERROR cannot be disabled. If there is an ON-unit associated with ERROR, upon its normal termination the standard system action is taken.

FINISH   This is raised by execution of STOP, and by execution of a RETURN in the main procedure. The standard system action is to do nothing. If an ON-unit is associated with FINISH, it is executed before program termination occurs. The ON-unit can avoid termination by jumping out of the ON-unit and continuing execution. FINISH cannot be disabled.

FIXEDOVERFLOW (FOFL) NOFIXEDOVERFLOW (NOFOFL)   This occurs when the length of a FIXED arithmetic operand exceeds 15 digits (or 31 bits).

NAME   Form: NAME(file-name) This is raised during execution of GET DATA when a name in the input cannot be referenced at the point GET DATA appears. The standard system action is to ignore the input item, print a message, and continue. Upon normal termination of an ON-unit, execution of GET DATA continues with the next item in the input. NAME cannot be disabled.

OVERFLOW (OFL) NOOVERFLOW (NOOFL)   This occurs when the magnitude of a floating point number exceeds approximately 10^{75} or 2^{252}.

SIZE NOSIZE   This occurs when the high-order (leftmost) significant bits or digits are lost in an assignment to a variable or temporary, or in an input-output operation. SIZE is raised when the size of the value exceeds the size declared for that variable, while FIXEDOVERFLOW is raised when the maximum allowed value for the computer is exceeded. In PL/I the default is NOSIZE.

STRINGRANGE (STRG) NOSTRINGRANGE (NOSTRG)   This is raised whenever the lengths of the arguments of SUBSTR don't follow the rules. The standard system action is to change the SUBSTR reference to fit the rules, by increasing or reducing the position and length arguments in a fairly obvious manner.

<u>SUBSCRIPTRANGE (SUBRG)</u> <u>NOSUBSCRIPTRANGE (NOSUBRG)</u>   This is raised when a subscript is evaluated and found to be outside its bounds.

<u>UNDEFINEDFILE (UNDF)</u>   Form: UNDEFINEDFILE(file-name)   This occurs if a file cannot be OPENed by execution of an OPEN statement. This may be caused by a conflict of attributes, no blocksize specified, no DD statement in the JCL for the file, and other similar reasons.

   Upon normal termination of the ON-unit, control is given to the statement following the statement that caused the interrupt. UNDEFINEDFILE cannot be disabled.

<u>UNDERFLOW (UFL)</u> <u>NOUNDERFLOW (NOUFL)</u>   This occurs when the magnitude of a floating point number is smaller than the minimum allowed -- approximately 10^{-78} or 2^{-260}. A 0 is used instead.

<u>ZERODIVIDE (ZDIV)</u> <u>NOZERODIVIDE (NOZDIV)</u>   This occurs when a division by zero is attempted.

Appendix B.8 Built-in Functions

We describe briefly the PL/I built-in functions as they are evaluated in the case where the values are maintained in the largest precision possible. More complete details can be found in IBMFM. Unless otherwise specified, an argument may be an array as well as a scalar value. The result is then an array with the same bounds. The values in the array are the result of applying the function to each of the individual values of the original array. If two or more arguments are arrays, they must have identical bounds.

String handling built-in functions

BIT(exp, [size]) -- The exp is converted to a bit string of length "size". "size" must be a decimal integer constant. If "size" is missing, the length of the result depends on the attributes of the exp.

BOOL(x, y, z) -- This is beyond the scope of this book.

CHAR(exp, [size]) -- The exp is converted to a character string representing the same value, of length "size". The same conventions apply for "size" as do with the function BIT.

HIGH(i) -- The result is a character string of length i, each character of which is the highest character in the collating sequence. i must be a decimal integer constant.

INDEX(string, config) -- string and config are bit or character strings. The result is a fixed binary integer which gives the leftmost position in string where the config begins. If config does not appear as a substring of string, the result is 0.

LENGTH(string) -- The result is a FIXED BINARY integer giving the length of the string.

LOW(i) -- The result is a character string of length i, each character of which is the lowest character in the collating sequence. i must be an integer constant.

REPEAT(string, i)   -- string is a character or bit string; i is
        a   decimal   constant.   The   result   is   "string"
        concatenatedd   with   itself   i   times.   Thus
        REPEAT('ABC',2) is 'ABCABCABC'.

STRING(x)   -- x is a variable, array name, or structure,
        composed entirely of character strings or entirely of
        bit strings. The result is the string resulting from
        concatenating all the elements of x together.

SUBSTR(string, i [, j])   -- The result is the substring of
        string beginning at character i and ending with
        character i+j-1. If j is missing, LENGTH(string)-i+1
        is used.

TRANSLATE(s, r [, p])   -- All arguments are bit strings or
        character strings. If p is missing, the string
        consisting of all 256 possible EBCDIC characters in
        ascending order is used (from hexadecimal 00 to FF).

        If r is shorter than p, r is extended with blanks
        (or zeros). The result is a string identical to s,
        except that any character of s which is also in p is
        replaced by the corresponding character in r.   Thus if
        character i of s is the same as character j of p, then
        character i of s is replaced by character j of r. For
        example, the result of

            TRANSLATE('XYZW', 'ABCD', 'VWXY')

        is the string 'CDZB'.

UNSPEC(x)   -- x is any expression. The result is a bit string
        containing the internal representation of x. The
        length depends on the attributes of x.

VERIFY(string, config)   -- string and config are both character
        strings or both bit strings. The result is a FIXED
        BINARY integer which indicates the position of the
        first character in string which is not in config. If
        all characters are in config, the result is 0. For
        example,

            VERIFY('ƁƁƁƁBC', 'Ɓ')   yields 5, while
            VERIFY('ƁƁƁƁBC', 'ABCƁ') yields 0.

Arithmetic Built-in Functions

    The result of an arithmetic built-in function is always an
arithmetic value. Unless otherwise noted, the attributes of the
result are the same as the attributes of the argument. If
conversion is necessary because arguments   differ,   the

conversions are performed as outlined for arithmetic operations in Appendix B.6.4.

Unless otherwise noted, an argument may be an array as well as a scalar value, as explained in the introduction to Appendix B.8. The argument to the functions BINARY, DECIMAL, FIXED, and FLOAT may not be strings. Use the GET statement with the STRING option to convert strings to arithmetic quantities.

We omit descriptions of the functions ADD, DIVIDE, MULTIPLY and PRECISION.

ABS(x)   -- The result is the absolute value of x.

BINARY(x)   --The value of x is converted to the binary base.

CEIL(x)   -- x must not be complex. The result is the smallest integer that is greater than or equal to x. CEIL(3.5) is 4; CEIL(-3.5) is -3.

COMPLEX(x, y)   -- The result is a complex number with real part x and imaginary part y. X and y must be real.

CONJG(x)   --The result is a complex number which is the conjugate of the complex number x.

DECIMAL(x) -- The argument is converted to base DECIMAL.

FIXED(x)   -- The argument x is converted to fixed point.

FLOAT(x)   -- The argument x is converted to floating point.

FLOOR(x)   -- x must not be complex. The result is the largest integer not greater than x. FLOOR(3.5) is 3; FLOOR(-3.5) is -4.

IMAG(x)   -- The result is the imaginary part of x.

MAX(x1, x2, ..., xn)   -- The result is the maximum value of the arguments x1, x2, ..., xn, converted to conform to the highest characteristics of all the arguments. (FLOAT is higher than FIXED, BINARY is higher than DECIMAL.) No argument may be complex.

MIN(x1, x2, ..., xn)   -- The result is the minimum value of the arguments, converted to the highest characteristics of all the arguments. (FLOAT is higher than FIXED, BINARY is higher than DECIMAL.) No argument may be complex.

MOD(x, y)   -- x and y may not be complex. The result is the remainder when dividing x by y. If x and y have different signs, the operation is performed on their absolute values, and the result is then ABS(y) -

remainder.   For example,   MOD(29,6)   is 5, while the
value of MOD(-29,6) is 1.

REAL(x)   -- the result is the real part of the complex value x.

ROUND(x, n)   -- n is an optionally signed integer constant. If
          n is 0, x is rounded to the nearest integer. If n >
          0, x is rounded at the nth digit to the right of the
          decimal (binary) point. If n < 0, x is rounded as the
          n+1th digit to the left of the decimal (binary) point.

          If x is floating point, n is ignored and the
          rightmost bit of the internal representation of x is
          set to 1.

SIGN(x)   -- x must not be complex.   The result is a fixed
          binary value equal to 1 if x>0, 0 if x=0, and -1 if
          x<0.

TRUNC(x) --x must not be complex. If x < 0 the result is
          CEIL(x); if x > 0 the result is FLOOR(x).

<u>Mathematical</u> <u>Built-in</u> <u>Functions</u> All arguments to the
mathematical built-in functions are floating point.   If not,
they will be converted to floating point.   Unless specifically
stated otherwise, an argument can be real or complex.   The
result is always a floating point value, with mode, base and
precision attributes the same as those of the argument.

    An argument may be an array, as described in the introduction
to Appendix B.8.

ATAN(x)   -- The result is the arctangent of x.   x must not be
          ±1I.

ATAN(x,y) --Both x and y must be real; they must not both be 0.
          The result is the arctangent of x/y.

ATAND(x,y)--x and y must be real, and not both be 0. The result
          is the arctangent of x/y, expressed in degrees.

ATANH(x) --The result is the hyperbolic tangent of x. ABS(x)
          must be greater than or equal to 1.

COS(x)   --The result is the cosine of x, where x is expressed
          in radians.

COSD(x)   -- The result is the cosine of x, where x is expressed
          in degrees.

COSH(x)   -- The result is the hyperbolic cosine of x.

ERF(x)   --x must be real. The result is 2/SQRT(PI) multiplied
          by the definite integral from 0 to x of e**(-t^2) dt.

ERFC(x)   --x must be real. The result is 1-ERF(x).

EXP(x)   --The result is e**x, where e is the base of the
            natural logarithm system.

LOG(x)   --If x is real, it must be greater than 0. If x is
            complex, it must not equal 0+0I. The result is the
            natural logarithm of x.

LOG10(x)   --x must be real and greater than 0. The result is
            the common logarithm of x (base 10).

LOG2(x)   --x must be real and greater than 0. The result is
            the logarithm to the base 2 of x.

SIN(x)   --The result is the sine of x, where x is expressed
            in radians.

SIND(x)   -- The result is the sine of x, where x is expressed
            in degrees.

SINH(x)   -- The result is the hyperbolic sine of x.

SQRT(x)   -- If x is real, it must be greater than or equal to
            0. The result is the square root of x.

TAN(x)   --The result is the tangent of x, where x is
            expressed in radians.

TAND(x)   -- The result is the tangent of x, where x is
            expressed in degrees.

TANH(x)   -- The result is the hyperbolic tangent of x.

Array Generic Functions

    All these functions require array arguments and return a
single scalar value.

ALL(x)   --must be an array of bit strings. The result is a
            bit string obtained by "and-ing" (as in the operator
            "&") all the bit strings of the array together.

ANY(x)   --x must be an array of bit strings. The result is
            the bit string obtained by "or-ing" (as in the
            operator "|") all the bit strings in the array
            together.

DIM(x,n)   --The result is a binary fixed integer giving the
            "extent" of the nth dimension of the array x.   The
            extent is the upper bound minus the lower bound, plus
            1.

HBOUND(x,n)   -- The result is the upper bound of the nth
         dimension of array x.

LBOUND(x,n)   -- The result is the lower bound of the nth
         dimension of array x.

POLY(a,x)   -- This is beyond the scope of the book.

PROD(x)   -- The result is the product of all the elements of
         array x.

SUM(x)   -- The result is the sum of all the elements of array x.

Condition Built-in Functions

These are: DATAFIELD, ONCHAR, ONCODE, ONCOUNT, ONFILE, ONKEY, ONLOC, and ONSOURCE. They are beyond the scope of this book.

Based Storage Built-in Functions

These are ADDR, EMPTY, NULL, and NULLO. They are beyond the scope of this book.

Multitasking Built-in Functions

These are COMPLETION(event-name), PRIORITY(task-name), and STATUS(event-name). They are beyond the scope of this book.

Miscellaneous Built-in Functions

ALLOCATION (x)   -- This is beyond the scope of the book.

COUNT(file-name) -- This is beyond the scope of the book.

DATE   -- The result is a character string of length 6, with the
         form yymmdd. yy is the current year, mm the current
         month, and dd the current day (e.g. 760530).

LINENO(file-name)   -- The result is the number of the current
         line in the named file.

TIME   -- The result is a character string of length 9 giving
         the current time of day. Its form is hhmmssttt, where
         hh is the current hour of the day, mm is the number of
         minutes, ss the number of seconds, and ttt the number
         of milliseconds in machine-dependent increments.

Appendix B.9 <u>Formats</u>

GET EDIT and PUT EDIT read and write values using a user-defined <u>format</u> to control the editing and formatting of the values. The format is a list of "data items" which specify the format of each individual value in turn -- how many characters it uses, where the decimal point should go, and so on. Interspersed between the data items may be "control items", which specify things like skipping to the next line or page.

Input-output is done under the control of the list of variables or expressions being read into or printed, as follows. The format is searched for the first data item; any control items encountered are executed immediately. When the first data item in the list is found, the first value is read or written using that data item. Next, if there is a second value to read or print, the format is searched again, beginning at the item following the one just used. Any control items encountered are executed immediately. Upon finding a data item, the second value is read or printed. This process continues until the last value has been read or printed. Any excess data items or control items in the format are not used.

To make formats more flexible, one may specify "iteration factors". Thus "3 A(2)" is equivalent to a list of three items "A(2), A(2), A(2)", while "2 (A(2), X(1))" is equivalent to the four items "A(2), X(1), A(2), X(1)". Simple examples of formats and their use are given in Part I.6.

A format has the form

(specification ¦, specification¦)

where each specification may be one of the following:

1.   item -- Items are described below.

2.   integer-constant item -- This is equivalent to "integer-constant" replications of the item. Thus "3 A(2)" is equivalent to "A(2), A(2), A(2)".

3.   (exp) item -- At the point the specification is to be used, the exp is evaluated and converted to an integer. If 0 or negative, the item is skipped. If exp > 0, this is equivalent to "exp" replications of the item. Thus, if I has the

value 4, "(I) A(3)" is equivalent to "A(3), A(3), A(3), A(3)". The expression is evaluated <u>each</u> time the specification is to be used to control editing.

4. integer-constant format -- This is equivalent to "integer-constant" replications of the format. Thus, "2 (A(2), X(1))" is equivalent to "A(2), X(1), A(2), X(1)". Note that this defines a format in terms of another format.

5. (exp) format -- The exp is evaluated as explained under specification 3 above. This is equivalent to "exp" replications of the format. If exp ≤ 0, the specification is skipped entirely.

   The following items may be used. Any expressions in the item are evaluated each time the item is to be used. w, d, and s are used for expressions.

1. A -- Print a character string, in the next n columns.   n is the current length of the string being written out.

2. A(w) -- Read or print a character string. For input, the next w columns of the input stream are assigned to the variable. If w ≤ 0, the null string is assigned and no columns are used in the input stream.

    For output, the character string value is printed, left-adjusted, in the next w columns of the output stream. The string is truncated if too long. If w ≤ 0, no output results.

3. B -- Print a bit string in the next n columns of the output stream. n is the length of the value being printed.

4. B(w) -- Read or print a bit string. For input, the next w columns of the input stream are read in and assigned to the corresponding bit variable. Blanks may occur before or after the bit string value in the input, but they may not be imbedded within the value. Only 1's and 0's are allowed in the input value. If w ≤ 0, the null string is assigned and no columns are skipped.

    For output, the corresponding bit string value is printed, left-adjusted, in the next w columns. If too long, the value is truncated on the right. If w ≤ 0, no output results.

5. C(real-format-item [, real-format-item]) -- Read or print a complex number. Each real-format-item is either F or E, as described below. If the second one is missing, it is assumed to be the same as the first.

For input, two numbers are read in and assigned to the real and imaginary part of the corresponding COMPLEX variable. No letter I may appear in the input. For output, the complex value is printed according to the format. No letter I is appended to it.

6. COLUMN(w) -- This control item causes columns to be skipped until column w of the current line is reached. On input, skipped columns are ignored; on output, they are filled with blanks. If the current line is already positioned <u>after</u> column w, the current line is completed and a new one started, in column w. If w ≤ 0, it is assumed to be 1. If w is greater than the size of a line, 1 is assumed.

7. E(w, d [, s]) -- Read or print a floating point number, in w columns. w must be large enough to include <u>all</u> parts of the number, including the preceding sign and the exponent. If the variable to be assigned or the value to be printed is not floating decimal, conversion will be performed on the number.

    For input, the value on the line should have the form

        [+ or -] mantissa [E [+ or -] yy]

    where yy is any 1 or 2 digit number. The mantissa is a fixed point constant. If the mantissa has no decimal point, the decimal point is assumed to be just before the rightmost d digits of the mantissa. If the exponent is missing, a zero exponent is assumed. Blanks may precede or follow the number in the field of w columns, but may not appear within the number. "s" is not used for input.

    For output, the number is printed in a field of w characters in the form

        [-] <s-d digits> . <d digits> E <+ or -> exponent

    s represents the number of significant digits and d the number of fractional digits. If s is missing, it is assumed to be d+1. Thus, one digit will be printed to the left of the decimal point. If d is 0 no decimal point is printed. s must be less than 17.

    If necessary, the number is rounded to fit the format.

8. F(w, d [, s]) -- Read or print a fixed-point decimal number, in w columns. If the variable being assigned or the value being printed is not fixed decimal, suitable conversion will be performed.

For input, the number is an optionally-signed decimal fixed-point constant. It may be preceded or followed by blanks, but can contain no embedded blanks. If the entire field is blank, the number is 0.

If the number contains no decimal point, an implied decimal point is inserted d digits from the right of the number. If s appears, the number is multiplied by 10**s, <u>after</u> it is read in but before it is assigned to the variable.

For output, the value to be printed is first converted to fixed decimal form. It is then rounded to fit the format and printed out, right-adjusted, in a field of w columns. If d does not appear, the integer part of the number is written without a decimal point. If d appears, d digits will be printed to the right of the decimal point. If s appears, before writing out the value, it is multiplied by 10**s.

9. LINE(exp) -- This control item causes blank lines to be inserted so that the current line is the expth line on the page. If exp ≤ 0, 1 is assumed. If the current line number ≥ exp, the ENDPAGE condition is raised (which usually causes a new page to be started).

10. PAGE -- This control item causes a new page to be started. It may be used for output only.

11. SKIP [(exp)] -- This control item causes exp lines (records) to be skipped (the current line counting as 1 skip). If exp is missing it is assumed to be 1. SKIP may cause the ENDPAGE condition to be raised (which usually causes a new page to be started on output).

On output, if exp ≤ 0, SKIP causes the same current line to be used, starting at the beginning. This does <u>not</u> erase the previous contents of the current line, but can be used to cause overprinting of characters.

12. X(w) -- This control item causes w columns to be skipped (on input) or w blank characters to be printed (on output). If w ≤ 0, it it is assumed to be 0.

Appendix B.10 <u>Simulating</u> <u>the</u> <u>Alternate</u> <u>Statement</u>

A possible formulation for a 4-alternate selection unit is

```
case I of
     1: S1
     2: S2
     3: S3
     4: S4
     endcase
```

To execute such a statement, variable I is evaluated and converted, if necessary, to an integer. If I<1 or I>4 execution is finished. If 1≤I≤4, the statement SI (the Ith one) is executed. Note that at most <u>one</u> of the four alternatives is executed.

In Section II.1.3 we discussed two possible implementations of the alternate statement, both using a sequence of IF statements. Here we give another possibility which uses PL/I <u>label</u> variables. This new implementation is usually more efficient, because it avoids execution of a <u>sequence</u> of conditional statements.

If one declares L using

DECLARE L(1:4) LABEL;

then L is an array of label variables, each of which can contain the label of some statement. For example, if L(1) contains the label LAB and we have the statement

LAB: X = X + Y;

then execution of GO TO L(1) causes control to pass to the statement X=X+Y;. Usually, label variables are a dangerous feature to use; they confuse the reader and are quite error prone. However, it is reasonable to use them in a restricted manner, as we do here to simulate a higher level construct.

One way to assign a label to L(1) is to use L(1) itself as the label of a statement:

L(1): X = X + Z;

Execution of GO TO L(1) now causes the statement X=X+Z; we use this technique to "simulate" the 4-alternate case statement shown above as follows:

```
/* SIMULATING A 4-ALTERNATIVE STATEMENT */
   IF (I<1) | (I>4) THEN GOTO TERM_SIM;
   GO TO L(I);

   L(1): S1
         GO TO TERM_SIM;
   L(2): S2
         GO TO TERM_SIM;
   L(3): S3
         GO TO TERM_SIM;
   L(4): S4
         GO TO TERM_SIM;
   TERM_SIM:;
```

Note that the <u>order</u> of the labeled substatements is immaterial,
since each is labeled. A label array that is assigned a value
by using L(1) as a label may <u>not</u> be declared STATIC or EXTERNAL.

INDEX